ABOUT THE EDITORS

ELEANOR MILLS is the editor ▓▓▓ ▓▓▓▓ ▓▓▓▓ ▓▓ he
Sunday Times, the UK's most popular ▓▓▓▓ ▓▓▓▓▓▓▓▓ on
and was educated at St Paul's and Westminster ▓▓▓ ng
English at Oxford. She trained to be a journalist on the ——————— he
was the only woman trainee in the newsroom. She then move ▓▓ *ily*
Telegraph where she became the youngest features editor in the ▓▓ r's
history. She joined the *Sunday Times* in 1998 where she did the paper's m in
interview every week for two years and is now its most senior female editor.
Aged thirty-four, she lives in London with her husband and two children.

KIRA COCHRANE was born in 1977 and studied American Literature
at the Universities of Sussex and California before starting work as a
writer/researcher on the *Sunday Times*'s News Review section in 2000.
She left in 2003 to concentrate on writing fiction and has since produced
two novels: *The Naked Season* (2003) and *Escape Routes for Beginners* (2004),
which was longlisted for the 2005 Orange Prize.

CUPCAKES AND KALASHNIKOVS

100 Years of the Best Journalism by Women

EDITED BY
ELEANOR MILLS WITH KIRA COCHRANE

CONSTABLE • LONDON

Constable & Robinson Ltd
3 The Lanchesters
162 Fulham Palace Road
London W6 9ER
www.constablerobinson.com

First published by Constable,
an imprint of Constable & Robinson Ltd 2005

A copy of the British Library Cataloguing in
Publication Data is available from the British Library

ISBN 1-84529-165-4

Printed and bound in the EU

1 3 5 7 9 10 8 6 4 2

For my daughters – Alice Lily and Laura

CONTENTS

ACKNOWLEDGEMENTS

My biggest thanks must go to Kira Cochrane who has spent exhaustive hours rummaging through stacks in all sorts of libraries to dig out many of these articles. There would be no collection without her brilliant research and nose for a top story, she is the best right-hand woman any editor could ever have. I must also thank my editor John Witherow at the *Sunday Times* for letting me edit this book and for his support and encouragement of my career. And my own mentor, Sarah Baxter, former editor of the *News Review* at the paper and now one of the first female Washington correspondents, for all her insights and belief; she is an inspiration.

I have been very encouraged by the enthusiasm, suggestions and knowledge of a range of wise women while putting together this book and during my journalistic career: Julia Langdon, Melanie Phillips, Lynn Barber, Rosie Boycott, Suzanne Moore, Gillian Tindall, India Knight, Margarette Driscoll, Lesley White, Christina Lamb, Gitta Sereny, Erin Pizzey, Ann Leslie, Rebecca Nicolson, Sarah Sands, Zadie Smith, Jilly Cooper, Georgia Garratt, Erica Jong, Tiffanie Darke and Kath Viner. And of course I am very grateful to Naomi Wolf for her unflagging encouragement and total belief in the worth of the project and for writing the introduction – her support has been invaluable.

I must also thank my team at the *Sunday Times*: Julia Margo, Giles Hattersley and Glenda Cooper particularly, but also Richard Bonfield in News International syndication. And thanks to Becky Hardie at Constable for being such a wise, kind and understanding editor.

Lastly I must pay tribute to my wonderful husband Derek who has put up with me rustling papers late at night with great stoicism and has been, as ever, my rock; and to my daughter Alice Lily for letting mummy send 'boring emails' when I should have been reading stories; and finally to the 'bump' for being well behaved enough to delay its arrival until this anthology was finished.

FOREWORD

Most of the world's great newspapers were established in the middle of the nineteenth century – or even before. In America the *New York Times* was established in 1861, in Britain *The Times* started to thunder in 1785 with the *Observer* and *Sunday Times* and even the tabloids such as the *News of the World* and the *People* coming on stream by 1881. A century ago, many of the titles which are familiar to readers from news stands today were up and running, including many of the periodicals. The golden age of journalism in many respects is seen to be between about 1880 and 1910 when newspapers really had a stranglehold on the news market and the technology to make their grip count.

But since then newspapers have undergone a rather different kind of revolution. What has changed dramatically in the last 100 years is the inclusion of women's voices. They are still not as widespread as they should be (a recent survey by the Center for Media Literacy in the US discovered that female bylines on the front pages averaged only 27 per cent of the stories there); but that is still nearly a third of all front page stories: a massive change in how things used to be.

I remember when I first became editor of the News Review section of the *Sunday Times* in London in 2001 having lunch with Godfrey Smith (the man who invented the first magazine supplement within a newspaper), who had worked for the paper for sixty years. 'When I first started,' he said, 'there was only one lady journalist on the staff: the woman's editor. She used to sweep in on Thursdays to conference, tell us what she was going to write – always dresses, or children's behaviour, and then disappear. We were absolutely terrified of her. Amazing how things change.'

Ever since then I've been fascinated by how women made their way into newspapers and by the history of the women – particularly writers – who came before me. Despite the millions of articles written by women all over the world, there is no anthology of the best of their contributions. I hope this volume will remedy that and bring some of their writing to a wider audience.

Of course, there are all sorts of journalism anthologies out there, but mostly from particular publications, so you get for instance 'the best of the American *Vogue* or *Cosmopolitan*, but nothing that gives the general reader an overview of the incredibly diverse journalism that women have been producing for over a century.

No single volume could do justice to this vast amount of material: but what I have tried to do in this book is to bring together some of the very greats – the 'must know abouts', if you like, such as Martha Gellhorn or

Rebecca West, whose reporting stands proud in any company – with some more obscure pieces which illustrate aspects of the female experience which still resonate today.

How does one define 'journalism'? The basic criteria for inclusion: the piece of writing should have been written for and first published in a newspaper or magazine. I wanted to reflect all the different sorts of articles in newspapers, so the anthology contains everything from first-hand accounts of battles, or events (such as Martha Gellhorn describing the horrors of Dachau or Ann Leslie witnessing the fall of the Berlin Wall) to book and film reviews, comment pieces, interviews, pamphlets, fiction (Bridget Jones began in a newspaper as a fictional diary about a singleton's life) and more personal features. Although women can report 'objectively' as well as any man, what women have really brought to newspapers is a more confessional, intimate voice. The strong voices of clever women warming to their themes and giving up details of their own lives and experiences in order to do so, comes across very clearly in this book. I am proud to have included such groundbreaking articles as Ruth Picardie's column written as she was dying of cancer, which spawned a whole subspecies of confessionals in imitation.

As an editor myself, I know the delight of commissioning a really top-class wordsmith, whether professional journalist or novelist, to write on the issue of the moment; many such pieces by well-known women writers appear in this collection. Some of the best journalism comes when you get a brilliant writer on a subject they feel passionately about. It is amazing how such gems survive the years and thunder on down the decades; I'm glad to rescue some of them from decaying old stacks of paper for new readers.

My aim was to make the scope of the anthology as broad as possible to reflect the range and different styles of women who have written for newspapers over the last 100 years. From the delights of making blackbird pie through the reality of birth to the ethics of the Nuremberg trials and the terrible tales of racism which led to the civil rights struggles in America, this collection shows the vast range of female voices in newspapers over the last century.

What is striking to me is the passion of the women and how ahead of their time they were in what they wrote and believed. Take for instance the radical Emma Goldman's articles, who called for birth control for women and whose attacks on prostitution made her a pariah at the time. Many took great risks in the social sphere by saying what they did and caused outrage, while many are just funny, humane and enduringly insightful about their lives and those of the people around them. This is not just a women's collection, it reflects the great dilemmas and struggles of humanity in the last century from an often new point of view.

We have kicked off with a section on war as it most vividly encapsulates how women's roles have changed. Before and during the First World War activists such as Sylvia Pankhurst wrote of the effects, on the ground and for civilians, of air raids on the East End, while the anarchist Emma Goldman wrote against 'The promoters of war mania' – with the ongoing protests about the situation in Iraq, her argument feels very modern. But a campaigning woman's role then was very much to write diatribes from the home front against the war: how different to women like Nancy Cunard who reported from the front in the Spanish Civil War with thrilling dispatches in the late 1930s, or Martha Gellhorn's inspirational World War Two reporting where she squeezed herself on to whatever troop transports she could to tell the world what was really happening. Or Rebecca West at the Nuremberg Trials, who reports brilliantly on the trials of the Nazi elite. Or Mary McCarthy's vivid dispatches from Vietnam from 1967. Here women are truly doing jobs that were formerly a male preserve, but bringing to them a particular woman's eye for detail and the sufferings of the local population. It is true that many of the women who wrote on war, particularly early on, were pacifists, which is perhaps overly reflected in the collection, but then objecting to the horror and pity of war has always been a woman's prerogative.

One of the very best and bravest of the modern female war reporters is Marie Colvin, whom I have had the honour to work with on the *Sunday Times*. She befriended the Palestinian leader, Yasser Arafat, over several decades and her article about his life is reprinted here. Even after losing an eye covering the Tamil rebellion in Sri Lanka, she has continued to report from hot spots around the world. What changes a century brings: where once all women could do was protest from the home front, or write letters to their husbands, it is now normal for women to report from war zones, bringing a new kind of sensibility to the writing of the first draft of history.

Journalism is by its nature ephemeral; today's newspapers is tomorrow's rubbish. So it is perhaps not surprising that many of us who come after have so little idea of what has been written on issues in newspapers before. But what has struck me most during the reading for this collection is how so many dilemmas that we think of as 'modern' are really no such thing. Take Maddy Vegtel's piece on having a baby at forty (first printed in the 1930s in American *Vogue*) – people's reactions to her being an 'old' mother and her own thoughts about it resonate just as strongly today. In fact when I first read it, I assumed it said 1980 and did a double take when I realized the true date.

This pattern was repeated over and over, particularly with regard to the great home v work dilemma which still haunts so many of us working mothers today. In 1924 *Good Housekeeping* magazine published an article called 'Should *Married* Women Work?' The essential problem Mrs Alfred

Sidgwick describes of how to spend enough time with children while carrying on a career outside the home and the broader social pressures women feel with regard to juggling a career and family has barely changed in the ninety years since. Over lunch with the columnist Melanie Phillips, I said how surprised I was that such 'having it all' dilemmas were being written about so long ago. 'That's because these problems have still not been resolved,' she said matter-of-factly, 'so they go on feeling new to every generation who encounters them.' I felt strangely comforted by the thought that women had been grappling with this one for a century.

From this *cri de coeur* in the 1920s, to Erica Jong's brilliant piece 'The Post-feminist Woman – is she Perhaps More Oppressed than Ever?' (*Seattle Times*, 1984), which describes hilariously the exhaustion of the working mother. I seem to wade through more articles on this subject than any other, but none surpassed Erica's from the early Eighties. Women are endlessly reinventing the wheel on these arguments so there is much to learn from what has been said before.

The struggle for emancipation and feminism has spawned some of the very best women's journalism. Every young woman who takes her vote for granted should read Djuna Barnes' account (from 1914) of how it feels to be forcibly fed. In one of the first instances of female 'gonzo' journalism, Barnes joined the women on hunger strike for female suffrage so she could write about what they were going through. She was not the first to use the technique of 'stunt' journalism to draw attention to a big issue; in 1888, the American journalist Nellie Bly describes a classically modern stunt of going undercover into an insane asylum in New York, which led to the authorities radically changing their provision for the mentally ill.

Women from the suffragette, Sylvia Pankhurst to the black writer, Alice Walker are represented in this anthology using journalism to campaign passionately on issues from votes for women to racism.

One aspect of this book that I found particularly frustrating was politics in its day-to-day sense: women have written extensively about the struggles of the women's movement, but certainly in Britain – and to some extent in America too – the scrum of domestic politics and the lobby in the House of Commons has been very much a man's world. There are notable exceptions: for instance Elizabeth Drew wrote brilliantly about the ins and outs of Washington and Watergate in the 1970s.

Over lunch with Julia Langdon, the first woman to be political editor of a national newspaper in Britain, I asked if I was missing some crucial women who had been key to British political coverage. 'No,' she said. 'It really was a gentleman's club.' She described how as recently as the 1980s she had been one of only two women in the press lobby at parliament. 'The men would come up to me and say, "Did you get that letter I was talking to you about yesterday?" I'd look blank and they'd insist that they'd given it to me. And then I'd realize that they'd given it to Eleanor (Goodman), the other woman in the lobby. We looked totally different but to the men we were interchangeable. It was extraordinary.'

Fortunately things are beginning to change and there is now a host of feisty young female lobby reporters and political columnists on both sides of the Atlantic. Unfortunately much of it needs so much contextualization that many articles I liked, I decided, ultimately, not to include.

There are some articles which once read have haunted me: particularly Audre Lorde's piece 'That Summer I Left Childhood was White'. Her description of a Washington where a black family couldn't be served an ice cream in a diner is a chilling reminder of what the civil rights struggles of the sixties in the US were all about. Angela Carter's 'Notes from a Maternity Ward' should be read by every expectant mother and Mary Stott's 'Learning to be a Widow' with its mixture of practical advice and raw grief still brings tears to the eyes.

The book can be read all the way through, or dipped into. One of the key criteria for inclusion was that it passed a very high threshold of excitement: the test was, could an article keep me reading late at night after a full day juggling the demands of my two-year-old, a tricky pregnancy and the *Sunday Times*?

There are a few pieces that I would have liked to have included but which were just too long: Lillian Ross's *New Yorker* interview with Ernest Hemingway was the main one, along with Isabel Hilton's 'The General,' an amazing account of trying to track down and finally meeting General Stroessner, Paraguay's fallen dictator. We also decided that rather than printing a small extract, we would exclude Gloria Steinem's 'I was a Playboy Bunny' as it is readily available elsewhere. I would have liked to include the moralist, Hannah Arendt, but much of her work was in German and this is a collection of journalism in English. Some pieces have been abridged; I hope readers will be encouraged to seek out the fuller versions themselves.

What kept me awake at night was the thought that there was someone totally brilliant we hadn't included; of course there are hundreds of other pieces we could have chosen. A collection like this can only ever be a starting point and some pieces were excluded to keep the anthology in balance. All I hope is that it opens as many windows into other times, lives and thinking for you as it has for me.

Eleanor Mills
London, April 2005

INTRODUCTION

It seems like such an extraordinarily necessary idea – an anthology collecting together, for the first time that I am aware of, the key voices of women journalists about the key issues of their times, leading up to the present. Thank goodness Eleanor Mills, who as News Review editor of the *Sunday Times* of London is in a position to assess weekly the leading contenders to write the first draft of history, and to see precisely how gender shapes or distorts the news, has collected these crucial essays reflecting what women reporters thought and said about the turning points in their own history.

In a sense, this collection is even more important and more illuminating than are the tomes we now have of thoroughly digested and meticulously thought-through historical analysis of women's place and sensibility over the past 150 years or so. Finished historical texts cannot begin to convey the flavour of the time from a woman reporter's point of view; it is one thing to read from a distance about the suffrage movement – another to have an account from Sylvia Pankhurst written before anyone knew that her campaign for women's equality would ever amount to more than a fanatic's fantasy.

It is one thing to read dispassionately a summary of the civil rights movement – another to see it from a child's-eye view from the vantage point of a writer as gifted as Audre Lorde.

This collection reminds us why both journalism and women's presence in journalism are so important. Journalism is so important simply because it is the first, most urgent and visceral glance at history: the relatively rough, impressionistic, almost breathless firsthand report – say, by Martha Gellhorn of Dachau, a confrontation with the evidence of human evil that stayed with that intrepid reporter for the rest of her life and led her into a prolonged existential crisis, according to her biographer – reawakens a sense of fresh horror in a way that a fifty-year-on commemoration of the now-familiar look of the camps can never do.

And women's voices in journalism are so important because, as this collection makes so painfully clear, it takes a century of first glances by waves of engaged, passionate minds at a single issue – such as domestic labour added to labour in the workforce, or the absence of child care, or the politics of sexuality – for those first glances and impassioned reactions to turn into a readiness for society as a whole to enact the kind of change that finally turns the historical page.

I would wish this collection to be given as a gift to every high school and college graduate, male and female; it is very, very hard to remain stupid about women's history and current situation after having absorbed this anthology.

Seeing the same issues reappear, decade after decade, byline after byline – each essay or article written, clearly, with some conviction that this, surely, will tip the social balance into reason – puts the long, stubborn resistance to women's equality into a sharper light than any polemic can manage.

I would wish Ms Mills' inspired collection on to every night table in the UK and the US simply because it is so delectable to take in, the quality of the writing so high and varied; lastly, I would wish it on the desks of every news editor; for surely reading about the issues of the day written in the first-person female voice, bringing new light to 'old stories', will jar any editor into awareness that male hegemony in the newsroom simply distorts the news and makes it frankly less interesting.

Ms Mills' anthology is better than history from the front lines; it is a blazing reminder of why it matters – to good writing and to good journalism – to get gender balance for the bylines who are tasked with writing history's first draft.

Naomi Wolf
New York, April 2005

WAR

EMMA GOLDMAN

1869–1940

Known to supporters and detractors alike as 'Red Emma', Russian-born Jew Emma Goldman was a revolutionary figure in the United States. She campaigned on a huge range of issues, including workers' rights, women's rights and freedom of speech and was repeatedly incarcerated for her views. In 1893 she was sentenced to a year in Blackwells Island penitentiary after urging the unemployed to take bread 'by force'. This was quickly followed by another sentence for distributing information about birth control. Her longest term came in 1917, when she was arrested for conspiring to obstruct the draft and was sentenced to serve two years, before being stripped of her citizenship and deported to Russia.

Her opposition to World War One had been typically strident, as is evident in the following article. This piece was first published in Goldman's own magazine, *Mother Earth*, which circulated from 1906–17 and published some of the most anarchic and radical writings in journalistic history.

The Promoters of the War Mania

March 1917, *Mother Earth*, vol XII, no. 1

At this most critical moment it becomes imperative for every liberty-loving person to voice a fiery protest against the participation of this country in the European mass murder. If the opponents of war, from the Atlantic to the Pacific, would immediately join their voices into a thunderous No!, then the horror that now menaces America might yet be averted. Unfortunately it is only too true that the people in our so-called Democracy are to a large extent a dumb, suffering herd rather than thinking beings who dare to give expression to a frank, earnest opinion.

Yet it is unthinkable that the American people should really want war. During the last thirty months they have had ample opportunity to watch the frightful carnage in the warring countries. They have seen universal murder, like a devastating pestilence, eat into the very heart of the peoples of Europe. They saw cities destroyed, entire countries wiped off the map, hosts of dead, millions of wounded and maimed. The American people could not help witnessing the spread of insane, motiveless hatred among the peoples of Europe. They must realize the extent of the famine, the suffering and anguish gripping the war-stricken countries.

They know, too, that while the men were killed off like vermin, the women and children, the old and the decrepit remained behind in helpless and tragic despair. Why then, in the name of all that is reasonable and humane, should the American people desire the same horrors, the same destruction and devastation upon American soil?

We are told that the 'freedom of the seas' is at stake and that 'American honor' demands that we protect that precious freedom. What a farce! How much freedom of the seas can the masses of toilers or the disinherited and the unemployed ever enjoy? Would it not be well to look into this magic thing, 'the freedom of the seas,' before we sing patriotic songs and shout hurrah?

The only ones that have benefitted by the 'freedom of the seas' are the exploiters, the dealers in munition and food supplies. The 'freedom of the seas' has served these unscrupulous American robbers and monopolists as a pretext to pilfer the unfortunate people of both Europe and America. Out of international carnage they have made billions; out of the misery of the people and the agony of women and children the American financiers and industrial magnates have coined huge fortunes.

Ask young Morgan. Will he dare admit his tremendous pecuniary gain from the export of munition and food supplies? Of course not. But the truth will out, sometimes. Thus a financial expert recently proved that even old Pierpont Morgan would be astounded could he see the dazzling profits gathered in by his son through war speculations. And, incidentally, do not let us forget that it is this speculation in murder and destruction which is responsible for the criminal increase in the cost of living in our own land. War, famine, and the capitalist class are the only gainers in the hideous drama called nationalism, patriotism, national honor, and freedom of the seas. Instead of putting a stop to such monstrous crimes, war in America would only increase the opportunities of the profit mongers. That and only that will be the result if the American people will consent to thrust the United States into the abyss of war.

President Wilson and other officials of the administration assure us that they want peace. If that claim held even one grain of truth, the government would have long ago carried out the suggestion of many true lovers of peace to put a stop to the export of munition and food stuffs. Had this shameful trade with the implements of slaughter been stopped at the beginning of the war, the good results for peace would have been manifold.

First, the war in Europe would have been starved out through the stoppage of food exports. Indeed, it is no exaggeration when I say that the war would have been at an end long ago had the American financiers been prevented from investing billions in war loans and had the American munition clique and food speculators not been given the opportunity to supply warring Europe with the means to keep up the slaughter.

Second, an embargo on exports would have automatically taken out American ships from the war and submarine zones and would have thus eliminated the much discussed 'reason' for war with Germany.

Third, and most important of all, the brazen, artificial increase in the cost of living, which condemns the toiling masses of America to semi-starvation, would be an impossibility were not the great bulk of American products shipped to Europe to feed the fires of war.

Peace meetings and peace protests have no meaning whatever unless the government is challenged to stop the continuance of exports. If for no other reason, this ought to be insisted upon, be it only to prove that Washington is capable of nice phrases, but that it has never made a single determined step for peace. That will help to demonstrate to the American people that the government represents only the capitalists, the International War and Preparedness Trust, and not the workers. Are then the people of America good enough only to pull the chestnuts out of the fire for the thieving trusts? That is all this wild clamor for war means as far as the masses are concerned.

The attempt to light the torch of the furies of war is the more mon-strous when one bears in mind that the people of America are cos-mopolitan. If anything, America should be the soil for international understanding, for the growth of friendship between all races. Here, all narrow, stifling national prejudices should be eradicated. Instead, the people are to be thrown into the madness and confusion of war, of racial antagonism and hatred.

True, there never was much love wasted in this country on the unfor-tunate foreigner, but what about the boast that the Goddess of Liberty holds high the beacon to all oppressed nations? What about America as the haven of welcome? Should all this now become the symbol of national persecution? What can result from it but the pollution of all social relationship? Think of it, war in this country is at present only a possibil-ity, and already the Germans and the Austrians are being deprived of employment, ostracized, and spied upon, persecuted and hounded by the jingoes. And that is only a small beginning of what war would bring in its wake.

I do not have to emphasize that I entertain not a particle of sympathy with the Germany of the Höhenzollern or the Austria of the Hapsburgs. But what have the Germans and the Austrians in America − or in their own country, for that matter − to do with the diplomacy and politics of Berlin or Vienna? It is nothing but blind, cruel national and patriotic madness which would make these people, who have lived, toiled, and suffered in this country, pay for the criminal plans and intrigues in Berlin and Vienna palaces.

These millions of Germans and Austrians, who have contributed more to the real culture and growth of America than all the Morgans and Rockefellers, are now to be treated like enemy aliens, just because Wall Street feels itself checked in its unlimited use of the seas for plunder, robbery, and theft from suffering America and bleeding Europe.

Militarism and reaction are now more rampant in Europe than ever before. Conscription and censorship have destroyed every vestige of liberty. Everywhere the governments have used the situation to tighten the militaristic noose around the necks of the people. Everywhere discipline has been the knout to whip the masses into slavery and blind obedience. And the pathos of it all is that the people at large have submitted without a murmur, though every country has shown its quota of brave men that would not be deluded.

The same is bound to take place in America should the dogs of war be let loose here. Already the poisonous seed has been planted. All the reactionary riffraff, propagandists of jingoism and preparedness, all the beneficiaries of exploitation represented in the Merchants and Manufacturers' Association, the Chambers of Commerce, the munition cliques, etc., etc., have come to the fore with all sorts of plans and schemes to chain and gag labor, to make it more helpless and dumb than ever before.

These respectable criminals no longer make a secret of their demand for compulsory military training. Taft, the spokesman of Wall Street, expressed it cynically enough that now, in face of the war danger, the time has come to demand the introduction of compulsory militarism. Subserviently echoing the slogan, principals and superintendents of our schools and colleges are hastening to poison the minds of their pupils with national 'ideals' and patriotic forgeries of history to prepare the young generation for 'the protection of national honor,' which really means the 'glory' of bleeding to death for the crooked transactions of a gang of legalized, cowardly thieves. Mr. Murray Butler, the lickspittle of Wall Street, is in the lead, and many others like him are crawling before the golden calf of their masters. Talk about prostitution! Why, the unfortunate girl in the street is purity itself compared with such mental degeneration.

Added to this process of poisoning are the huge appropriations rushed through by Congress and the state legislatures for the national murder machinery. Sums reaching into the hundreds of millions for the Army and Navy fly through the air within such enticing reach that the Steel Trust and other corporations manufacturing ammunition and war supplies are dissolving in patriotic sentiment and enthusiasm and have already offered their generous services to the country.

Hand in hand with this military preparedness and war mania goes the increased persecution of the workers and their organizations. Labor went wild with enthusiasm and gratitude to the President for his supposed humanity in proclaiming the eight-hour law before election, and now it develops that the law was merely a bait for votes and a shackle for labor. It denies the right to strike and introduces compulsory arbitration. Of course it is common knowledge that strikes have long since been made ineffective by antipicketing injunctions and the prosecution of strikers, but the federal eight-hour law is the worst parody on the right to organize and to strike, and it is going to prove an additional fetter on labor. In connection with this arbitrary measure goes the proposition to give the President full power in case of war to take control of the railroads and their employees, which would mean nothing less than absolute subserviency and industrial militarism for the workers.

Then there is the systematic, barbarous persecution of radical and revolutionary elements throughout the land. The horrors in Everett, the conspiracy against labor in San Francisco, with Billings and Mooney already sacrificed – are they mere coincidences? Or do they not rather signify the true character of the war which the American ruling class has been waging against labor?

The workers must learn that they have nothing to expect from their masters. The latter, in America as well as in Europe, hesitate not a moment to send hundred thousands of the people to their death if their interests demand it. They are ever ready that their misguided slaves should have the national and patriotic banner over burning cities, over devastated countrysides, over homeless and starving humanity, just as long as they can find enough unfortunate victims to be drilled into mankillers, ready at the bidding of their masters to perform the ghastly task of bloodshed and carnage.

Valuable as the work of the Women's Peace Party and other earnest pacifists may be, it is folly to petition the President for peace. The workers, they alone, can avert the impending war; in fact, all wars, if they will refuse to be a party to them. The determined antimilitarist is the only pacifist. The ordinary pacifist merely moralizes; the antimilitarist acts; he refuses to be ordered to kill his brothers. His slogan is: 'I will not kill, nor will I lend myself to be killed.'

It is this slogan which we must spread among the workers and carry into the labor organizations. They need to realize that it is monstrously criminal to voluntarily engage in the hideous business of killing. It is terrible enough to kill in anger, in a moment of frenzy, but it is still more so to blindly obey the command of your military superiors to commit murder. The time must come when slaughter and carnage through blind obedience will not only not receive rewards, monuments, pensions, and eulogies, but will be considered the greatest horror and shame of a barbaric, bloodthirsty, greed-obsessed age; a dark, hideous blotch upon civilization.

Let us understand this most valuable truth: A man has the power to act voluntarily only as long as he does not wear the uniform. Once you have donned the garb of obedience, the 'voluntary' soldier becomes as much a part of the slaughter machine as his brother who was forced into military service. It is still time in our land to decide against militarism and war, to hold out determinately against compulsory military service for the murder of your fellow men. After all, America is not yet like Germany, Russia, France, or England in the throes of a military regime with the mark of a Cain upon her brow. The determined stand which the workers can take individually, in groups and organizations against war, will still meet with ready and enthusiastic response. It would arouse the people all over the land. As a matter of fact, they want no war. The cry for it comes from the military cliques, the munition manufacturers, and their mouthpiece, the press, this most degenerate criminal of all criminals. They all stand by the flag. Oh, yes; it's a profitable emblem that covers a multitude of sins.

It is still time to stem the bloody tide of war by word of mouth and pen and action. The promoters of war realize that we have looked into their cards and that we know their crooked, criminal game. We know they want war to increase their profits. Very well, let them fight their own wars. We, the people of America, will not do it for them. Do you think war would then come or be kept up? Oh, I know it is difficult to arouse the workers, to make them see the truth back of the nationalistic, patriotic lie. Still we must do our share. At least we shall be free from blame should the terrible avalanche overtake us in spite of our efforts.

I for one will speak against war so long as my voice will last, now and during war. A thousand times rather would I die calling to the people of America to refuse to be obedient, to refuse military service, to refuse to murder their brothers, than I should ever give my voice in justification of war, except the one war of all the peoples against their despots and exploiters – the Social Revolution.

NANCY CUNARD

1896–1965

The daughter of Sir Bache Cunard, scion of the English shipping family, Nancy Cunard grew up on her father's estate in Leicestershire, before attending a number of exclusive schools in London, France and Germany. She began writing poetry in 1916, with her volumes including *Outlaws* (1921) and *Sublunary* (1923). In 1928, she founded the Hours Press, which published writers including Ezra Pound and Samuel Beckett.

An occasional journalist, Cunard travelled to Spain at the start of the Civil War and began reporting regularly for the *Manchester Guardian*. The following is one of her early reports.

Report from the Spanish Civil War

9 February 1939, *Manchester Guardian*

At Le Perthus, from nine o'clock this morning until 4.30, I have been watching soldiers pass between the two stone posts that are actually the frontier-line. They have come by in thousands and thousands, in groups, singly, and in numberless lorries. At the posts stand the French soldiers, who immediately search them for arms. The Spanish soldiers give up their arms in an orderly fashion. The pile of rifles, revolvers, cartridge belts, dirks, and even a knife or two grow throughout the day. Two machine-guns have been brought in; farther up, an armoured car.

But all this is only the beginning; we are told: 'Tomorrow the rearguard of the army, and afterwards – the army that has fought.' On the mountains each side they come, so that the whole landscape seems to be moving. Soldiers on horseback, wounded men, women, children, a whole population, and cars and ambulances. Many of the ambulances are British and of the 'Centrale Internationale Sanitaire', one of whose doctors tells me of the appalling lack of supplies, of staff, and of help.

In fact, there is enough of nothing save the now excellently distributed food rations which are made by France. There was a good supply of food at La Junquera, as the food parcels that had been intended for parts of Catalonia now taken by the enemy were being used there. All medical centres and staffs are over-powered, however; at Cerbere, for instance, a doctor told me, are 1,500 wounded soldiers with hardly any sanitary necessities at all. Lack of sufficient transport for them is another difficulty. Dr Audrey Russell, who is well known for her fine work in Spain for many months, said that she had just been able to get her last canteen into French territory.

General Molesworth was another English worker at Le Perthus, where he was indefatigably trying to get the internationals together. 'Only a handful have come through so far,' the General told me.

Some of the camps to which the Spanish refugees are going are not fit to receive human beings. The problem has been too vast to be dealt with as yet.

At the great central camp at Le Boulou are thousands of men, women, and children. On one side of the road is an enclosure with wire fencing. On the other the refugees who walked down from Le Perthus yesterday are lying, sitting, standing, doing nothing this cold end of a February afternoon. It is a horrible sight, and all of them, men, women and children, are in the utmost depression. This 'camp' is a large, flat, bare area, the grass trodden down into a sort of grey compost. They sleep here, in the open. A few have rigged up some vague kind of shelter.

As for medical aid – just one case I saw will show the state of things. A woman lamented that she could do nothing for her child. She took off the little girl's bonnet and said: 'These dreadful sores are the result of typhus.' They come and stand around you and talk; they argue among themselves in front of you: 'Are we worse off here today than we might be in Spain?' Then a woman cries out, 'I shall never get into a train without knowing where it is going, for I have heard that they want to send us back to Franco.' Other voices broke out: 'Ninety-five per cent of us want to go to Mexico – anything rather than return to Spain as it will be under the fascists.' At the village town hall a girl I knew in Spain says she thinks the women she is one of in a long queue may get a permit to go to Perpignan some time soon. All the men, says a French guard, are going to Argeles; when? No one knows. In all of this families get separated; the men are taken from their families in some cases. Every phrase ends in 'I don't know.' As for the wounded – they are lying in the ditch among their crutches; a man limps by in obvious agony.

Somehow one becomes accustomed to such sights after ten days. But they become more real again when I try to set down just a fraction here and compare this mass-wretchedness with the 'business-eye' of some Marseilles white-slave traffickers who have made their appearance. There are many pretty girls in the Spanish migration.

HELEN KIRKPATRICK
1909–1997

As the lone female on the international staff of the *Chicago Daily News*, American reporter Helen Kirkpatrick braved some of the worst conditions of World War Two to establish herself as a major war reporter.

In 1944, for instance, she accompanied the American troops as they stormed the Normandy beaches. This commitment to her writing impressed both readers and the authorities, and, post-war, Kirkpatrick was awarded the French Legion of Honour and the US Medal of Freedom.

The following article is a good example of the personal style that she often brought to her reports and describes how she managed to dodge the Luftwaffe's raids and survive the London blitz.

On Surviving the London Blitz

9 September 1940, *Chicago Daily News*

London still stood this morning, which was the greatest surprise to me as I cycled home in the light of early dawn after the most frightening night I have ever spent. But not all of London was still there, and some of the things I saw this morning would scare the wits out of anyone.

When the sirens first shrieked on Saturday, it was evident we were in for something, but dinner proceeded calmly enough. It was when the first screaming bomb started on its downward track that we decided the basement would be healthier.

The whole night was one of moving from the basement to the first floor, with occasional sallies to make sure that no incendiaries had landed on the rooftop.

That was perhaps more frightening than the sound of constant bombs punctuated by guns near and far. For the London air was heavy with the burning smell. The smoke sometimes brought tears to the eyes, and the glow around the horizon certainly looked as though the entire city might be up in flames any minute.

On one occasion I dropped off to sleep on a basement floor and slept probably forty-five minutes, when two screamers sounding as though they had landed right next door brought me, startled, to my feet. A few minutes later a couple of incendiaries arrived just around the corner, but the fire equipment came within seconds.

Most of the time we felt that the entire center of the city had probably been blasted out of existence and we ticked off each hit with 'That must be Buckingham Palace – that's Whitehall.' It was staggering, to say the least, to cycle for a mile through the heart of London and fail to see even one pane of glass shattered and eventually to find one's own house standing calm and in one piece.

A later tour, however, showed that while none of the bombs hit any objectives we had picked out, they had landed squarely on plenty of places. I walked through areas of rubble and debris in southeastern London this morning that made it seem incredible that anyone could be alive, but they were, and very much so. Fires for the most part were put out or were well under control by early morning.

It was a contrast to find one section of 'smart London' that had as bad a dose as the tenement areas. Near one of many of Sir Christopher Wren's masterpieces, houses were gutted structures with windowpanes hanging out, while panes in a church were broken in a million pieces.

It is amazing this morning to see London traffic more like New York theater traffic than the slow dribble it had been during past months, but it is most amazing to see that there is any London to have traffic at all, it is pretty incredible, too, to find people relatively unshaken after the terrific experience.

There is some terror, but nothing on the scale that the Germans may have hoped for and certainly not on a scale to make Britons contemplate for a moment anything but fighting on.

Fright becomes so mingled with a deep almost uncontrollable anger that it is hard to know when one stops and the other begins. And on top of it all London is smiling even in the districts where casualties must have been very heavy.

MARTHA GELLHORN
1908–98

Quitting university after just a year, Gellhorn had a prodigious start to her writing career, contributing to publications including the *New Republic* whilst still in her late teens. Determined to become a foreign correspondent, she then moved to France in her twenties to work for the United Press bureau in Paris.

Thus started a brilliant career, which saw Gellhorn bring her pacifist-tinged views to reports on conflicts ranging from the Spanish Civil War to Vietnam, and, finally, the wars in Central America. Some of her most striking writing came from the period of World War Two, when, in Gellhorn's words, she 'followed the war wherever I could reach it'. The following article, her May 1945 account of the prisoner of war camp, Dachau, is startling in both its detail and humanity.

Dachau

1945, The Face of War

MAY 1945—We came out of Germany in a C-47 carrying American prisoners of war. The planes were lined up on the grass field at Regensburg and the passengers waited, sitting in the shade under the wings. They would not leave the planes; this was a trip no one was going to miss. When the crew chief said all aboard, we got in as if we were escaping from a fire. No one looked out the windows as we flew over Germany. No one ever wanted to see Germany again. They turned away from it, with hatred and sickness. At first they did not talk, but when it became real that Germany was behind forever they began talking of their prisons. We did not comment on the Germans; they are past words, there is nothing to say. 'No one will believe us,' a soldier said. They agreed on that; no one would believe them.

'Where were you captured, miss?' a soldier asked.

'I'm only bumming a ride; I've been down to see Dachau.'

One of the men said suddenly, 'We got to talk about it. We got to talk about it, if anyone believes us or not.'

Behind the barbed wire and the electric fence, the skeletons sat in the sun and searched themselves for lice. They have no age and no faces; they all look alike and like nothing you will ever see if you are lucky. We crossed the wide, crowded, dusty compound between the prison barracks and went to the hospital. In the hall sat more of the skeletons, and from them came the smell of disease and death. They watched us but did not move; no expression shows on a face that is only yellowish, stubbly skin, stretched across bone. What had been a man dragged himself into the doctor's office; he was a Pole and he was about six feet tall and he weighed less than a hundred pounds and he wore a striped prison shirt, a pair of unlaced boots, and a blanket which he tried to hold around his legs. His eyes were large and strange and stood out from his face, and his jawbone seemed to be cutting through his skin. He had come to Dachau from Buchenwald on the last death transport. There were fifty boxcars of his dead travelling companions still on the siding outside the camp, and for the last three days the American Army had forced Dachau civilians to bury these dead. When this transport had arrived, the German guards locked the men, women and children in the boxcars and there they slowly died of hunger and thirst and suffocation. They screamed and they tried to fight their way out; from time to time, the guards fired into the cars to stop the noise.

This man had survived; he was found under a pile of dead. Now he stood on the bones that were his legs and talked and suddenly he wept. 'Everyone is dead,' he said, and the face that was not a face twisted with pain or sorrow or horror. 'No one is left. Everyone is dead. I cannot help myself. Here I am and I am finished and cannot help myself. Everyone is dead.'

The Polish doctor who had been a prisoner here for five years said, 'In four weeks, you will be a young man again. You will be fine.'

Perhaps his body will live and take strength, but one cannot believe that his eyes will ever be like other people's eyes.

The doctor spoke with great detachment about the things he had watched in this hospital. He had watched them and there was nothing he could do to stop them. The prisoners talked in the same way – quietly, with a strange little smile as if they apologized for talking of such loathsome things to someone who lived in a real world and could hardly be expected to understand Dachau.

'The Germans made here some unusual experiments,' the doctor said. 'They wished to see how long an aviator could go without oxygen, how high in the sky he could go. So they had a closed car from which they pumped the oxygen. It is a quick death,' he said. 'It does not take more than fifteen minutes, but it is a hard death. They killed not so many people, only eight hundred in that experiment. It was found that no one can live above thirty-six thousand feet altitude without oxygen.'

'Whom did they choose for this experiment?' I asked.

'Any prisoner,' he said, 'so long as he was healthy. They picked the strongest. The mortality was one hundred per cent, of course.'

'It is very interesting, is it not?' said another Polish doctor.

We did not look at each other. I do not know how to explain it, but aside from the terrible anger you feel, you are ashamed. You are ashamed for mankind.

'There was also the experiment of the water,' said the first doctor. 'This was to see how long pilots could survive when they were shot down over water, like the Channel, let us say. For that, the German doctors put the prisoners in great vats and they stood in water up to their necks. It was found that the human body can resist for two and a half hours in water eight degrees below zero. They killed six hundred people in this experiment. Sometimes a man had to suffer three times, for he fainted early in the experiment, and then he was revived and a few days later the experiment was again undertaken.'

'Didn't they scream, didn't they cry out?'

He smiled at that question. 'There was no use in this place for a man to scream or cry out. It was no use for any man ever.'

A colleague of the Polish doctor came in; he was the one who knew about the malaria experiments. The German doctor, who was chief of the Army's tropical medicine research, used Dachau as an experimental station. He was attempting to find a way to immunize German soldiers against malaria. To that end, he inoculated eleven thousand prisoners with tertiary malaria. The death rate from the malaria was not too heavy; it simply meant that these prisoners, weakened by fever, died more quickly afterward from hunger. However, in one day three men died of overdoses of Pyramidon, with which, for some unknown reason, the Germans were then experimenting. No immunization for malaria was ever found.

Down the hall, in the surgery, the Polish surgeon got out the record book to look up some data on operations performed by the SS doctors. These were castration and sterilization operations. The prisoner was forced to sign a paper beforehand, saying that he willingly undertook this self-destruction. Jews and gypsies were castrated; any foreign slave laborer who had had relations with a German woman was sterilized. The German women were sent to other concentration camps.

The Polish surgeon had only his four front upper teeth left, the others on both sides having been knocked out by a guard one day, because the guard felt like breaking teeth. This act did not seem a matter of surprise to the doctor or to anyone else. No brutality could surprise them any more. They were used to a systematic cruelty that had gone on, in this concentration camp, for twelve years.

The surgeon mentioned another experiment, really a very bad one, he said, and obviously quite useless. The guinea pigs were Polish priests. (Over two thousand priests passed through Dachau; one thousand are alive.) The German doctors injected streptococci germs in the upper leg of the prisoners, between the muscle and the bone. An extensive abscess formed, accompanied by fever and extreme pain. The Polish doctor knew of more than a hundred cases treated this way; there may have been more. He had a record of thirty-one deaths, but it took usually from two to three months of ceaseless pain before the patient died, and all of them died after several operations performed during the last few days of their life. The operations were a further experiment, to see if a dying man could be saved; but the answer was that he could not. Some prisoners recovered entirely, because they were treated with the already known and proved antidote, but there were others who were now moving around the camp, as best they could, crippled for life.

Then, because I could listen to no more, my guide, a German Socialist who had been a prisoner in Dachau for ten and a half years, took me across the compound to the jail. In Dachau, if you want to rest from one horror you go and see another. The jail was a long clean building with small white cells in it. Here lived the people whom the prisoners called the NN. NN stands for *Nacht und Nebel*, which means night and mist. Translated into less romantic terms, this means that the prisoners in these cells never saw a human being, were never allowed to speak to anyone, were never taken out into the sun and the air. They lived in solitary confinement on water soup and a slice of bread, which was the camp diet. There was of course the danger of going mad. But one never knew what happened to them in the years of their silence. And on the Friday before the Sunday when the Americans entered Dachau, eight thousand men were removed by the SS on a final death transport. Among these were all the prisoners from the solitary cells. None of these men has been heard of since. Now in the clean empty building a woman, alone in a cell, screamed for a long time on one terrible note, was silent for a moment, and screamed again. She had gone mad in the last few days; we came too late for her.

In Dachau if a prisoner was found with a cigarette butt in his pocket he received twenty-five to fifty lashes with a bull whip. If he failed to stand at attention with his hat off, six feet away from any SS trooper who happened to pass, he had his hands tied behind his back and he was hung by his bound hands from a hook on the wall for an hour. If he did any other little thing which displeased the jailers he was put in the box. The box is the size of a telephone booth. It is so constructed that being in it alone a man cannot sit down, or kneel down, or of course lie down. It was usual to put four men in it together. Here they stood for three days and nights without food or water or any form of sanitation. Afterward they went back to the sixteen-hour day of labor and the diet of water soup and a slice of bread like soft gray cement.

What had killed most of these people was hunger; starvation was simply routine. A man worked those incredible hours on that diet and lived in such overcrowding as cannot be imagined, the bodies packed into airless barracks, and woke each morning weaker, waiting for his death. It is not known how many people died in this camp in the twelve years of its existence, but at least forty-five thousand are known to have died in the last three years. Last February and March, two thousand were killed in the gas chamber because, though they were too weak to work, they did not have the grace to die; so it was arranged for them.

The gas chamber is part of the crematorium. The crematorium is a brick building outside the camp compound, standing in a grove of pine trees. A Polish priest had attached himself to us and as we walked there he said, 'I started to die twice of starvation but I was very lucky. I got a job as a mason when we were building this crematorium, so I received a little more food, and that way I did not die.' Then he said, 'Have you seen our chapel, madame?' I said I had not, and my guide said I could not; it was within the zone where the two thousand typhus cases were more or less isolated. 'It is a pity,' the priest said. 'We finally got a chapel and we had Holy Mass there almost every Sunday. There are very beautiful murals. The man who painted them died of hunger two months ago.'

Now we were at the crematorium. 'You will put a handkerchief over your nose,' the guide said. There, suddenly, but never to be believed, were the bodies of the dead. They were everywhere. There were piles of them inside the oven room, but the SS had not had time to burn them. They were piled outside the door and alongside the building. They were all naked, and behind the crematorium the ragged clothing of the dead was neatly stacked, shirts, jackets, trousers, shoes, awaiting sterilization and further use. The clothing was handled with order, but the bodies were dumped like garbage, rotting in the sun, yellow and nothing but bones, bones grown huge because there was no flesh to cover them, hideous, terrible, agonizing bones, and the unendurable smell of death.

We have all seen a great deal now; we have seen too many wars and too much violent dying; we have seen hospitals, bloody and messy as butcher shops; we have seen the dead like bundles lying on all the roads of half the earth. But nowhere was there anything like this. Nothing about war was ever as insanely wicked as these starved and outraged, naked, nameless dead. Behind one pile of dead lay the clothed healthy bodies of the German soldiers who had been found in this camp. They were shot at once when the American Army entered. And for the first time anywhere one could look at a dead man with gladness.

Just behind the crematorium stood the fine big modern hothouses. Here the prisoners grew the flowers that the SS officers loved. Next to the hothouses were the vegetable gardens, and very rich ones too, where the starving prisoners cultivated the vitamin foods that kept the SS strong. But if a man, dying of hunger, furtively pulled up and gorged himself on a head of lettuce, he would be beaten until he was unconscious. In front of the crematorium, separated from it by a stretch of garden, stood a long row of well-built, commodious homes. The families of the SS officers lived here; their wives and children lived here quite happily, while the chimneys of the crematorium poured out unending smoke heavy with human ashes.

The American soldier in the plane said, 'We got to talk about it.' You cannot talk about it very well because there is a kind of shock that sets in and makes it almost unbearable to remember what you have seen. I have not talked about the women who were moved to Dachau three weeks ago from their own concentration camps. Their crime was that they were Jewish. There was a lovely girl from Budapest, who somehow was still lovely, and the woman with mad eyes who had watched her sister walk into the gas chamber at Auschwitz and been held back and refused the right to die with her sister, and the Austrian woman who pointed out calmly that they all had only the sleazy dresses they wore on their backs, they had never had anything more, and that they worked outdoors sixteen hours a day too in the long winters, and that they too were 'corrected,' as the Germans say, for any offense, real or imaginary.

I have not talked about how it was the day the American Army arrived, though the prisoners told me. In their joy to be free, and longing to see their friends who had come at last, many prisoners rushed to the fence and died electrocuted. There were those who died cheering, because that effort of happiness was more than their bodies could endure. There were those who died because now they had food, and they ate before they could be stopped, and it killed them. I do not know words to describe the men who have survived this horror for years, three years, five years, ten years, and whose minds are as clear and unafraid as the day they entered.

I was in Dachau when the German armies surrendered unconditionally to the Allies. The same half-naked skeleton who had been dug out of the death train shuffled back into the doctor's office. He said something in Polish; his voice was no stronger than a whisper. The Polish doctor clapped his hands gently and said, 'Bravo.' I asked what they were talking about.

'The war is over,' the doctor said. 'Germany is defeated.'

We sat in that room, in that accursed cemetery prison, and no one had anything more to say. Still, Dachau seemed to me the most suitable place in Europe to hear the news of victory. For surely this war was made to abolish Dachau, and all the other places like Dachau, and everything that Dachau stood for, and to abolish it forever.

MARGUERITE HIGGINS
1920–66

Hired by the *New York Herald Tribune* in 1942, Marguerite Higgins was always determined to be a war reporter, and, after two years of lobbying her editor, was sent first to London and then mainland Europe. During these early years of her career she showed a unique ability to dodge both enemy bullets and male biases, accompanying the GIs as they occupied Berlin and becoming one of the first reporters into both Dachau and Buchenwald Nazi war camps.

By the time the following article was written her career and reputation as one of the foremost American war reporters was, therefore, well underway. Her account of wading onto Red Beach with the marines is just one of the many vivid descriptions of the front which went on to win her the Pulitzer Prize for International Reporting in 1951.

On the American Invasion of Inchon, Korea

18 September 1950, *New York Herald Tribune*

Heavily laden US marines, in one of the most technically difficult amphibious landings in history, stormed at sunset today over a ten-foot sea wall in the heart of the port of Inchon and within an hour had taken three commanding hills in the city.

I was in the fifth wave that hit 'Red Beach,' which in reality was a rough, vertical pile of stones over which the first assault troops had to scramble with the aid of improvised landing ladders topped with steel hooks.

Despite a deadly and steady pounding from naval guns and airplanes, enough North Koreans remained alive close to the beach to harass us with small-arms and mortar fire. They even hurled hand grenades down at us as we crouched in trenches, which unfortunately ran behind the sea wall in the inland side.

It was far from the 'virtually unopposed' landing for which the troops had hoped after hearing of the quick capture of Wolmi Island in the morning by an earlier Marine assault. Wolmi is inside Inchon harbor and just off 'Red Beach.' At H-hour minus seventy, confident, joking Marines started climbing down from the transport ship on cargo nest and dropping into small assault boats. Our wave commander, Lieutenant R. J. Schening, a veteran of five amphibious assaults, including Guadalcanal, hailed me with the comment, 'This has a good chance of being a pushover.'

Because of tricky tides, our transport had to stand down the channel and it was more than nine miles to the rendezvous point where our assault waves formed up.

The channel reverberated with the earsplitting boom of warship guns and rockets. Blue and orange flames spurted from the 'Red Beach' area and a huge oil tank, on fire, sent great black rings of smoke over the shore. Then the fire from the big suns lifted and the planes that had been circling overhead swooped low to rake their fire deep into the sea wall.

The first wave of our assault troops was speeding toward the shore by now. It would be H-hour (5:30 P.M.) in two minutes. Suddenly, bright-orange tracer bullets spun out from the hill in our direction.

'My God! There are still some left,' Lieutenant Schening said. 'Everybody get down. Here we go!'

It was H-hour plus fifteen minutes as we sped the last two thousand yards to the beach. About halfway there the bright tracers started cutting across the top of our little boat. 'Look at their faces now,' said John Davies of the Newark *News*. I turned and saw that the men around me had expressions contorted with anxiety.

We struck the sea wall hard at a place where it had crumbled into a canyon. The bullets were whining persistently, spattering the water around us. We clambered over the high steel sides of the boat, dropping into the water and, taking shelter beside the boat as long as we could, snaked on our stomachs up into a rock-strewn dip in the sea wall.

In the sky there was good news. A bright, white star shell from the high ground to our left and an amber cluster told us that the first wave had taken their initial objective, Observatory Hill. But whatever the luck of the first four waves, we were relentlessly pinned down by rifle and automatic-weapon fire coming down on us from another rise on the right.

There were some thirty Marines and two correspondents crouched in the gouged-out sea wall. Then another assault boat swept up, disgorging about thirty more Marines. This went on for two more waves until our hole was filled and Marines lying on their stomachs were strung out all across the top of the sea wall.

An eerie colored light flooded the area as the sun went down with a glow that a newsreel audience would have thought a fake. As the dusk settled, the glare of burning buildings all around lit the sky.

Suddenly, as we lay there intent on the firing ahead, a sudden rush of water came up into the dip in the wall and we saw a huge LST (Landing Ship, Tank) rushing at us with the great plank door half down. Six more yards and the ship would have crushed twenty men. Warning shouts sent every one speeding from the sea wall, searching for escape from the LST and cover from the gunfire. The LST's huge bulk sent a rush of water pouring over the sea wall as it crunched in, soaking most of us.

The Marines ducked and zigzagged as they raced across the open, but enemy bullets caught a good many in the semi-darkness. The wounded were pulled aboard the LSTs, six of which appeared within sixty-five minutes after H-hour.

As nightfall closed in, the Marine commanders ordered their troops forward with increasing urgency, for they wanted to assure a defensible perimeter for the night.

In this remarkable amphibious operation, where tides played such an important part, the Marines were completely isolated from outside supply lines for exactly four hours after H-hour. At this time the outrushing tides – they fluctuate thirty-one feet in twelve-hour periods – made mud flats of the approaches to 'Red Beach.' The LSTs bringing supplies simply settled on the flats, helpless until the morning tides would float them again.

At the battalion command post the news that the three high-ground objectives – the British Consulate, Cemetery Hill, and Observatory Hill – had been taken arrived at about H-hour plus sixty-one minutes. Now the important items of business became debarking tanks, guns, and ammunition from the LSTs.

Every cook, clerk, driver, and administrative officer in the vicinity was rounded up to help in the unloading. It was exciting to see the huge M-26 tanks rumble across big planks onto the beach, which only a few minutes before had been protected only by riflemen and machine gunners. Then came the bulldozers, trucks, and jeeps.

It was very dark in the shadow of the ships, and the unloaders had a hazardous time dodging bullets, mortar fire, and their own vehicles.

North Koreans began giving up by the dozens by this time and we could see them, hands up, marching across the open fields toward the LSTs. They were taken charge of with considerable glee by a Korean Marine policeman, Captain Woo, himself a native of Inchon, who had made the landing with several squads of men who were also natives of the city. They learned of the plan to invade their home town only after they had boarded their ship.

Tonight, Captain Woo was in a state of elation beyond even that of the American Marines who had secured the beachhead. 'When the Koreans see your power,' he said, 'they will come in droves to our side.'

As we left the beach and headed back to the Navy flagship, naval guns were booming again in support of the Marines. 'This time,' said a battalion commander, 'they are preparing the road to Seoul.'

MARY McCARTHY
1912–89

Novelist, theatre critic, memoirist and travel writer, Mary McCarthy is still perhaps best known for her political essays, which covered an estimable range of subjects, including sexual emancipation, the nuclear threat, communism and the Watergate crisis. Having embraced communism in the early 1930s, she swiftly lost her taste for it, later writing, 'I realized, with a certain wistfulness, that it was too late for me to become any kind of Marxist. Marxism, I saw, from the learned young man I listened to at Committee meetings, was something you had to take up young, like ballet dancing.'

With the Vietnam war underway, there was much demand from various editors for her to cover the conflict first hand. The following article records her experiences on first arriving in Saigon and her opposition to the war being waged there.

Report from Vietnam

I   THE HOME PROGRAM

20 April 1967, *New York Review of Books*

I confess that when I went to Vietnam early in February I was looking for material damaging to the American interest and that I found it, though often by accident or in the process of being briefed by an official. Finding it is no job; the Americans do not dissemble what they are up to. They do not seem to feel the need, except through verbiage: e.g., napalm has become 'Incinder-jell,' which makes it sound like Jello. And defoliants are referred to as weed-killers – something you use in your driveway. The resort to euphemism denotes, no doubt, a guilty conscience or – the same thing nowadays – a twinge in the public-relations nerve. Yet what is most surprising to a new arrival in Saigon is the general unawareness, almost innocence, of how what 'we' are doing could look to an outsider.

At the airport in Bangkok, the war greeted the Air France passengers in the form of a strong smell of gasoline, which made us sniff as we breakfasted at a long table, like a delegation, with the Air France flag planted in the middle. Outside, huge Esso tanks were visible behind lattice screens, where US bombers, factory-new, were aligned as if in a salesroom. On the field itself, a few yards from our Caravelle, US cargo planes were warming up for take-off; US helicopters flitted about among the swallows, while US military trucks made deliveries. The openness of the thing was amazing (the fact that the US was using Thailand as a base for bombing North Vietnam was not officially admitted at the time); you would have thought they would try to camouflage it, I said to a German correspondent, so that the tourists would not see. As the Caravelle flew on toward Saigon, the tourists, bound for Tokyo or Manila, were able to watch a South Vietnamese hillside burning while consuming a 'cool drink' served by the hostess. From above, the bright flames looked like a summer forest fire; you could not believe that bombers had just left. At Saigon, the airfield was dense with military aircraft; in the 'civil' side, where we landed, a passenger jetliner was loading GI's for Rest and Recreation in Hawaii. The American presence was overpowering, and, although one had read about it and was aware, as they say, that there was a war on, the sight and sound of that massed American might, casually disposed on foreign soil, like a corporal having his shoes shined, took one's breath away. 'They don't try to hide it!' I kept saying to myself, as though the display of naked power and muscle ought to have worn some cover of modesty. But within a few hours I had lost this sense of incredulous surprise, and, seeing the word, 'hide,' on a note-pad in my hotel room the next morning, I no longer knew what I had meant by it (as when a fragment of a dream, written down on waking, becomes indecipherable) or why I should have been pained, as an American, by this high degree of visibility.

As we drove into downtown Saigon, through a traffic jam, I had the fresh shock of being in what looked like an American city, a very shoddy West Coast one, with a Chinatown and a slant-eyed Asiatic minority. Not only military vehicles of every description, but Chevrolets, Chryslers, Mercedes Benz, Volkswagens, Triumphs, and white men everywhere in sport shirts and drip-dry pants. The civilian take-over is even more astonishing than the military. To an American, Saigon today is less exotic than Florence or the Place de la Concorde. New office buildings of cheap modern design, teeming with teazed, puffed secretaries and their Washington bosses, are surrounded by sandbags and guarded by MP's; new, jerrybuilt villas in pastel tones, to rent to Americans, are under construction or already beginning to peel and discolor. Even removing the sandbags and the machine guns and restoring the trees that have been chopped down to widen the road to the airport, the mind cannot excavate what Saigon must have been like 'before.' Now it resembles a gigantic PX. All those white men seem to be carrying brown paper shopping bags, full of whiskey and other goodies; rows of ballpoints gleam in the breast pockets of their checked shirts. In front of his villa, a leathery oldster, in visored cap, unpacks his golf clubs from his station wagon, while his cotton-haired wife, in a flowered print dress, glasses slung round her neck, stands by, watching, her hands on her hips. As in the American vacation-land, dress is strictly informal; nobody but an Asian wears a tie or a white shirt. The Vietnamese old men and boys, in wide, conical hats, pedaling their Cyclos (the modern version of the rickshaw) in and out of the traffic pattern, the Vietnamese women in high heels and filmy ao-dais of pink, lavender, heliotrope, the signs and Welcome banners in Vietnamese actually contribute to the Stateside impression by the addition of 'local' color, as though you were back in a Chinese restaurant in San Francisco or in a Japanese suki-yaki place, under swaying paper lanterns, being served by women in kimonos while you sit on mats and play at using chopsticks.

Perhaps most of all Saigon is like a stewing Los Angeles, shading into Hollywood, Venice Beach, and Watts. The native stall markets are still in business, along Le Loi and Nguyen Hue Streets, but the merchandise, is, for Asia, exotic. There is hardly anything native to buy, except flowers and edibles and fire-crackers at Têt time and – oh yes – souvenir dolls. Street vendors and children are offering trays of American cigarettes and racks on racks of Johnnie Walker, Haig & Haig, Black & White (which are either black market, stolen from the PX, or spurious, depending on the price); billboards outside car agencies advertise Triumphs, Thunderbirds, MG's, Corvettes, 'For Delivery here or Stateside, Payment on Easy Terms'; non-whites, the less affluent ones, are mounted on Hondas and Lambrettas. There are photo-copying services, film-developing services, Western tailoring and dry-cleaning services, radio and TV repair shops, air-conditioners, Olivetti typewriters, comic books, *Time, Life,* and *Newsweek*, airmail paper – you name it, they have it. Toys for Vietnamese children (there are practically no American kids in Vietnam) include US-style jackknives, pistols, and simulated-leather belts, with holsters – I did not see any cowboy suits or Indian war-feathers. Pharmaceuticals are booming, and a huge bill-board all along the top of a building in the central marketplace shows, for some reason, a smiling Negro with very white teeth advertising a toothpaste called Hynos.

If Saigon by day is like a PX, at night, with flares overhead, it is like a World's Fair or Exposition in some hick American city. There are Chinese restaurants, innumerable French restaurants (not surprising), but also La Dolce Vita, Le Guillaume Tell, the Paprika (a Spanish restaurant on a rooftop, serving paella and sangría). The national cuisine no American wants to sample is the Vietnamese. In February, a German circus was in town. 'French' wine is made in Cholon, the local Chinatown. In the nightclubs, if it were not for the bar girls, you would think you were on a cruise ship: a *chanteuse* from Singapore sings old French, Italian, and American favorites into the microphone; an Italian magician palms the watch of a middle-aged Vietnamese customer; the band strikes up 'Happy Birthday to You,' as a cake is brought in. The 'vice' in Saigon – at least what I was able to observe of it – has a pepless *Playboy* flavor.

As for virtue, I went to church one Sunday in the Cathedral (a medley of Gothic, Romanesque, and vaguely Moorish) on John F. Kennedy Square, hoping to hear the mass in Vietnamese. Instead, an Irish-American priest preached a sermon on the hemline to a large male white congregation of soldiers, construction-workers, newspaper correspondents; in the pews were also some female secretaries from the Embassy and other US agencies and a quotient of middle-class Vietnamese of both sexes. The married men present, he began, did not have to be told that the yearly rise or fall in skirt lengths was a 'traumatic experience' for a woman, and he likened the contemporary style centers – New York, Chicago, San Francisco – to the ancient 'style centers' of the Church – Rome, Antioch, Jerusalem. His point seemed to be that the various rites of the Church (Latin, Coptic, Armenian, Maronite – he went into it very thoroughly) were only *modes* of worship. What the Sunday-dressed Vietnamese, whose hemline remains undisturbed by changes emanating from the 'style centers' and who were hearing the Latin mass in American, were able to make of the sermon, it was impossible to tell. Just as it was impossible to tell what some very small Vietnamese children I saw in a home for war orphans were getting out of an American adult TV program they were watching at bedtime, the littlest ones mother-naked. Maybe TV too is catholic, and the words do not matter.

Saigon has a smog problem, like New York and Los Angeles, a municipal garbage problem, a traffic problem, power failures, inflation, juvenile delinquency. In short, it meets most of the criteria of a modern Western city. The young soldiers do not like Saigon and its clip joints and high prices. Everybody is trying to sell them something or buy something from them. Six-year-old boys, cute as pins, are plucking at them: 'You come see my sister. She Number One fuck.' To help the GI resist the temptations of merchants – and soak up his buying power – diamonds and minks are offered him in the PX, tax free. (There were no minks the day I went there, but I did see a case of diamond rings, the prices ranging up to 900-odd dollars.) Unfortunately, the PX presents its own temptation – that of resale. The GI is gypped by taxidrivers and warned against Cyclo men, (probably VC) and he may wind up in a Vietnamese jail, like some of his buddies, for doing what everybody else does – illegal currency transactions. If he walks in the center after nightfall, he has to pick his way among whole families who are cooking their unsanitary meal or sleeping, right on the street, in the filth. When he rides in from the airport, he has to cross a bend of the river, bordered by shanties, that he has named, with rich American humor, Cholera Creek.

To the servicemen, Saigon stinks. They would rather be in base camp, which is clean. And the JUSPAO press officer has a rote speech for arriving correspondents: 'Get out of Saigon. That's my advice to you. Go out into the field.' As though the air were purer there, where the fighting is.

That is true in a way. The Americanization process smells better out there, to Americans, even when perfumed by napalm. Out there, too, there is an enemy a man can respect. For many of the soldiers in the field and especially the younger officers, the Viet Cong is the only Vietnamese worthy of notice. 'If we only had them fighting on our side, instead of the goddamned Arvin [Army of the Vietnamese Republic], we'd *win* this war' is a sentiment the newspapermen like to quote. I never heard it said in those words, but I found that you could judge an American by his attitude toward the Viet Cong. If he called them 'Charlie' (cf. John Steinbeck), he was either an infatuated civilian, a low-grade primitive in uniform, or a fatuous military mouthpiece. Decent soldiers and officers called them 'the VC.' The same code of honor applied in South Vietnamese circles; with the Vietnamese, who are ironic, it was almost a pet name for the enemy. Most of the American military will praise the fighting qualities of the VC, and the more intellectual (who are not necessarily the best) praise them for their 'motivation.' Americans have become very incurious, but the Viet Cong has awakened the curiosity of the men who are fighting them. From within the perimeter of the camp, behind the barbed wire and the sand-bags, they study their habits, half-amused, half-admiring; gingerly a relationship is established with the unseen enemy, who is probably carefully fashioning a booby trap a few hundred yards away. This relation does not seem to extend to the North Vietnamese troops, but in that case contact is rarer. The military are justly nervous of the VC, but unless they have been wounded out on a patrol or have had the next man killed by a mine or a mortar, they do not show hatred or picture the black-pajama saboteur as a 'monster,' a word heard in Saigon offices.

In the field, moreover, the war is not questioned: it is just a fact. The job has to be finished – that is the attitude. In Saigon, the idea that the war can ever be finished appears fantastic: the Americans will be there forever, one feels; if they go, the economy will collapse. What postwar aid program could be conceived – or passed by Congress – that would keep the air in the balloon? And if the Americans go, the middle-class Saigonese think, the Viet Cong will surely come back, in two years, five years, ten, as they come back to a 'pacified' hamlet at Têt time, to leave, as it were, a calling-card, a reminder – we are still here. But, at the same time, in Saigon the worth of the American presence, that is, of the war, seems very dubious, since the actual results, in uglification, moral and physical, are evident to all. The American soldier, bumping along in a jeep or a military truck, resents seeing all those Asiatics at the wheels of new Cadillacs. He knows about corruption, often firsthand, having contributed his bit to it, graft, theft of AID and military supplies from the port. He thinks it is disgusting that the local employees steal from the PX and then stage a strike when the manageress makes them line up to be searched on leaving the building. And he has heard that these 'apes,' as some men call them, are salting away the profits in Switzerland or in France, where De Gaulle, who is pro-VC, has just run the army out.

Of course, all wars have had their profiteers, but it has not usually been so manifest, so inescapable. The absence of the austerity that normally accompanies war, of civilian sacrifices, rationing, shortages, blackouts (compare wartime London or even wartime New York, twenty-five years ago) makes this war seem singularly immoral and unheroic to those who are likely to die in it – for what? So that the Saigonese and other civilians can live high off the hog? The fact that the soldier or officer is living pretty high off the hog himself does not reconcile him to the glut of Saigon; rather the contrary. Furthermore, an atmosphere of sacrifice is heady; that – and danger – is what used to make wartime capitals gay. Saigon is not gay. The peculiar thing is that with all those young soldiers wandering about, all those young journalists news-chasing, Saigon seems so middle-aged – inert, listless, bored. That, I suppose, is because everyone's principal interest there is money, the only currency that is circulating, like the stale air moved by ceiling-fans and air-conditioners in hotels and offices.

The war, they say, is not going to be won in Saigon, nor on the battlefield, but in the villages and hamlets. This idea, by now trite (it was first discovered in Diem's time and has been rebaptized under a number of names – New Life Hamlets, Rural Construction, Counter Insurgency, Nation-Building, Revolutionary Development, the Hearts and Minds Program), is the main source of inspiration for the various teams of missionaries, military and civilian, who think they are engaged in a crusade. Not just a crusade against Communism, but something *positive*. Back in the Fifties and early Sixties, the war was presented as an investment: the taxpayer was persuaded that if he stopped Communism *now* in Vietnam, he would not have to keep stopping it in Thailand, Burma, etc. That was the domino theory, which our leading statesmen today, quite comically, are busy repudiating before Congressional committees – suddenly nobody will admit to ever having been an advocate of it. The notion of a costly investment that will save money in the end had a natural appeal to a nation of homeowners, but now the assertion of an American 'interest' in Vietnam has begun to look too speculative as the stake increases ('When is it going to pay off?') and also too squalid as the war daily becomes more savage and destructive. Hence the 'other' war, proclaimed by Johnson in Honolulu, which is simultaneously pictured as a strategy for winning War Number One and as a top priority in itself. Indeed, in Vietnam, there are moments when the 'other' war seems to be viewed as the sole reason for the American presence, and it is certainly more congenial to American officials, brimming with public spirit, than the war they are launching from the skies. Americans do not like to be negative, and the 'other' war is constructive.

To see it, of course, you have to get out of Saigon, but, before you go, you will have to be briefed, in one of those new office buildings, on what you are going to see. In the field, you will be briefed again, by a military man, in a district or province headquarters, and frequently all you will see of New Life Hamlets, Constructed Hamlets, Consolidated Hamlets, are the charts and graphs and maps and symbols that some ardent colonel or brisk bureaucrat is demonstrating to you with a pointer, and the mimeographed hand-out, full of statistics, that you take away with you, together with a supplement on Viet Cong Terror. On paper and in chart form, it all sounds commendable, especially if you are able to ignore the sounds of bombing from B-52s that are shaking the windows and making the charts rattle. The briefing official is enthusiastic, as he points out the progress that has been made, when, for example, the activities organized under AID were reorganized under OCO (Office of Civilian Operations). You stare at the chart on the office wall in which to you there is no semblance of logic or sequence ('Why,' you wonder, 'should Youth Affairs be grouped under Urban Development?'), and the official rubs his hands with pleasure: 'First we organized it *vertically.* Now we've organized *horizontally!'* Out in the field, you learn from some disgruntled officer that the AID representatives, who are perhaps now OCO representatives without knowing it, have not been paid for six months.

In a Saigon 'backgrounder,' you are told about public health measures undertaken by Free World Forces. Again a glowing progress report. In 1965, there were 180 medical people from the 'Free World' in Vietnam treating patients; in 1966, there were 700 – quite a little escalation, almost four times as many. The troop commitment, of course, not mentioned by the briefer, jumped from 60,000 to 400,000 – more than six-and-a-half times as many. That the multiplication of troops implied an obvious escalation in the number of civilian patients requiring treatment is not mentioned either. Under questioning, the official, slightly irritated, estimates that the civilian casualties comprise between 7½ and 15 per cent of the surgical patients treated in hospitals. He had 'not been interested particularly, until all the furore,' in what percentage of the patients were war casualties. And naturally he was not interested in what percentage of civilian casualties never reached a hospital at all.

But the treatment of war victims, it turned out, was not one of the medical 'bull's eyes' aimed at in the 'other' war. Rather a peacetime-type program, 'beefing up' the medical school, improvement of hospital facilities, donation of drugs and antibiotics (which, as I learned from a field worker, are in turn sold by the local nurses to the patients for whom they have been prescribed), the control of epidemic diseases, such as plague and cholera, education of the population in good health procedures. American and allied workers, you hear, are teaching the Vietnamese in the government villages to boil their water, and the children are learning dental hygiene. Toothbrushes are distributed, and the children are shown how to use them. If the children get the habit, the parents will copy them, a former social worker explains, projecting from experience with first-generation immigrants back home. There is a campaign on to vaccinate and immunize as much of the population as can be got to cooperate; easy subjects are refugees and forced evacuees, who can be lined up for shots while going through the screening process and being issued an identity card – a political health certificate.

All this is not simply on paper. In the field, you are actually able to see medical teams at work, setting up temporary dispensaries under the trees in the hamlets for the weekly or bi-weekly 'sick call' – distributing medicines, tapping, listening, sterilizing, bandaging; the most common diagnosis is suspected tuberculosis. In Tay Ninh Province, I watched a Philcag (Filipino) medical team at work in a Buddhist hamlet. One doctor was examining a very thin old man, who was stripped to the waist; probably tubercular, the doctor told me, writing something on a card which he gave to the old man. 'What happens next?' I wanted to know. Well the old man would go to the province hospital for an X-ray (that was the purpose of the card), and if the diagnosis was positive, then treatment should follow. I was impressed. But (as I later learned at a briefing) there are only sixty civilian hospitals in South Vietnam – for nearly 16 million people – so that the old man's total benefit, most likely, from the open-air consultation was to have learned, gratis, that he might be tubercular.

Across the road, some dentist's chairs were set up, and teeth were being pulled, very efficiently, from women and children of all ages. I asked about the toothbrushes I had heard about in Saigon. The Filipino major laughed. 'Yes, we have distributed them. They use them as toys.' Then he reached into his pocket – he was a kindly young man with children of his own – and took out some money for all the children who had gathered round to buy popsicles (the local equivalent) from the popsicle man. Later I watched the Filipino general, a very handsome tall man with a cropped head, resembling Yul Brynner, distribute Têt gifts and candy to children in a Cao Dai orphanage and be photographed with his arm around a little blind girl. A few hours earlier, he had posed distributing food in a Catholic hamlet – 'Free World' surplus items, such as canned cooked beets. The photography, I was told, would help sell the Philcag operation to the Assembly in Manila, where some leftist elements were trying to block funds for it. Actually, I could not see that the general was doing any harm – unless not doing enough is harm, in which case we are all guilty – and he was more efficient than other Civic Action leaders. His troops had just chopped down a large section of jungle (we proceeded through it in convoy, wearing bullet-proof vests and bristling with rifles and machine-guns, because of the VC), which was going to be turned into a New Life Hamlet for resettling refugees. They had also built a school, which we stopped to inspect, finding, to the general's surprise, that it had been taken over by the local district chief for his office headquarters.

The Filipino team, possibly because they were Asians, seemed to be on quite good terms with the population. Elsewhere – at Go Cong, in the delta – I saw mistrustful patients and heard stories of rivalry between the Vietnamese doctor, a gynecologist, and the Spanish and American medical teams; my companion and I were told that we were the first 'outsiders,' including the resident doctors, to be allowed by the Vietnamese into *his* wing – the maternity, which was far the cleanest and most modern in the hospital and contained one patient. Similar jealousies existed of the German medical staff at Hue. In the rather squalid surgical wing of the Go Pong hospital, there were two badly burned children. Were they war casualties, I asked the official who was showing us through. Yes, he conceded, as a matter of fact they were. How many of the patients were war-wounded, I wanted to know. 'About four' of the children, he reckoned. And one old man, he added, after reflection.

The Filipinos were fairly dispassionate about their role in pacification: this may have been because they had no troops fighting in the war (those leftist elements in the Assembly!) and therefore did not have to act like saviors of the Vietnamese people. The Americans, on the contrary, are zealots, above all the blueprinters in the Saigon offices, although occasionally in the field, too, you meet a true believer – a sandy, crew-cut, keen-eyed army colonel who talks to you about 'the nuts and bolts' of the program, which, he is glad to say, is finally getting the 'grass roots' support it needs. It is impossible to find out from such a man what he is doing, concretely; an aide steps forward to state, 'We sterilize the area prior to the insertion of the RD teams,' whose task, says the colonel, is to find out 'the aspirations of the people.' He cannot tell you whether there has been any land reform in his area – that is a strictly Vietnamese pigeon – in fact he has no idea of *how* the land in the area is owned. He is strong on coordination: all his Vietnamese counterparts, the colonel who 'wears two hats' as province chief, the mayor, a deposed general are all 'very fine sound men,' and the Marine general in the area is 'one of the finest men and officers' he has ever met. For another army zealot every Vietnamese officer he deals with is 'an outstanding individual.'

These springy, zesty, burning-eyed warriors, military and civilian, engaged in AID or Combined Action (essentially pacification) stir faraway memories of American college presidents of the fund-raising type; their diction is peppery with oxymoron ('When peace breaks out,' 'Then the commodities started to hit the beach'), like a college president's address to an alumni gathering. They see themselves in fact as educators, spreading the American way of life, a new *propaganda fide*. When I asked an OCO man in Saigon what his groups actually did in a Vietnamese village to prepare – his word – the people for elections, he answered curtly, 'We teach them Civics 101.'

The American taxpayer who thinks that aid means help has missed the idea. Aid is, first of all, to achieve economic stability within the present system, i.e., political stability for the present ruling groups. Loans are extended, under the counterpart fund arrangement, to finance Vietnamese imports of American capital equipment (thus aiding, with the other hand, American industry). Second, aid is *education*. Distribution of canned goods (instill new food habits), distribution of seeds, fertilizer, chewing-gum and candy (the Vietnamese complain that the GI's fire candy at their children, like a spray of bullets), lessons in sanitation, hog-raising, and crop-rotation. The program is designed, not just to make Americans popular but to shake up the Vietnamese, as in some 'stimulating' freshman course where the student learns to question the 'prejudices' implanted in him by his parents. 'We're trying to wean them away from the old barter economy and show them a market economy. Then they'll really *go*.'

'We're teaching them free enterprise,' explains a breathless JUSPAO official in the grim town of Phu Cuong. He is speaking of the 'refugees' from the Iron Triangle, who were forcibly cleared out of their hamlets, which were then burned and leveled, during Operation Cedar Falls ('Clear and Destroy'). They had just been transferred into a camp, hastily constructed by the ARVN with tin roofs painted red and white, to make the form, as seen from the air, of a giant Red Cross – 1,651 women, 3,754 children, 582 men, mostly old, who had been kindly allowed to bring some of their furniture and pots and pans and their pigs and chickens and sacks of their hoarded rice; their cattle had been transported for them, on barges, and were now sickening on a dry, stubbly, sandy plain. 'We've got a captive audience!' the official continued excitedly. 'This is our big chance!'

To teach them free enterprise and, presumably, when they were 'ready' for it, Civics 101; for the present, the government had to consider them 'hostile civilians.' These wives and children and grandfathers of men thought to be at large with the Viet Cong had been rice farmers only a few weeks before. Now they were going to have to pitch in and learn to be vegetable farmers; the area selected for their eventual resettlement was not suitable for rice-growing, unfortunately. Opportunity was beckoning for these poor peasants, thanks to the uprooting process they had just undergone. They would have the chance to buy and build their own homes on a pattern and of materials already picked out for them; the government was allowing them 1700 piasters toward the purchase price. To get a new house free, even though just in the abstract, would be unfair to them as human beings: investing their own labor and their own money would make them feel that the house was really *theirs.*

In the camp, a schoolroom had been set up for their children. Interviews with the parents revealed that more than anything else they wanted education for their children; they had not had a school for five years. I remarked that this seemed queer, since Communists were usually strong on education. The official insisted. 'Not for five years.' But in fact another American, a young one, who had actually been working in the camp, told me that strangely enough the small children there knew their multiplication tables and possibly their primer – he could not account for this. And in one of the razed villages, he related, the Americans had found, from captured exercise books, that someone had been teaching the past participle in English, using Latin models – defectors spoke of a high school teacher, a Ph.D. from Hanoi.

Perhaps the parents, in the interviews, told the Americans what they thought they wanted to hear. All over Vietnam, wherever peace has broken out, if only in the form of a respite, Marine and army officers are proud to show the schoolhouses their men are building or rebuilding for the hamlets they are patrolling, rifle on shoulder. At Rach Kien, in the delta (a Pentagon pilot-project of a few months ago), I saw the little schoolhouse Steinbeck wrote about, back in January, and the blue school desks he had seen the soldiers painting. They were still sitting outside, in the sun; the school was not yet rebuilt more than a month later – they were waiting for materials. In this hamlet, everything seemed to have halted, as in 'The Sleeping Beauty,' the enchanted day Steinbeck left; nothing had advanced. Indeed, the picture he sketched, of a ghost town coming back to civic life, made the officers who had entertained him smile – 'He used his imagination.' In other hamlets, I saw schoolhouses actually finished and one in operation. 'The school is dirty,' the colonel in charge barked at the Revolutionary Development director – a case of American tactlessness, though he was right. A young Vietnamese social worker said sadly that he wished the Americans would stop building schools. 'They don't realize – we have no teachers for them.'

Yet the little cream schoolhouse is essential to the American dream of what we are doing in Vietnam, and it is essential for the soldiers to believe that in *Viet Cong* hamlets no schooling is permitted. In Rach Kien I again expressed doubts, as a captain, with a professionally shocked face, pointed out the evidence that the school had been used as 'Charlie's' headquarters. 'So you really think that the children here got no lessons, *nothing*, under the VC?' 'Oh, indoctrination courses!' he answered with a savvy wave of his pipe, In other words, VC Civics 101.

If you ask a junior officer what he thinks our war aims are in Vietnam, he usually replies without hesitation: 'To punish aggression.' It is unkind to try to draw him into a discussion of what constitutes aggression and what is defense (the Bay of Pigs, Santo Domingo, Goa?), for he really has no further ideas on the subject. He has been indoctrinated, just as much as the North Vietnamese POW, who tells the interrogation team he is fighting to 'liberate the native soil from the American aggressors' – maybe more. Only the young American does not know it; he probably imagines that he is *thinking* when he produces that formula. And yet he does believe in something profoundly, though he may not be able to find the words for it: free enterprise. A parcel that to the American mind wraps up for delivery hospitals, sanitation, roads, harbors, schools, air travel, Jack Daniel, convertibles, Stimmudents. That is the C-ration that keeps him going. The American troops are not exactly conscious of bombing, shelling, and defoliating to defend free enterprise (which they cannot imagine as being under serious attack), but they plan to come out of the war with their values intact. Which means that they must spread them, until everyone is convinced, by demonstration, that the American way is better, just as American seed-strains are better and American pigs are better. Their conviction is sometimes baldly stated. North of Da Nang, at a Marine base, there is an ice-cream plant on which is printed in large official letters the words: 'ICE-CREAM PLANT: ARVN MORALE BUILDER.' Or it may wear a humanitarian disguise, e.g., OPERATION CONCERN, in which a proud little town in Kansas airlifted 110 pregnant sows to a humble little town in Vietnam.

Occasionally the profit motive is undisguised. Flying to Hue in a big C-130, I heard the pilot and the co-pilot discussing their personal war aim, which was to make a killing, as soon as the war was over, in Vietnamese real estate. From the air, while they kept an eye out for VC, they had surveyed the possibilities and had decided on Nha Trang – 'beautiful sand beaches' – better than Cam Ranh Bay – a 'desert.' They disagreed as to the kind of development that would make the most money: the pilot wanted to build a high-class hotel and villas, while the co-pilot thought that the future lay with low-cost housing. I found this conversation hallucinating, but the next day, in Hue, I met a Marine colonel who had returned to the service after retirement; having fought the Japanese, he had made his killing as a 'developer' in Okinawa and invested the profits in a frozen-shrimp import business (from Japan) supplying restaurants in San Diego. War, a cheap form of mass tourism, opens the mind to business opportunities.

All these developers were Californians. In fact, the majority of the Americans I met in the field in Vietnam were WASPS from Southern California; most of the rest were from the rural South. In nearly a month I met *one* Jewish boy in the services (a nice young naval officer from Pittsburgh), two Boston Irish, and a captain from Connecticut. Given the demographic shift toward the Pacific in the United States, this Californian ascendancy gave me the peculiar feeling that I was seeing the future of our country as if on a movie screen. Nobody has dared make a war movie about Vietnam, but the prevailing unreality, as experienced in base camps and headquarters, is eerily like a movie, a contest between good and evil, which is heading toward a happy ending, when men with names like 'Colonel Culpepper,' 'Colonel Derryberry,' 'Captain Stanhope,' will vanquish Victor Charlie. The state that has a movie actor for governor and a movie actor for US senator seemed to be running the show.

No doubt the very extensive press and television coverage of the war has made the participants very conscious of 'exposure,' that is, of role-playing. Aside from the usual networks, Italian television, Mexican television, the BBC, CBC were all filming the 'other' war during the month of February, and the former Italian Chief of Staff, General Liuzzi, was covering it as a commentator for the *Corriere della Sera*. The effect of all this attention on the generals, colonels, and lesser officers was to put a premium on 'sincerity.'

Nobody likes to be a villain, least of all a WASP officer, who feels he is playing the heavy in Vietnam through some awful mistake in type-casting.

He *knows* he is good at heart, because everything in his home environment – his TV set, his paper, his Frigidaire, the President of the United States – has promised him that, whatever shortcomings he may have as an individual, collectively he is good. The 'other' war is giving him the chance to clear up the momentary misunderstanding created by those bombs, which, through no fault of his, are happening to hit civilians. He has *warned* them to get away, dropped leaflets saying he was coming and urging 'Charlie' to defect, to join the other side; lately, in pacified areas, he has even taken the precaution of having his targets cleared by the village chief before shelling or bombing, so that now the press officer giving the daily briefing is able to reel out: 'OPERATION BLOCKHOUSE. 29 civilians reported wounded today. Two are in 'poor' condition. Target had been approved by the district chief.' Small thanks he gets, our military hero, for that scrupulous restraint. But in the work of pacification, his real self comes out, clear and true. Digging wells for the natives (too bad if the water comes up brackish), repairing roads ('Just a jungle trail before we came,' says the captain, though his colonel, in another part of the forest, has just been saying that the engineers had uncovered a fine stone roadbed built eighty years ago by the French), building a house for the widow of a Viet Cong (so far unreconciled; it takes time).

American officers in the field can become very sentimental when they think of the good they are doing and the hard row they have to hoe with the natives, who have been brainwashed by the Viet Cong. A Marine general in charge of logistics in I-Corps district was deeply moved when he spoke of his Marines: moving in to help rebuild some refugee housing with scrap lumber and sheet tin (the normal materials were cardboard boxes and flattened beer cans); working in their off-hours to build desks for a school; giving their Christmas money for a new high school; planning a new marketplace. The Marine Corps had donated a children's hospital, and in that hospital, up the road, was a little girl who had been wounded during a Marine assault. 'We're nursing her back to health,' he intoned, with prayerful satisfaction – a phrase he must have become attached to by dint of repetition; his PIO (Information Officer) nodded three times. In the hospital, I asked to see the little girl. 'Oh, she's gone home,' said the PIO. 'Nursed her back to health.' In reality the little girl was still there, but it was true, her wounds were nearly healed.

A young Marine doctor, blue-eyed, very good-looking, went from bed to bed, pointing out what was the matter with each child and showing what was being done to cure it. There was only the one war casualty; the rest were suffering from malnutrition (the basic complaint everywhere), skin diseases, worms; one had a serious heart condition; two had been badly burned by a stove, and one, in the contagious section, had the

plague. The doctor showed us the tapeworm, in a bottle, he had extracted
from one infant. A rickety baby was crying, and a middle-aged corpsman
picked it up and gave it its bottle. They were plainly doing a good job,
under makeshift conditions and without laboratory facilities. The children
who were well enough to sit up appeared content; some even laughed,
shyly. No amusements were provided for them, but perhaps it was
sufficient amusement to be visited by tiptoeing journalists. And it could
not be denied that it was a break for these children to be in a Marine hospital, clean, well-fed, and one to a bed. They were benefiting from the
war, at least for the duration of their stay; the doctor was not sanguine, for
the malnutrition cases, about what would happen when the patients went
home. 'We keep them as long as we can,' he said, frowning. 'But we can't
keep them forever. They have to go back to their parents.'

Compared to what they were used to, this short taste of the American way
of life must have been delicious for Vietnamese children. John Morgan in
the London *Sunday Times* described another little Vietnamese girl up near
the DMZ – do they have one to a battalion? – who had been wounded by
Marine bullets ('A casualty of war,' that general repeated solemnly. 'A casualty of war') and whom he saw carried in one night to a drinking party in
sick bay, her legs bandaged, a spotlight playing on her, while the Marines
pressed candy and dollar bills into her hands and had their pictures taken
with her; she had more dolls than Macy's, they told him – 'that girl is real
spoiled.' To spoil a child war victim and send her back to her parents, with
her dolls as souvenirs, is patently callous, just as it is callous to fill a child's
stomach and send it home to be hungry again. The young doctor, being
a doctor, was possibly conscious of the fakery – from a responsible medical
point of view – of the 'miracle' cures he was effecting; that was why he
frowned. Meanwhile, however, the Marine Corps brass could show the
'Before' and 'After' to a captive audience. In fact two. The studio audience
of children, smiling and laughing and clapping, and the broader audience
of their parents, who, when allowed to visit, could not fail to be impressed,
if not awed, by the 'other' side of American technology. And beyond that
still a third audience – the journalists and their readers back home, who
would recognize the Man in White and his corpsman, having brought
them up, gone to school with them, seen them on TV, in soap opera. I felt
this myself, a relieved recognition of the familiar face of America. These
are the American boys we know at once, even in an Asian context, bubbling an Asian baby. We do not recognize them, helmeted, in a bomber
aiming cans of napalm at a thatched village. We have a credibility gap.

Leaving the hospital, I jolted southward in a jeep, hanging on, swallowing dust; the roads, like practically everything in Vietnam, have been

battered, gouged, scarred, torn up by the weight of US material. We passed
Marines' laundry, yards and yards of it, hanging outside native huts – the
dark green battle cloth spelled money. Down the road was a refugee camp,
which did not form part of the itinerary. This, I realized, must be 'home'
to some of the children we had just seen; the government daily allowance
for a camp family was ten piasters (six cents) a day – sometimes twenty if
there were two adults in the family. Somebody had put a streamer, in
English, over the entrance: 'REFUGEES FROM COMMUNISM.'

   This was a bit too much. The children's hospital had told the story the
Americans were anxious to get over. Why put in the commercial? And
who was the hard sell aimed at? Not the refugees, who could not read
English and who, if they were like all the other refugees, had fled, some
from the Viet Cong and some from the Americans and some because their
houses had been bombed or shelled. Not the journalists, who knew better.
Whoever carefully lettered that streamer, crafty Marine or civilian, had
applied all his animal cunning to selling himself.

JULIE FLINT

1948–

As a freelance journalist, Julie Flint has reported from the Middle East for the past twenty years, including her most recent reports on the humanitarian disaster in the Sudan. In this account of what she calls a 'non-camp' for refugees just across the border of north-west Iraq, she brings to life the horrific conditions prompted by Saddam Hussein's 1991 expulsion of the Kurdish people.

Mountainsides of Hell

14 April 1991, *Observer*

It rained all night long, at first spottily but then with extraordinary energy. No one slept for the crying of hungry, frozen children terrified by the wind and lightning. In the morning, what the world is pleased to call a 'refugee camp' was a giant mudbath set at a 45-degree angle with every-thing on it, animal and vegetable, clinging on for dear life.

By midday, six little graves marked out by stones recorded the night's death toll in just one corner of this human ant-heap. In the tent where she had given birth to her first child two days earlier, crammed in with 14 other women and children after an 80-mile walk from Iraq, a 24-year-old Kurdish woman held out a sneezing, wheezing bundle. 'Take it to England,' she implored. Her husband, a teacher, looked on speechless, unable to relinquish his first-born but equally unable to condemn the baby to near-certain death. Outside the tent, a two-year-old with a grossly dis-tended stomach stood howling in the mud, bent double, bottom bare and legs covered in diarrhoea.

Nothing prepares you for the awfulness of this non-camp just across the border of north-west Iraq, one of more than half-a-dozen refugee con-centrations along the border and arguably the worst. None of the televi-sion pictures does it justice. No words convey the misery of it – except, perhaps, the laconic observation of a man in a green dressing-gown that 'this place is no good even for animals'.

Two weeks after the first Kurdish refugees spilled over the Turkish border, pursued by Saddam Hussein's helicopter gunships and T-72 tanks, this mountainside looks like a page torn from Vietnam. Down in the valley, Huey helicopters land in showers of mud, supplying the Turkish army; up on the mountain crest, Hercules transport planes drop relief packages that have already crushed six refugees to death and that confuse countless others. ('What is this?' a young man asks, holding up a packet of Dextrose. 'Aspirin?' Disabused, he tosses it into the mud. 'Dextrose? What's that?') The slippery ridges in between look like something out of Dante's *Inferno*, covered in the smoke of a thousand bonfires and carpeted with the horns, hooves and bloated entrails of slaughtered goats. Blackened by smoke, and amputated for firewood, trees look as if they have been napalmed.

There is no natural shelter for the 250,000 refugees estimated to be on both sides of the Uludere mountain, no natural materials with which to build shelter, no water apart from small springs on the highest slopes.

'It is the worst physical location I have ever seen,' says Hugo Slim, of Save the Children. 'The worst weather, the worst level of shelter.' 'A cross between Ethiopia and the Somme,' says David Jones, deputy director of Oxfam. 'Imagine there are suddenly a million people on the highest mountains of the North of Scotland, only allowed a few hundred metres below the snow line. What government committee could deal with that? It is not a place where you can have anyone. It is inhuman to keep people in these conditions.'

It is especially difficult for refugees who are, in their vast majority, townspeople and who lack the communal support systems and outdoor habits of most Kurdish villagers. 'Everything is missing here,' a middle-aged man says in all seriousness. 'Especially the WC.' On this mountain, people are packed so tightly that some walked for miles to find a nook where they can squat in privacy; others, lacking the strength to walk that far, defecate between the tents. There is diarrhoea everywhere.

Those who have blankets have to choose between wrapping themselves in them, selfishly, or using them to make a tent that can shelter an entire family.

In this vast bog, cemented by a sense of shock and something bordering on despair, there are pockets of manic energy: a woman sweeps the mud; a man looking for firewood digs up a giant root in preference to a dozen more accessible branches; a group of exhausted children play tag with a ball made from a piece of plastic. But most people sit quietly, adults looking inquiringly at foreigners – 'Doctor?' – and little children gazing out like catatonics.

They all look like weathered tramps and it comes as a shock when a filthy, ragged man says in perfect English: 'We are very dirty, but most of us here have Masters. I myself have an MA in Arabic Literature.'

The mountainside shakes off its lethargy whenever a tractor laden with supplies donated by local Kurds claws its way up the only path there is. Young men attack it like piranhas, oblivious of the Turkish soldiers who whip them with wooden switches and club them with rifle butts; oblivious, too, of anything that is not a bag of bread, a box of biscuits or a sack of macaroni. *Observer* photographer Dod Miller was dragged off one tractor and needed stitches for a head wound. A colleague was buried under a pile of 20 or 30 men before being pulled free, glasses smashed and coat and sweater ripped off. 'Please excuse our people,' said a young teacher among the rescuers. 'We don't have food, water or blankets. We don't have anything.'

This is the 'camp' that Turkish officers said was deemed too dreadful for US Secretary of State James Baker to visit. As the Red Crescent set up the first medical centre, refugees were fighting each other with knives to get the first snatch at the tractors, first shot at the parachuted supplies which, in the absence of any organisation on the ground, only encouraged the survival of the fittest.

Despite the cold and the hunger, water is the biggest problem. As the days tick by and winter snows melt, increasingly few have the energy to climb high into the mountains to pack no-longer-virgin snow into vegetable bags that look horribly like body bags. They turn instead to rivers that are thick with mud – good enough for washing feet, shoes and clothes, but not good enough for filling babies' bottles, although many do.

In the absence of water, one woman cooked macaroni in a bone-dry pan. Beside her a family that had just killed its last goat cut it up by smashing it with rocks. At the bottom of the hill a tractor tried to drag a water trailer up the path, but got stuck in the mud. 'Can you believe,' said an old man, 'that this is the end of the twentieth century?'

While the international community masters the logistical nightmare presented by this avalanche in Turkey's backward south-eastern corner, the supplies being sent by local people, for the moment the bulk of the refugees' sustenance, often miss the mark.

All along the mountain paths brightly-coloured clothes are trampled into the mud, flung aside in the frenzied rush for food. Dozens of wooden cradles are abandoned with every truckload, too large for the makeshift tents and no substitute for a mother's warmth in the nights when temperatures drop below freezing. Broken loaves of bread lie everywhere: distribution is a problem even when supply is not.

The Turkish commandos who control the border and have set up camp at the bottom of the mountain make it quite clear that they have only one duty – security. 'We are just here to keep the people safe,' says a lieutenant, who passes his time playing chess. 'We are not responsible for food or water. Our work is to keep people safe from terrorism.'

Relations between the troops and the refugees are bad, with the Kurds' consensus being that 'we have left a large prison for a small one'.

Commandos line the mountain track from top to bottom, with regular encampments on the lower side to ensure that no one gets off the mountain. If they have sympathy for the refugees, they do not show it. They all carry switches torn from trees and flick the Kurds like cattle whenever they break the unwritten rules of this non-camp. No one is allowed down the mountain – even to collect firewood – and few are permitted more than a few hundred yards down the path, even to reach the water truck when it manages to negotiate the mud.

The Kurds claim they can buy their way with dollars and cigarettes. They say more than a dozen refugees have been killed by the commandos.

The commandos have [a low] opinion of the Kurds, failing to see the doctors, teachers and engineers beneath the mud-drenched clothes and having, with few exceptions, no common language in which to communicate. 'Write another paragraph,' says a septuagenarian refugee. 'We don't want to stay in Turkey. We want to go to another country.'

As we left the border, their wretchedness was summed up in the tiny figure of a little boy weeping, with great gulping sobs, by the roadside. If he had a family, it was nowhere to be seen.

'Baaaa,' said a Turkish soldier, prodding him with a stick.

SUSAN SONTAG
1933–2004

Born in New York, where she also spent most of her adult life, Susan Sontag was a novelist, and, most pre-eminently, an essayist. Her first collection of essays, *Against Interpretation and Other Essays*, announced her arrival as a public intellectual in 1966 and introduced her view that 'the project of interpretation is largely reactionary'.

Throughout her career she returned regularly to the subject of photography, and, specifically, whether photographs could ever actually be what they claimed: a definitive slice of the truth. The following article proved to be one of her last, and is an extensive analysis of the torture photographs that emerged from the American-held Abu Ghraib prison in Iraq, during the second Gulf War.

Regarding the Torture of Others

23 May 2004, *New York Times*

I.—For a long time – at least six decades – photographs have laid down the tracks of how important conflicts are judged and remembered. The Western memory museum is now mostly a visual one. Photographs have an insuperable power to determine what we recall of events, and it now seems probable that the defining association of people everywhere with the war that the United States launched pre-emptively in Iraq last year will be photographs of the torture of Iraqi prisoners by Americans in the most infamous of Saddam Hussein's prisons, Abu Ghraib.

The Bush administration and its defenders have chiefly sought to limit a public-relations disaster – the dissemination of the photographs – rather than deal with the complex crimes of leadership and of policy revealed by the pictures. There was, first of all, the displacement of the reality onto the photographs themselves. The administration's initial response was to say that the president was shocked and disgusted by the photographs – as if the fault or horror lay in the images, not in what they depict. There was also the avoidance of the word 'torture.' The prisoners had possibly been the objects of 'abuse,' eventually of 'humiliation' – that was the most to be admitted. 'My impression is that what has been charged thus far is abuse, which I believe technically is different from torture,' Secretary of Defense Donald Rumsfeld said at a press conference. 'And therefore I'm not going to address the "torture" word.'

Words alter, words add, words subtract. It was the strenuous avoidance of the word 'genocide' while some 800,000 Tutsis in Rwanda were being slaughtered, over a few weeks' time, by their Hutu neighbors 10 years ago that indicated the American government had no intention of doing anything. To refuse to call what took place in Abu Ghraib – and what has taken place elsewhere in Iraq and in Afghanistan and at Guantanamo Bay – by its true name, torture, is as outrageous as the refusal to call the Rwandan genocide a genocide. Here is one of the definitions of torture contained in a convention to which the United States is a signatory: 'any act by which severe pain or suffering, whether physical or mental, is intentionally inflicted on a person for such purposes as obtaining from him or a third person information or a confession.' (The definition comes from the 1984 Convention Against Torture and Other Cruel, Inhuman or Degrading Treatment or Punishment. Similar definitions have existed for some time in customary law and in treaties, starting with Article 3 – common to the four Geneva conventions of 1949 – and many recent human rights conventions.) The 1984 convention declares, 'No exceptional circumstances whatsoever, whether a state of war or a threat of war, internal political instability or any other public emergency, may be invoked as a justification of torture.' And all covenants on torture specify that it includes treatment intended to humiliate the victim, like leaving prisoners naked in cells and corridors.

Whatever actions this administration undertakes to limit the damage of the widening revelations of the torture of prisoners in Abu Ghraib and elsewhere – trials, courts-martial, dishonorable discharges, resignation of senior military figures and responsible administration officials and substantial compensation to the victims – it is probable that the 'torture' word will continue to be banned. To acknowledge that Americans torture their prisoners would contradict everything this administration has invited the public to believe about the virtue of American intentions and America's right, flowing from that virtue, to undertake unilateral action on the world stage.

Even when the president was finally compelled, as the damage to America's reputation everywhere in the world widened and deepened, to use the 'sorry' word, the focus of regret still seemed the damage to America's claim to moral superiority. Yes, President Bush said in Washington on May 6, standing alongside King Abdullah II of Jordan, he was 'sorry for the humiliation suffered by the Iraqi prisoners and the humiliation suffered by their families.' But, he went on, he was 'equally sorry that people seeing these pictures didn't understand the true nature and heart of America.'

To have the American effort in Iraq summed up by these images must seem, to those who saw some justification in a war that did overthrow one of the monster tyrants of modern times, 'unfair.' A war, an occupation, is inevitably a huge tapestry of actions. What makes some actions representative and others not? The issue is not whether the torture was done by individuals (i.e., 'not by everybody') – but whether it was systematic. Authorized. Condoned. All acts are done by individuals. The issue is not whether a majority or a minority of Americans performs such acts but whether the nature of the policies prosecuted by this administration and the hierarchies deployed to carry them out makes such acts likely.

II.—Considered in this light, the photographs are us. That is, they are representative of the fundamental corruptions of any foreign occupation together with the Bush administration's distinctive policies. The Belgians in the Congo, the French in Algeria, practiced torture and sexual humiliation on despised recalcitrant natives. Add to this generic corruption the mystifying, near-total unpreparedness of the American rulers of Iraq to deal with the complex realities of the country after its 'liberation.' And add to that the overarching, distinctive doctrines of the Bush administration, namely that the United States has embarked on an endless war and that those detained in this war are, if the president so decides, 'unlawful combatants' – a policy enunciated by Donald Rumsfeld for Taliban and Qaeda prisoners as early as January 2002 – and thus, as Rumsfeld said, 'technically' they 'do not have any rights under the Geneva Convention,' and you have a perfect recipe for the cruelties and crimes committed against the thousands incarcerated without charges or access to lawyers in American-run prisons that have been set up since the attacks of September 11, 2001.

So, then, is the real issue not the photographs themselves but what the photographs reveal to have happened to 'suspects' in American custody? No: the horror of what is shown in the photographs cannot be separated from the horror that the photographs were taken – with the perpetrators posing, gloating, over their helpless captives. German soldiers in the Second World War took photographs of the atrocities they were committing in Poland and Russia, but snapshots in which the executioners placed themselves among their victims are exceedingly rare, as may be seen in a book just published, 'Photographing the Holocaust,' by Janina Struk. If there is something comparable to what these pictures show it would be some of the photographs of black victims of lynching taken between the 1880s and 1930s, which show Americans grinning beneath the naked mutilated body of a black man or woman hanging behind them from a tree. The lynching photographs were souvenirs of a collective action whose participants felt perfectly justified in what they had done. So are the pictures from Abu Ghraib.

The lynching pictures were in the nature of photographs as trophies – taken by a photographer in order to be collected, stored in albums, displayed. The pictures taken by American soldiers in Abu Ghraib, however, reflect a shift in the use made of pictures – less objects to be saved than messages to be disseminated, circulated. A digital camera is a common possession among soldiers. Where once photographing war was the province of photojournalists, now the soldiers themselves are all photographers – recording their war, their fun, their observations of what they find picturesque, their atrocities – and swapping images among themselves and e-mailing them around the globe.

There is more and more recording of what people do, by themselves. At least or especially in America, Andy Warhol's ideal of filming real events in real time – life isn't edited, why should its record be edited? – has become a norm for countless Webcasts, in which people record their day, each in his or her own reality show. Here I am – waking and yawning and stretching, brushing my teeth, making breakfast, getting the kids off to school. People record all aspects of their lives, store them in computer files and send the files around. Family life goes with the recording of family life – even when, or especially when, the family is in the throes of crisis and disgrace. Surely the dedicated, incessant home-videoing of one another, in conversation and monologue, over many years was the most astonishing material in 'Capturing the Friedmans,' the recent documentary by Andrew Jarecki about a Long Island family embroiled in pedophilia charges.

An erotic life is, for more and more people, that which can be captured in digital photographs and on video. And perhaps the torture is more attractive, as something to record, when it has a sexual component. It is surely revealing, as more Abu Ghraib photographs enter public view, that torture photographs are interleaved with pornographic images of American soldiers having sex with one another. In fact, most of the torture photographs have a sexual theme, as in those showing the coercing of prisoners to perform, or simulate, sexual acts among themselves. One exception, already canonical, is the photograph of the man made to stand on a box, hooded and sprouting wires, reportedly told he would be electrocuted if he fell off. Yet pictures of prisoners bound in painful positions, or made to stand with outstretched arms, are infrequent. That they count as torture cannot be doubted. You have only to look at the terror on the victim's face, although such 'stress' fell within the Pentagon's limits of the acceptable. But most of the pictures seem part of a larger confluence of torture and pornography: a young woman leading a naked man around on a leash is classic dominatrix imagery. And you wonder how much of the sexual tortures inflicted on the inmates of Abu Ghraib was inspired by the vast repertory of pornographic imagery available on the Internet – and which ordinary people, by sending out Webcasts of themselves, try to emulate.

III.—To live is to be photographed, to have a record of one's life, and therefore to go on with one's life oblivious, or claiming to be oblivious, to the camera's nonstop attentions. But to live is also to pose. To act is to share in the community of actions recorded as images. The expression of satisfaction at the acts of torture being inflicted on helpless, trussed, naked victims is only part of the story. There is the deep satisfaction of being photographed, to which one is now more inclined to respond not with a stiff, direct gaze (as in former times) but with glee. The events are in part designed to be photographed. The grin is a grin for the camera. There would be something missing if, after stacking the naked men, you couldn't take a picture of them.

Looking at these photographs, you ask yourself, How can someone grin at the sufferings and humiliation of another human being? Set guard dogs at the genitals and legs of cowering naked prisoners? Force shackled, hooded prisoners to masturbate or simulate oral sex with one another? And you feel naive for asking, since the answer is, self-evidently, People do these things to other people. Rape and pain inflicted on the genitals are among the most common forms of torture. Not just in Nazi concentration camps and in Abu Ghraib when it was run by Saddam Hussein. Americans, too, have done and do them when they are told, or made to feel, that those over whom they have absolute power deserve to be humiliated, tormented. They do them when they are led to believe that the people they are torturing belong to an inferior race or religion. For the meaning of these pictures is not just that these acts were performed, but that their perpetrators apparently had no sense that there was anything wrong in what the pictures show.

Even more appalling, since the pictures were meant to be circulated and seen by many people: it was all fun. And this idea of fun is, alas, more and more – contrary to what President Bush is telling the world – part of 'the true nature and heart of America.' It is hard to measure the increasing acceptance of brutality in American life, but its evidence is everywhere, starting with the video games of killing that are a principal entertainment of boys – can the video game 'Interrogating the Terrorists' really be far behind? – and on to the violence that has become endemic in the group rites of youth on an exuberant kick. Violent crime is down, yet the easy delight taken in violence seems to have grown. From the harsh torments inflicted on incoming students in many American suburban high schools – depicted in Richard Linklater's 1993 film, 'Dazed and Confused' – to the hazing rituals of physical brutality and sexual humiliation in college fraternities and on sports teams, America has become a country in which the fantasies and the practice of violence are seen as good entertainment, fun.

What formerly was segregated as pornography, as the exercise of extreme sadomasochistic longings – as in Pier Paolo Pasolini's last, near-unwatchable film, 'Salo' (1975), depicting orgies of torture in the Fascist redoubt in northern Italy at the end of the Mussolini era – is now being normalized, by some, as high-spirited play or venting. To 'stack naked men' is like a college fraternity prank, said a caller to Rush Limbaugh and the many millions of Americans who listen to his radio show. Had the caller, one wonders, seen the photographs? No matter. The observation – or is it the fantasy? – was on the mark. What may still be capable of shocking some Americans was Limbaugh's response: 'Exactly!' he exclaimed. 'Exactly my point. This is no different than what happens at the Skull and Bones initiation, and we're going to ruin people's lives over it, and we're going to hamper our military effort, and then we are going to really hammer them because they had a good time.' 'They' are the American soldiers, the torturers. And Limbaugh went on: 'You know, these people are being fired at every day. I'm talking about people having a good time, these people. You ever heard of emotional release?'

Shock and awe were what our military promised the Iraqis. And shock and the awful are what these photographs announce to the world that the Americans have delivered: a pattern of criminal behavior in open contempt of international humanitarian conventions. Soldiers now pose, thumbs up, before the atrocities they commit, and send off the pictures to their buddies. Secrets of private life that, formerly, you would have given nearly anything to conceal, you now clamor to be invited on a television show to reveal. What is illustrated by these photographs is as much the culture of shamelessness as the reigning admiration for unapologetic brutality.

IV.—The notion that apologies or professions of 'disgust' by the president and the secretary of defense are a sufficient response is an insult to one's historical and moral sense. The torture of prisoners is not an aberration. It is a direct consequence of the with-us-or-against-us doctrines of world struggle with which the Bush administration has sought to change, change radically, the international stance of the United States and to recast many domestic institutions and prerogatives. The Bush administration has committed the country to a pseudo-religious doctrine of war, endless war – for 'the war on terror' is nothing less than that. Endless war is taken to justify endless incarcerations. Those held in the extralegal American penal empire are 'detainees'; 'prisoners,' a newly obsolete word, might suggest that they have the rights accorded by international law and the laws of all civilized countries. This endless 'global war on terrorism' – into which both the quite justified invasion of Afghanistan and the unwinnable folly in Iraq have been folded by Pentagon decree – inevitably leads to the

demonizing and dehumanizing of anyone declared by the Bush administration to be a possible terrorist: a definition that is not up for debate and
is, in fact, usually made in secret.

The charges against most of the people detained in the prisons in Iraq
and Afghanistan being nonexistent – the Red Cross reports that 70 to
90 percent of those being held seem to have committed no crime other
than simply being in the wrong place at the wrong time, caught up in some
sweep of 'suspects' – the principal justification for holding them is 'interrogation.' Interrogation about what? About anything. Whatever the
detainee might know. If interrogation is the point of detaining prisoners
indefinitely, then physical coercion, humiliation and torture become
inevitable.

Remember: we are not talking about that rarest of cases, the 'ticking time
bomb' situation, which is sometimes used as a limiting case that justifies
torture of prisoners who have knowledge of an imminent attack. This is
general or nonspecific information-gathering, authorized by American
military and civilian administrators to learn more of a shadowy empire of
evildoers about whom Americans know virtually nothing, in countries
about which they are singularly ignorant: in principle, any information at
all might be useful. An interrogation that produced no information (whatever information might consist of) would count as a failure. All the more
justification for preparing prisoners to talk. Softening them up, stressing
them out – these are the euphemisms for the bestial practices in American
prisons where suspected terrorists are being held. Unfortunately, as Staff Sgt.
Ivan (Chip) Frederick noted in his diary, a prisoner can get too stressed out
and die. The picture of a man in a body bag with ice on his chest may well
be of the man Frederick was describing.

The pictures will not go away. That is the nature of the digital world in
which we live. Indeed, it seems they were necessary to get our leaders to
acknowledge that they had a problem on their hands. After all, the con-
clusions of reports compiled by the International Committee of the Red
Cross, and other reports by journalists and protests by humanitarian organizations about the atrocious punishments inflicted on 'detainees' and 'suspected terrorists' in prisons run by the American military, first in
Afghanistan and later in Iraq, have been circulating for more than a year.
It seems doubtful that such reports were read by President Bush or Vice
President Dick Cheney or Condoleezza Rice or Rumsfeld. Apparently it
took the photographs to get their attention, when it became clear they
could not be suppressed; it was the photographs that made all this 'real' to
Bush and his associates. Up to then, there had been only words, which are
easier to cover up in our age of infinite digital self-reproduction and self-
dissemination, and so much easier to forget.

So now the pictures will continue to 'assault' us – as many Americans are bound to feel. Will people get used to them? Some Americans are already saying they have seen enough. Not, however, the rest of the world. Endless war: endless stream of photographs. Will editors now debate whether showing more of them, or showing them uncropped (which, with some of the best-known images, like that of a hooded man on a box, gives a different and in some instances more appalling view), would be in 'bad taste' or too implicitly political? By 'political,' read: critical of the Bush administration's imperial project. For there can be no doubt that the photographs damage, as Rumsfeld testified, 'the reputation of the honorable men and women of the armed forces who are courageously and responsibly and professionally defending our freedom across the globe.' This damage – to our reputation, our image, our success as the lone super-power – is what the Bush administration principally deplores. How the protection of 'our freedom' – the freedom of 5 percent of humanity – came to require having American soldiers 'across the globe' is hardly debated by our elected officials.

Already the backlash has begun. Americans are being warned against indulging in an orgy of self-condemnation. The continuing publication of the pictures is being taken by many Americans as suggesting that we do not have the right to defend ourselves: after all, they (the terrorists) started it. They – Osama bin Laden? Saddam Hussein? what's the difference? – attacked us first. Senator James Inhofe of Oklahoma, a Republican member of the Senate Armed Services Committee, before which Secretary Rumsfeld testified, avowed that he was sure he was not the only member of the committee 'more outraged by the outrage' over the photographs than by what the photographs show. 'These prisoners,' Senator Inhofe explained, 'you know they're not there for traffic viol-ations. If they're in Cellblock 1-A or 1-B, these prisoners, they're mur-derers, they're terrorists, they're insurgents. Many of them probably have American blood on their hands, and here we're so concerned about the treatment of those individuals.' It's the fault of 'the media' which are pro-voking, and will continue to provoke, further violence against Americans around the world. More Americans will die. Because of these photos.

There is an answer to this charge, of course. Americans are dying not because of the photographs but because of what the photographs reveal to be happening, happening with the complicity of a chain of command – so Maj. Gen. Antonio Taguba implied, and Pfc. Lynndie England said, and (among others) Senator Lindsey Graham of South Carolina, a Republican, suggested, after he saw the Pentagon's full range of images on May 12. 'Some of it has an elaborate nature to it that makes me very suspicious of whether or not others were directing or encouraging,' Senator Graham said. Senator Bill Nelson, a Florida Democrat, said that viewing an uncropped version of one photo showing a stack of naked men in a hallway – a version that revealed how many other soldiers were at the scene, some not even paying attention – contradicted the Pentagon's assertion that only rogue soldiers were involved. 'Somewhere along the line,' Senator Nelson said of the torturers, 'they were either told or winked at.' An attorney for Specialist Charles Graner Jr., who is in the picture, has had his client identify the men in the uncropped version; according to the *Wall Street Journal*, Graner said that four of the men were military intelligence and one a civilian contractor working with military intelligence.

V.—But the distinction between photograph and reality – as between spin and policy – can easily evaporate. And that is what the administration wishes to happen. 'There are a lot more photographs and videos that exist,' Rumsfeld acknowledged in his testimony. 'If these are released to the public, obviously, it's going to make matters worse.' Worse for the administration and its programs, presumably, not for those who are the actual – and potential? – victims of torture.

The media may self-censor but, as Rumsfeld acknowledged, it's hard to censor soldiers overseas, who don't write letters home, as in the old days, that can be opened by military censors who ink out unacceptable lines. Today's soldiers instead function like tourists, as Rumsfeld put it, 'running around with digital cameras and taking these unbelievable photographs and then passing them off, against the law, to the media, to our surprise.' The administration's effort to withhold pictures is proceeding along several fronts. Currently, the argument is taking a legalistic turn: now the photographs are classified as evidence in future criminal cases, whose outcome may be prejudiced if they are made public. The Republican chairman of the Senate Armed Services Committee, John Warner of Virginia, after the May 12 slide show of image after image of sexual humiliation and violence against Iraqi prisoners, said he felt 'very strongly' that the newer photos 'should not be made public. I feel that it could possibly endanger the men and women of the armed forces as they are serving and at great risk.'

But the real push to limit the accessibility of the photographs will come from the continuing effort to protect the administration and cover up our misrule in Iraq – to identify 'outrage' over the photographs with a campaign to undermine American military might and the purposes it currently serves. Just as it was regarded by many as an implicit criticism of the war to show on television photographs of American soldiers who have been killed in the course of the invasion and occupation of Iraq, it will increasingly be thought unpatriotic to disseminate the new photographs and further tarnish the image of America.

After all, we're at war. Endless war. And war is hell, more so than any of the people who got us into this rotten war seem to have expected. In our digital hall of mirrors, the pictures aren't going to go away. Yes, it seems that one picture is worth a thousand words. And even if our leaders choose not to look at them, there will be thousands more snapshots and videos. Unstoppable.

HOME & FAMILY

EVELYN SHARP
1869–1955

A prolific novelist and journalist, Evelyn Sharp was the first regular columnist on the *Manchester Guardian's* women's page. An early suffragette she was imprisoned for breaking government windows and for refusing to leave the House of Commons after the then-Home Secretary ignored a delegation she was heading. Part of the United Suffragettes, Sharp was editor of its journal *Votes for Women* and insisted that the movement keep up its activism throughout World War One. In the following article she argues for an end to the tradition of spring-cleaning.

The Rebel on the Hearth

4 March 1924, *Manchester Guardian*

Spring-cleaning always seems to me a confession of failure. Obviously, if the house is dirty enough to require special cleaning in the spring, the implication is that it has not been kept clean in the preceding summer, autumn and winter, and to clean it with a flourish of dusters at one season is not to guarantee it will not need cleaning again during the other three. Indeed, spring-cleaning acts rather as a deterrent than otherwise. For weeks beforehand it seems hardly worth while to clean the house since it is going to be turned upside down shortly; and after the dreadful event is over to start cleaning it again is like going to church on Easter Monday or making a speech the day after the poll.

There are so many rebels on the hearth in these emancipated days that an organised revolt against spring-cleaning ought to be easy to provoke. It should certainly be one of those so-called women's movements that should have the hearty co-operation of all the men of the household, for the wail of the husband, father or brother is the recognised accompaniment to this yearly disaster. Spring-cleaning is quite an important part of the traditional jest about women, but there is no reason why it should be an essential part, and if there still remain some mockers who would sooner suffer the inconvenience of spring-cleaning than lose one chance of laughing at the absurdities of women, they would be largely outnumbered by those in favour of abolition, and as everybody knows, the next best thing to defeating the enemy is to divide the enemy's ranks.

But many will still be found to defend this ancient custom. Chimneys have to be swept, they will say, and the sweep alone entails a spring-cleaning.

But does he? At this one season of the year he may, with truth be said to 'come to dust'. But where there is a kitchen chimney the sweep comes at other seasons of the year, too, and except at springtime does not disorganise the whole household. In the case of all other chimneys, the sweep is even an active argument against spring-cleaning – for there are still archaic housewives who permit no fire to be lighted after the chimney has been swept at spring time; and if the sweep could come and go unobtrusively at other times of the year, as the window-cleaner does, whole families would not shiver before a fireless grate in the bitter winds of an English summer.

If spring-cleaning is to be abolished the psychological motives underlying it cannot be ignored. One must allow for the sense of novelty and excitement that seems to be satisfied by this yearly outbreak of cleanliness. Nothing is duller than to keep a house clean by removing a little dirt every day; it is as wearing to the spirit as it would be to sew one stitch – an impossible feat in any case – in order to save problematic nine. The house may be no cleaner after a week's onslaught upon 51 weeks of accumulated dirt, than if the dirt had never been allowed to accumulate, but the difference between making a house clean and keeping it clean is the difference between having loved and lost and never having loved at all. Clearly, if the spring-cleaner is ever to be converted from this annual orgy of domesticity, domesticity must be itself rendered more exciting and adventurous from day to day.

The elemental desire to wallow in dirt in order fully to enjoy converting it into driven snow is not, however, the only motive underlying the universal love of spring-cleaning. Equally universal, though a little more subtle, is the feeling in the early part of the year – long before the weather justifies it – that 'summer is i'comen in'. It makes us do all sorts of mad and delightful and pleasant and poetic things; but unfortunately the means for satisfying it in poetic and pleasant ways are not so universal as the feeling. The housewife in the straitened city dwelling, the charwoman who comes in by the day, the domestic servant with her Sunday and her evening out, are all victims of the age-long desire to do something new in the springtime, something to celebrate the renewal of life after death. To make the house smell of furniture polish and soap from top to bottom, to put up clean curtains on the assumption that the sun is waiting to come in, to make the place temporarily unlivable in, and to try to wipe out in a week the neglect of a year, is merely the spring-cleaners' way of welcoming the eternal miracle of Mother Earth. And that was never done in olden times without a human sacrifice. But if spring-cleaning seems rather inadequate as the charwoman's Saturnalia, the only cure for her and for all spring-cleaners is to provide other ways of celebrating the return of spring. Until we do that she will continue to worship the fetish of spring-cleaning, and the house will be more or less dirty for eleven and a half months a year.

CRYSTAL EASTMAN

1881–1928

At the time of her death, one of Eastman's friends wrote that 'she was for thousands a symbol of what a free woman might be'. Foremost an activist, she carried out the first ever in-depth investigation of industrial accidents, drafted New York State's first workers' compensation law, formed the Congressional Union for Women Suffrage, as well as the American Union Against Militarism. With her brother, Max, she worked on the radical journal, the *Masses*, which was forcibly closed down in 1917 due to its outspoken opposition to World War One. By 1920, her campaigning was reaching its peak, and, with a host of other radicals, she formed the American Civil Liberties Union (ACLU) which is still burgeoning today.

The following article was part of a series in the *Nation* magazine, which asked seventeen women to explain the personal sources of their feminism. In Eastman's case, she chose to write about her mother's life. Written in 1927, it is a thoroughly modern piece.

Mother-worship

16 March 1927, *Nation*

The story of my background is the story of my mother. She was a Middle-Western girl, youngest, cleverest, and prettiest of six daughters – children of an Irish gunsmith and a 'Pennsylvania Dutch' woman of good family and splendid character. The gunsmith was a master of his trade but a heavy drinker, always ugly and often dangerous. My mother got away from home as soon as she could. After a year in a nearby coeducational college she taught school for a while and then married. The man she chose (for she was the sort of girl who has many chances) was a penniless but handsome and idealistic Yankee divinity student whom she met during that one college year. When he had secured his first parish, they were married.

For about eight years, during which there were four different parishes and four children were born, my mother was a popular, active, and helpful minister's wife. Then my father, who had always struggled against ill-health, suffered a complete nervous breakdown. He was forced to give up his church and his chosen profession. My mother had to support the family.

She began by teaching English literature in a girls' school. Before long she was giving Sunday-evening talks at the school. Then she began to fill outside engagements and finally she became a sort of supply-preacher to nearby country churches. About the year 1890, though she had had no theological education, she was ordained as a Congregational minister and called to be the pastor of a fairly large church in a well-to-do farming community. After three or four successful years, she and my father (who by this time had lost a good bit of money trying to be a farmer and a grocer but had begun to regain his health) were called as associate pastors to a big liberal church in a city of 40,000. It was my mother's reputation as a preacher that brought them this opportunity and she proved equal to the larger field. In time my father's health improved so that he could carry his share of the work, but my mother was always the celebrated member of the family.

I have a vivid memory of my mother when I was six years old. We are standing, my brother and I, in front of a run-down farmhouse on the edge of the town which had become our home. We have just said goodbye to our mother and now we are watching her trip off down the hill to the school where she goes every day to teach. She turns to smile at us – such a beaming smile, such a bright face, such a pretty young mother. When the charming, much-loved figure begins to grow small in the distance, my brother, who is younger and more temperamental than I, begins to cry. He screams as loud as he can, until he is red in the face. But he cannot make her come back. And I, knowing she will be worried if she hears him, try to drag him away. By the time I was ten my mother had become a preacher.

Life was never ordinary where my mother was. She was always trying something new. She had an eager, active mind, and tremendous energy. She was preeminently an initiator. From the time I was thirteen we spent our summers like most middle-class, small-town American families, in a cottage beside a lake. And our life there, I suppose, would have been much like the life in thousands of other such summer communities, except for the presence of my mother. For one thing, she organized a system of cooperative housekeeping with three other families on the hillside, and it lasted for years. A cook was hired jointly, but the burden of keeping house, planning meals, buying meat and groceries from the carts that came along three times a week, getting vegetables and fruit from the garden, collecting the money, keeping track of guests, and paying the bills, shifted every week. At first it was only the mothers who took their turn at housekeeping. But as the children grew older they were included in the scheme, boys as well as girls. Toward the end we had all the fun of eating in a big jolly group and only one or two weeks of housekeeping responsibility during the whole summer.

We used to have Sunday night music and singing for the whole hillside at our cottage, with the grown-ups in the big room, and the children lying outside on the porch couches or off on the grass. We had 'church' Sunday mornings, too, in our big room; after all we were the minister's family. But it was a very short informal 'church' followed by a long swim, and any one who wanted to could preach. We took turns at preaching as well as at keeping house, and we could choose the subjects of our own sermons.

Then one summer my mother started 'symposiums.' Once a week the mothers and older children and any fathers who happened to be around would gather on somebody's porch, listen to a paper, and then discuss it. I read a paper on 'Woman' when I was fifteen, and I believe I was as wise in feminism then as I am now, if a little more solemn.

'The trouble with women,' I said, 'is that they have no impersonal interests. They must have work of their own, first because no one who has to depend on another person for his living is really grown up; and, second, because the only way to be happy is to have an absorbing interest in life which is not bound up with any particular person. Children can die or grow up, husbands can leave you. No woman who allows husband and children to absorb her whole time and interest is safe against disaster.'

The proudest and happiest moment of my college days was when I met my mother in New York, as I did once a year, and went with her to a big banquet in connection with some ministers' convention she had come down to attend. She always spoke at the banquet, and she was always the best speaker. She was gay, sparkling, humorous, intimate, adorable. I would sit and love her with all my heart, and I could feel all the ministers loving her and rejoicing in her.

Almost always it is painful to sit in the audience while a near relative preaches, prays, or makes a speech. Husbands, wives, brothers, sisters, and children of the performers ought to be exempt from attending such public functions. My brothers and I always suffered when father preached, although, as preachers go, he was pretty good. At any rate he was beautiful to look at and had a large following of enthusiastic admirers. But when my mother preached we hated to miss it. There was never a moment of anxiety or concern; she had that secret of perfect platform ease which takes all strain out of the audience. Her voice was music; she spoke simply, without effort, almost without gestures, standing very still. And what she said seemed to come straight from her heart to yours. Her sermons grew out of her own moral and spiritual struggles. For she had a stormy, troubled soul, capable of black cruelty and then again of the deepest generosities. She was humble, honest, striving, always beginning again to try to be good.

With all her other interests she was thoroughly domestic. We children loved her cooking as much as we loved her preaching. And she was all kinds of devoted mother, the kind that tucks you in at night and reads you a story, and the kind that drags you to the dentist to have your teeth straightened. But I must leave her now and try to fill out the picture. My father, too, played a large part in my life. He was a generous man, the kind of man that was a suffragist from the day he first heard of a woman who wanted to vote. One evening, after mother had been teaching for some time and had begun to know her power as a public speaker, she came to him as he lay on his invalid's couch.

'John,' she said, 'I believe I could preach!'

'Mary!' he cried, jumping up in his excitement, 'I *know* you could!'

This was in those early days when he had given up his own career as a minister, when he had cheerfully turned small farmer and had begun, on days when he was well enough, to peddle eggs and butter at the back doors of his former parishioners. From the moment he knew that my mother wanted to preach, he helped and encouraged her. Without his coaching and without his local prestige, it is doubtful if she could have been ordained. And my father stood by me in the same way, from the time when I wanted to cut off my hair and go barefoot to the time when I began to study law. When I insisted that the boys must make their beds if I had to make mine, he stood by me. When I said that if there was dishwashing to be done they should take their turn, he stood by me. And when I declared that there was no such thing in our family as boys' work and girls' work, and that I must be allowed to do my share of wood-chopping and outdoor chores, he took me seriously and let me try.

Once when I was twelve and very tall, a deputation of ladies from her church called on my mother and gently suggested that my skirts ought to be longer. My mother, who was not without consciousness of the neighbors' opinions, thought she must do something. But my father said, 'No, let her wear them short. She likes to run, and she can't run so well in long skirts.'

A few years later it was a question of bathing suits. In our summer community I was a ringleader in the rebellion against skirts and stockings for swimming. On one hot Sunday morning the other fathers waited on my father and asked him to use his influence with me. I don't know what he said to them but he never said a word to me. He was, I know, startled and embarrassed to see his only daughter in a man's bathing suit with bare brown legs for all the world to see. I think it shocked him to his dying day. But he himself had been a swimmer; he knew he would not want to swim in a skirt and stockings. Why then should I?

Beyond the immediate circle of my family there were other influences at work. My mother, among her other charms, had a genius for friendship. There were always clever, interesting, amusing women coming in and out of our house. I never thought of women as dull folk who sat and listened while the men talked. The little city where we lived was perhaps unusual. It was the home of six or seven distinguished persons, and not all of them were men.

In this environment I grew up confidently expecting to have a profession and earn my own living, and also confidently expecting to be married and have children. It was fifty-fifty with me. I was just as passionately determined to have children as I was to have a career. And my mother was the triumphant answer to all doubts as to the success of this double role. From my earliest memory she had more than half supported the family and yet she was supremely a mother.

I have lived my life according to the plan. I have had the 'career' and the children and, except for an occasional hiatus due to illness or some other circumstance over which I had no control, I have earned my own living. I have even made a certain name for myself. If I have not fulfilled the promise of my youth, either as a homemaker or as a professional woman, I have never wavered in my feminist faith. My mother has always been a beacon to me, and if today I sometimes feel a sense of failure it may be partly because I have always lived in the glow of her example. In their early struggle for survival against narrow-minded and prejudiced parents some of my contemporaries seem to have won more of the iron needed in the struggle of life than I got from my almost perfect parents.

MADDY VEGTEL

In writing about her pregnancy at the age of forty, Maddy Vegtel underlines the ongoing social concern (and sometimes outright hysteria) surrounding the subject of late motherhood. It is hard to believe the article was written in the 1930s and shows how some dilemmas that we perceive as 'modern' have been around for longer than we think.

Forty – when the Baby was Born

1930s, American *Vogue*

When a middle-aged woman, that is biologically speaking middle-aged, announces to the world that she is going to have a baby, the response to this announcement is terrifically un-enthusiastic.

Friends lift eyebrows, pull down mouths, and exclaim, 'My dear! No! Aren't you taking a terrible risk . . . ?' Others remark, very brightly, 'Well, of course, I do know a woman who had no trouble at all, even the baby turned out to be all right, but still . . .' Others are very, very gay about it. They scream, 'Darling! How divine! How too marvellous!' And can't get away fast enough to tell their friends that it is positively suicide, completely reckless, and besides in a couple of years, my God, she'll be taken for its grandmother!

A few, but very few people will say calmly, sincerely, 'I am so glad. I think you are a very lucky person.'

It is also lucky for the prospective mother that she is so completely satisfied about the matter herself, otherwise this lack of friendly enthusiasm, this sinister atmosphere of foreboding would be a trifle hard to bear.

She knows as well as any one the disadvantages of having a first child late in life. The physical ones: it is a greater risk for herself; it may take a long time before she feels perfectly all right again; the child may not be as healthy as it should be, etc., etc. These depressing thoughts will race up and down through her head in the first months of pregnancy, dismal thoughts indeed! But as the months progress, she will find to her surprise that happier thoughts pop up, too; that there are not only disadvantages, but definite advantages as well. I know – my son is almost a year old, and he was born when I was forty.

What are the advantages of having a child at the age of, let us say, forty? Well, most important of all, a woman at that age definitely knows that she wants the child, otherwise she just wouldn't have it. There is no doubt. At that age, she knows herself, her husband, as well as she ever will; she has some idea of what kind of a father, what kind of a mother, he and she will make. She knows if she is a slothful sort, or a pernickety housekeeper; if she is the overly anxious, or the just too, too casual type. In any case, she can take herself firmly in hand and say, 'This will not do . . .'

At her age, she also knows what type of life she enjoys most and is therefore the most successful at, or vice versa; she has probably tried out several different types by now. For years she may have had a nine-to-five job, with dashing madly home to dash madly out again far into the night. She has managed a comfortable country place 'so wonderful for weekend parties,' she has travelled and travelled with husband and without, and now finally she is settled in a charming apartment 'so easy to do over every now and then.'

Suddenly at the approaching forties she admits to herself that she never wants to have a job again, that she loves home life, loves to keep house for her husband and herself, but is bored with seeing her home always with an eye to entertaining. That what she really wants, and wants now, is a home for a child to grow up in. To have happy memories of, for after being in the world for quite a while, she knows how very important a normal, happy childhood is. It will not only be fun for herself to buy candles for a birthday-cake or candles for the Christmas-tree (it was getting to be a little silly doing that just for her husband and herself), but it will be *right*. For a Christmas-tree and a birthday-cake are those simple things which are remembered with a fine, delicious glow all through life.

It no longer excites her to think up a new way to arrange flowers for dinner conversation, or to unearth a special little wine for Mr. A.B.C., who knows everything there is to know about little wines; no – she now wants some day to hear her child say, 'Mother, I like the way we eat at a round table with the lamp on it . . . it's cozy.'

Knowing all this, it is hardly likely that after the baby is born she'll decide that what she really is cut out for is to run an artificial flower shop or that she needs a complete change of husband, which may eventually lead to the child having, besides a father and mother, a couple of stepmothers and stepfathers as well, and cause general emotional upset.

At peace then with husband and home, she expects her baby with calm content. Immediately there will be some woman who exclaims, 'You'll feel simply dismal for months, and you'll miss so much and those frightful clothes . . .' It is likely that this woman, being about your own age, had her children some fifteen years ago.

In fifteen years, a great many discoveries have been made, all helping to make child-bearing much less of an ordeal. There are, first of all, all these wonderful medicines; pills, capsules, injections. Capsules full of vitamins to keep roses in your cheeks; pills of calcium so that your teeth will stay in and your hair won't fall out, your nails remain glossy; injections so that you need hardly feel nauseated at all.

Then there are simply thousands of quite charming dresses full of artful pleats and drawstrings . . . but far more important than all the artificial aid is the fact that a prospective mother of twenty-five and one of forty do not think alike. At twenty-five, one might tear one's hair at having to miss a divine party and shriek when you find that you just simply can't wear that little tulle any longer. At forty, you certainly don't. You've worn a lot of tulle, have gone to a lot of parties, have drunk a great many drinks; at forty, you simply do not care.

All you want during these months is to be comfortable, to see those few people whom you really want to see, and to dream your little dreams.

Naturally, the years have made you less and less dependent on people and on their opinions. You yourself have done a great many foolish things, but some decent ones, too; you've laughed, cried, had tantrums, known real grief, real happiness. You've known a great many people, read a great many books, listened to music, seen pictures. You have, in other words, lived.

So now at forty you are a definite person; you've done away with that lovely, lazy slogan of youth, '*tout savoir c'est tout pardonner.*' You now have your own standard, your taste, ideas. You say, 'I like this . . . I don't like that . . .' regardless of what someone else may say. You are independent, and this independence does not forsake you now. And you'll need it now more than ever, if only in trifles at first.

You are lying on a couch. A friend drops in and says, 'Oh, you should be taking a firm, brisk walk . . .'

You are taking a firm, brisk walk, and another friend says, 'You really should be at home, lying down . . .' Do you get flustered? No! Do you take their advice? No! You smile and say, 'I suppose I should . . .' And go on doing exactly what you want to do.

A mother of four tells you that you will need short-sleeved and long-sleeved vests for the child, also belly-bands, *positively* belly-bands. Your doctor said, 'No belly-bands . . .' So again you smile and say, 'I think that I have everything I'll need.'

They lend you books. Masses of books on prenatal care, on infant care. You look through one of them and read, 'Your child should from the very first year wear long woollen stockings.' Another volume says, 'Always remember when in doubt, ask your doctor . . .' That sounds very sensible; so finally that book becomes your treasure, *the Book.*

And once the baby is there, that serenity does not forsake you. A grain of salt . . . you add it to your own daily life so why not the baby's? You don't believe in every single word a psychoanalyst says about your own self, so why should you take his every word on the baby as gospel truth? You don't follow every new food fad, so why should the poor child have to? Depriving it of meat purées and broths is just as silly as doing without meat yourself. Oranges are very healthy, but a diet of oranges will do no more for an infant than it did for you when you went in for *that* nonsense years ago! A well-balanced diet is exactly as important for a baby as it is for you. Far more important than being a little late with its bottle now and then, for you realize soon enough that that won't harm the child, just as you realize that a simply dreadful pimple on its eyelid does not mean permanent disfigurement or that a fall out of the crib is not always followed by a concussion.

As to pets . . . Dogs have fleas. Well, it may as well get used to seeing a flea now and then, and decent cats do not scratch babies.

No one believes in slapping a child any more, but if your temper does get the better of you once in a while and you suddenly wake up and find that *you have slapped your child*, you do not believe that this incident is going to leave it with a horrible complex which may eventually get cleared up by 1969. At your age, you take things calmly; you simply can not imagine disasters where there are only trifles! And as the child grows older, it can not help but benefit by your calm outlook, by that blessing which comes with age: a sense of value.

These are happy thoughts – to remember when you are suddenly, quite horribly struck by the disadvantages of having a child late in life. Your little boy will not grow into manhood saying (as all sensitive males in fiction always do) ' . . . Ah! how well I remember my mother when she'd come and kiss me good-night before going to a ball. . . . She'd wear a pink bouffant frock, and in her golden hair she'd have a tiny, shining butterfly! And her perfume . . . I can still smell that delicious perfume . . . .'

He may remember perfume, of course, but the bouffant frock and the golden hair are out, I am afraid!

Your little girl will probably remark someday, 'Mother, you look much older than Dorothy's and Ann's mothers do. Why?' And, 'Mother, were you always grey?'

You will probably not feel up to a swim with your child at 7 a.m. in the morning, or for a three hours' hike through the woods. Someday you will have to feign great interest at a football game while you can hardly wait to get home to a fire and a drink. Or you will be begged to go along skiing, a sport which always does something to your back. Or to go . . . But will you? Will you be asked these things? Perhaps your child will not ask his old mother to join these strenuous activities at all, perhaps all your child will ask is just to find you home when he or she and all their friends get there!

MARJORIE KINNAN RAWLINGS
1896–1953

A journalist, short-story writer and novelist, Rawlings' best-known work is the 1939 Pulitzer Prize-winning novel, *The Yearling*, which she wrote whilst living in rural Florida. The following article is a description of her instinctive approach to cookery, and includes her directions for making blackbird pie, complete from the shooting of the birds in the marsh-grass to the table.

I Sing While I Cook

1930s, American *Vogue*

It has been a matter of pure joy to me, a very serious woman, to find that the properly planned and prepared food brings acolytes into my life who are unimpressed by my abilities either as a novelist or as a *femme fâtale*. Writing is my profession, my exaltation, and my torture. I write as an introvert, attempting to turn an intangible loveliness into a tangible conception. But I cook as an extrovert, singing at the top of my lungs, in ecstasy and the certainty of fulfilment. My black Adrina says, 'I sho' loves to see you cut loose in the kitchen.'

Suppose we leave out of the picture, for the moment, the pale neurotics who genuflect before dreary diets or the this-that-and-t'other caloried or documented eating. Let us consider only the pleasing of normal, lusty folk who, after two or three cocktails, sit down with well-bred greediness to my careless and carefree table on my Florida veranda. For these, I dote on planning a meal that shall first titillate, then satisfy, then ease. I play to the gourmet, never to the gourmand.

To my notion, the most pleasant way of playing is to make the most of local materials. I can do wonders with asparagus, but asparagus in Florida comes from California, from Colorado, or New York, and is a withered memory of its own early days. So, instead of asparagus with Hollandaise, I stimulate a menu with fresh okra, direct from the field. I use only the young crisp pods, boil them whole, briskly, for ten minutes by the stop-watch – one minute too long destroys their integrity. Then I arrange the pods on individual, small, hot plates like the spokes of a wheel, their firm green tips pointed in thirstily toward the individual tiny bowls of Hollandaise. We dip the still firm okra into the sauce, holding it by the uncut stem end, as unhulled strawberries are dipped in powdered sugar.

Perhaps the loveliest of my local dishes is my Crab Newburgh. I can not possibly give proportions, for I never have, twice, the same amount of fresh crabmeat. Robert Frost says in one of his orchard poems, 'Something has to be left to God.' And in cooking, something has to be left to the instinct, or experience, of the cook, who goes at such dishes not by measure, but by the look and the holy feel of the mixture. In describing my Newburgh at its best, I must stand humbly and acknowledge two miracles that go into its composition. One is Dora, my Jersey cow, who has the rottenest disposition and gives the richest cream in the world. The other miracle is the nature of the crabmeat.

In the middle of a desolate nowhere in Florida, whose location I refuse to reveal lest tourists make a path to its shore, we have the phenomenon of a spring bubbling suddenly from subterranean depths to form a stream that runs into a river, and thence to the sea. In that spring and that stream are found the largest, the sweetest blue crabs I have ever encountered. The cooked meat from them is as white as the breast of a virgin, and as tender. The large flakes fall as exquisitely from the shell as the white garments fall from the bride.

I take whatever measure I may have, then, of these unviolated morsels, and toss them into an iron skillet, half-inch deep in Dora's butter. I turn them gently. They must not brown, they must not change the colour of their innocence, but they must absorb the butter as a flower absorbs the sun. Then I add lemon-juice, approximately one tablespoonful to a heaping cupful of crabmeat. I toy again. I add salt, a dash of clove, a fainter dash of nutmeg, and a wisp of a dash of red pepper. I pour on, slowly, devilish-Dora's cream, thick and golden. I let simmer. I call for a ritual cocktail. The rest of the meal is ready. The guests are warned to powder their noses, to take their last drink, and to assemble.

I beat eggs. How can I say how many? Probably three eggs to a pint of cream. I fold in the eggs. I uncork the sherry, which should be as dry as possible. I pour slowly, stirring meanwhile as feverishly as though the Prince of Wales were waiting. How much sherry? How should I know? Just enough to thin the thickened blend to something a shade beyond the original thickness of the cream.

Adrina cries out, 'Supper comin' up!'

The guests seat themselves. I add two or three tablespoonfuls of cognac brandy, I turn the Newburgh into a red-hot, deep serving-dish, I rush it to the table. Toast points are ready, and parsley for garnishing. I serve. I pray. The Newburgh is tasted – a sip of Chablis behind it. Strong men who have admitted that they have not read my writings, who have indicated all too plainly that there are sirens in their lives past my power to dethrone, grope for my hand to kiss its blistered finger-tips. Women who would knife me in the back, if I turned it, murmur, 'Darling – .' This, then, is a Newburgh.

My blackbird pie, however, came close to costing me a friend. I carried my use of local ingredients, to say nothing of a childish innocence, almost too far. I sat Sam Byrd, the actor, of *Tobacco Road* and *Of Mice and Men* fame, down to a pie of blackbirds. I think it really held twenty-four, for there were four of us at table, and I always allow six of the tiny things per person.

Sam said, 'You don't mean – blackbirds?'

'Why, yes. It does seem evil to shoot them, doesn't it? Their chirping is so gay in the rushes.'

'Not blackbirds?'

'The little red-winged blackbirds. The females are drab and are sometimes mistaken for rice-birds. I suppose I should really explain why I began shooting them for pie. I am a rotten shot, and one cold, foggy morning in a duck-blind on Orange Lake back of my place, I had simply missed too many ducks. I was in a fury of frustration. And all around me in the marsh-grass the red-winged blackbirds were cheeping and chirring by the hundreds. I slipped No. 10 shot in my double-barreled twenty-gauge, and two shots dropped a dozen birds. Pie for two.'

'And what possessed you – pardon me – how did it occur to you that they might be edible?'

I stared at him.

'Why, people have always eaten blackbird pie, haven't they? Don't you remember, "Four and twenty blackbirds baked in a pie?"'

'But that was a nursery rhyme – .'

And it came to me then for the first time that I might indeed be serving something beyond the pale.

'But it's delicious. I make it often. Whenever the blackbirds are around in quantities.'

He shuddered. Like a novice in the snake department at the zoo, he poked at his portion. He cut a piece of the small, succulent brown breast. He buried it between two wisps of flaky crust, brushed it with gravy – holy water, I presume, against the devil – closed his eyes, and swallowed it. He opened his eyes. He blinked them. He laid his hand on mine.

He said in a low voice, 'My dear friend. To think I didn't trust you –.'

He wrote one day asking for the recipe for the Sam Byrd cook-book. Here it is:

Like the recipe for rabbit, you must, of course, first shoot your blackbirds. Pluck them dry if you have the patience or the services of a little Negro boy. Split them down the back and dress them, but leave them whole. Roll them in flour. In plenty of butter in a deep kettle, brown the floured birds; and with them a tablespoonful or so of minced onion and minced green pepper. When brown, cover with hot water. Add salt, pepper, a bay-leaf, and a dash of allspice. Simmer gently about two hours, or until the birds are tender. Add tiny whole onions, potatoes cut in balls or small squares, and carrots cut in the shape and size of shoe-string potatoes. When the onions are nearly tender, remove the bay-leaf, add a tablespoonful of minced parsley, thicken slightly, turn into a deep casserole, add a few tablespoonfuls of sherry, cover with thick, rich pastry crust, and bake in a hot oven. Serve with a dry red wine, an endive and kumquat salad, and follow with tangerine sherbet.

This is the way I cook my small squab-sized chickens when I'm tired of waiting for them to reach broiler size:

Dress whole. Stuff with browned buttered crumbs and pecans. Roll in flour, well seasoned with salt and pepper. Brown on all sides in butter. Arrange in baking-dish. Almost cover with hot water that has been poured into skillet containing the butter in which chickens were browned. Add sherry, one-eighth cupful to each chicken. Cover tightly and bake until very tender, when chickens will have absorbed most of the liquid. I some-times prepare in this fashion the smaller game birds, quail, doves, snipe; squirrel; small individual pot roasts of venison; or chicken too large for frying, cut into portions.

I am sorry I cannot here discuss frogs' legs; or the time my pet raccoon grew instantly to manhood by imbibing one whole Alexander cocktail; and how, after sleeping it off on the pillows of my bed, he came swagger-ing to the dinner-table and fell growling on a pair of frogs' legs tossed him by an alarmed guest whose leg he tried to climb; how he ate – after all his previous life on warm milk from the nursing bottle – six pairs; how the guest said:

'But, after all, frogs' legs are his natural diet, aren't they?'

'Yes,' I answered, 'but not French fried – .'

ELEANOR ROOSEVELT
1884–1962

With her campaigning zeal and willingness to use all media outlets – press conferences, radio broadcasts, lecture tours – to publicize her views, Roosevelt broke with precedent as American first lady and transformed the role irrevocably.

One of the keys to her public visibility was her work as a journalist, writing the syndicated column 'My Day' six days a week, from 1935 to 1962. In these articles she covered a huge range of topics, including race, politics and women's issues.

Another of her main themes was her relationship with her own family and, specifically, her children. In addressing this subject she asserts the normality of her day-to-day life, underlining the fact that her concerns are much the same as those of the general populace.

My Day

11 November 1938, United Feature Syndicate Inc

HYDE PARK, NOVEMBER 11—My journeys are over, and I hardly realized that I have covered so much territory and seen so many of my children and grandchildren.

A newspaperwoman on one of my stops tried to catechize me on the proper relationship between parents and their children. It grew out of [a] remark I made that I was horribly neat, and she wanted to know if one could be too neat. Because I had nothing better to say, I answered, 'Yes, if one nags one's family too much on the subject, and makes life miserable for everyone.' Thereupon she asked if I had succeeded in making my children as neat as I was myself. She had brought her son down to meet me, so I gathered she found it very difficult to make him live up to her own standards.

The answer, of course, is that having children is, perhaps, the beginning of an education for them, but it is certainly the beginning of an education for their parents. All their young lives their parents are learning self-control, patience, a sense of values, how to respect other people's personalities and yet not neglect teaching some things which, if they are not learned young, must be learned in later life with far greater hardship.

When these early years are over, this type of education comes to an end. The parents think they have done all they can do in the way of home discipline and education, and a new phase of mutual education begins. Parents then find that having developed individuals, they must permit those individuals to live their own lives, to have their own experiences, to make their own decisions, sometimes to make their own mistakes.

I don't know how other parents are, but I know that for myself, I can stand back and look at my children and what they do and think, once they are grown up, with a certain amount of objectivity. On the other hand, I know quite well that there is a bond between us and that, right or wrong, that bond could never be broken. I am proud of them when I think they have acquitted themselves well, regardless of what the rest of the world may think. Even when I disagree and feel impelled to tell them so, I know that I understand them better than anyone else, perhaps. They are always my children, with the right to call upon me in case of need.

The greatest contribution the older generation can give, I think, to the younger generation, is the feeling that there is someone to fall back upon, more especially when the hard times of life come upon them. That is so even when we know that we have brought those hard times upon ourselves.

Funny that a newspaperwoman, in a casual interview at an airport, should force me to think of one of the most binding relationships in life. I have been immersed in personal things for several days, and it is rather a strange transition back to a life which is completely taken up with public affairs.

DAPHNE du MAURIER
1907–89

The prolific London-born writer's best-known works include the novels *My Cousin Rachel* and *Jamaica Inn*, as well as her 1938 classic, *Rebecca*, which brought her huge international acclaim.

The following article is her sensitive analysis of how to write a letter to a husband on the frontline: which subjects are acceptable and which completely taboo? It gives an interesting insight into the difficulties for the women left behind, as they attempt to second-guess their husbands' feelings and respond appropriately; and of the attitudes towards women and wifely roles at the time and courage and strength of the women left behind.

Letter Writing in Wartime

September 1940, *Good Housekeeping*

What sort of letters did we write, in the old, forgotten days before the war? Those of us who even then had a husband, or a lover, or a son living away from home, and possibly abroad, would sit down comfortably on mail day and scribble pages of light-hearted gossip without that dumb anguish at the back of the mind that perhaps the letter would never find its reader. We talked of the children, of the Browns who were coming over on Sunday, of a possible cold in the head, of a rumoured engagement between old friends, 'Fancy old Pat getting off at last,' and lastly of approaching plans for the future summer or winter holiday, when reunion was a definite and settled possibility. The envelope was sealed, the Air Mail stamp pressed on the right-hand corner, and then, with one letter to the Bank and another to a London store, the little collection would be left on a salver in the hall for the parlour-maid to take away.

And to-day? The desk stands as it has always stood, beside the fireplace with the window on the right. Paper, pen, and ink are there before us. But the photograph on the top of the desk stares at us with a new depth, a new intensity – so much so that we cannot bear to look at it too closely, and instead reach for our pen in a rather breathless hurry, only to find we have no words to say.

It is possible that the children have said something funny, that the Browns are still coming over on Sunday, and that a cold in the head does not make for clear thinking – but are these things enough, now? What does he want to be told, this husband, this lover, this son? This is a problem that every individual wife, sweetheart, or mother must solve for herself. No hard rules can be laid down. One thing is certain, though. Any murmur of 'self-pity' will not be helpful to the writer. The woman who dares to write, 'This agony of separation is too much for me to bear,' cannot be forgiven. Whatever she does, and must feel in her heart, of strain and anxiety, no sign of it should appear in any of her letters. Men are not always the sturdy, stalwart creatures we imagine, and a yearning letter from home may bring the nervy, highly-strung type to breaking-point. We are not the only ones to wonder, at odd and fearful moments, if the separation is to be final. And so there must be no weakness in these letters of ours, no poor and pitiful hinting at despair. We must be strong, and confident, and full of faith, so that some measure of the spirit we would show will find its way to that reader far away, bringing him comfort, and hope, and a quiet peace even in the midst of very great horror and distress. He will want home news, of course, and local news, too. Here we can be helpful. No rumours, no grim hearsay gossip from the friend-of-a-friend, but news that will give courage and a renewed determination to endure. The retreat from Dunkirk, wrongly described, would make a fighting-man in another part of the battle feel that the Allied cause was lost, and that nothing was in store for him and his companions but annihilation or grim surrender. Told properly, by someone with understanding and a faith in miracles, the story would read as one of the greatest epics in English history, and fill any man who had not actually experienced it himself with wonder, and pride, and fresh faith in God and his fellow-men.

We must not forget, in our letters, that there is comedy in war as well as tragedy, and that there is a certain sense of fun, essentially English in its quality, that can turn the dullest and drabbest incident – and even serious incidents, too – into a thing of laughter. There is much armchair criticism, on the home front, that can be observed and re-told in a letter, with the proverbial tongue in the cheek; and how many of us, during the last twelvemonth, must have come back from our First Aid lectures, A.R.P. practice, and weekly working parties, in a state bordering on hysteria, only to find an empty house and no companion to chuckle with us from the opposite chair at the tale we have to tell. All these things we can put into our letters – Mrs. Jones who reached for her smelling-bottle when arteries were mentioned – the collapse of the stretcher under a fourteen-stone V.A.D. who had offered herself as victim to our blundering hands – the fanatical gas instructor who whipped a small bottle containing Lewisite under our quailing noses only to be knocked out herself – the lecturer who came to talk on National Savings, and being absent-minded and having mislaid her notes, read a treatise on *Preparing for Baby* to a gathering of spinsters. It is these things that we want to remember in wartime, the idiotic and the heroic, the ridiculous and the sublime, so that we can make a hotch-potch of them in our letters when we write, and the man who reads them will breathe, for one moment, something of our unchanging, foolish world. The grumbles are best forgotten, the rumours of ill-omen, the bitter scraps of criticism, the complacency and selfishness combined. These, alas, have always existed and will continue to exist, but they have never made history! The man to whom we write and who may yet give his life for his country, does not shed his blood for the little things. When he fights for England he does not think of the blunders, the omissions, the jealousies that governments have shown, and will always show, to the end of time – he sees instead the quiet, intangible things.

MARY STOTT
1907–2002

As editor of the *Guardian* women's page from 1956 to 1972, Mary Stott reinvented the concept of such sections, throwing out the usual articles on fashion and home furnishings, in favour of substantial features that spoke to women's genuine concerns. The page was campaigning and political, necessarily reflecting Stott's rejection of discrimination in any form, but never predictable. Although obviously pro-women, Stott took issue with many of the feminist positions bubbling up in the late 1960s and early 1970s, including the Labour Party's use of a compulsory quota system for women candidates and the prevalent use of the term 'Ms'.

One of Stott's notable contributions was to encourage women who weren't professional journalists to write about their difficult personal experiences – with breast cancer, for example, post-natal depression and domestic violence – in the belief that the pieces would speak directly to readers in the same situation. In light of this, Stott included this article of her own on the page in 1968, after the untimely death of her husband Ken. In dealing with both the practical and emotional responsibilities of being a widow, the piece is informative, but also affecting. Over the years it brought her an ongoing response, and began her involvement with the National Association of Widows.

Learning to be a Widow

27 July 1968, *Guardian*

It may come suddenly or far, far too slowly, but from the day we are born death is a certainty. So why do those of us who are agnostics or atheists and cannot believe in any kind of personal survival shove the thought of death into a dark cupboard and refuse to look at it? Why do people even say 'How morbid!' when one talks quietly or with tension-easing jokes, of hearses and wills and estate duties?

This is about learning to be a widow and it is for men as well as for women, but people who think such an article is either exhibitionist or depressing had better stop here. It is intended, simply and rather urgently to help with the hard fact of life that the chances are much higher than evens that a woman will survive her husband. Women who don't face this, or whose husbands don't, are in for a far harder time than those who do. To start with three practical points:

It is best to accept quite early in one's married life (a friend of mine came back from her honeymoon a widow) that it is necessary to make a will and to leave all family and household documents tidily in a place known to both. You need birth certificate, marriage certificate, the name and address of the building society, national insurance number . . . and all sorts of addresses and particulars. Do you know where they are? No woman should have to cope with the hell of scrabbling blindly through drawers and pockets to find these things when she is distracted, numb, or exhausted.

Every woman should have money of her own that she can get at quickly, even if it is no more than £50 in the Post Office. The most thoughtful and far-seeing husband may crash his car just before pay day when funds are low, and anyway, his money may not be immediately available to his wife. How does a woman pay the butcher or buy food for the people who will come to the funeral unless she has ready money? Has she to humiliate herself by borrowing from her friends, or to trudge to the Ministry of Social Security, which may only be open from 10 a.m. to 4 p.m. and be closed on Saturdays. Employers should immediately offer help, even if it is no more than an advance on wages, to every employee, every employee's widow.

Given that to the very young death is an outrageous thing, a denial of meaningful personality, an impossible idea to accept, it should not be so once the first uncle or aunt, let alone the first parent, has died. From that time on the thought should be explored, gingerly at first, and then more openly, and often with laughter, for jokes are no less funny for being macabre and help to make intolerable jobs just about tolerable . . . summoning the undertaker, getting the death certificate, arranging the funeral. People want to say goodbye in dignity and fellowship and the only place to do this yet is in a church. Most ministers of religion understand the strong need for this kind of help and give it generously. But if one knows beforehand which minister, what form of service, it is one strain the less, and a help to one's friends.

The other things are harder to say: It has happened. The human being with whom your life was inextricably bound up is now, incredibly, an undertaker's job. You are liable to be alone in the house in the middle of the night, or be knocked up by a well-meaning policeman. And so, of course, you may be terrified, helpless or entirely out of your mind. The thing to hang on to is that human beings are basically kind. The newest neighbour, the merest acquaintance, will make your telephone calls, summon help, prop you up with tea or brandy until your own people can be with you. You have only to raise a finger and someone will cope for you, glad, grateful to serve your need. This is something one can absolutely rely on.

Most widows manage bravely until the funeral is over – and should be told so because it helps. But then what? Alas, no one can say. Not only are we all different people, differently equipped, suffering in different ways and degrees, but none of us can know in advance how we shall react to grief and shock. The strong and capable may suffer a total collapse of the will to live. The gentle, even the flabby, may find a life force exerting itself almost right away. One woman may need to hide, one to run to friends, one to stay alone where she is. One may clutch at work, one be incapable of it. Thinking ahead about this won't help much and shock may numb the wits for quite a while. One does as one must.

But one must find one's own way back, as the numbness wears off. One must fight the thought 'Why did it happen to me?'. However appalling it was, it was worse for someone else. So your husband died on a business trip to Bulgaria, or collapsed in the loo, or you saw him walk under a bus, or you were driving the car, or you called the doctor too late or you saw him wrestle agonisingly with death for days, or linger, unconscious or senile for weeks or even months. So it was beyond bearing. But other women bore this and more. Lapses into self-pity and into a kind of hatred for the care-free, the untouched, are inevitable, but to make self-pity a way of life is unreasonable and almost unforgivable. There are so many of us and none of us is entitled to think 'No-one suffered as I suffer'.

However smug and trite it may sound, it is true that the best therapy is ungrudgingly responding, as soon as one can, to other people's needs, accepting that they have their lives to live, their troubles to cope with. In time of grief and loss one is driven to lay a burden on one's friends, for one has a great and continuing need for support, company, affection, practical help, but it helps a great deal if one can spread the load and remember not to lean too much on any one shoulder, not to ask too much, and manage to give a little, here and there.

This, I think is what one ought to learn during one's married life. The most devotedly loved wives are not by any means always the most desolate widows. What he was, what he gave you, what you became because of him, what you learned in the way of unselfishness, what you earned together in the way of friends, may well be enough to see you through.

ANGELA CARTER
1940–92

Novelist, short-story writer and essayist, Carter excelled in all literary mediums to become one of the pre-eminent writers of her generation. Always quirky, often dark, her work presented a unique and perfectly developed worldview, shocking in its originality.

Pregnant with her first and only child, aged forty-one, Carter wrote the following piece about her experience of giving birth in a South London Hospital for the *New Statesman*. In it, she brilliantly depicts the way in which mothers of any age can be patronized and coddled, a subject as relevant now as ever.

Notes from a Maternity Ward

December 1983, *New Statesman*

Towards the end of the thirty-eighth week, I grow bored with saying: 'Fine,' when asked at the ante-natal clinic how I'm doing. So I try a little joke. It backfires. God, how it backfires. 'How do you feel?' 'A bit apprehensive,' I say. 'Not so much about the birth itself as about the next twenty or thirty years.' The consultant, an unreconstructed Thatcher clone – that is, she looks like Thatcher minus the peroxide and the schlap – turns on me a face costive with high moral seriousness. 'You have done the right thing in not having an abortion,' she says. 'But there is still time. If you have any doubts at all, I urge you to seriously discuss adoption with your husband – I know he's only a common-law husband, of course.'

I'm overwhelmed by incredulity. Had I ever mentioned abortion in connection with this incipient cherub? Are my compañero and I not the Darby and Joan of our circle? Should I say we just got hitched? What business is it of hers, anyway? I lapse into outraged silence. Later, I will weep with fury, but, if I do so now, who can tell how she will misinterpret that. I seethe. Who does she think she is; or I am? And if she delivers this kind of unsolicited advice to the white middle-class – to a member of it who has given her occupation as 'journalist', to boot – then what manner of abuse does she feel free to dish out to the black proletariat? How come she's lived so long? And why don't I punch her in the nose?

I'll tell you why. Because she's chosen to insult me when I'm flat on my back, dress pulled up, knickers down, vulnerable, helpless, undignified.

I would publish her name to the four winds, and gladly. But the hell of it is, she turns out to be a good doctor, as far as the mechanics are concerned. Callous and insensitive perhaps; but quick to spot a malfunction. A gift not to be sneezed at. And, furthermore, a woman so strait-jacketed by self-righteousness I doubt she'd ever understand why I want to crucify her. After all, her concern was only for what was best for the baby. And hadn't I virtually said I didn't want him? When she sees me, all pale and proud, on the ward after he's born – he chuckling in a glass box like a very expensive orchid – she's as nice as pie. Well done, she says.

'She'. Note how this consultant is female. I'm lying in at the embattled South London Hospital for Women, the last place I expected to be insulted. But there you go. Here, women treat women and she's the only one of them who treated me like a piece of shit.

I haven't been in hospital for thirty years, so I can't comment on the decline in the standards of the NHS; the floors aren't polished until they turn into lethal ice-rinks any more, which is no bad thing. The food has certainly improved, in comparison with the early fifties. The sheer wonder of the NHS remains; that they will do the best they can for us, that we are not at the mercy of a free market economy, that the lovely nurses smile as if they meant it and hug you when you are sad.

Inevitably, this particular hospital is scheduled for the axe. No amount of special pleading on behalf of women whose religion specifies they be treated by doctors of the same sex seems likely to save it; it is due to close down next April, its various wards – it's a general hospital – distributed around other local hospitals. The staff seems scarcely able to believe that some miracle won't save the place. If the Minister of Health turns into a woman tomorrow, there might be a chance, especially if (s)he then converted to Islam.

It is a rather elegant, red-brick building convenient for Clapham South tube station (the Northern line). It overlooks green and pleasant Clapham Common. It is, obviously, very well equipped; only needs a coat or two of paint and a few vases of plastic flowers to be fit for – who? The young woman in the bed next to me made a shrewd guess as to what would happen to the building once the NHS moved out. 'They'll sell it to bloody BUPA, won't they,' she opined.

The midwife shows me how to put the baby to the nipple. 'Look deep into his eyes,' she says. 'It helps with the bonding.' Good grief! Aren't we allowed any choice in the matter, he and I? Can't I learn to love him for himself, and vice versa, rather than trust to Mother Nature's psycho-physiological double bind? And what of his relationship with his father, who has no breasts? Besides, it's very difficult to look him in the eye. He fastens on the nipple with the furtive avidity of a secret tippler hitting the

British sherry, glancing backwards to make sure nobody else gets there first. When he strikes oil, he instantly becomes comatose. Am I supposed to poke him into consciousness: 'Hey, baby, don't nod off, we're supposed to be bonding.' More like bondage. Constrained affection; what resentment it will breed, in time. It's all part of the mystification in which the whole process of childbirth is so richly shrouded. For he is doomed to love us, at least for a significant initial period, because we are his parents. The same goes for us. That is life. That's the hell of it.

Somebody gave us an American publication called *Giving Birth*. A collection of photographs of mothers and fathers sharing the experience. (Where's the lesbian couple? Discrimination!) The parents look ecstatic; radiant; touchingly, comically startled and so on. Lots of shots of little heads poking out of vulvas. Also quotes from participants: 'I felt I had to be very focused. It was almost like meditation,' says one mother. It is compiled by somebody called Mary Motley Kalergis, another name on my post-partural hit-list. (Isn't one allowed a year's justifiable homicide after the event?) The photographs are all in black and white, please note. And, indeed, colour film would have made souvenir snaps of the finale of my own *accouchement* look like stills from a Hammer horror film. While what was going on next door, an emergency Caesarian, well, *that* certainly wasn't like meditation, not half it wasn't! This truly nauseating book is designed to mystify. It is about as kitsch as a fluffy blue bunny, and as much to do with the realities of parturition as a fluffy blue bunny has to do with a real live baby.

OK, OK. So this notebook has submerged under a sea of babyshit. Mao Tse-tung called a pig 'a manure factory on four legs'. A baby is much the same, except it remains stationary. Some people suggest you chuck soiled disposables on the compost heap. There are a few other suggestions for utilising the formidable quantities of ordure produced by the average baby and heedlessly thrown away every day. To say nothing of the valuable amounts of methane they emit. At the end of *War and Peace*, Tolstoy has Natasha ankle-deep in baby shit; impossible not to read something vindictive into that, although he does make Pierre soil his hands, too. Anyway, there is nothing wrong with babyshit. The TV news gobs out fresh horrors into the living room every evening; insulted by the specific urgencies of the neonate, that appalling dichotomy – the one between our lives as we live them and the way that forces outside ourselves shape them for us – seems less desperate than usual. Under the circumstances, a mercy.

RUTH PICARDIE
1964–97

The British journalist Ruth Picardie was just thirty-two when she was first diagnosed with breast cancer. Shortly afterwards (on finding that the cancer was terminal) she began a ground breaking series of columns in the *Observer*. Entitled 'Before I Say Goodbye', these took her readers on a poignant journey through her experience.

When first published, this was a uniquely confessional column, and it quickly proved influential, leading to a string of copycats as, journalists charted their struggles with alcoholism, depression, pregnancy etc, as well as other accounts of disease.

As the first of these confessional columns, Picardie's was also, arguably, the best. The following column was sadly her last, and is finished, as she wished, by her sister, Justine.

Before I Say Goodbye

24 August 1997, *Observer*

As every pop-psychologist knows, denial is the first stage of coming to terms with death. 'Among the over 200 dying patients we have interviewed,' writes Elisabeth Kubler-Ross in her classic work *On Death and Dying*, 'most reacted to the awareness of a terminal illness at first with the statement, "No, not me, it cannot be true".' Apparently, patients then move on, over a period of months, to anger, bargaining, depression and finally acceptance.

Me? I used to think I was a fast-track kind of girl, the sort who began a diet on a Monday (muesli for breakfast); stuck to it really well until Wednesday (baked potato, no butter for lunch); accidentally ate some garlic bread with a bowl of low-calorie gazpacho on Thursday; decided on Saturday that a bowl of raspberries (fresh, unlimited) couldn't really be eaten without a small tub of cream (M&S extra thick); and by Sunday realised that, actually, calorie-counting put your metabolism in starvation mode. Months? Pooey. I used to be the sort of superwoman who spent a mere week moving through the five well-known stages of coming to terms with having a spare tyre: depression, anger, bargaining, denial, acceptance. What else do you expect from an evolved, post-feminist chick? Sadly, being diagnosed with cancer seems to have arrested my capacity for high-powered psychological evolution. For a shocking 10 months since Diagnosis Day I have become convinced that I am, in fact, pregnant. Which, on the face of it, is down there in the kindergarten of denial, or possibly the mania of bargaining, or at the very best the delusion of depression.

However, I need only to refer you to one of the pregnancy manuals dusting up my shelves: the vomiting, the weird stuff growing inside you, the endless waiting for the big day.

This is where Ruth's column ends, though it is not the ending she intended [writes her sister, Justine Picardie]. She is now in a hospice, too ill to finish this article, though I think I know what she intended to say. Her twins, Lola and Joe, were born two years ago this week. The similarity between those hot August days before she gave birth, and now, is perhaps not as far-fetched as it seems. Friends telephone, wanting to know the news, though there is nothing yet to tell; flowers arrive, as if in anticipation; the sticky afternoons drift by; the nights seem to last forever.

But unlike two years ago, there is no fixed due date. There have been times in the past few days when Ruth has fallen asleep in her hospital bed, and I've wondered if she will ever wake up again. Then she opens her eyes, and ruminatively eats another chocolate biscuit. She has talked about leaving the hospice in time for Lola and Joe's birthday party, about future shopping expeditions and trips to the theatre, about writing another column.

So this is not a neat conclusion, nor even rough prediction of what to expect next. Last Sunday, I sat with Ruth in the hospice, and she added a handwritten note to the bottom of her unfinished column. 'So here I am, still waiting for the big day which I hope and half-hope won't come.'

DANIELLE CRITTENDEN
1963–

A prominent conservative writer and thinker, Toronto-born Crittenden was launch-editor of the *Women's Quarterly* in the early 1990s and has been published in a huge range of publications. Her controversial response to the feminist movement, 'What Our Mothers Didn't Tell Us: Why Happiness Eludes The Modern Woman', brought her much attention on its publication in 1999, and her profile grew when she was appointed to write the *Wall Street Journal's* first ever piece of serialized fiction.

The result was the light-hearted but pithy 'AmandaBright@home' which described the life of a highly educated, working, Washington mother who gives it all up to stay at home and tend her children. The following article is the story's first instalment.

AmandaBright@home

25 May 2001, *Wall Street Journal*

CHAPTER 1

It happened whenever Amanda returned from Christine's: She felt asphyx-iated by the cramped chaos of her own tiny house.

It was your typical Cleveland Park row house, a narrow brick job from the '20s crammed alongside other narrow brick jobs from the '20s. There was not much to recommend it except that it was not, repeat not, a tract house in the suburbs.

They'd bought it during the Washington real-estate slump of the mid-1990s. Never mind that if Amanda and Bob were different sorts of people they could then have afforded a Palladian-windowed, multilevel, four-bedroomed, two-and-a-half-bathroomed 'Manor Home' in a develop-ment named something like Badger Run Estates. They had looked at one of those places precisely once during their transition from apartment-dwelling, one-child family to house-dwelling, two-child family. They had driven away so quickly their car left tire tracks in the newly planted sod.

'I don't want to spend my life commuting,' Bob muttered as they sat waiting for an interminable light change at a six-lane intersection near a shopping center where you could buy, right away, with no money down, a reclining mattress.

'I never want to be more than a two-block walk from a good cup of coffee,' replied Amanda, and that's all they said for the next 45 minutes until the bridge that took them back over the Potomac hove mercifully into view.

That was before she knew Christine Saunders and her two-acre ravine lot, her cherry-lined driveway and her commodious, mock-Georgian brick mansion with its massive 'media' room, 'chef's' kitchen and skylit halls. Everything vanished in that house: the children, the toys, even Christine's husband, who kept an office somewhere in the basement. The few times Amanda had actually met him were as he emerged, blinking like a ferret, to ask if anyone had seen his car keys.

Amanda struggled with the lock on her front door while trying to balance Emily on her hip and save Ben's fingers from amputation by the hinges of the outer screen. The inner door opened with a rush, and the three of them tumbled over a pile of rubber boots and stuffed animals.

'Ugh! Kids! Why do you leave these things right here, where Mommy can trip?!' Amanda dropped her bags beside the mess. 'OK, just *go* – go upstairs, do something, watch a video, I don't care.' The children ran off hooting in triumph.

She still felt a bit tipsy from the Chardonnay she'd drunk at Christine's. They had spent the afternoon by the swimming pool at Christine's country club. Afterward they had repaired to Christine's backyard, where the kids laid claim to an elaborate play set and the two women settled into their sun chairs brandishing plastic picnic glasses filled with wine.

Amanda rarely drank in the afternoon, but in the Saunders' household the afternoon bottle was something of a ritual, even on a weekday. She couldn't say she strenuously objected to this ritual; indeed, the wine worked upon her like a mild anesthetic and quelled the anxiety Amanda had felt all afternoon watching the other women at the club.

She'd stood knee deep in the kiddy pool in her faded and stretched bikini trying to look dignified while Ben spat water and Emily screamed in terror at the tiny ripples lapping at her waist. For some reason Amanda and her children were the only ones creating a spectacle. The other mothers lay upon their chaises longues as still and majestic as the gilded figures on Egyptian sarcophagi, their wrists and necks banded in gold, their possessions propped around them. Or they wandered serenely over the lush, landscaped lawns, their groomed hair glinting in the sunlight, a genetically perfect clone or two trotting along obediently at their heels.

They reminded Amanda of prized thoroughbreds retired from the track, content in their new vocation as brood mares. Personal trainers kept their bodies buffed and toned purely for aesthetic pleasure, not because the women had any need to exert themselves physically. Where would they exert themselves if they could? Out here in the Maryland suburb of Potomac, there were not even sidewalks. When these women were not at the club they were chauffeuring kids around (preferably in a Mercedes station wagon), flexing, at most, their right foot upon a gas pedal.

Yet it was not so much the wealth of Christine and her clubmates that Amanda envied. It was their apparent sense of ease. Every single one of these women had been raised, like Amanda herself, to spend her life steadily climbing a trajectory toward some professional goal. They'd gone to college; they'd devoted their 20s to succeeding in some company; and then, boom, here they were applying their highly trained brains to the problems of toddler management and running their homes with the skill and organization with which they'd run entire departments.

Yet it didn't seem to bother them – certainly not the way it still bothered Amanda, a full three years after she'd left her job at the National Endowment for the Arts. Nor did it seem to bother Christine.

It had been almost a year since Amanda and Christine first met at the parents' coffee at their children's pre-school. In all that time she'd never once heard Christine express a doubt about having thrown over a promising career as an intellectual property lawyer. Bob told Amanda that his colleagues at the Department of Justice still cited an article Christine had written 10 years ago for the *Chicago Law Review*. Yet the only time Christine made reference to her former career was to joke how poorly it prepared her for dealing with children. 'It's not like knowing the doctrine of contributory infringement helps me get Vaseline out of Victoria's hair.'

Now, re-entering her own narrow, disorganized house only increased the nasty pressure inside Amanda's head. There were Legos strewn about the small living room and a half-finished puzzle in the hallway. A pull-toy left on the stairs just screamed lawsuit.

But it wasn't only the child clutter: There was grown-up clutter too, clutter in which she had once taken a defiant pride: *I'm not a housewife. I am at home to care for my children – not to 'make a home.' One day I will be returning to the office where I belong. Until then we can get by with the fiberboard bookshelves from college and the loveseat we bought when we moved in together, and the lamp from my grandmother, and the milk crates we once thought made funky record holders.* It was the same pride she'd taken in driving the old Volvo instead of trading it in for the suburbanite's vehicle of choice, the minivan. Now it all seemed to her – well, cheap.

God, it was a quarter to six. She'd have to get dinner started. Maybe they should just get take-out – although it would be the second time this week. How was she going to justify it to Bob? 'Sorry but I spent all afternoon at Christine's club and didn't have time to make dinner.' 'We were at Christine's house drinking and I forgot to stop at the Safeway.'

No, this was not going to do. Amanda opened the fridge. It was overflowing with cartons and plastic containers but nothing that could be used to prepare dinner for two adults: peanut butter, bread, yogurt, juice boxes, eggs, leftover macaroni and cheese, the congealed remains of a cheese pizza ordered in the night before. She searched through the drawers but came up with only a spoiled head of Boston lettuce, a bunch of celery, some lemons and an unripe avocado. Her elbow knocked over a container of grated parmesan cheese, sprinkling everything with a fine white powder like freshly fallen snow.

'Damn!'

'Uh-oh, Mommy use a bad word.' Emily wandered into the kitchen stark naked, trailing one of Amanda's scarves.

'*Emily*,' said Amanda tensely, 'why did you take off your clothes?'

'I'm playing Indians with Ben,' Emily replied complacently, shaking her long brown curls. 'I'm an Indian princess. Will you tie this on me, Mommy?' She held up the scarf.

'No, Mommy will *not* tie this on you, Emily; it is Mommy's good scarf,' Amanda said, snatching the scarf away. 'And you are *not* Indians,' she added irritably, 'you are *Native Americans*.'

Emily burst into tears. Amanda sighed and took the child into her arms.

'B-b-but I want to b-b-be a-a-n-Ind-d-d,' Emily sobbed, 'a-a-a Natif Merkan *princess*.'

Amanda wiped her daughter's tears with her sleeve and draped the scarf around the thin, shivering body, arranging it, as artfully as she could, to resemble a three-year-old's conception of what Natif Merkan princesses wore if Natif Merkan princesses shopped at Nordstrom's.

'Just this once, Emily,' Amanda warned. 'Next time use a towel.'

'Natif Merkins don't wear *towels*,' Emily said indignantly.

'Well, they don't wear Mommy's scarves either, sweetie. Off you go.'

'I'm hungry,' she replied, not moving.

The telephone rang. Emily did not budge. Upstairs, Ben began shrieking for his lost princess.

'Go!' said Amanda pleadingly.

'I'm hungry!'

Amanda answered the phone. It was Bob.

'Hi, hon. What's going on there? It sounds like you're surrounded by Apaches.'

'Actually, I am,' said Amanda, pushing Emily out the kitchen door and closing it behind her, setting off a second set of shrieks to join in chorus with the first.

'Can you talk for a minute? I've got some great news.'

'Uh, yeah – sure.'

'Do you think you and I could go out for dinner alone tonight?'

Amanda brightened immediately. 'I'll have to find a sitter – '

'Maybe Hannah could come over from next door. We won't stay out late.'

'OK, I'll ask and call you back. What's the news – tell me quickly.'

Bob was unusually breathless. 'It looks like the DOJ is finally going after Megabyte. The whole antitrust thing. It's war. And I'm going to be in charge – well, sort of. I'll tell you more at dinner.'

'Oh, Bob!'

'Yes – very exciting. Call me back.'

And it was exciting, yes. But as Amanda struggled to untangle the vacuum from the hall closet (stepping over the weeping Emily and ignoring the yelling upstairs that was growing closer), she wondered why Bob's news left her feeling suddenly bereft. At the very moment the walls of the house seemed to be caving in, it seemed as if her one ally and partner had just been dropped a rope to pull himself up, out and away from her.

Amanda switched on the vacuum and began to suck up the cheese. The only upside about vacuuming, she realized, was that it drowned out the screams.

SARAH BAXTER

1959–

Living in America and France as a child, Baxter was then educated in England. Her distinguished career as political editor of the *New Statesman*; presenter of the BBC's *Midnight Hour* political show and Channel Four's *The Parliament Programme*; Assistant Editor of the *Observer* and Editor of the *Sunday Times News Review* led her to the US.

In 2001 Baxter took up her new post as New York correspondent for the *Sunday Times*. She had been there only a few weeks when the 9/11 attacks occurred. She had arranged to meet a contact near the Twin Towers at 9 a.m. that morning so when the drama unfurled she was right on the spot and had to flee for her life with thousands of other New Yorkers when they collapsed, worried all the time about whether she would ever get back to her children in Brooklyn. Below is her gripping account of that day.

My Brave, Wounded New World

11 November 2001, *Sunday Times*

Too much of a good thing can be wonderful, but I didn't always appreciate it. Could I have been undergoing some kind of mid-life crisis when I decided to uproot to New York last summer? I had two beautiful children aged three and one, a husband I loved, a new home in a leafy part of London and a stimulating job as editor of the *News Review* section of the *Sunday Times*.

Somehow that wasn't enough. My life felt so contented that I wondered if it would ever change. My husband Jez, a photographer, travels on assignments all over the world. I was a sedentary career woman with children, a nanny and one day, probably, a dog.

My mother is American, my father half-French. I had the uneasy feeling that I was squandering my international heritage and becoming irreversibly English. After the birth of my son last year, I returned to my desk but began to wonder whether there was a job out there for me that would be enjoyable for my family yet shake up our lives. This perplexed me for some time until I hit upon the perfect posting: New York. It would be an exciting, risk-free adventure.

I had lived for three years as a child in America and knew that Billie, my daughter, and Max, my son, would lap up all that it had to offer. America was enjoying its longest period of economic expansion and although there were the first warnings of recession it still seemed a place of unparalleled opportunity. Jez was all for it. My mother was thrilled with this unexpected reclamation of her roots.

We arrived in mid-July to a brownstone in Brooklyn Heights. Before going to sleep at night, Jez and I would gaze at the skyscrapers of lower Manhattan out of our bedroom window. On the next floor down, from our kitchen, the twin towers of the World Trade Center were still visible.

Billie really fell for the city. We would laugh about all the flags that were around even then. 'The Americans are so proud of their flag,' I told her. Unprompted, she told everybody she liked living in New York better than in our old house.

On a glorious September morning, Jez took photographs of Billie, Max and me under the Brooklyn Bridge with the twin towers in the background. They were for a *Sunday Times* article on property hunting. Later that day Jez had to catch a flight to London. We kissed and waved goodbye gaily. The property piece never ran: two days after the pictures were taken the World Trade Center was gone.

I woke up early on September 11 thinking about my grandmother. In 1900 she had come as a young girl from central Europe to Ellis Island, the immigrants' gateway to New York. I was intending to catch the first ferry to the museum on Ellis Island to be interviewed about her by the BBC. The boat leaves from Battery Park on the southern tip of Manhattan.

Emerging from the subway a few hundred yards from the World Trade Center, I heard a great boom and knew at once that I would be witnessing a tragedy. I ran towards the noise thinking that an enormous bomb had gone off. As I turned the corner both towers were on fire: I had missed the first plane and heard the second.

Everybody has viewed the distressing images on television. From a street or two away they were even more haunting. Covered in dust, I evacuated the area after the first tower collapsed. I didn't want to hang around for the second to fall on me. I was scared of leaving my children alone in a foreign country with their nanny. Trivial thoughts raced through my head. I felt angry about the alteration of the skyline. I wondered if New York had been spoilt for ever for my family. I couldn't grasp the scale of the disaster.

Jez, meanwhile, was in his office in London. A British friend rang him after the first plane struck. He immediately telephoned the house and spoke to our Czech nanny. She answered the phone in the kitchen, looked up and saw the second plane slam in.

Jez asked her what she was going to tell Billie. She suggested that a firework had exploded. He thought Billie deserved something a little more realistic. She was told a plane had crashed. Had I been home, I am not sure what I would have said. I felt guilty and relieved that I wasn't put on the spot as I was unable to get through to the house on my mobile.

I was longing to see my children, but it hadn't occurred to me until I got home that they would have seen the burning skyscrapers. Three hours after the disaster when I entered the door, still covered in ash, Billie said tearfully: 'It's so sad, mummy, about the towers. They were so beautiful.' I gave her a big cuddle and told her they had to be brought down for reasons of safety. Only later did I learn that she had pestered her nanny into taking her out on the deck to have a good look.

I was afraid to ask Billie about her feelings. Instead I quickly showered and rushed out to sign her up for ballet lessons. It had been on my mind all morning: you had to enrol at the gym on a first come, first served basis. I was desperate to secure for her two months of innocent pleasure. Of course, when I got there the enrolment had been cancelled.

After that I plunged into work but at the back of my mind was a horrifying thought: had I, in pursuit of having it all, placed my children at risk? One night a plane screamed across the sky and I woke up trembling. All planes were supposed to be grounded. Were we under attack again?

Then came the warnings from the White House of more terrorist attacks. Al Qaeda threatened: keep your children away from skyscrapers. The café on the corner was suddenly up for sale. The owner's wife had seen the second plane crash from her window and took her two-year-old boy that day to her mother's in Ohio. She sent her husband an ultimatum: the restaurant or your family.

As soon as the bombing of Afghanistan started, I stocked up on mineral water, tinned food and nappies. I thought about my own relatives in Ohio, to whom perhaps I could send my children should the city become a war zone.

My mother rang. 'I can't believe you are still there,' she said. She felt we should have left town with Billie and Max, at least for a few days, to see how the war panned out. I explained that there was nothing to be afraid of and, anyway, I was a reporter. It was my job to be here. But when the first cases of anthrax emerged, I felt more nervous than when I had stood beneath the towers. Knowing nothing about biological terrorism, I wondered if going to the scene of an outbreak could lead me to bring a few spores home to my children. I am still not entirely clear on this point. Anthrax may not be contagious but it has the ability to jump from one location to another.

Some of my anxieties returned about Billie. She never brings up the subject of the towers but she knows more than she lets on. At Hallowe'en her teacher proposed reading a scary story to the class. Suddenly lots of little voices piped up: how terrible it was that the planes crashed, how sad it was that all those people died. It was as if they had been given permission to mention what had frightened them.

Later that day Billie and I went trick-or-treating. We passed our nearest fire house, a favourite haunt for handing out sweets. The men were out on call. We peeped in, looked at their coats and hats and carried on enjoying ourselves. She told her dad afterwards: 'They'd gone on a job. They're so brave. Some of them are alive and some of them are dead. Can you be brave when you're dead?' Neither of us had ever mentioned the missing firemen to her.

This was not the carefree all-American childhood I had imagined for her and Max. I thought back to my own time as a girl in Montgomery, Alabama, in the 1960s when the civil rights movement was at its height. I knew dimly about the ugliness of racism and segregation, but I was happy. Later I took pride in having lived through a moment of history even though it had passed me by. I hope my children will feel the same way about what they saw as toddlers out of the kitchen window.

As my memories of September 11 recede and the anthrax cases subside, my fears for our family seem a little foolish. Max has used up his emergency nappy supply and we've eaten several of the tins of food. Billie loves her school, has made friends and is deliberately trying to acquire an American accent as fast as she can. She calls me 'Mommy' teasingly. The truth is we like living in New York. It's more adventurous than we planned but it is what I asked for.

Had I known that the biggest attack on America would take place on my doorstep, I would not have wanted to bring my children here. But Jez and I are more pro-American than we ever were. I have held an American passport all my life, but only after the terrorist attacks did I begin to think of myself as a citizen. Last week Jez got his green card; in due course he may apply for citizenship so that he can be a dual national, too.

We didn't hang the Stars and Stripes in our window after September 11, but we understood the sentiment in a way that many foreigners did not. It was an expression of sympathy with the families of the missing, pride in the sacrifice of the firemen and an affirmation of 'e pluribus unum' – out of the many, one. It wasn't about nuking Osama Bin Laden.

Jez and I were still too British to want to buy a flag from the street vendors who sprang up overnight with patriotic wares. We're thinking of getting one, though, in time for independence day on the Fourth of July.

INDIA KNIGHT

1965–

One of Britain's top columnists and a bestselling novelist (*My Life on a Plate*, 2000 and *Don't You Want Me*, 2002) Knight went to Cambridge University where she read English. In her early twenties she had two young sons. She worked for *The Times*, the *Mail on Sunday*, *Today* and the *Observer* before becoming a columnist on the *Sunday Times*.

This moving article tracks the dilemmas of her third pregnancy. Her daughter, Nell, was born with a heart defect and a chromosomal disorder which might have been picked up if she had had an amniocentesis. The piece produced much debate.

Thank God I Let my Baby Live

25 April 2004, *Sunday Times*

Unfortunately, I am not particularly pro-choice. Abortion is a subject I normally button my lip about: saying that you are pro-life is considered illiberal and anti-feminist. So I keep quiet about the fact that I believe with all my heart (and what passes for my brain) that life starts at the moment of conception.

This seems to me to be simple biological truth. A dead baby is a dead baby, whether it is a 6-week- or 20-week-old 'foetus'. I understand and accept that this may be a minority view, though nothing will persuade me to believe that the majority of people feel it is in any way right to kill, as is currently legal, a 24-week-old unborn baby – one that sucks its thumb, kicks its legs, smiles to itself, hiccups.

I feel so strongly and categorically about the subject that piping up only leads to the more unpleasant kind of arguments. Religious persuasion is usually invoked (I am a semi-lapsed Catholic who uses contraception, but I would be pro-life, I think, regardless of faith or the lack of it). However, after Channel 4's *My Foetus* programme last week, which showed a doctor performing a vacuum-pump termination, I want to say my piece.

Eleven weeks ago I gave birth to a lovely little daughter. On Wednesday morning she will be having open-heart surgery to correct a congenital condition called truncus arteriosus, aka common arterial trunk: her pulmonary artery and aorta are conjoined. Being told, as we were when Nell was one day old, that your baby has a serious and life-threatening heart defect is an experience so brutally devastating that I cannot describe it.

Nell has common arterial trunk because of a chromosomal malfunction called 22q deletion – bits of genetic material have fallen off the 22nd chromosome. She could, in theory, be pretty badly handicapped: there are a possible 180 symptoms of the syndrome, including heart defects. So far, thank God, our beautiful girl has shown no sign of any of the really serious ones, aside from her heart condition – but since she's only tiny, that doesn't mean we're out of the woods by any stretch.

I am 38, and as a 38-year-old I was scanned repeatedly throughout my pregnancy. Everything was, as my obstetrician put it, 'boringly normal'. Nell's heart has four chambers and fully functioning valves – that's all the scan can see. I had a nuchal fold test to determine the baby's chances of having Down's syndrome: it came back as a one in 1,600 chance. Pretty remote, so I didn't have an amniocentesis – it seemed pointlessly invasive, given that I would not abort a child if it had Down's. If I had had the test, though, it would have picked up the chromosomal abnormality – and since this is often indicative of heart defects, my boyfriend and I would perhaps have known about this too.

Imagine thinking you are carrying a healthy baby and being told that, actually, she may have 180 diverse handicaps and a life-threatening heart condition. What would you do? I like to think that I would have brushed off any suggestion of a termination. But I don't know: it is possible that I would have performed a quick ideological U-turn and yelled, or sobbed, for the abortionist. Mercifully, this was never an option: we didn't know anything was wrong.

The only point at which I waver in my unwavering stance on abortion is in the case of babies born so severely handicapped that, we imagine, their life will barely be 'worth living'. Since having Nell, and joining e-mail groups and discussion boards, I have changed the greater part of my mind: what my boyfriend and I are going through is a picnic compared with what some families must endure. And their children are happy – I've looked at their photographs and seen them wearing party hats on their birthdays, or playing in the garden, beaming with joy. A beam of joy is a beam of joy, no matter how sick you are. Some of these children have severe learning difficulties, some have serious physical anomalies; one or two are so ill that it hurts your heart to look at them.

But they all have one thing in common: they are alive, and enjoying their lives and, above all, they are all loved.

Who are we to say what does or does not constitute a life 'worth living'? Should all these children have been sucked out and ended up in some hospital bin? And what do you do if your perfect child is horribly burnt or is involved in a hideous car crash when she is 10 years old? Do you quietly dig a hole in the garden because, suddenly, her life is no longer 'worth living' either?

When I was in my late teens and early twenties and militantly pro-choice about a woman's 'right to choose', having an abortion was in some quarters seen as a badge of, if not quite honour, then a commendable, almost sexy kind of feminist bad girlhood.

As a reasonably bad girl myself, I remember feeling left out – how puerile that seems now – because I managed to have sex and not get pregnant. My friends referred to their terminations as 'abos', thought of themselves as rather rock'n'roll, and liked airing the old chestnut that terminating their baby's life was as easy as having a tooth out.

It has been my unhappy experience to escort two women to an abortion clinic in London, friendship being stronger than moral conviction. One fainted straight afterwards; the other cried before, during and after, and every day for the next six months.

I'll never forget seeing the other half-dozen women in the waiting room waiting to go upstairs and have their baby removed and thrown away. In both my friends' cases, the abortion was chosen because, well, you know, having a baby wasn't terribly convenient at the time.

My daughter is the most wonderful thing to have happened to my boyfriend and me. She has fat little cheeks and huge blue eyes and tufts of black hair, and every time she smiles her gummy smile I am so overwhelmed that I just stand there grinning back and want to explode with love. It breaks my heart to think that there are people who abort children like her, and it breaks my heart to think that I may once have been one of them.

There is no point in sitting on the fence on this subject. Like everybody, I try to see that morality is personal, that everything is a matter of choice. But if you believe something is wrong for you and wrong in general then you might as well call what you hold true a moral principle.

Tony Blair once told the late Cardinal Winning that though he was personally opposed to abortion, he didn't want to impose that view on others. Winning couldn't believe his ears.

'On what other policies do you apply such a logic?' he asked. Winning thought Blair's fence-sitting was shallow, and we might all be guilty of such fence-sitting when forced to address this most emotional of subjects.

But let me just tell you: our baby smiles at us and the sun comes out. She could have ended up as bits of human tissue in a bowl of water, like the baby terminated in *My Foetus*.

You might take the view that the thing in the bowl is merely a collection of cells – but surely every intelligent person knows in their heart that this is ethical flimflam. Do what you will with your pregnancy – I am not calling for the criminalisation of abortion – but have the moral courage to clearly understand what it is that you are doing.

I have spent my life listening to women voicing their right to choose, and I've supported them often in that choice. But I want to call for another right: the right to name the thing lying in the bowl. It is the same thing as the one lying downstairs in a cot. It is a baby.

POLITICS, RACE & SOCIETY

NELLIE BLY
1864–1922

Born Elizabeth Jane Cochrane in Apollo, Pennsylvania, Bly began her career after her parents' deaths, when she wrote a letter to the editor of the *Pittsburgh Dispatch*. The letter – signed simply, 'Lonely orphan girl' – piqued the editor, George Madden's, interest. She persuaded Madden to let her write for him, and he suggested that she change her name to Nellie Bly – taken from a popular song of the time.

Not content with the usual women's articles – stories of social gatherings and parties – Bly immediately began her investigative career, pioneering this form brilliantly. She became an expert on the social issues that affected women, and wrote thorough investigations of the divorce laws and factory conditions.

Bly quickly established herself as a leading American journalist and her fame was guaranteed when she was sent on an assignment to travel around the world as quickly as possible, achieving the task in a record-breaking seventy-two days. Crowds met her on her return and she became a minor celebrity.

Another article was particulary influential. Feigning insanity, Bly was committed to New York's Blackwell's Island asylum, from which she reported on the horrific, rat-infested and abusive conditions being experienced by the women incarcerated there. The article, published in the *New York World*, led to a slew of letters, and forced the City of New York to spend $1,000,000 more per annum on the care of the insane. In this extract, Nellie spends her first night in the asylum. It is probably the first piece of 'stunt' journalism by a woman.

Ten Days in a Madhouse

1888, *New York World*

IN BELLEVUE HOSPITAL

The ambulance stopped with a sudden jerk and the doctor jumped out. 'How many have you?' I heard some one inquire. 'Only one, for the pavilion,' was the reply. A rough-looking man came forward, and catching hold of me attempted to drag me out as if I had the strength of an elephant and would resist. The doctor, seeing my look of disgust, ordered him to leave me alone, saying that he would take charge of me himself. He then lifted me carefully out and I walked with the grace of a queen past the crowd that had gathered curious to see the new unfortunate. Together with the doctor I entered a small dark office, where there were several men. The one behind the desk opened a book and began on the long string of questions which had been asked me so often.

I refused to answer, and the doctor told him it was not necessary to trouble me further, as he had all the papers made out, and I was too insane to be able to tell anything that would be of consequence. I felt relieved that it was so easy here, as, though still undaunted, I had begun to feel faint for want of food. The order was then given to take me to the insane pavilion, and a muscular man came forward and caught me so tightly by the arm that a pain ran clear through me. It made me angry, and for a moment I forgot my *role* as I turned to him and said:

'How dare you touch me?' At this he loosened his hold somewhat, and I shook him off with more strength than I thought I possessed.

'I will go with no one but this man,' I said, pointing to the ambulance-surgeon. 'The judge said that he was to take care of me, and I will go with no one else.'

At this the surgeon said that he would take me, and so we went arm in arm, following the man who had at first been so rough with me. We passed through the well-cared-for grounds and finally reached the insane ward. A white-capped nurse was there to receive me.

'This young girl is to wait here for the boat,' said the surgeon, and then he started to leave me. I begged him not to go, or to take me with him, but he said he wanted to get his dinner first, and that I should wait there for him. When I insisted on accompanying him he claimed that he had to assist at an amputation, and it would not look well for me to be present. It was evident that he believed he was dealing with an insane person. Just then the most horrible insane cries came from a yard in the rear. With all my bravery I felt a chill at the prospect of being shut up with a fellow-creature who was really insane. The doctor evidently noticed my nervousness, for he said to the attendant: 'What a noise the carpenters make.'

Turning to me he offered me explanation to the effect that new build-ings were being erected, and that the noise came from some of the workmen engaged upon it. I told him I did not want to stay there without him, and to pacify me he promised soon to return. He left me and I found myself at last an occupant of an insane asylum.

I stood at the door and contemplated the scene before me. The long, uncarpeted hall was scrubbed to that peculiar whiteness seen only in public institutions. In the rear of the hall were large iron doors fastened by a padlock. Several still-looking benches and a number of willow chairs were the only articles of furniture. On either side of the hall were doors leading into what I supposed and what proved to be bedrooms. Near the entrance door, on the right-hand side, was a small sitting-room for the nurses, and opposite it was a room where dinner was dished out. A nurse in a black dress, white cap and apron and armed with a bunch of keys had charge of the hall. I soon learned her name, Miss Ball.

An old Irishwoman was maid-of-all-work. I heard her called Mary, and I am glad to know that there is such a good-hearted woman in that place. I experienced only kindness and the utmost consideration from her. There were only three patients, as they are called. I made the fourth. I thought I might as well begin work at once, for I still expected that the very first doctor might declare me sane and send me out again into the wide, wide world. So I went down to the rear of the room and introduced myself to one of the women, and asked her all about herself. Her name, she said, was Miss Anne Neville, and she had been sick from overwork. She had been working as a chambermaid, and when her health gave way she was sent to some Sisters' Home to be treated. Her nephew, who was a waiter, was out of work, and, being unable to pay her expenses at the Home, had had her transferred to Bellevue.

'Is there anything wrong with you mentally as well?' I asked her.

'No,' she said. 'The doctors have been asking me many curious questions and confusing me as much as possible, but I have nothing wrong with my brain.'

'Do you know that only insane people are sent to this pavilion?' I asked.

'Yes, I know; but I am unable to do anything. The doctors refuse to listen to me, and it is useless to say anything to the nurses.'

Satisfied from various reasons that Miss Neville was as sane as I was myself, I transferred my attentions to one of the other patients. I found her in need of medical aid and quite silly mentally, although I have seen many women in the lower walks of life, whose sanity was never questioned, who were not any brighter.

The third patient, Mrs. Fox, would not say much. She was very quiet, and after telling me that her case was hopeless refused to talk. I began now to feel surer of my position, and I determined that no doctor should convince me that I was sane so long as I had the hope of accomplishing my mission. A small, fair-complexioned nurse arrived, and, after putting on her cap, told Miss Ball to go to dinner. The new nurse, Miss Scott by name, came to me and said, rudely:

'Take off your hat.'

'I shall not take off my hat,' I answered. 'I am waiting for the boat, and I shall not remove it.'

'Well, you are not going on any boat. You might as well know it now as later. You are in an asylum for the insane.'

Although fully aware of that fact, her unvarnished words gave me a shock. 'I did not want to come here; I am not sick or insane, and I will not stay,' I said.

'It will be a long time before you get out if you don't do as you are told,' answered Miss Scott. 'You might as well take off your hat, or I shall use force, and if I am not able to do it, I have but to touch a bell and I shall get assistance. Will you take it off?'

'No, I will not. I am cold, and I want my hat on, and you can't make me take it off.'

'I shall give you a few more minutes, and if you don't take it off then I shall use force, and I warn you it will not be very gentle.'

'If you take my hat off I shall take your cap off; so now.'

Miss Scott was called to the door then, and as I feared that an exhibition of temper might show too much sanity I took off my hat and gloves and was sitting quietly looking into space when she returned. I was hungry, and was quite pleased to see Mary make preparations for dinner. The preparations were simple. She merely pulled a straight bench up along the side of a bare table and ordered the patients to gather 'round the feast; then she brought out a small tin plate on which was a piece of boiled meat and a potato. It could not have been colder had it been cooked the week before, and it had no chance to make acquaintance with salt or pepper. I would not go up to the table, so Mary came to where I sat in a corner, and while handing out the tin plate, asked:

'Have ye any pennies about ye, dearie?'

'What?' I said, in my surprise.

'Have ye any pennies, dearie, that ye could give me. They'll take them all from ye any way, dearie, so I might as well have them.'

I understood it fully now, but I had no intention of feeing Mary so early in the game, fearing it would have an influence on her treatment of me, so I said I had lost my purse, which was quite true. But though I did not give Mary any money, she was none the less kind to me. When I objected to the tin plate in which she had brought my food she fetched a china one for me, and when I found it impossible to eat the food she presented she gave me a glass of milk and a soda cracker.

All the windows in the hall were open and the cold air began to tell on my Southern blood. It grew so cold indeed as to be almost unbearable, and I complained of it to Miss Scott and Miss Ball. But they answered curtly that as I was in a charity place I could not expect much else. All the other women were suffering from the cold, and the nurses themselves had to wear heavy garments to keep themselves warm. I asked if I could go to bed. They said 'No!' At last Miss Scott got an old gray shawl, and shaking some of the moths out of it, told me to put it on.

'It's rather a bad-looking shawl,' I said.

'Well, some people would get along better if they were not so proud,' said Miss Scott. 'People on charity should not expect anything and should not complain.'

So I put the moth-eaten shawl, with all its musty smell, around me, and sat down on a wicker chair, wondering what would come next, whether I should freeze to death or survive. My nose was very cold, so I covered up my head and was in a half doze, when the shawl was suddenly jerked from my face and a strange man and Miss Scott stood before me. The man proved to be a doctor, and his first greetings were:

'I've seen that face before.'

'Then you know me?' I asked, with a great show of eagerness that I did not feel.

'I think I do. Where did you come from?'

'From home.'

'Where is home?'

'Don't you know? Cuba.'

He then sat down beside me, felt my pulse, and examined my tongue, and at last said:

'Tell Miss Scott all about yourself.'

'No, I will not. I will not talk with women.'

'What do you do in New York?'

'Nothing.'

'Can you work?'

'No, *señor*.'

'Tell me, are you a woman of the town?'

'I do not understand you,' I replied, heartily disgusted with him.

'I mean have you allowed the men to provide for you and keep you?'

I felt like slapping him in the face, but I had to maintain my composure, so I simply said:

'I do not know what you are talking about. I always lived at home.'

After many more questions, fully as useless and senseless, he left me and began to talk with the nurse. 'Positively demented,' he said. 'I consider it a hopeless case. She needs to be put where some one will take care of her.'

And so I passed my second medical expert.

After this, I began to have a smaller regard for the ability of doctors than I ever had before, and a greater one for myself. I felt sure now that no doctor could tell whether people were insane or not, so long as the case was not violent.

Later in the afternoon a boy and a woman came. The woman sat down on a bench, while the boy went in and talked with Miss Scott. In a short time he came out, and, just nodding good-bye to the woman, who was his mother, went away. She did not look insane, but as she was German I could not learn her story. Her name, however, was Mrs. Louise Schanz. She seemed quite lost, but when the nurses put her at some sewing she did her work well and quickly. At three in the afternoon all the patients were given a gruel broth, and at five a cup of tea and a piece of bread. I was favored; for when they saw that it was impossible for me to eat the bread or drink the stuff honored by the name of tea, they gave me a cup of milk and a cracker, the same as I had had at noon.

Just as the gas was being lighted another patient was added. She was a young girl, twenty-five years old. She told me that she had just gotten up from a sick bed. Her appearance confirmed her story. She looked like one who had had a severe attack of fever. 'I am now suffering from nervous debility,' she said, 'and my friends have sent me here to be treated for it.' I did not tell her where she was, and she seemed quite satisfied. At 6.15 Miss Ball said that she wanted to go away, and so we would all have to go to bed. Then each of us – we now numbered six – were assigned a room and told to undress. I did so, and was given a short, cotton-flannel gown to wear during the night. Then she took every particle of the clothing I had worn during the day, and, making it up in a bundle, labeled it 'Brown,' and took it away. The iron-barred window was locked, and Miss Ball, after giving me an extra blanket, which, she said, was a favor rarely granted, went out and left me alone. The bed was not a comfortable one. It was so hard, indeed, that I could not make a dent in it; and the pillow was stuffed with straw. Under the sheet was an oilcloth spread. As the night grew colder I tried to warm that oilcloth. I kept on trying, but when morning dawned and it was still as cold as when I went to bed, and had reduced me too, to the temperature of an iceberg, I gave it up as an impossible task.

I had hoped to get some rest on this my first night in an insane asylum. But I was doomed to disappointment. When the night nurses came in they were curious to see me and to find out what I was like. No sooner had they left than I heard some one at my door inquiring for Nellie Brown, and I began to tremble, fearing always that my sanity would be discovered. By listening to the conversation I found it was a reporter in search of me, and I heard him ask for my clothing so that he might examine it. I listened quite anxiously to the talk about me, and was relieved to learn that I was considered hopelessly insane. That was encouraging. After the reporter left I heard new arrivals, and I learned that a doctor was there and intended to see me. For what purpose I knew not, and I imagined all sorts of horrible things, such as examinations and the rest of it, and when they got to my room I was shaking with more than fear.

'Nellie Brown, here is the doctor; he wishes to speak with you,' said the nurse. If that's all he wanted I thought I could endure it. I removed the blanket which I had put over my head in my sudden fright and looked up. The sight was reassuring.

He was a handsome young man. He had the air and address of a gentleman. Some people have since censured this action; but I feel sure, even if it was a little indiscreet, that the young doctor only meant kindness to me. He came forward, seated himself on the side of my bed, and put his arm soothingly around my shoulders. It was a terrible task to play insane before this young man, and only a girl can sympathize with me in my position.

'How do you feel to-night, Nellie?' he asked, easily.

'Oh, I feel all right.'

'But you are sick, you know,' he said.

'Oh, am I?' I replied, and I turned my head on the pillow and smiled.

'When did you leave Cuba, Nellie?'

'Oh, you know my home?' I asked.

'Yes, very well. Don't you remember me? I remember you.'

'Do you?' and I mentally said I should not forget him. He was accompanied by a friend who never ventured a remark, but stood staring at me as I lay in bed. After a great many questions, to which I answered truthfully, he left me. Then came other troubles. All night long the nurses read one to the other aloud, and I know that the other patients, as well as myself, were unable to sleep. Every half-hour or hour they would walk heavily down the halls, their boot-heels resounding like the march of a private of dragoons, and take a look at every patient. Of course this helped to keep us awake. Then as it came toward morning, they began to beat eggs for breakfast, and the sound made me realize how horribly hungry I was. Occasional yells and cries came from the male department, and that did not aid in making the night pass more cheerfully. Then the ambulance-gong, as it brought in more unfortunates, sounded as a knell to life and liberty. Thus I passed my first night as an insane girl at Bellevue.

MARY HEATON VORSE
1874–1966

'I love my golden wings and I want to fly right into the sun until they are all draggled and battered.' So wrote Vorse as a young woman, before fleeing her wealthy New England family to settle in New York's Greenwich Village in the early 1900s. Here, she became involved with a number of burgeoning political movements – libertarian socialism, suffragism and pacifism – writing about these issues for the radical magazine, *The Masses*.

Later, as a war correspondent, Vorse would travel to Lenin's Russia and Hitler's Germany, before becoming America's foremost pioneer of Labour journalism. In the following article she describes a textiles strike in Passaic in 1926, in which she acted as publicity director for the 11,000 protestors. Unsurprisingly perhaps, at the time of Vorse's death her FBI file was said to be bulging . . .

The War in Passaic

17 March 1926, *Nation*

The strike of the textile workers in Passaic, New Jersey, is a strike of hunger. It is the direct result of a 10 per cent slash in wages already far below a level of decent living. The pay of the textile workers is the lowest in American industry. They get from $12 to $22 a week. Heads of families work for $20, $17.50, and $15. It seems incredible that wages as low as these should have been cut by companies whose mills are among the richest in the country. But that is what happened. That is what has sent ten thousand textile workers streaming out of the mills. That is why after weeks of strike the picket line numbers thousands. That is why processions of workers march from Passaic to Garfield and Clifton singing. Never has a strike of such small numbers shown such mass picketing and such parades. Half the picket line is composed of young people. Mothers with children by the hand, older women and high-school boys and girls stream along, their heads thrown back, singing 'Solidarity forever, the union makes us strong' to the tune of 'John Brown's Body.' The singing picket line has hope in it. Passaic sprawling in its winter slush and snow watches its mill-workers make a full-hearted protest against the intolerable conditions in the mills, against the inhuman and unbearable wage cut.

During the first weeks of the strike the numbers of strikers rolled up like a snowball. The Botany Mill came out first. One mill after another joined the strikers until nearly all the mills were involved. One day they formed a parade of twelve thousand to march from Passaic into Clifton. What a parade! Processions of baby carriages, bands of youngsters, older women, an old grandma of eighty-one. The undimmed, enthusiastic mill children, the youngsters in their teens.

This peaceful parade was set upon by the police as they tried to cross a bridge marching from one town to another. Clubbings of such brutal nature occurred that the daily press was filled with pictures of prostrate strikers and policemen with riot clubs in air. This clubbing did not dim their spirit. The big parade gave them a sense of power and solidarity. They had been striking against the wage cut – only that. Now they voiced demands: a 10 per cent increase over the old wage scale, the return of money taken from them by wage cut, time and a half for over-time, a forty-hour week, decent sanitary working conditions, no discrimination against union workers, and recognition of the union. Then came a further triumph, the Forstmann-Huffmann Mills with their four thousand workers joined the walk-out.

The outside world began to notice the strike. Noted ministers, writers, representatives of labor organizations, supporters of civil liberties streamed into Passaic. The town of Garfield invited the strikers to a meeting and the city council indorsed the strikers' demands completely, the only dissenting voices being those of the mayor and the chief of police.

At the beginning of the sixth week the mayor of Passaic menaced the strikers with a force of three hundred mounted policemen. This proved to be only a bugaboo. The picket line, two thousand strong, was practically unmolested, while the aged horses upon which a few policemen were mounted brought laughter from the crowd. Again the strikers formed a parade in the afternoon and marched into Garfield. Throughout all these demonstrations perfect order was preserved.

Then the authorities decided to break the peace. With tear bombs, mounted patrolmen, and a company of sixty-five foot police they tried to disperse a crowd of 2,000 strikers. They failed. The workers jeered and laughed at them. But finally, with the help of five fire companies battering the crowd with powerful streams of water the guardians of order broke the ranks of the strikers, smashing them with clubs when they attempted to halt in their flight or to reform their ranks. The next day the police did better still. They charged a crowd of 3,000 strikers, bludgeoned many men, women, and children, and smashed with deliberate intent the persons and cameras of the news photographers and motion-picture men present. That was their last victory. The strikers, armed with gas masks, helmets, and their unbending courage, defied the police successfully – and paraded in peace. Photographers took pictures through the slits in armored cars or from the safe vantage of a swooping airplane. The authorities were, temporarily at least, confounded. As a result of the disorders of the week Justice of the Peace Katz issued warrants for the arrest of Chief of Police Zober and two patrolmen charged with clubbing orderly and inoffensive men and women. To the date of writing warrants are still hovering over the heads of these guardians of the public peace; none of their fellow-officers can be induced to serve them. Meantime the fight goes on and the picket line, an army of thousands, defies the police and greets the few remaining workers when the mill gates open.

The present Passaic strike is only a phase of the long fight of the textile workers for organization and a living wage. These million people who weave our cloth have always lived on the fringe of destitution. Employed by some of the richest corporations in America, their poverty is a by-word. The conditions under which they live is a disgrace to this rich country. We are indicted, tried, and condemned by our textile workers. From time to time they remind us of this fact by a strike.

Fourteen years ago all of us who saw the strike in Lawrence were horrified at the conditions we found. Heads of families were working for $9, for $12. People lived in dwellings that were no better than rat-holes. It was then that Vida Scudder, professor in Wellesley College, stated that the women of this country would refuse to wear cloth manufactured under such conditions if they knew the price in human life being paid for it.

Now after fourteen years we see people whose real wages are but little higher than those of Lawrence days. We see them living in tenements so ill-ventilated, in rooms so dark with walls that sweat so much moisture that the tenements of New York seem pleasant, airy places in comparison. Even in 1912 the laws of Massachusetts prevented some of the scandalous conditions of Passaic. Children under sixteen were not allowed to work in the mills. Passaic children of fourteen are permitted to work an eight-hour day. Night work for women was not permitted in Massachusetts. In Passaic we have the spectacle of hundreds upon hundreds of women, the most overburdened of all the population, the mothers of large families, forced by their husbands' low wages to work in the mills. These women, who may have six, seven, and eight children, go to work at night. They work for ten hours a night, five nights a week. They have no dinner hour. At midnight a recess of fifteen minutes is accorded them. They return home in the morning to get the children off to school and to do the housework. Most of them have children under school age as well and these they must attend to during the day – rest or no rest.

It is this night-work in the mills that marks the difference between the bright-looking, eager girls and the dragged, hopeless, tired older faces which one sees, faces blurred by fatigue. The bearing of many children, the constant fight against poverty, the existence in over-crowded, unaired rooms, the long, grilling, inhuman hours of night-work make these women's lives a nightmare of fatigue.

A law was passed by the legislature of New Jersey forbidding night-work of women. A group of women mill workers appeared at Trenton and begged to have this law repealed. Of course they did. How can a family of nine people live on $20? Of course these women will clamor to be allowed to kill themselves with night-work rather than forego the pittance which they make.

The recent wage cut was written in terms of life and death. The textile workers live so near the margin of destitution that 10 per cent taken from them means undernourishment and disease and eventually death. The men and women in Passaic have met the conditions imposed on them with heroism and have tried for their children's sake to make good homes out of nothing. In the miserable dark rooms in which they live you will find bright hangings, touching bunches of gay paper flowers, often spotless cleanliness, always an attempt at beauty. Through their strike the textile workers have again questioned our civilization.

It would be impossible for any right-thinking man or woman to go into the homes of Passaic and talk to the women who work on the night shift without feeling that a personal responsibility had been laid upon him or her. When there is such want and suffering, when conditions of toil are so degrading, when the places that human beings live in are so indecent it becomes the concern of the public at large to make its power felt and to see that this state of things is altered.

AUDRE LORDE
1934–92

Born in Harlem to parents from Grenada, Lorde rose to huge acclaim as a novelist, teacher, poet and essayist. She began her career in 1968 with her poetry collection, *The First Cities*, and went on to publish a number of other volumes, including *From a Land Where Other People Live*, which was nominated for the 1974 National Book Award.

In 1980, Lorde published the autobiographical *Cancer Journals*, in which she wrote about her own mastectomy and chronicled her decision to pursue alternative treatment. The following piece is one of the essays she collected in a second autobiographical work, two years later, *Zami: A New Spelling of My Name*. In it she provides a haunting description of the racism she experienced when visiting Washington as a child.

That Summer I Left Childhood was White

1982, Zami: A New Spelling of My Name

The first time I went to Washington, D.C. was on the edge of the summer when I was supposed to stop being a child. At least that's what they said to us all at graduation from the eighth grade. My sister Phyllis graduated at the same time from high school. I don't know what she was supposed to stop being. But as graduation presents for us both, the whole family took a Fourth of July trip to Washington, D.C., the fabled and famous capital of our country.

It was the first time I'd ever been on a railroad train during the day. When I was little, and we used to go to the Connecticut shore, we always went at night on the milk train, because it was cheaper.

Preparations were in the air around our house before school was even over. We packed for a week. There were two very large suitcases that my father carried, and a box filled with food. In fact, my first trip to Washington was a mobile feast; I started eating as soon as we were comfortably ensconced in our seats, and did not stop until somewhere after Philadelphia. I remember it was Philadelphia because I was disappointed not to have passed by the Liberty Bell.

My mother had roasted two chickens and cut them up into dainty bite-size pieces. She packed slices of brown bread and butter and green pepper and carrot sticks. There were little violently yellow iced cakes with scalloped edges called 'marigolds,' that came from Cushman's Bakery. There was a spice bun and rock-cakes from Newton's, the West Indian bakery across Lenox Avenue from St. Mark's School, and iced tea in a wrapped mayonnaise jar. There were sweet pickles for us and dill pickles for my father, and peaches with the fuzz still on them, individually wrapped to keep them from bruising. And, for neatness, there were piles of napkins and a little tin box with a washcloth dampened with rosewater and glycerine for wiping sticky mouths.

I wanted to eat in the dining car because I had read all about them, but my mother reminded me for the umpteenth time that dining car food always cost too much money and besides, you never could tell whose hands had been playing all over that food, nor where those same hands had been just before. My mother never mentioned that Black people were not allowed into railroad dining cars headed south in 1947. As usual, whatever my mother did not like and could not change, she ignored. Perhaps it would go away, deprived of her attention.

I learned later that Phyllis's high school senior class trip had been to Washington, but the nuns had given her back her deposit in private, explaining to her that the class, all of whom were white, except Phyllis, would be staying in a hotel where Phyllis 'would not be happy,' meaning, Daddy explained to her, also in private, that they did not rent rooms to Negroes. 'We will take you to Washington, ourselves,' my father had avowed, 'and not just for an overnight in some measly fleabag hotel.'

American racism was a new and crushing reality that my parents had to deal with every day of their lives once they came to this country. They handled it as a private woe. My mother and father believed that they could best protect their children from the realities of race in America and the fact of American racism by never giving them name, much less discussing their nature. We were told we must never trust white people, but *why* was never explained, nor the nature of their ill will. Like so many other vital pieces of information in my childhood, I was supposed to know without being told. It always seemed like a very strange injunction coming from my mother, who looked so much like one of those people we were never supposed to trust. But something always warned me not to ask my mother why she wasn't white, and why Auntie Lillah and Auntie Etta weren't, even though they were all that same problematic color so different from my father and me, even from my sisters, who were somewhere in-between.

In Washington, D.C. we had one large room with two double beds and an extra cot for me. It was a back-street hotel that belonged to a friend of my father's who was in real estate, and I spent the whole next day after Mass squinting up at the Lincoln Memorial where Marian Anderson had sung after the D.A.R. refused to allow her to sing in their auditorium because she was Black. Or because she was 'Colored,' my father said as he told us the story. Except that what he probably said was 'Negro,' because for his times, my father was quite progressive.

I was squinting because I was in that silent agony that characterized all of my childhood summers, from the time school let out in June to the end of July, brought about by my dilated and vulnerable eyes exposed to the summer brightness.

I viewed Julys through an agonizing corolla of dazzling whiteness and I always hated the Fourth of July, even before I came to realize the travesty such a celebration was for Black people in this country.

My parents did not approve of sunglasses, nor of their expense.

I spent the afternoon squinting up at monuments to freedom and past presidencies and democracy, and wondering why the light and heat were both so much stronger in Washington, D.C. than back home in New York City. Even the pavement on the streets was a shade lighter in color than back home.

Late that Washington afternoon my family and I walked back down Pennsylvania Avenue. We were a proper caravan, mother bright and father brown, the three of us girls step-standards in between. Moved by our historical surroundings and the heat of the early evening, my father decreed yet another treat. He had a great sense of history, a flair for the quietly dramatic and the sense of specialness of an occasion and a trip.

'Shall we stop and have a little something to cool off, Lin?'

Two blocks away from our hotel, the family stopped for a dish of vanilla ice cream at a Breyer's ice cream and soda fountain. Indoors, the soda fountain was dim and fan-cooled, deliciously relieving to my scorched eyes.

Corded and crisp and pinafored, the five of us seated ourselves one by one at the counter. There was I between my mother and father, and my two sisters on the other side of my mother. We settled ourselves along the white mottled marble counter, and when the waitress spoke at first no one understood what she was saying, and so the five of us just sat there.

The waitress moved along the line of us closer to my father and spoke again. 'I said I kin give you to take out, but you can't eat here. Sorry.' Then she dropped her eyes looking very embarrassed, and suddenly we heard what it was she was saying all at the same time, loud and clear.

Straight-backed and indignant, one by one, my family and I got down from the counter stools and turned around and marched out of the store, quiet and outraged, as if we had never been Black before. No one would answer my emphatic questions with anything other than a guilty silence. 'But we hadn't done anything!' This wasn't right or fair! Hadn't I written poems about Bataan and freedom and democracy for all?

My parents wouldn't speak of this injustice, not because they had con-tributed to it, but because they felt they should have anticipated it and avoided it. This made me even angrier. My fury was not going to be acknowledged by a like fury. Even my two sisters copied my parents' pre-tense that nothing unusual and anti-American had occurred. I was left to write my angry letter to the president of the United States all by myself, although my father did promise I could type it out on the office typewriter next week, after I showed it to him in my copybook diary.

The waitress was white, and the counter was white, and the ice cream I never ate in Washington, D.C. that summer I left childhood was white, and the white heat and the white pavement and the white stone monu-ments of my first Washington summer made me sick to my stomach for the whole rest of that trip and it wasn't much of a graduation present after all.

NANCY MITFORD

1904–73

Born to an aristocratic English family, Mitford took up writing in her late twenties, 'to relieve the boredom of the intervals between the recreations established by social convention'. She went on to have considerable success with her fourth novel, the autobiographical *The Pursuit of Love* (1945), as well as later works including *Love in a Cold Climate*.

Along with her fiction, Mitford was also a prolific journalist and essayist, and, indeed, many of her admirers felt that her vibrant, witty writing style was more suited to this medium than any other. The following article is perhaps her most famous and in it she sets out the terms by which people can be considered 'U' (upper class), and 'non-U' (decidedly not). It's testament to the influence of this piece that these terms still crop up regularly in newspapers and books as shorthand for the class divide in Britain. This is an extract.

The English Aristocracy

September 1955, *Encounter Magazine*

The English aristocracy may seem to be on the verge of decadence, but it is the only real aristocracy left in the world today. It has real political power through the House of Lords and a real social position through the Queen. An aristocracy in a republic is like a chicken whose head has been cut off: it may run about in a lively way, but in fact it is dead. There is nothing to stop a Frenchman, German, or Italian from calling himself the Duke of Carabosse if he wants to, and in fact the Continent abounds with invented titles. But in England the Queen is the fountain of honours and when she bestows a peerage upon a subject she bestows something real and unique.

The great distinction between the English aristocracy and any other has always been that, whereas abroad every member of a noble family is noble, in England none are noble except the head of the family. In spite of the fact that they enjoy courtesy titles, the sons and daughters of lords are commoners – though not so common as baronets and their wives who take precedence after honourables. (So, of course, do all knights, except Knights of the Garter who come after the eldest sons and the daughters of barons, but before the younger sons.) The descendants of younger sons, who, on the Continent would all be counts or barons, in England have no titles and sit even below knights. Furthermore, the younger sons and daughters of the very richest lords receive, by English custom, but little money from their families, barely enough to live on. The sons are given the same education as their eldest brother and then turned out, as soon as they are grown up, to fend for themselves; the daughters are given no education at all, the general idea being that they must find some man to keep them – which, in fact, they usually do. The rule of primogeniture has kept together the huge fortunes of English lords; it has also formed our class system. [. . .]

Most of the peers share the education, usage, and point of view of a vast upper middle class, but the upper middle class does not, in its turn, merge imperceptibly into the middle class. There is a very definite border line, easily recognizable by hundreds of small but significant landmarks.

When I speak of these matters I am always accused of being a snob, so, to illustrate my point, I propose to quote from Professor Alan Ross of Birmingham University. Professor Ross has written a paper, printed in Helsinki in 1954, for the *Bulletin de la Société Néo-philologique de Helsinki*, on 'Upper Class English Usage.' Nobody is likely to accuse either this learned man or his Finnish readers of undue snobbishness. The Professor, pointing out that it is solely by their language that the upper classes nowadays are distinguished (since they are neither cleaner, richer, nor better-educated than anybody else) has invented a useful formula: U (for upper class) speaker versus non-U-speaker. Such exaggeratedly non-U usage as 'serviette' for 'napkin' he calls non-U indicators. Since 'a piece of mathematics or a novel written by a member of the upper class is not likely to differ in any way from one written by a member of another class . . . in writing it is in fact only modes of address, postal addresses and habits of beginning and ending letters that serve to demarcate the class.' . . . The names of many houses are themselves non-U; the ideal U-address is PQR where P is a place name, Q a describer, and R the name of a county, as 'Shirwell Hall, Salop.' (Here I find myself in disagreement with Professor Ross – in my view abbreviations such as Salop, Herts, or Glos, are decidedly non-U. Any sign of undue haste, in fact, is apt to be non-U, and I go so far as preferring, except for business letters, not to use air mail.) [. . .]

He speaks of the U-habit of silence, and perhaps does not make as much of it as he might. Silence is the only possible U-response to many embarrassing modern situations: the ejaculation of 'cheers' before drinking, for example, or 'it was so nice seeing you,' after saying goodbye. In silence, too, one must endure the use of the Christian name by comparative strangers and the horror of being introduced by Christian and surname without any prefix. This unspeakable usage sometimes occurs in letters – Dear XX – which, in silence, are quickly torn up, by me.

After discoursing at some length on pronunciation, the professor goes on to vocabulary and gives various examples of U and non-U usage.

Cycle is non-U against U *bike*.

Dinner: U-speakers eat *luncheon* in the middle of the day and *dinner* in the evening.

Non-U-speakers (also U-children and U-dogs) have their *dinner* in the middle of the day.

Greens is non-U for U *vegetables*.

Home: non-U – 'they have a lovely *home*'; U – 'they've a very nice *house*.'

Ill: 'I was *ill* on the boat' is non-U against U *sick*.

Mental: non-U for U *mad*.

Note paper: non-U for U *writing paper*.

Toilet paper: non-U for U *lavatory paper*.

Wealthy: non-U for U *rich*. To these I would add:

Sweet: non-U for U *pudding*.

Dentures: non-U for U *false teeth*. This, and *glasses* for *spectacles*, almost amount to non-U indicators.

Wire: non-U for U *telegram*.

Phone: a non-U indicator.

(One must add that the issue is sometimes confused by U-speakers using non-U indicators as a joke. Thus Uncle Matthew in *The Pursuit of Love* speaks of his *dentures*.)

Finally Professor Ross poses the question: Can a non-U-speaker become a U-speaker? His conclusion is that an adult can never achieve complete success 'because one word or phrase will suffice to brand an apparent U-speaker as originally non-U (for U-speakers themselves never make mistakes).' I am not quite sure about this. Usage changes very quickly and I even know undisputed U-speakers who pronounce girl 'gurl,' which twenty years ago would have been unthinkable. All the same, it is true that one U-speaker recognizes another U-speaker almost as soon as he opens his mouth, though U-speaker A may deplore certain lapses in the conversation of U-speaker B.

ELIZABETH DREW

1935–

Whilst granted significant opportunities to report on war and crime, political reporting has been one of the most difficult fields for women journalists to break into, a situation that persists to the present day. As a wide-ranging essayist, biographer and broadcaster, Drew was one of the first full-time female political reporters, acting as Washington Correspondent for the *Atlantic Monthly* from 1967–73 and subsequently transferring to the *New Yorker*, where she held the same post until 1992.

In this article, Drew provides one of the most in-depth accounts of the Watergate scandal, expertly capturing the atmosphere of the nation's capital throughout May 1973.

A Watergate Diary

Notes of a Washington correspondent during the month of May, 1973

August 1973, *Atlantic Monthly*

'Whoever wants to see a brick must look at its pores, and must keep his eyes close to it. But whoever wants to see a cathedral cannot see it as he sees a brick. This demands a respect for distance.'

–José Ortega y Gasset

MAY 2—One of the most bizarre aspects of living through this time is the way in which seemingly diverse threads suddenly connect. As one reads the news, flashbacks recur. The connecting threads and flashbacks are at once confusing, and help to make it all of a piece. For example: preparing for an interview with Murray Chotiner . . . In the clippings about Chotiner's role in the milk fund case, there, astonishingly, is the name 'Howard Hunt.' Milk producers had raised funds for the President's re-election through some hundred-odd dummy committees, and then the Administration had raised the price support of milk. Chotiner, now a Washington lawyer, had helped to raise the money. One of the dummy committees, the clippings say, was headed by Howard Hunt.

Hunt, the White House 'plumber,' is one of the mesmerizing and unifying figures in this whole business. Once connected with the CIA, a participant in the Bay of Pigs invasion, Hunt is a character out of his own adventure novels. Hunt's name in the address books of two of the men caught in the Watergate first linked the break-in to the White House. It was reported that Hunt, wearing a red wig, had gone out to Denver to see Dita Beard of ITT. The mind kept going back to that: a man on the White House payroll putting on a red wig and going across the country to see a sick, disgraced lobbyist. When Hunt's wife, Dorothy, was killed in a plane crash, $10,000 in $100 bills had been found in her purse. The $100 bills found on the men in the Democratic headquarters, and traced, via Mexico, to campaign donors, symbolized the central elements in the whole affair: money, much of it given in exchange for, or hope of, government favors, and some of it used for espionage and sabotage against those considered dangerous to the Administration, including potential political opponents. Hunt and Gordon Liddy, a Watergate co-conspirator, had raided the files of Daniel Ellsberg's psychiatrist. Material from Hunt's White House file, including a report on Chappaquiddick, had been given by Ehrlichman and Dean to Acting FBI Director Pat Gray to burn, which he did, thus compromising Gray. And now here, in the Chotiner clippings, was Howard Hunt, head of a milk fund.

Through all of the details there is a stark simplicity. It comes down to two themes that have been shadows on Richard Nixon's political career: aggression against the opposition, and money. Thinking about Murray Chotiner put it in focus. Chotiner was there in the early, controversial Nixon campaigns against Jerry Voorhis and Helen Gahagan Douglas. The Chotiner theory of politics, he once explained, is that 'if you do not deflate the opposition candidate before your own candidate gets started, the odds are you're doomed to defeat.' When Nixon was under fire for 'the Nixon fund' in 1952, Chotiner urged him to counterattack with 'the Checkers speech.' A dog and a cloth coat entered American political history. After Nixon became President, Chotiner worked in the White House for a while, through the 1970 mid-term elections. (Among the Democratic senators up for reelection were Edward Kennedy and Edmund Muskie.) It was said that Haldeman and Ehrlichman got Chotiner out of the White House in 1971 because they thought he might embarrass the President.

MAY 4—The bombing of Cambodia grows – about sixty B-52 strikes today.

MAY 5—At a cocktail party, word spreads that the next *Newsweek* will say that John Dean has information implicating the President in the Watergate cover-up. [. . .] How much information does Dean really have? Will he – should he – be believed?

Every once in a while, there is a shift in the way that the Watergate affair is perceived. Its proportions seem larger, and so do its implications. Suddenly, now there are conversations about the procedures for impeachment, and resignation. There is no precise reason for this shift; the atmospherics of Washington often defy rational explanation. But there is a sense that more is coming, and that no one knows where it will end. The concepts of 'impeachment' or 'resignation' suggest a resolution, a definition of what has happened. We seem to find it hard to live without definitions or resolutions.

MAY 6—The Sunday *New York Times* says John Dean told the FBI that the following items were found in Hunt's office: a 'Colt revolver, one clip for the revolver, one holster, three shoulder harnesses, three belt harnesses, four rechargeable Bell and Howell batteries, one tear gas cannister, two microphones in simulated Chapstick containers. Three antenna leads, four antennas, six jack wires, one shoulder harness with white lead wire and phone jack, three operating instructions for a Bell and Howell portable transmitter. There was also one copy of the book, "The Pentagon Papers"; six brown envelopes containing classified material relating to the Pentagon Papers; one tan folder marked "Ellsberg"; one tan folder marked "Pentagon Papers"; one folder marked "John Paul Vann"; folders marked "Time and Pay Records," which contained verification of hours worked at the White House, and a folder marked "Press Contacts."'

The *Times* reports that Hunt has told the federal grand jury that the CIA supplied some of the equipment.

Flashback: Richard Helms was replaced as Director of the CIA after the election; it was never very clear why.

MAY 7—Ordinarily, *Time* and *Newsweek* are read on Tuesdays, when the subscription copies arrive. But now, copies are bought as soon as they reach the newsstands on Monday morning. *Newsweek*'s story about Dean is more carefully hedged than the weekend stories about it suggested. [. . .]

The FBI is now a shambles. The factionalism into which it began to deteriorate in Hoover's last years threatens anyone who tries to succeed him, and could even destroy the agency itself. On one level, it is a set of bureaucratic battles of Hoover men against anti-Hoover men, and of agents in the field against those in Washington. On another level, it is a morality play: FBI agents, with information about the espionage and sabotage and cover-up, weighing their responsibilities to the bureaucracy, to the institution, to the Administration, and to the public. Motivated by both patriotism and petty rivalries, the FBI has become an important source of leaks to the press. Hoover men are believed to have provided information which sand-bagged Pat Gray. An agency trained in obtaining sensitive information and double-dealing and blackmail is now, using these capacities, devouring itself.

Can we train people in the black arts and then control their practice of their craft?

ALICE WALKER
1944–

The youngest of eight children, Walker was born to impoverished African-American sharecroppers in rural Georgia, at a time of huge racial tumult and violence. She won a scholarship to Georgia's Spelman College, and then another to Sarah Lawrence College in New York, which was then an overwhelmingly white institution.

As an activist in the Civil Rights movement, Walker first won attention for her writing with an acclaimed essay, *The Civil Rights Movement: What Good Was It?* Since then she has published collections of short stories and poetry and a number of novels, including *Meridian*, *The Temple of My Familiar*, and her most popular work, *The Color Purple*, which won her the Pulitzer Prize.

Throughout her life and writing, Walker has been an outspoken activist, known for her involvement with a large variety of causes, including the Women's movement and the environmental lobby. The following article brings many of her key concerns powerfully to the fore as she writes about the abortion debate and attacks white men's power as lawmakers.

The Right to Life: what can the White Man ... Say to the Black Woman?

22 May 1989, *Nation*

What is of use in these words I offer in memory and recognition of our common mother. And to my daughter.

What can the white man say to the black woman?
For four hundred years he ruled over the black woman's womb.

Let us be clear. In the barracoons and along the slave shipping coasts of Africa, for more than twenty generations, it was he who dashed our babies' brains out against the rocks.

What can the white man say to the black woman?
For four hundred years he determined which black woman's children would live or die.

Let it be remembered. It was he who placed our children on the auction block in cities all across the eastern half of what is now the United States, and listened to and watched them beg for their mother's arms, before being sold to the highest bidder and dragged away.

What can the white man say to the black woman?

We remember that Fannie Lou Hamer, a poor sharecropper on a Mississippi plantation, was one of twenty-one children; and that on plantations across the South black women often had twelve, fifteen, twenty children. Like their enslaved mothers and grandmothers before them, these black women were sacrificed to the profit the white man could make from harnessing their bodies and their children's bodies to the cotton gin.

What can the white man say to the black woman?

We see him lined up on Saturday nights, century after century, to make the black mother, who must sell her body to feed her children, go down on her knees to him.

Let us take note:

He has not cared for a single one of the dark children in his midst, over hundreds of years.

Where are the children of the Cherokee, my great grandmother's people?

Gone.

Where are the children of the Blackfoot?

Gone.

Where are the children of the Lakota?

Gone.

Of the Cheyenne?

Of the Chippewa?

Of the Iroquois?

Of the Sioux?

Of the Mandinka?

Of the Ibo?

Of the Ashanti?

Where are the children of the 'Slave Coast' and Wounded Knee?

We do not forget the forced sterilizations and forced starvations on the reservations, here as in South Africa. Nor do we forget the smallpox-infested blankets Indian children were given by the Great White Fathers of the United States government.

What has the white man to say to the black woman?

When we have children you do everything in your power to make them feel unwanted from the moment they are born. You send them to fight and kill other dark mothers' children around the world. You shove them onto public highways in the path of oncoming cars. You shove their heads through plate glass windows. You string them up and you string them out.

What has the white man to say to the black woman?
From the beginning, you have treated all dark children with absolute hatred.

Thirty million African children died on the way to the Americas, where nothing awaited them but endless toil and the crack of a bullwhip. They died of a lack of food, of lack of movement in the holds of ships. Of lack of friends and relatives. They died of depression, bewilderment and fear.
What has the white man to say to the black woman?
Let us look around us: Let us look at the world the white man has made for the black woman and her children.

It is a world in which the black woman is still forced to provide cheap labor, in the form of children, for the factories and on the assembly lines of the white man.

It is a world into which the white man dumps every foul, person-annulling drug he smuggles into creation.

It is a world where many of our babies die at birth, or later of malnutrition, and where many more grow up to live lives of such misery they are forced to choose death by their own hands.
What has the white man to say to the black woman, and to all women and children everywhere?
Let us consider the depletion of the ozone; let us consider homelessness and the nuclear peril; let us consider the destruction of the rain forests – in the name of the almighty hamburger. Let us consider the poisoned apples and the poisoned water and the poisoned air and the poisoned earth.

And that all of our children, because of the white man's assault on the planet, have a possibility of death by cancer in their almost immediate future.

What has the white, male lawgiver to say to any of us? To those of us who love life too much to willingly bring more children into a world saturated with death?

Abortion, for many women, is more than an experience of suffering beyond anything most men will ever know; it is an act of mercy, and an act of self-defense.

To make abortion illegal again is to sentence millions of women and children to miserable lives and even more miserable deaths.

Given his history, in relation to us, I think the white man should be ashamed to attempt to speak for the unborn children of the black woman. To force us to have children for him to ridicule, drug and turn into killers and homeless wanderers is a testament to his hypocrisy.
What can the white man say to the black woman?
Only one thing that the black woman might hear.

Yes, indeed, the white man can say, Your children have the right to life. Therefore I will call back from the dead those 30 million who were tossed overboard during the centuries of the slave trade. And the other millions who died in my cotton fields and hanging from my trees.

I will recall all those who died of broken hearts and broken spirits, under the insult of segregation.

I will raise up all the mothers who died exhausted after birthing twenty-one children to work sunup to sundown on my plantation. I will restore to full health all those who perished for lack of food, shelter, sunlight, and love; and from my inability to see them as human beings.

But I will go even further:

I will tell you, black woman, that I wish to be forgiven the sins I commit daily against you and your children. For I know that until I treat your children with love, I can never be trusted by my own. Nor can I respect myself.

And I will free your children from insultingly high infant mortality rates, short life spans, horrible housing, lack of food, rampant ill health. I will liberate them from the ghetto. I will open wide the doors of all the schools and hospitals and businesses of society to your children. I will look at your children and see not a threat but a joy.

I will remove myself as an obstacle in the path that your children, against all odds, are making toward the light. I will not assassinate them for dreaming dreams and offering new visions of how to live. I will cease trying to lead your children, for I can see I have never understood where I was going. I will agree to sit quietly for a century or so, and meditate on this.

This is what the white man can say to the black woman.
We are listening.

ANN LESLIE

Born and raised in India and Pakistan, British journalist Leslie went on to study at Oxford before joining the staff of the *Express* newspaper. There she was given a column at the prodigious age of twenty-two, but soon resigned, protesting that she wanted to be a proper reporter.

This proved a wise choice and Leslie has since gone on to become a highly respected and garlanded foreign correspondent, contributing to the *Daily Mail* for more than three decades. This period has seen her cover a huge variety of world events, including wars and massacres as well as Nelson Mandela's final walk to freedom. Amidst all these, the one she describes as her most exciting is the fall of the Berlin Wall. The following article is her account of that moment, bringing to life all its implicit passion and hope.

Report on the Fall of the Berlin Wall

1989, *Daily Mail*

Checkpoints at the Berlin Wall erupted into a huge carnival last night.

Thousands of East Germans flooded through, brandishing champagne and beer bottles.

Many danced on top of the wall near Checkpoint Charlie with good-humoured border guards making no attempt to remove them or break up the bedlam.

Hours earlier, the Wall had been consigned to the history books as the infamous symbol of a divided Europe. East Germany's new leaders said their citizens could now emigrate freely and directly to West Germany.

On both sides of the Wall there was celebration that Checkpoint Charlie – dramatic backcloth of countless spy films and novels – was now nothing more than a tourists' turnstile. Crowds of East Germans hurried through the no man's land where, hours earlier, they would have been shot at by guards. Thousands more crossed at other checkpoints, simply by showing their identity cards.

The developments surprised the West as much as the East. When, in June 1987, Ronald Reagan stood at the Wall built by Erich Honecker and called out: 'Mr Gorbachev, tear this Wall down' no one imagined that within two years it would be defunct. Mr Reagan's successor, President

Bush said of the news: 'I feel good about it.' He advised East Germans to stay on and 'participate in the reforms that are taking place.'

At first, a trickle of citizens arrived at the border in East Berlin. It soon became a deluge. In Bornholmer Strasse, border police gave up and let everybody through without checking, and first-aid teams were on hand to help some people who fainted with emotion.

On the West Berlin side, crowds shot off fireworks and clapped as the East Berliners surged through.

At one o'clock this morning, I spoke to Uta Ruhrdanz and four student friends at the Friedrichstrasse checkpoint in East Berlin. 'We've just been to the West – for 20 minutes!' cried Uta. 'It's unbelievable! Still we can't understand how this happened and why, but for the moment we are just so excited and happy that we can't think much further!

'As soon as we heard the news we thought, "Can it be true – let's go and see." When we arrived the border guards said, "OK you can go across tonight and come back if you want. But tomorrow morning you should go and get your police stamp." There were lots of us crowding on to the train to West Berlin and we were all singing and laughing and some were trying to dance.

'And some people were still a little bit scared: they were saying, "Perhaps it's all a trick, perhaps they won't let us come back again." We, too, felt a little bit frightened and so when we were in West Berlin we rushed out into the Kurfustendamm and bought souvenirs and then rushed back again. I think we were not believing completely that all this is true – but here we are. We are back and there has been no problem. It is so wonderful!'

As I returned to my hotel cars were honking, people were shouting greetings and a middle-aged couple came up to me and embraced me, beaming with excitement.

It had taken several hours since the historic announcement before East Berliners really began to believe what was now possible. Half-an-hour after the announcement. I had gone to Checkpoint Charlie where I interviewed a border guard.

A fine drizzle fell, draping his cap with diamonds of light from the floodlights at the Wall: the scene was straight out of a spy thriller. But this border guard in his huge greatcoat had suddenly been transformed from a creature of totalitarian nightmare into an affable East German bloke clearly delighted to know that the more murderous part of his role was, as of half an hour earlier, effectively over.

Around me the people were gathering, some toasting the great news with champagne. The guard looked up the road where foreign cars were lined up already.

'Isn't it great?' an East German friend with me asked him. 'Wouldn't it have been wonderful if they'd announced this four months ago?' 'Yes – it is wonderful but I don't think it's too late now. I think now there is hope for the country!' he replied. 'Oh, but you know that 43,000 people have left since the weekend?' my friend informed him. The border guard looked aghast. 'As many as that? I didn't realise.'

I asked him whether he was happy at the developments. He smiled ruefully. 'Personally, no – because it's going to mean I have to work much harder coping with the enormous queues that will be coming.'

The queue at the Friedrichstrasse checkpoint was growing by the minute. The people – young, old, middle-aged – were laughing, crying, embracing and all were telling each other (and me) exactly how and where they heard the news.

It had been yet another astonishing day in the city. Even yesterday I found that East Germans, for so long terrorised by the state security – the hated Stasi – would hesitate before speaking to me. They had developed a fear that even the walls in the streets were listening to them. But last night that fear seemed finally to have gone. In the queue at Friedrichstrasse one woman said: 'They are still spying on us – look at that man listening over there. He is Stasi!'

In fact he turned out to be a harmless Swedish reporter and even though people in the queue had looked at him you could tell that they suddenly didn't care whether he was Stasi or not.

The Wall still exists physically but in effect it has been destroyed. The psychological symbol of the Wall with its watch towers and its terrible no man's land had entered deeply into every East Berliner's soul. Now that the symbol, if not the physical presence, had been removed I found East Berliners looking on it as a simple border marker.

'I don't think they should pull the wall down yet.' said my East German friend. 'After all every country marks its border. But of course people on both sides should be able to pass to and fro – and now, at last, that is happening. This has been the most exciting day of my life.'

When we parted she flung her arms round me and kissed me, crying: 'Who would ever have believed that this would happen today!'

ERICA JONG

1942–

Poet, novelist, teacher and memoirist, Erica Jong exploded on to the literary scene in 1973 with her first novel (written in just six weeks), *Fear of Flying*. A partly autobiographical study of a frustrated young wife's experiences during the sexual revolution of the late 1960s and early 1970s, it changed public perceptions of female sexuality by suggesting that women could enjoy casual encounters (famously termed the 'zipless fuck') just as much as men. On publication, Henry Miller wrote that 'this book will make literary history – because of it women are going to find their own voice and give us great sagas of sex, life, joy, and adventure.'

From this point onwards, Jong became a prominent cultural commentator, providing a voice that is political, entertaining, incisive and often very provocative. In the following article she considers the Clinton marriage as the couple face Bill's second term in office. The piece compares Hillary Clinton to Eleanor Roosevelt and outlines the many impossible trials meted out to gifted women who become First Lady.

Hillary's Husband Re-elected: the Clinton Marriage of Politics and Power.

25 November 1996, *Nation*

Here we are, two minutes after the last American presidential election in the twentieth century, and Hillary Rodham Clinton is still the most problematic First Lady in American history – admired abroad, hated at home, mistrusted by women journalists even though this Administration has actually done much good for women. Suspected of being a megalomaniac, embroiled in document losing, spy-hiring, the suicide of an aide conjectured to be her lover, and possible perjury; pilloried in the press and jeered at in political cartoons; distrusted even by her admirers – can't Hillary do anything right? Why does she get no credit for all the positive things she has done?

The old campaign button that trumpeted 'Elect Hillary's Husband in '92' showed a picture of Hillary, not Bill. Indeed, it's hard to remember it 'now. It's even hard to remember how Hillary flouted the rules decreed for political wives: the obligatory Stepford Wife impersonation, the fake flirtatious flattery that makes wives seem feminine and nonthreatening; the willingness to pretend to be the power behind the throne; the diplomatic surrender to the role of First Lady.

The kaleidoscope of Hillary images and the frequently self-destructive behavior of the First Lady are particularly regrettable because both the Clinton Administration and the Clinton marriage are historic. As a couple, the Clintons raise important issues about both electoral and sexual politics. It is clear that without H.R.C.'s participation, Bill Clinton would have gone right down the Gary Hart sewer. Because his wife stood by him in that first Barbara Walters interview in 1992, because he did not exactly deny 'causing pain' in the marriage while Hillary held his hand supportively, the first Clinton campaign was able to weather and rise above what had been killing sexual crises for other presidential candidates. Unlike France, America does not coddle public adulterers. Only 'the little woman' can save them. She forgives, we forgive.

In those days – the first Clinton campaign – we were still hearing a lot about getting two for the price of one. Elect one, get one free. Hillary was the freebie. Never before in American politics had any couple campaigned this way. The very American ideal of a 'power couple' who add up to more than the sum of their parts was put on the ballot in the 1992 election. America was enthusiastic about it then. Indeed, the Clinton candidacy looked bravely feminist compared with the fuddy-duddy aura of Bush and Mrs Bush. But misogyny was far from dead, as we were soon to see.

The subsequent assault on Hillary demonstrated the entrenched woman-hating both of the American press and the bigoted public it so badly serves. When William Safire of the *New York Times* called H.R.C. 'a congenital liar,' surely he was subjecting her to a different standard from the one to which he had held other First Ladies. Can anyone in the laser glare of the public eye be expected to be candid all the time? Did anyone ask Pat Nixon what she thought of her husband's destruction of evidence? Was Nancy Reagan interrogated about Irangate? Certainly not. But H.R.C.'s gene pool was impugned at the drop of a document. With the roasting of Hillary it became clear that when we wish women to fail, we decree for them endless and impossible ordeals, like those that were devised for witches by their inquisitors. If they drown, they are innocent; if they float, they are guilty. This has pretty much been the way America has gotten rid of its cleverest political women, from the feminists Victoria Woodhull and Emma Goldman to Eleanor Roosevelt and the unsuccessful vice-presidential candidate Geraldine Ferraro. And there is no doubt that many people still wish H.R.C. to fail. Even now.

Clinton strategists – including the disgraced Dick Morris – kept Hillary out of the limelight for most of the campaign. She was only seen (but not heard) in proper 'helpmeet' photo-ops like the Atlanta Olympics, the

Wyoming vacation and the exotic ports of call she visited with First Daughter Chelsea. America preferred – 58 per cent of men told pollsters that their view of Hillary was unfavorable – the duplicitous Southern charms of Elizabeth Hanford Dole: a driven career woman with no children who claims she is 'pro-life,' a chief Red Cross administrator who uses her powerful charity as a political tool of the Republican Party, a soft-spoken, flirtatious belle married to an old man, a saccharine public speaker who used the Republican convention in San Diego as an excuse to drown the delegates in treacle. Duplicity in women makes America comfortable; straightforwardness does not. There was even, I learned, heated debate in the White House about whether H.R.C. should speak at the Democratic convention or remain out of sight and earshot. After Liddy Dole's San Diego seduction, it was decided that, however risky, Hillary had to speak. What a far cry from 1992, when Hillary was considered an asset! By the summer of 1996, she was a liability to be hidden. This is what four years of Hillary-hating had accomplished.

The deal of the Clinton marriage fascinates me and I suspect it fascinates a good portion of the electorate. It reflects our period better than any political marriage I can think of. Clearly Hillary figured out in law school that if the time was not yet ripe for a woman President, it was likely to be ripe for a guy as driven and smart and personable as Bill Clinton. And she could be his chief adviser, patron (she made the money – with no small help from his political position) and disciplinarian. However much she warmed to his Southern charm, no matter how much she loved him, his political ambition turned her on just as much.

Not that there is anything wrong with a marital deal. You might even say that the more things that bind a couple together, the better chance they have of staying together. But theirs is a radical deal for an American political marriage. H.R.C. has never staked out highway beautification as her bailiwick (as did Lyndon Baines Johnson's wife, Lady Bird) or crusaded to put warning labels on rock albums (once the one-woman campaign of Second Lady Tipper Gore). On the contrary, she has claimed center stage with top policy issues – however politically naive she may have been.

This audacity dazzled at first. But then, why should a First Lady stick to so-called women's issues? Hillary was always policy-minded, always loath to be ghettoized ideologically. She was always far more serious than Bill, even in college and law school. He was a people pleaser. She was a woman who put intellect first, which meant automatically that many men – and women – would not be pleased by her. One of the reasons she hooked up with Bill was that he was the first man who seemed not to be afraid of her intellect but rather challenged and attracted by it. He was determined 'to get the smartest girl in the class,' as an old Arkansas buddy of his told

Roger Morris. He was sick of beauty queens. 'If it isn't Hillary, it's nobody,' he informed his mother, cautioning her to be nice to Hillary before he brought her to meet the family in 1972. Though he apparently had nostalgia – and a use – for those beauty queens after he and Hillary were married, at the time of their courtship Hillary's brains thrilled him more. She excited him. Maybe she still does. After all, many powerful men yearn for the sting of a dominatrix's whip now and then; it seems to be a sovereign tonic for hubris.

One of the difficulties of being a smart, driven woman is finding men who are turned on by brains. Hillary's initial attachment to Bill probably had a lot to do with the excitement of finding such a fearless man. Later, it seems, she had invested so much of herself in the marriage and in the daughter they shared that she wasn't willing to throw it all away even if faced with compulsive, repeated infidelities. The stresses on H.R.C. have been extreme, and one must say that despite them she has proved an exemplary mother. She has protected Chelsea from the media, allowed her the space to grow into womanhood, put her education ahead of politics. As the mother of a teenage daughter, I honor H.R.C. for what she has achieved.

Still, we have to look at the strangeness of the public image put forward by this revolutionary presidential couple: they were elected as a team but have absolutely refused to make the terms of their marriage public except to admit that he 'caused pain.' It is the inconsistency of this position that has accounted for a great deal of the trouble. If you vote for a couple, you feel entitled to know about the bonds that hold them together. But Hillary has insisted that those bonds are private. People resent her determination to have it both ways. But how on earth could the Clintons own up to the details of Bill's sex life? The fact that they have quashed the issue thus far is nothing short of a miracle.

The more you read about Bill Clinton, the more it seems evident that not only were there affairs but that he used his position as governor to facilitate them, using state troopers as beards and panderers, getting them to pick up frilly little gifts at Victoria's Secret. But I assume that his erotic life is no better and no worse than any other male politician's. I am, in general so disillusioned with male politicians that I actually prefer Bill Clinton the womanizer to Bob Dole the deadbeat dad who dumped the first wife who nursed him through his famous war wounds. (Dole actually got his political cronies to arrange an 'emergency divorce' so he could jettison the old wife and family more cheaply.) Fucking is fucking, but failing to pay child support is a real crime. At least Bill Clinton didn't abandon his wife and child.

Hillary's history is full of paradoxes. A baby boomer who grew up in a straight-arrow Methodist Republican registered family in a white, upwardly mobile suburb of Chicago, she became a left-leaning Democrat at Wellesley College. At Yale Law School she WAS studious, solitary, solemn, given to wearing flannel shirts and thick glasses, noted for her brilliance and hard work. Her mother, a closet Democrat, had compromised with her life and did not want Hillary to compromise – a familiar mother-daughter story. Her father was stern, unambiguously Republican, tight with money and difficult to please. Imagine a girl like that winning the good ol' boy who has been dating beauty queens! It gives you an idea of how much his 'locking in on her' (as one old friend put it) must have meant to her.

Hillary is an appealing figure to me because her life shows the strange compromises gifted women make. She had already changed her politics, drifted away from her parents' reactionary attitudes. What lay ahead were other complete makeovers – looks, name, ideals. Everything would have to change for the greater glory of Bill Clinton and the pillow power he bestowed. If she has often come across as angry and unsettled, as constantly remaking her image, it is because this is the truth. How could she not be angry? Like an ancient Chinese noblewoman with bound feet, she has had to deform even her anatomy to get where she needed to go. She hobbled her own fierce ambitions to transplant herself to Arkansas and defend his. She gave up her end-of-sixties indifference to female fashion, her passion for social justice and her native disgust with hypocrisy. Then, while he used her feminism as a shield to cover his philandering, he proceeded to make a mockery of everything she believed in.

Since Bill Clinton had always been clear about his ambition to be a top Arkansas politician and then President, his path never changed. Hers changed constantly – and with it her hair, her eyes, her weight, her name. At some point she must have had to decide that all those changes were worth it. How else can a smart woman justify such a metamorphosis? She had to recommit herself over and over to life with him. No wonder she demanded paybacks, such as running health care reform and his public life. She would have felt demolished otherwise. One sympathizes with her strength to make demands. But the power struggle of the marriage inevitably influenced the power politics of the nation, and that is what is so radically new about the Clinton presidency.

George Bush used his first day in the presidency to congratulate 'right to life' marchers, even while insinuating that First Lady Barbara Bush did not agree with him. No such stand for Bill Clinton. He and Hillary were joined at the hip politically, however much stress their marriage might be under. Their presidency has redefined public and private. Both Clintons' policies are in lockstep, even though their marriage may be chronically on the rocks.

'We cared deeply about a lot of the same things,' Hillary told an interviewer for the campaign film *The Man From Hope* in 1992. This revealing quote, edited out of the final film, makes the deal of the marriage clear. 'Bill and I really are bound together in part because we believe we have an obligation to give something back and to be part of making life better for other people,' she went on (as quoted by Bob Woodward in *The Choice*). The tragedy of their story is that such idealism had to be replaced by a ruthless commitment to politics, and this deformation of principle came much harder to her than to him. Hillary's image problem has several root causes. One is undoubtedly the ineptness of her staff. Another is the undeniable fact that there is no way for a smart woman to be public without being seen as a treacherous Lady Macbeth figure or bitch goddess (our failing, more than Hillary's). But the deepest problem is that Hillary comes across on television as cold and too controlled because that is the truth. She has rejigged her image so often, retailored it so much to please the spin doctors, that it comes across as inauthentic. It is.

The truth is that Bill is what he is – warm, tear-jerkingly populist, dying to please, woo and pander. He's a born salesman, 'riding on a smile,' in the immortal words of Arthur Miller. Hillary, meanwhile, is a brainy girl trying to look like an Arkansas beauty queen, a corporate lawyer trying to look like a happy housewife, a fierce feminist who has submerged her identity in her husband's ambitions. It doesn't add up – too many contradictions – which is why we don't believe it. The pearls and pink put on for the campaign – as well as the new, practiced smiling – are not totally convincing either. We expect Lady Macbeth to reappear, rubbing the blood from her hands.

We should weep for Hillary Clinton rather than revile her. She is a perfect example of why life is so tough for brainy women. The deformations of her public image reveal the terrible contortions expected of American women. Look pretty but be (secretly) smart. Conform in public; cry in private. Make the money but don't seem to be aggressive. Swallow everything your husband asks you to swallow, but somehow keep your own identity. Hillary shows us just how impossible all these conflicting demands are to fulfill.

For Hillary and her generation, 'no single act came to symbolize so vividly her role and sacrifice as the surrender of her maiden name,' as Roger Morris points out in *Partners in Power*. Refusing to be submerged in the identity of wife is a burning issue for our generation. A woman can give up on this outwardly and continue to seethe inwardly. As with so many other Hillary transformations, the stress shows. I'm glad it does. It shows that she still has her conscience intact, if not her soul. She is not the consummately smooth performer her husband is.

Besides the constant hair transformations, nothing has shown Hillary's discomfort with her role as much as her choice of Jean Houston and

Mary Catherine Bateson as spiritual guides. For all the idiocies of the American press, which cheaply depicted Hillary's spiritual quests as 'seances,' Houston and Bateson are serious figures. Bateson is a writer and anthropologist, who, like her mother, Margaret Mead, is fascinated with the changing roles of twentieth-century women. Like her father, the English-born anthropologist Gregory Bateson, she also has a deep interest in spirituality in the modern world. Houston is a respected spiritual teacher and author. It is to Hillary's credit that she sought guidance from such interesting women. It also shows her deep need for reassurance in the midst of the nonstop Hate Hillary campaign that has been the salient feature of her public life. As Bob Woodward suggests, 'Hillary's sessions with Houston reflected a serious inner turmoil that she had not resolved.'

Apparently, Houston encouraged Hillary to take heart from her role model, Eleanor Roosevelt, and to use the technique of imaginary conversations with a mentor to confront her own deep hurt about the attacks, jealousy and misunderstanding she has encountered as First Lady. This is an ancient technique for building self-knowledge and resolve. It was used during the Italian Renaissance by Machiavelli. Nevertheless, Hillary has been ridiculed as the dupe of seance-mongers for her very human need to reach out for help. This is beyond unkind. It is cruel and unusual punishment. I would rather put my faith in leaders who acknowledge their human need for guidance than in those who will accept none. Hillary remains deeply troubled on many levels; I wish she could open herself to psychological help. But then, of course, she might have to leave Bill!

Hillary herself is in great speaking form these days: passionate, strong, determined. She has even learned to soften political discourse with smiles. Once again her hair has been redesigned, her jewelry is smaller and more 'feminine' – the safety of pearls – and some adviser has connived to dress her in pastels. You could say she's on the Dole. She has been Liddyized. She frequently says, 'My husband and I believe' or 'the President believes,' and she allows no public space for those who would divide them. She is poised, cool, in control. The anger does not show. All that is missing is the sense of the real woman underneath the pretty makeup and softly tailored suit.

One wants to say Hillary is the hollow woman – but in fact the opposite is true: She is a seething mass of contradictions, so she dares let none of her feelings show. 'Relaxed' is not a word you would use about her even now. She gives off an aura of discipline and ferocious tenacity. It's impossible to glimpse the human being beneath the mask. Yet all those stories of her breaking down in tears or rage in private after this perfect composure in public seem wholly believable. She seems to be holding herself together with hairspray.

What is familiar about this picture? A woman is sacrificed to her husband's ambitions. Her personality is deformed. She takes almost all the flak in the press while he gets away with murder. You might almost say she is taking the punishment for him, and for all women who step outside the lines prescribed for paper-doll political wives – in fact, for all contemporary women. Hillary Rodham Clinton looks more to me like Joan of Arc every day. She is burned as a witch week in and week out so that her husband can rise in the polls. She is the scapegoat half of the Clinton duo, the rear end that gets whipped so the smiling Clinton head can triumph. She is Agamemnon's Iphigenia sacrificed for a propitious wind, Euripides' Alcestis going across the Styx instead of her husband.

And this is the way the Clinton presidential couple is conventional rather than revolutionary. Yes, they dared to present themselves as a team. But once again it's the female half that gets trashed while the male half is forgiven for all his transgressions and winds up being President. Bill Clinton owes Hillary. Big. The only difference between him and other guys is that he seems to know it. History has burdened Hillary Clinton with changing the way powerful women are perceived in our culture. But if she can see herself as part of a historical continuum, as a pathfinder opening the way for her daughter's generation, she may be able to rise above the pain of daily crucifixions in the media.

With a second Clinton Administration, H.R.C. has the rare opportunity to triumph over her detractors. She has already fulfilled her wish to be an Eleanor Roosevelt for the end of the century. In many ways her mainstreaming of feminism has prepared us to accept a woman President in the twenty-first century. By acting as a lightning rod she has gotten us comfortable with women who talk back in public, don't hide their brains, don't hide their passionate mothering. H.R.C. is the latest incarnation of Miss Liberty. I'm glad she's a survivor. Her survival means I can survive. If the next Clinton ticket is H.R.C. and Al Gore, I intend to vote for them more happily than I voted for Bill Clinton on Tuesday.

BARBARA EHRENREICH
1941–

A doctor of biology, Ehrenreich began her career writing science articles in professional journals, but soon found her concern with social change superseding this interest. She quickly began writing more political articles – often concerned with America's intrinsic class and wealth stratifications – and was soon contributing investigative and campaigning pieces to magazines including *Ms*, the *Nation* and the *New Republic*.

This piece represents some of the most extensive and personal investigative work ever written, and was prompted by a conversation over lunch in 1998 with *Harper's* editor, Lewis Lapham. Ehrenreich wondered aloud about the recent slew of welfare reforms, and asked how four million former welfare recipients would get by on a wage of $6 an hour. 'Someone,' she suggested, 'ought to do the old-fashioned kind of journalism – you know, go out there and try it themselves.' Lapham's reply was prophetic. 'You.'

Ehrenreich subsequently left her comfortable Florida Keys home for the next two years and survived solely on the wages from a series of low-paid jobs, including cleaning, waitressing and assisting in a Walmart store. Below, she recounts the beginning of this experience.

Nickel-and-Dimed
On (Not) Getting By in America

January 1999, *Harper's Magazine*

At the beginning of June 1998 I leave behind everything that normally soothes the ego and sustains the body – home, career, companion, reputation, ATM card – for a plunge into the low-wage workforce. There, I become another, occupationally much diminished 'Barbara Ehrenreich' – depicted on job-application forms as a divorced homemaker whose sole work experience consists of housekeeping in a few private homes. I am terrified, at the beginning, of being unmasked for what I am: a middle-class journalist setting out to explore the world that welfare mothers are entering, at the rate of approximately 50,000 a month, as welfare reform kicks in. Happily, though, my fears turn out to be entirely unwarranted: during a month of poverty and toil, my name goes unnoticed and for the most part unuttered. In this parallel universe where my father never got out of the mines and I never got through college, I am 'baby,' 'honey,' 'blondie,' and, most commonly, 'girl.'

My first task is to find a place to live. I figure that if I can earn $7 an hour – which, from the want ads, seems doable – I can afford to spend $500 on rent, or maybe, with severe economies, $600. In the Key West area, where I live, this pretty much confines me to flophouses and trailer homes – like the one, a pleasing fifteen-minute drive from town, that has no air-conditioning, no screens, no fans, no television, and, by way of diversion, only the challenge of evading the landlord's Doberman pinscher. The big problem with this place, though, is the rent, which at $675 a month is well beyond my reach. All right, Key West is expensive. But so is New York City, or the Bay Area, or Jackson Hole, or Telluride, or Boston, or any other place where tourists and the wealthy compete for living space with the people who clean their toilets and fry their hash browns.[1] Still, it is a shock to realize that 'trailer trash' has become, for me, a demographic category to aspire to.

So I decide to make the common trade-off between affordability and convenience, and go for a $500-a-month efficiency thirty miles up a two-lane highway from the employment opportunities of Key West, meaning forty-five minutes if there's no road construction and I don't get caught behind some sun-dazed Canadian tourists. I hate the drive, along a roadside studded with white crosses commemorating the more effective head-on collisions, but it's a sweet little place – a cabin, more or less, set in the swampy back yard of the converted mobile home where my landlord, an affable TV repairman, lives with his bartender girlfriend. Anthropologically speaking, a bustling trailer park would be preferable, but here I have a gleaming white floor and a firm mattress, and the few resident bugs are easily vanquished.

Besides, I am not doing this for the anthropology. My aim is nothing so mistily subjective as to 'experience poverty' or find out how it 'really feels' to be a long-term low-wage worker, I've had enough unchosen encounters with poverty and the world of low-wage work to know it's not a place you want to visit for touristic purposes; it just smells too much like fear. And with all my real-life assets – bank account, IRA, health insurance, multiroom home – waiting indulgently in the background,

1 According to the Department of Housing and Urban Development, the 'fair-market rent' for an efficiency is $551 here in Monroe County, Florida. A comparable rent in the five boroughs of New York City is $704; in San Francisco, $713; and in the heart of Silicon Valley, $808. The fair-market rent for an area is defined as the amount that would be needed to pay rent plus utilities for 'privately owned, decent, safe, and sanitary rental housing of a modest (non-luxury) nature with suitable amenities.'

I am, of course, thoroughly insulated from the terrors that afflict the genuinely poor.

No, this is a purely objective, scientific sort of mission. The humanitarian rationale for welfare reform – as opposed to the more punitive and stingy impulses that may actually have motivated it – is that work will lift poor women out of poverty while simultaneously inflating their self-esteem and hence their future value in the labor market. Thus, whatever the hassles involved in finding child care, transportation, etc., the transition from welfare to work will end happily, in greater prosperity for all. Now there are many problems with this comforting prediction, such as the fact that the economy will inevitably undergo a downturn, eliminating many jobs. Even without a downturn, the influx of a million former welfare recipients into the low-wage labor market could depress wages by as much as 11.9 percent, according to the Economic Policy Institute (EPI) in Washington, D.C.

But is it really possible to make a living on the kinds of jobs currently available to unskilled people? Mathematically, the answer is no, as can be shown by taking $6 to $7 an hour, perhaps subtracting a dollar or two an hour for child care, multiplying by 160 hours a month, and comparing the result to the prevailing rents. According to the National Coalition for the Homeless, for example, in 1998 it took, on average nationwide, an hourly wage of $8.89 to afford a one-bedroom apartment, and the Preamble Center for Public Policy estimates that the odds against a typical welfare recipient's landing a job at such a 'living wage' are about 97 to 1. If these numbers are right, low-wage work is not a solution to poverty and possibly not even to homelessness.

It may seem excessive to put this proposition to an experimental test. As certain family members keep unhelpfully reminding me, the viability of low-wage work could be tested, after a fashion, without ever leaving my study. I could just pay myself $7 an hour for eight hours a day, charge myself for room and board, and total up the numbers after a month. Why leave the people and work that I love? But I am an experimental scientist by training. In that business, you don't just sit at a desk and theorize; you plunge into the everyday chaos of nature, where surprises lurk in the most mundane measurements. Maybe, when I got into it, I would discover some hidden economies in the world of the low-wage worker. After all, if 30 percent of the workforce toils for less than $8 an hour, according to the EPI, they may have found some tricks as yet unknown to me. Maybe – who knows? – I would even be able to detect in myself the bracing psychological effects of getting out of the house, as promised by the welfare wonks at places like the Heritage Foundation. Or, on the other hand, maybe there would be unexpected costs – physical, mental, or financial – to throw off all my calculations. Ideally, I should do this with two small children in tow, that being the welfare average, but mine are grown and no one is willing to lend me theirs for a month-long vacation in penury. So this is not the perfect experiment, just a test of the best possible case: an unencumbered woman, smart and even strong, attempting to live more or less off the land.

On the morning of my first full day of job searching, I take a red pen to the want ads, which are auspiciously numerous. Everyone in Key West's booming 'hospitality industry' seems to be looking for someone like me – trainable, flexible, and with suitably humble expectations as to pay. I know I possess certain traits that might be advantageous – I'm white and, I like to think, well-spoken and poised – but I decide on two rules: One, I cannot use any skills derived from my education or usual work – not that there are a lot of want ads for satirical essayists anyway. Two, I have to take the best-paid job that is offered me and of course do my best to hold it; no Marxist rants or sneaking off to read novels in the ladies' room. In addition, I rule out various occupations for one reason or another: Hotel front-desk clerk, for example, which to my surprise is regarded as unskilled and pays around $7 an hour, gets eliminated because it involves standing in one spot for eight hours a day. Waitressing is similarly something I'd like to avoid, because I remember it leaving me bone tired when I was eighteen, and I'm decades of varicosities and back pain beyond that now. Telemarketing, one of the first refuges of the suddenly indigent, can be dismissed on grounds of personality. This leaves certain supermarket jobs, such as deli clerk, or housekeeping in Key West's thousands of hotel and guest rooms. Housekeeping is especially appealing, for reasons both atavistic and practical: it's what my mother did before I came along, and it can't be too different from what I've been doing part-time, in my own home, all my life.

So I put on what I take to be a respectful-looking outfit of ironed Bermuda shorts and scooped-neck T-shirt and set out for a tour of the local hotels and supermarkets. Best Western, Econo Lodge, and HoJo's all let me fill out application forms, and these are, to my relief, interested in little more than whether I am a legal resident of the United States and have committed any felonies. My next stop is Winn-Dixie, the supermarket, which turns out to have a particularly onerous application process, featuring a fifteen-minute 'interview' by computer since, apparently, no human on the premises is deemed capable of representing the corporate point of view. I am conducted to a large room decorated with posters illustrating how to look 'professional' (it helps to be white and, if female, permed) and warning of the slick promises that union organizers might try to tempt me with. The interview is multiple choice: Do I have anything, such as child-care problems, that might make it hard for me to get to work on time? Do I think safety on the job is the responsibility of management? Then, popping up cunningly out of the blue: How many dollars' worth of stolen goods have I purchased in the last year? Would I turn in a fellow employee if I caught him stealing? Finally, 'Are you an honest person?'

Apparently, I ace the interview, because I am told that all I have to do is show up in some doctor's office tomorrow for a urine test. This seems to be a fairly general rule: if you want to stack Cheerio boxes or vacuum hotel rooms in chemically fascist America, you have to be willing to squat down and pee in front of some health worker (who has no doubt had to do the same thing herself). The wages Winn-Dixie is offering – $6 and a couple of dimes to start with – are not enough, I decide, to compensate for this indignity.[2]

I lunch at Wendy's, where $4.99 gets you unlimited refills at the Mexican part of the Super-bar, a comforting surfeit of refried beans and 'cheese sauce.' A teenage employee, seeing me studying the want ads, kindly offers me an application form, which I fill out, though here, too, the pay is just $6 and change an hour. Then it's off for a round of the locally owned inns and guest-houses. At 'The Palms,' let's call it, a bouncy manager actually takes me around to see the rooms and meet the existing housekeepers, who, I note with satisfaction, look pretty much like me – faded ex-hippie types in shorts with long hair pulled back in braids. Mostly, though, no one speaks to me or even looks at me except to proffer an application form. At my last stop, a palatial B&B, I wait twenty minutes to meet 'Max,' only to be told that there are no jobs now but there should be one soon, since 'nobody lasts more than a couple weeks.' (Because none of the people I talked to knew I was a reporter I have changed their names to protect their privacy and, in some cases perhaps, their jobs.)

Three days go by like this, and, to my chagrin, no one out of the approximately twenty places I've applied calls me for an interview. I had been vain enough to worry about coming across as too educated for the jobs I sought, but no one even seems interested in finding out how overqualified I am. Only later will I realize that the want ads are not a reliable measure of the actual jobs available at any particular time. They

---

2 According to the *Monthly Labor Review* (November 1996), 28 percent of work sites surveyed in the service industry conduct drug tests (corporate workplaces have much higher rates), and the incidence of testing has risen markedly since the Eighties. The rate of testing is highest in the South (56 percent of work sites polled), with the Midwest in second place (50 percent). The drug most likely to be detected - marijuana, which can be detected in urine for weeks - is also the most innocuous, while heroin and cocaine are generally undetectable three days after use. Prospective employees sometimes try to cheat the tests by consuming excessive amounts of liquids and taking diuretics and even masking substances available through the Internet.

are, as I should have guessed from Max's comment, the employers' insurance policy against the relentless turnover of the low-wage workforce. Most of the big hotels run ads almost continually, just to build a supply of applicants to replace the current workers as they drift away or are fired, so finding a job is just a matter of being at the right place at the right time and flexible enough to take whatever is being offered that day. This finally happens to me at one of the big discount hotel chains, where I go, as usual, for housekeeping and am sent, instead, to try out as a waitress at the attached 'family restaurant,' a dismal spot with a counter and about thirty tables that looks out on a parking garage and features such tempting fare as 'Pollish [sic] sausage and BBQ sauce' on 95-degree days. Phillip, the dapper young West Indian who introduces himself as the manager, interviews me with about as much enthusiasm as if he were a clerk processing me for Medicare, the principal questions being what shifts can I work and when can I start. I mutter something about being woefully out of practice as a waitress, but he's already on to the uniform: I'm to show up tomorrow wearing black slacks and black shoes; he'll provide the rust-colored polo shirt with HEARTHSIDE embroidered on it, though I might want to wear my own shirt to get to work, ha ha. At the word 'tomorrow,' something between fear and indignation rises in my chest. I want to say, 'Thank you for your time, sir, but this is just an experiment, you know, not my actual life.'

So begins my career at the Hearthside, I shall call it, one small profit center within a global discount hotel chain, where for two weeks I work from 2:00 till 10:00 P.M. for $2.43 an hour plus tips.[3] In some futile bid for gentility, the management has barred employees from using the front door, so my first day I enter through the kitchen, where a red-faced man with shoulder-length blond hair is throwing frozen steaks against the wall and yelling, 'Fuck this shit!' 'That's just Jack,' explains Gail, the wiry middle-aged waitress who is assigned to train me. 'He's on the rag again' – a condition occasioned, in this instance, by the fact that the cook on the morning shift had forgotten to thaw out the steaks. For the next eight hours, I run after the agile Gail, absorbing bits of instruction along with fragments of personal tragedy. All food must be trayed, and the reason she's so tired today is that she woke up in a cold sweat thinking of her boyfriend, who killed himself recently in an upstate prison. No refills on lemonade.

3 According to the Fair Labor Standards Act, employers are not required to pay 'tipped employees,' such as restaurant servers, more than $2.13 an hour in direct wages. However, if the sum of tips plus $2.13 an hour falls below the minimum wage, or $5.15 an hour, the employer is required to make up the difference. This fact was not mentioned by managers or otherwise publicized at either of the restaurants where I worked.

And the reason he was in prison is that a few DUIs caught up with him, that's all, could have happened to anyone. Carry the creamers to the table in a monkey bowl, never in your hand. And after he was gone she spent several months living in her truck, peeing in a plastic pee bottle and reading by candlelight at night, but you can't live in a truck in the summer, since you need to have the windows down, which means anything can get in, from mosquitoes on up.

At least Gail puts to test any fears I had of appearing overqualified. From the first day on, I find that of all the things I have left behind, such as home and identity, what I miss the most is competence. Not that I have ever felt utterly competent in the writing business, in which one day's success augurs nothing at all for the next. But in my writing life, I at least have some notion of procedure: do the research, make the outline, rough out a draft, etc. As a server, though, I am beset by requests like bees: more iced tea here, ketchup over there, a to-go box for table fourteen, and where are the high chairs, anyway? Of the twenty-seven tables, up to six are usually mine at any time, though on slow afternoons or if Gail is off, I sometimes have the whole place to myself. There is the touch-screen computer-ordering system to master, which is, I suppose, meant to minimize server-cook contact, but in practice requires constant verbal fine-tuning: 'That's gravy on the mashed, okay? None on the meatloaf,' and so forth – while the cook scowls as if I were inventing these refinements just to torment him. Plus, something I had forgotten in the years since I was eighteen: about a third of a server's job is 'side work' that's invisible to customers – sweeping, scrubbing, slicing, refilling, and restocking. If it isn't all done, every little bit of it, you're going to face the 6:00 P.M. dinner rush defenseless and probably go down in flames. I screw up dozens of times at the beginning sustained in my shame entirely by Gail's support – 'It's okay, baby, everyone does that sometime' – because, to my total surprise and despite the scientific detachment I am doing my best to maintain, I care. [. . .]

When I wake up at 4:00 A.M. in my own cold sweat, I am not thinking about the writing deadlines I'm neglecting; I'm thinking about the table whose order I screwed up so that one of the boys didn't get his kiddie meal until the rest of the family had moved on to their Key Lime pies. That's the other powerful motivation I hadn't expected – the customers, or 'patients,' as I can't help thinking of them on account of the mysterious vulnerability that seems to have left them temporarily unable to feed themselves. After a few days at the Hearthside, I feel the service ethic kick in like a shot of oxytocin, the nurturance hormone. The plurality of my customers are hard-working locals – truck drivers, construction workers, even housekeepers from the attached hotel – and I want them to have the closest to a 'fine dining' experience that the grubby circumstances will allow. No 'you guys' for me; everyone over twelve is 'sir' or 'ma'am.' I ply them with iced tea and coffee refills; I return, mid-meal, to inquire how everything is; I doll up their salads with chopped raw mushrooms, summer squash slices, or whatever bits of produce I can find that have survived their sojourn in the cold-storage room mold-free.

ELEANOR MILLS
1970–

Beginning her career as a journalist writing about tanks (bulk liquid transportation, not the bang bang kind) for *Tank World* magazine, Mills quickly fled to the *Observer*. She became Features Editor of the *Daily Telegraph* aged twenty-six (the youngest they'd ever had) and then moved to the *Sunday Times* where she did the paper's main interview every week. Soon after, July 2001, she became editor of the *News Review* – the paper's weekly comment, analysis and features section.

This interview with Benazir Bhutto was one of her weekly encounters and sums up how Bhutto's glittering early career as a beacon to other women politicians turned tawdry as the corruption allegations kept on coming.

Putting her Best Face on a Murky Business

10 October 1999, *Sunday Times*

Benazir Bhutto was once the very model of a Third World leader. The scion of a political dynasty, the Oxford-educated beauty with democratic ideals seemed the answer to Pakistan's prayers. In 1988 she became the first woman to head a Muslim nation and the first to give birth while in office. She embodied a new, more optimistic, era.

But a decade is a long time in politics. These days Bhutto is mired in a corruption scandal that looks set to finish her career for good. In April, she was convicted of embezzling more than £1 billion. Tomorrow, her lawyers will go to the supreme court of Pakistan in a final appeal. If they fail, she faces five years in jail, a £5.2m fine, disqualification from holding public office and confiscation of all her property – Pakistan's high society is already gleefully awaiting the 'sale of the century'.

At present, Bhutto is in the throes of moving into a rented flat in South Kensington – 'It is all boxes, chaos, impossible,' she says – so we arrange to meet at her sister's place nearby. I arrive early and after a cursory greeting am left alone in a grand sitting room – mahogany furniture, cream silk curtains across three big windows. There are two large photographs. One is an official portrait of Benazir the prime minister with an inscription, 'To my darling Sunny'. (Bit formal for a sister?) The other is of their father, Zulfikar Ali Bhutto, founder of the Pakistan's People's Party (PPP), who was hanged by President Zia in 1979. 'My sister,' Bhutto confesses later, 'would like me to give up politics' – considering their two brothers were murdered and the fate of their father, I am not surprised.

Suddenly, the door bell rings. I expect Bhutto but discover two lawyers who have come to monitor what she says. Finally, she arrives in an elegant whirl of red and white (white cashmere jersey, silk skirt covered with red roses, crimson lipstick) and large black sunglasses. Her skin glows and her hair shines; not bad for a 46-year-old woman on the verge of losing everything.

Bhutto immediately denies all charges of corruption. She is, she claims, the victim of an elaborate conspiracy conducted by 'the theocrats of Pakistan' – she pronounces it 'Park-is-tarn'. 'There is a dangerous clique in the military and the judiciary, which includes the prime minister Nawaz Sharif, which wants to turn Pakistan into a theocratic state, modelled on the Taliban. They have thrown more and more mud at me hoping it will stick.' She repeatedly insists – to approving nods from the lawyers – that all charges are politically motivated. 'They have not one shred of evidence. Dictators in Pakistan abuse the judicial process to eliminate popular leaders, it happened to my father. Now they want to eliminate me.'

Since democracy was restored in Pakistan in 1988 (when Bhutto and the PPP were elected) power has alternated between it and the Muslim League. Pakistani politics is a dirty and violent business – Bhutto's husband, Asif Zardari, has been in prison for three years accused of corruption and murdering one of her brothers. I feel sure there are no clean hands here, but having read the independent view provided by Sir John Morris QC, the former British attorney-general, it certainly seems that Bhutto's trial has been unfair in some respects. It cannot be right, for instance, that she was convicted by the son of the man who ordered her father's execution.

Yet whatever the wrongs she has suffered during the legal proceedings, in a society like Pakistan where corruption is endemic (in a recent survey it was found to be even worse than that well-known kleptocracy, Nigeria) it is hard to believe that Bhutto and her husband (once the minister for investment) are as innocent as they claim. He was, after all, dubbed 'Mr 10%' in her first term in office and 'Mr 40%' in her second (she claims this was 'a slur on an innocent man by my political enemies'). And the splendour of the couple's many homes (palatial pads in Karachi and Islamabad, a private zoo, not to mention a disputed multi-million mansion in Surrey) have led some to question the loot's origin.

Bhutto is adamant that her money is 'family money, we have been wealthy for centuries'. But in a country where the majority live on the poverty line, such wealth inevitably arouses suspicions.

She is still by no means short of cash. Surreally, she says she has just been gazumped on a 'beautiful house in Osterley with lots of space for my mother (who has Alzheimer's), a big garden, lots of bedrooms, dining room, living room, study.' Such houses are not cheap – nor are rented flats in Queen's Gate. Can she put her hand on her heart and swear that neither she nor her husband ever took kickbacks?

'Yes, I can,' she says, 'because my husband never asked me once. He could have come to me and said 'I want you to do this, I want you to do that', but he never did. People say he could have done it behind my back – 'I say, show me the proof. People are innocent until proven guilty.' Despite her insistent tone and initial conviction, this sounds like a rather half-hearted denial. Indisputable, however, is the appallingly high personal cost Bhutto has paid for her time in power. She has not seen her husband – 'we care for each other deeply' – since a prison visit in April. And for the past two and a half years her three children (aged 11, 9 and 6) have been living in Dubai 'for their own safety' where she could see them only inter-mittently. They were supposed to be back in Dubai last month, but she has installed them in schools here while she fights her appeal.

'Like most working women,' she begins – with what I soon realise is phony humility – 'I often wonder whether my job has robbed my chil-dren of what was their right. But I feel that if I had not been what I am, I would not have been happy and, as an unhappy mother, my children would have grown up neurotic. Now they don't have my time, but they do have the attention of a woman who is satisfied that she is working for a higher cause. In that sense I am a better person and a better mother.'

She says she is happy 'to have this period together with them in England' and for the first time I don't feel like I am being spun a line. 'The best thing is I am here when the tooth fairy has to visit . . . the fairy often forgets when I am not there. The most fulfilling relationship is that of a mother because children love you unconditionally.' For a moment, she looks sad. In her high-octane whirl, there can't have been much space for normal family life.

'What they have done to my family is inhuman, it has caused me immense mental agony,' she says. There is a pause. Then the official Bhutto is back on message. 'But I am not going to let them succeed. I am going to fight,' she says briskly. 'Obviously the price is too high when you lose your brothers and your father but I had a task to do.'

She continues in this vein for a while before saying more wistfully: 'You know, Eleanor, being back in England, seeing friends from my time at Oxford makes me think how extraordinary my own life has been. Their lives have had stability; husbands, wives, children, jobs. Whereas I have achieved great heights of fame, but have paid dearly. I only entered poli-tics out of duty when my father was in prison. I thought it was temporary, that I would be a diplomat again when he was released. But he wasn't.'

There is no stopping her now. 'All my life I have been looking for an exit route. But the more I tried to get out of politics, the more it embraced me. In 1997, I thought, enough: I have small children, my mother is sick, I will tend to my personal affairs. But then my party said, "There is no one else who can lead us, you must fight on." I have been prime minister twice, to do it a third time holds little charm, but my people would vote me back tomorrow.'

This spiel is vintage Bhutto. Nothing is her fault, forces have acted upon her; the corruption charges are a political conspiracy; she is a politician only out of 'duty'. It is a touching portrait, but I just don't buy it. She is just not the 'poor little me' type. I have never met such an imperious woman; Blair's babes fade into insignificance in comparison. She is just too smooth, the setting too opulent, the 'I am a woman of the people' line just a bit rich coming from such a privileged mouth. As an undergraduate – she was president of the Oxford Union – she drove a yellow MG, hung out in the south of France and worked closely with Peter Mandelson on student politics.

Her 'good friend Peter', the king of spin himself, would be proud of the way Bhutto is trying to whitewash herself now. But, tellingly, her old pal has not been rallying to the cause. 'No, I haven't seen him,' says Bhutto, 'I feel inhibited to see old friends who are now powerful men because I don't want it to be misconstrued.' Our own iron lady has – perhaps unsurprisingly – been much more helpful. 'Margaret Thatcher has been very kind to me, she understands how it is to be a woman in a man's world. I visit her sometimes for advice and support, she is very good at that.' General Pinochet, Benazir Bhutto – what interesting affairs Thatcher's tea parties are becoming. And how sad that Bhutto, who began by flying the flag for a new generation, should wind up in their has-beens club.

MELANIE PHILLIPS
1951–

One of the most controversial voices in British journalism, Phillips began her career as a scion of the left, as News Editor of the *Guardian*, Britain's most influential liberal newspaper. She quickly became disenchanted with the lack of rigour in the left's view and began to question all its holy grails. She has since become a columnist whom her former friends love to hate but have to respect. After writing for the *Guardian* she moved to the *Observer* and then the *Sunday Times*, leaving there to write for the right-wing tabloid the *Daily Mail*.

This article attacking the idea that in education 'all must have prizes' sums up much of her critique.

Everybody Wins and All Must Have Prizes

22 September 2003, *Daily Mail*

Surely, in the immortal words of John McEnroe, they cannot be serious? Alas, the latest pronouncement from those in charge of our exam system is truly beyond satire.

Their new idea for boosting examination success is to abolish the very idea of failure, along with the difference between the right and the wrong answer to a question.

The Qualifications and Curriculum Authority has told those marking the school curriculum tests that 'F' for 'Fail' is to be replaced by 'N' for 'Nearly', and that maths questions are to be marked 'creditworthy' or 'not creditworthy' instead of correct or incorrect. A QCA spokesman said – apparently with a straight face – that if pupils don't pass these tests it doesn't mean they have failed, because they will have 'nearly reached the target'.

This may seem ridiculous beyond parody (will the Conservatives now claim they 'nearly' won the Brent East by-election?). Tragically, however, it is merely the logical outcome of an education system which is steadily destroying the concept of achievement itself.

A-level standards have now become so degraded, with universities unable to distinguish between pupils obtaining vast numbers of top grades, that the Government has floated the preposterous suggestion of admission by lottery. Tomorrow Professor Steven Schwartz, the Government's adviser on university admissions, is expected to propose that the universities lower the A-level grades required of children from sink schools.

This grossly unjust proposal reflects the neanderthal view that real intellectual achievement is a conspiracy against the working class. The Government has dismally failed to correct the appalling standards which act as the real bar to university for able pupils from many schools in poor areas. It also refuses to accept that many pupils at such schools understandably believe that a university degree is of less use than proper training for a skilled job.

Actual facts like these, however, can't be expected to block the path of an ideological fixation. Professor Schwartz wants to set up a two-tier admissions procedure to shoe-horn into university the pupils that both he and the Government unfairly assume are discriminated against – a travesty that will destroy the worth of such qualifications altogether.

Labour's obsession with identical educational achievement is strongly echoed by the entrenched belief in the education world that sheep must never be sorted from goats. Getting the correct answer or passing an exam is not as important as preventing pupils from having their feelings hurt.

Such political and education ideologues believe that the education system has failed if it fails anyone. That's why the government wants half the population to have a university degree.

Schools Minister, David Miliband, condemns as elitist those who argue that only relatively few can benefit from a university education. Expect to hear a lot more of such ministerial class-war sneering as the university top-up fees argument rages. Yet top-up fees have only become necessary because successive governments have hugely expanded university numbers.

This expansion has itself reduced achievement and caused rampant exam grade inflation, as standards are lowered to funnel more students into higher education. Those who have blown the whistle on this corruption are either denounced or ignored. Only recently David Kent, a senior maths examiner, revealed how he was forced to lower the GCSE pass mark to avoid failing too many students because their performance was so poor.

The progressive loss of any reliable, objective measure of achievement, along with a widening choice of soft subjects, means that ever more students are apparently qualified for university but with ever less knowledge. The result is not just an explosion of absurd degree courses, but the standard of proper subjects is also being forced downwards.

Universities are now heavily into remedial work for the many students who haven't learnt enough to keep up. But since these institutions receive funds in proportion to the numbers getting good degrees, the standard of those qualifications is going down.

These students can't do the work because the A-level has been dumbed down. That's because the GCSE, the exam 'no-one could fail', has in turn been of such a low standard: and the reason for that was to give the majority of 16-year-olds a qualification.

The futility of that particular aim was shown up by last week's OECD figures which revealed Britain's dismal international education performance at 16, despite many more students going to university.

Against the background of our ruined A-levels, Professor Schwartz is expected to propose US-style intelligence tests as a university entrance requirement. But crucially, such tests do not require evidence of an appropriate level of knowledge.

This is a proposal that has nothing to do with concern over education standards, and everything to do with forcing up the proportion of working-class students. Indeed, the universities will only be able to charge top-up fees if they prove they are taking more children from poor schools.

In this way, ministers will effectively put a gun to the universities' heads to reduce standards, in order to promote the government's programme of crude social engineering at the expense of academic rigour. And to cap this destruction of the education system, students will be forced to pay for the privilege.

The mess in which the government is in over top-up fees is deepening into wild incoherence. Thus the Education Secretary Charles Clarke lets it be known that he will exempt the poorest students – while the Prime Minister confides that he is most worried about resistance from the middle classes.

Such political pain is particularly pointless, since top-up fees will solve nothing. They will need to be set far higher if the universities are to stave off bankruptcy. They will tighten still further the government's grip on the universities' windpipes. And they will be subsidising useless degree courses and declining educational achievement.

The collapse in education and the corruption of the universities can only be halted if these institutions are set free from government control. That would mean they would have to charge fees. Fair access could be ensured by channelling higher education funds into weighted vouchers which could then be topped up, supplemented by scholarships and bursaries. Putting power into the hands of education consumers would spell an end to meaningless degree courses and create more pressure for high quality vocational training.

Those who say this is elitist are themselves responsible for making qualifications at every stage increasingly worthless. In fact they are the real elitists, since their charge that it is wrong to deprive people of a university education reveals that they think any other qualification is demeaning and without merit.

The Prime Minister insists he will not be deflected over top-up fees. He thinks he is being radical by introducing the market into higher education. He does not realise that his whole education policy is utterly wrong and misguided, hijacked by the very ideology of levelling down that he appears to imagine he is opposing.

Tony Blair made education reform the litmus test of his government's success. With his policy descending into farce, he will doubtless continue to delude himself that he is 'nearly' becoming 'creditworthy'. The rest of us may conclude instead that he has simply failed.

MARIE COLVIN

1957–

Born and raised in New York, Colvin's career as a war correspondent for Britain's *Sunday Times* has seen her cover conflicts in the Balkans, Chechnya and East Timor, where she helped to save the lives of 1,500 women and children besieged by Indonesian troops.

In 2001 she lost an eye while on assignment as the first foreign reporter to enter northern Sri Lanka (a Tamil-held territory) for six years.

One of the most fearless of all contemporary war reporters, Colvin has nurtured strong relationships with the leaders and rebels behind the headlines. In this article, written just after Yasser Arafat's death, she describes the reality of this complex man and his chaotic entourage.

The Arafat I Knew

14 November 2004, *Sunday Times*

When I first met Yasser Arafat, the legend was larger than the reality. He was described both as a charismatic terrorist chieftain and an inspirational national leader. In reality he was a small, obsessive figure who appeared happiest behind a desk and seemed unlikely to be leader of anything, let alone one of the most fractious political movements on earth.

It took me years to figure out why this unprepossessing man was the undisputed father of the Palestinian nation.

I first met Arafat in 1987 when he was living in exile in a bougainvillea-draped villa in Tunis. He had created a mini-world within a world. Most of the big cheeses of the Palestine Liberation Organisation lived nearby, and most slept all day while the Tunisians went about their business.

The key was to adopt PLO time: everything happened after dark, mostly at 3 am, it seemed. I remember thinking that the key to Arafat's success was that he simply tired everyone out.

They were places of camaraderie, these houses of waiting for Arafat. I would sit up all night, sipping coffee, smoking endless cigarettes, listening to stories of Palestine and Beirut and the venting of frustration about Arafat. The complaints were tinged with respect and even fear. The apocryphal story everyone told was of a Japanese journalist who had waited so long for an interview with Arafat that he had enough time to learn Arabic.

Arafat had not always wielded such authority. Abu Iyad, his number three and the architect of the notorious Black September group, got so frustrated in one meeting that he threw a shoe at the Palestinian leader, a grave insult in the Arab world – 'You are lower than my shoe' is the worst thing you can say without bringing in someone's mother.

He returned from this meeting (I was still waiting for my interview) to tell me ruefully about the early days in the 1960s when the underground Palestinian leaders had put Arafat up as their public face because he had so much energy but so little authority. They wanted to continue the revolution out of the glare of attention from either the press or intelligence agencies and they thought he would be a weak figurehead while they ran the show.

'And look where we are now!' Iyad sputtered in exasperation. 'Arafat, Arafat, Arafat.'

When I finally met him it was in a setting that he would obsessively replicate wherever he went, and that I would see for the next 15 years in different countries.

He sat behind a desk in a scruffy room laden with symbols, rather like a medieval painting. Behind him was a mural of Jerusalem's golden dome of the Haram al-Sharif, the Muslims' third most holy place in the city he claimed as the Palestinian capital.

A television was in the corner, which in Tunis ran Tom and Jerry cartoons. Later, in Gaza, after he had returned from exile under the 1993 Oslo peace accord with Israel, it was tuned to CNN World.

On his desk, always, were a Palestinian flag and a 2ft-high pile of papers. He was in a uniform of his own creation, with obscure medals – the one he most liked explaining was the golden pin of a phoenix, whose mythical rise from the fire symbolised to him the Palestinian people.

And always the black and white keffiyeh (headscarf), pristine and pressed, pinned exactly over his right shoulder in the shape of the future state of Palestine.

The call to see him would always come after midnight. It would be brief: Abu Ammar, as he was known to all Palestinians, wants you. After the hours of waiting, there would then be a drive at terrifying speed through darkened streets.

Why? It became clear that he never planned ahead but when he gave an order he expected immediate obedience.

I later realised that this could sum up all of his dealings with everyone from the lowliest bodyguard to the American president. He could have towering rages.

Whatever house in whatever country would shake with his tirades, expletives in his Egyptian accent. One waited out the storm.

On that first visit I walked into his Tunis villa through a lounging crowd of smoking, uniformed men with machineguns and revolvers casually at their hips. His room was brightly lit. Behind the desk was a tiny man with big lips, a scraggly chin growth that was not quite a beard (he once told me exactly how many minutes he saved a year by shaving only every five days), bulging eyes behind oversize black-rimmed glasses and no obvious charisma.

I think his first words to me were, 'And what do you want?' As if he didn't know. It was like meeting a fussy hotel clerk in a provincial capital.

He was a difficult interview. I came to realise this was because at all times he was speaking to four constituencies – Palestinians in exile, Palestinians in the West Bank and Gaza, the Arab world and finally a western audience.

Years later I found myself unexpectedly sympathising with Madeleine Albright, the American Secretary of State, when I sat in on his end of a telephone conversation with her. She was trying to persuade him to stand down Palestinian demonstrations against a new Jewish settlement. He said he couldn't stop the violence until the Israeli bulldozers stopped.

Albright said: 'Let's not get into a discussion of which came first, the chicken or the egg.' To which Arafat's cryptic reply was: 'But not to forget in the end there is the hen and there is the egg.' There was a silence on her side – boy, did I understand.

When he was not in a formal situation, a different, earthy, even funny person emerged. It was travelling in a plane with him to Washington, to Norway for the Nobel peace prize, to see Colonel Muammar Gadaffi in Libya, and in his convoy as he crossed into Gaza in 1994 as the returning leader, that I came to understand him better.

On the plane to Libya, he worked through a mass of papers, always with his green pen. Without a break of stride after landing, he got into the limousine to the hotel Gadaffi had assigned him. But when Gadaffi then did not see him for 12 hours, Arafat took it as an insult.

He sent me in his convoy back to the airport. It was a feint. The call immediately came that the Libyan leader wanted to see him, so my driver drove at 100mph to join him at Gadaffi's headquarters.

Gadaffi, in his finest robes, greeted Arafat then turned and noticed me. 'Mary,' he asked (I knew him, too, but he has never been able to pronounce my name), 'what are you doing here?' It was as if I had wandered in off the street.

'She's with me,' Arafat said proudly, as if we were at a London film premiere. He then went on to lie outrageously about the state of my nose, which at the time was on the wrong side of my face. Arafat told Gadaffi the Israelis had broken it. The truth was that Palestinian demonstrators had thrown a rock through the window of my car when I was posing as a Jewish settler on a reporting assignment.

It was on this trip that I also discovered the secret of Arafat's unusual uniforms. I used to wonder where he got them and why they were always so well laundered – until I stayed with him in a VIP villa after flying in from Gaza.

This is what would happen: his bodyguards (all male, one of whom he raised from orphanhood) would go out shopping – they all knew Arafat's size. They would buy presents for their families and then they would stop by an army surplus shop.

There always was one, whether they were in an African capital or in Stockholm. There they would purchase a crisp, second-hand uniform and return with it to add to his ever-growing stock.

On the plane, they undressed him. There was no embarrassment. They took off his uniform, and he got into a track suit. Senior members of his leadership found this the best time to talk to him, the only time there were no interruptions. Last to come off was his keffiyeh. And yes, he was totally bald.

These once-young bodyguards, some now middle-aged, ironed his keffiyeh, kept his uniform clean and put him to bed. They slept outside his door.

I think it was this intimacy that sparked the Israeli propaganda that Arafat was homosexual. But intimacy is very different from sexuality, and Arafat was always ferociously heterosexual.

He loved saying to me, 'I am married to Palestine.' But there was always a woman. There was the Palestinian woman with impeccable revolutionary credentials and the big hips he so liked. Then there was the Egyptian, who travelled with him and descended the presidential plane with inappropriate red high heels.

And then there was Suha. Everyone around him reacted to the emergence of Suha Tawil, the daughter of a Palestinian businessman, with the jealousy of lovers.

Their male world was disrupted: Arafat had actually publicly acknowledged a woman. Not only that: he married her, after a showdown with her mother.

I remember my first intimation that this French-coutured, buxom blonde might be more than a secretary and translator, which was how she first joined his circle.

We were on a plane, it was dark and he had taken off the Chelsea boots he always wore. She had taken off her court heels. In the dark, I saw that they were playing footsie as his bodyguards slept.

A few months later, Arafat crashed in a desert storm in Libya and suffered the head injury that led to brain surgery in Jordan and the shakes be suffered afterwards. Among the photographs found in his pocket was one that showed Arafat dancing with abandon, twirling his keffiyeh as he held Suha's hand.

She was disliked in his circle, though I always thought this was unfair. Most of the criticism was for things that any woman – raised as she had been in exile with her wealthy parents in bourgeois circles in Paris – thought normal. She had married a president, and she liked the red carpet. She wanted a decent house, not a home that was a doss house for his extended entourage.

To Arafat, womanly ways were a mystery. I remember when I drove into Gaza with him on his return from exile that Suha's first impulse was to find a hairdresser. She came back with hair that was, to put it kindly, a greeny orange rather than blonde. Arafat came into their bedroom and joked, 'Women! They are always changing the colour of their hair. Every time you see them!' He had no idea that Suha was mortified by the appalling coiffure.

He was mystified by all the unguents and creams that filled their bathroom; even more so by the black lace lingerie that would be hanging in the shower to dry.

When we were flying to Oslo, where he and Shimon Peres would receive the Nobel peace prize, the pilot of his plane came on the intercom to say: 'Ladies and gentlemen, I am proud to be flying the president of Palestine . . .' Arafat interrupted him, shouting from his back seat like a schoolboy at the back of the bus: 'There are no ladies here!' and giggling to the accompaniment of guffaws from around the plane.

They could not have been more different. Suha wanted to live in the biggest house in Gaza, but Arafat would have none of it. He eventually agreed to rent a three-bedroom home: he thought even that a bit of an extravagance but probably necessary if one had a woman around.

He loved his baby daughter, Zahwa, named after his mother, but played with her as if she was an exotic marmoset, unrelated to his own species – much less of his blood.

One of his outstanding characteristics was his complete indifference to creature comforts. He lived a spartan life by choice: he wore the same thing every day, ate the same thing every day. He liked his honey, put hot tea on his cornflakes (how could he?) and always had a healthy lunch of chicken, fish and vegetables – to the dismay of his aides, who had to eat with him and got bored with the presidential fare.

If his home in Tunis was virtually a public thoroughfare, the changes after he moved back to Gaza took adjusting to. I remember late at night at the new presidential home/office there, standing around with his aides, smoking as one always did. I put a cigarette out on the floor, unthinking, as had always been the custom in all of his abodes.

A small, elderly man left his seat (there were always rooms of people waiting for Arafat, whatever the hour, wherever he was, and he always saw all of them) and said with dignity: 'Please pick up your cigarette. This is the house of the president.'

I was embarrassed. It was a new world, one he never really changed to fit in with. Unlike Arafat and the other returning exiles, men in Gaza and the West Bank lived with their families, went to jobs in the daytime and cared about education and road maintenance.

The only time I saw Arafat nervous was the night before that return to Gaza. There had been protests by Hamas, the Islamic fundamentalist group, which saw its power and influence being challenged by the return of the PLO. Arafat's photograph had been torn up on television. He was unsure of his welcome and thought he might be attacked by Hamas on his return. 'I am ready to die,' he said that night as he unwound his keffiyeh.

The homecoming was a huge event. Palestinians in Gaza had lived for years on the legends of the virile young PLO fighters in exile, and the crowds went wild when the buses carrying the returning heroes arrived. The cheers turned to gasps, however, when the doors opened and a motley crew of fat, pot-bellied, middle aged men stepped down from the buses. The fighters had grown old in their exile.

Appearances were deceptive. Shortly afterwards, Hamas did attack, attempting an assault on Arafat's house. But, on his orders, the pot-bellies easily fought off the fundamentalists, killing about a dozen.

One of the greatest problems with Arafat was that he really was ready to die. That was when he was happiest. Most recently, when I saw him in his Ramallah headquarters on the West Bank, it was under Israeli shellfire, but he would repeat: 'I am ready to be a martyr.'

The prospect seemed to invigorate him. Months before, over lunch, he had seemed diminished, suddenly old and frail. There were non-sequiturs and long gaps in conversation. He would start to answer a question, then look into space for four minutes or so before continuing. Four minutes is a long time in a conversation, but the aides who always lunched with him kept quiet until he resumed speaking.

His skin had turned almost translucent, and he showed me his hands – always tiny and neat – and said: 'I don't get enough sun. I need sun.' I joked about Tunis, when his need for sun had led him to buy a sun lamp and, in a very Arafat way, to ignore the instructions for caution and leave his hands under the sun lamp for half an hour. They were burned and mottled for years after that. He didn't like my joke.

But during the Ramallah siege, he suddenly looked and acted 20 years younger. His shakes stopped. His voice strengthened. Sometimes, when I would come into his office, he would be marching around the conference table, arms swinging, eyes fixed on the carpet, wearing the heavy wool military jacket he wore in all seasons, at the same pace he had held when in Tunis he marched around the swimming pool in which he never swam.

It was his only exercise and he was impervious to the facile metaphor that marching in circles was how he was leading the Palestinian people.

In Ramallah the Israelis reduced his world to four rooms surrounded by a moonscape of rubble, which he could never leave without his old enemy Ariel Sharon trying to deport him. When I last saw him, in a cramped room in these Muqata headquarters, he was at his most relaxed. He leaned back in an oversized chair, sipped a cup of sweet milky tea, and offered a plate of Arabic pastries that had been dropped off with his guards by a well-wisher.

In this mad landscape, it was typical Arafat to talk about the mundane details of his confinement. When I asked him what had changed in his leadership, he said: 'Much more paperwork. Nobody can travel to see me because of the Israeli siege of our cities. So they send a report, as you see.'

He was reading through a by now 3ft pile of papers, initialling every one with his trademark green pen.

So, who was Yasser Arafat? I've thought about that question a lot in the past week as Suha got her revenge and banned everyone from his deathbed.

'Finally, I control my husband,' was her message, but it was ill-judged.

I remember when I was on his tiny plane flying from Tunis to Washington in 1993 for the White House handshake with Yitzhak Rabin and Bill Clinton that sealed the Oslo accords and the return from exile. Arafat's guards put him to bed in the back seat. Then they came to ask me: 'Marie, will we have to fight when we land?'

This question says everything about the Palestinians. As a western reporter, I thought the idea that they would land in America and find guns blazing absurd. But they believed it probable and had got on the plane ready to die for Arafat.

What few westerners realise is that the Palestinians are hated throughout the Arab world (and that absolutely nobody dresses like Arafat). He could smarm the Saudis and then blackmail them; he could escape Hafez al-Assad after the Syrian leader jailed him and sentenced him to death; and he kissed everyone far too much, both Saddam Hussein and me. When he kissed me 17 times after my eye was injured, and even kissed my eye patch, his bodyguards intervened and said, 'Enough, Abu Ammar.'

The only time I ever got him really talking was when he reminisced about his childhood in British-occupied Jerusalem. (He was actually born in Cairo, but after his mother died he spent years in Jerusalem and later claimed he was born there.) He was beloved by the Palestinians, all flaws included, because he created their identity and nationality out of what had previously been simply a horde of unwanted refugees. Even though he dressed as no Palestinian would, they were recognised around the world by the symbol of this strange little man with big glasses.

The key to his success in winning the loyalty of the Palestinians lay in his absolute self-belief, boundless energy and inability to feel embarrassed. He had utter faith in himself as the personification of the nation he had conjured up; and he would go anywhere, do anything, say anything to further this cause. He also had no compunction about using violence both against Hamas and the Israelis.

He privately said he opposed suicide bombings but his failure to stop them was part of his greater failure. He had created the Palestinian nation but ultimately could not control the forces he unleashed.

Nor did he have the vision to turn his creation into a state. Those uniforms spoke volumes: he would not give up being a guerrilla leader to become the statesman the Palestinians so badly need.

EMANCIPATION &
HAVING IT ALL

DJUNA BARNES
1892–1982

Poet, playwright, novelist and illustrator, Djuna Barnes produced a huge variety of work, beginning with her groundbreaking journalism of the early 1900s. One of the very first writers to break with the journalistic tradition of objectivity and distance, she insinuated herself directly into her work, helping to invent the experiential style which would later become known as 'gonzo' and be lauded in the work of writers such as Tom Wolfe and Hunter S. Thompson.

The following article is a strong example of this technique, and also shows off the impressionistic writing style that Barnes developed throughout her fiction. Although never part of the suffragist movement herself, their struggles were garnering huge attention and Barnes decided that she could best communicate these by sharing in the experience of being force-fed. She was clearly prepared to suffer for her art . . .

How It Feels to be Forcibly Fed

6 September 1914, *New York World*

I have been forcibly fed!

In just what relation to the other incidents in my life does this one stand? For me it was an experiment. It was only tragic in my imagination. But it offered sensations sufficiently poignant to compel comprehension of certain of the day's phenomena.

The hall they took me down was long and faintly lighted. I could hear the doctor walking ahead of me, stepping as all doctors step, with that little confiding gait that horses must have returning from funerals. It is not a sad or mournful step; perhaps it suggests suppressed satisfaction.

Every now and then one of the four men that followed turned his head to look at me; a woman by the stairs gazed wonderingly – or was it contemptuously – as I passed.

They brought me into a great room. A table loomed before me; my mind sensed it pregnant with the pains of the future – it was the table whereon I must lie.

The doctor opened his bag, took out a heavy, white gown, a small white cap, a sheet, and laid them all upon the table.

Out across the city, in a flat, frail, coherent yet incoherent monotone, resounded the song of a million machines doing their bit in the universal whole. And the murmur was vital and confounding, for what was before me knew no song.

I shall be strictly professional, I assured myself. If it be an ordeal, it is familiar to my sex at this time; other women have suffered it in acute reality. Surely I have as much nerve as my English sisters? Then I held myself steady. I thought so, and I caught sight of my face in the glass. It was quite white; and I was swallowing convulsively.

And then I knew my soul stood terrified before a little yard of red rubber tubing.

The doctor was saying, 'Help her upon the table.'

He was tying thin, twisted tapes about his arm; he was testing his instruments. He took the loose end of the sheet and began to bind me: he wrapped it round and round me, my arms tight to my sides, wrapped it up to my throat so that I could not move. I lay in as long and unbroken lines as any corpse – unbroken, definite lines that stretched away beyond my vision, for I saw only the skylight. My eyes wandered, outcasts in a world they knew.

It was the most concentrated moment of my life.

Three of the men approached me. The fourth stood at a distance, looking at the slow, crawling hands of a watch. The three took me not unkindly, but quite without compassion, one by the head, one by the feet; one sprawled above me, holding my hands down at my hips.

All life's problems had now been reduced to one simple act – to swallow or to choke. As I lay in passive revolt, a quizzical thought wandered across my beleaguered mind: This, at least, is one picture that will never go into the family album.

Oh, this ridiculous perturbation! – I reassured myself. Yet how imagination can obsess! It is the truth that the lights of the windows – pictures of a city's skyline – the walls, the men, all went out into a great blank as the doctor leaned down. Then suddenly the dark broke into a blotch of light, as he trailed the electric bulb up and down and across my face, stopping to examine my throat to make sure I was fully capable of swallowing.

He sprayed both nostrils with a mixture of cocaine and disinfectant. As it reached my throat, it burned and burned.

There was no progress on this pilgrimage. Now I abandoned myself. I was in the valley, and it seemed years that I lay there watching the pitcher as it rose in the hand of the doctor and hung, a devilish, inhuman menace. In it was the liquid food I was to have. It was milk, but I could not tell what it was, for all things are alike when they reach the stomach by a rubber tube.

He had inserted the red tubing, with the funnel at the end, through my nose into the passages of the throat. It is utterly impossible to describe the anguish of it.

The hands above my head tightened into a vise, and like answering vises the hands at my hips and those at my feet grew rigid and secure.

Unbidden visions of remote horrors danced madly through my mind. There arose the hideous thought of being gripped in the tentacles of some monster devil fish in the depths of a tropic sea, as the liquid slowly sensed its way along innumerable endless passages that seemed to traverse my nose, my ears, the inner interstices of my throbbing head. Unsuspected nerves thrilled pain tidings that racked the area of my face and bosom. They seared along my spine. They set my heart at catapultic plunging.

An instant that was an hour, and the liquid had reached my throat. It was ice cold, and sweat as cold broke out upon my forehead.

Still my heart plunged on with the irregular, meaningless motion that sunlight reflected from a mirror casts upon a wall. A dull ache grew and spread from my shoulders into the whole area of my back and through my chest.

The pit of my stomach had lapsed long ago, had gone out into absolute vacancy. Things around began to move lethargically; the electric light to my left took a hazy step or two toward the clock, which lurched forward to meet it; the windows could not keep still. I, too, was detached and moved as the room moved. The doctor's eyes were always just before me. And I knew then that I was fainting. I struggled against surrender. It was the futile defiance of nightmare. My utter hopelessness was a pain. I was conscious only of head and feet and that spot where someone was holding me by the hips.

Still the liquid trickled irresistibly down the tubing into my throat; every drop seemed a quart, and every quart slid over and down into space. I had lapsed into a physical mechanism without power to oppose or resent the outrage to my will.

The spirit was betrayed by the body's weakness. There it is — the outraged will. If I, playacting, felt my being burning with revolt at this brutal usurpation of my own functions, how they who actually suffered the ordeal in its acutest horror must have flamed at the violation of the sanctuaries of their spirits.

I saw in my hysteria a vision of a hundred women in grim prison hospitals, bound and shrouded on tables just like this, held in the rough grip of callous warders while white-robed doctors thrust rubber tubing into the delicate interstices of their nostrils and forced into their helpless bodies the crude fuel to sustain the life they longed to sacrifice.

Science had at last, then, deprived us of the right to die.

Still the liquid trickled irresistibly down the tubing into my throat.

Was my body so inept, I asked myself, as to be incapable of further struggle? Was the will powerless to so constrict that narrow passage to the life reservoir as to dam the hated flow? The thought flashed a defiant command to supine muscles. They gripped my throat with strangling bonds. Ominous shivers shook my body.

'Be careful – you'll choke,' shouted the doctor in my ear.

One could still choke, then. At least one could if the nerves did not betray.

And if one insisted on choking – what then? Would they – the callous warders and the servile doctors – ruthlessly persist, even with grim death at their elbow?

Think of the paradox: those white robes assumed for the work of prolonging life would then be no better than shrouds; the linen envelope encasing the defiant victim a winding sheet.

Limits surely there are to the subservience even of those who must sternly execute the law. At least I have never heard of a militant choking herself into eternity.

It was over. I stood up, swaying in the returning light; I had shared the greatest experience of the bravest of my sex. The torture and outrage of it burned in my mind; a dull, shapeless, wordless anger arose to my lips, but I only smiled. The doctor had removed the towel about his face. The little, red mustache upon his upper lip was drawn out in a line of pleasant understanding. He had forgotten all but the play. The four men, having finished their minor roles in one minor tragedy, were already filing out at the door.

'Isn't there any other way of tying a person up?' I asked. 'That thing looks like – '

'Yes, I know,' he said, gently.

SYLVIA PANKHURST
1882–1960

Along with her mother, Emmeline, and sister, Christabel, the British suffragette, Sylvia Pankhurst, is best known for her committed and ultimately successful struggle to win the vote for women. A profilic writer and activist, she also campaigned on a range of other issues, and in 1914 created her own newspaper, *The Woman's Dreadnought*, in which to air these views. In the following article she explains the thinking behind her drive for women's suffrage, the cause for which she would soon become famous, if not legendary.

Human Suffrage

18 December 1915, *The Woman's Dreadnought*

Before the War large numbers of women and men were giving all their thought and energy to securing a million votes for the women of the British Isles – a million votes for thirteen million women!

The demand was recommended on account of its 'moderation.' In the light of the great world conflict does it not seem miserably inadequate, timidly weak and mean?

'I believe that a woman should have a vote if she pays rates and taxes.' How that phrase jars and wearies one? Can any tax count beside the toil of hand and brain that a human worker gives in a life time, or in comparison with the bringing into the world of another living, sentient human being, whose thoughts and deeds may add immeasurably to the common stock? When a man goes out to take part in the hideous slaughter of the battlefield the paying of rates and taxes is a forgotten thought to him; the fact that he has paid cannot buy him off, and his being too poor for taxing will not save him from being sent to the front if Conscription comes.

Cast away the trivial ideas of the professional politician. The world conflict, with its dehumanising hate and violence, and the widespread peril and loss that draw poor mothers and wives together, should cause our minds to dwell only on real, vital things.

What is a vote but a voice in the affairs that concern us all? Surely there was never a time in which we could see so clearly as now that the interests of all the people are closely interwoven, and that everyone of us must have a vote in the management of our world.

Cast away the idea that it is expedient to ask for an instalment of justice in accordance with some petty, ill-drafted, fugitive politician's rule, instead of basing our demand on the infinite and eternal fact of our common humanity.

In the hard, hungry days that followed the Napoleonic wars, the brave old reformers did not want the vote for merely academic reasons. They fought for it because they saw in it a means of giving all the people the power to free themselves from gaunt and urgent want, and to protect themselves from cruel exploitation and harsh injustice. They wanted to give every man an equal chance to share in controlling the destinies of the nation.

Those old reformers asked for no half-measures, suggested no paltering compromises, but demanded Universal Suffrage. They were determined to wring from the autocrats in power as much justice as they could, and not to abate their demands until they had got all they asked. Theirs is a spirit that we may well emulate. Our experiences are likely to reproduce theirs in many things.

The War, with its waste and destruction, is intensifying the international strife that is always with us, the struggle of human evolution towards a higher development of social life.

In every nation the forces of reaction are gaining ground because of War conditions. Militarism is becoming more strongly entrenched.

Unorganised individualism is shown to be wasteful, and the extraordinary strain which war is putting upon human energy and material resources, has necessitated, and after the War will continue to necessitate, in every country more extensive control and co-ordination by the central government than has hitherto been known.

State action may be of two kinds. It may mean compulsory regulation of the bulk of the population by a small official class, in the interests of the powerful wealthy few who pull the strings – the vast mass of the people being used as mere pawns in an almost limitless army. Or State action may mean the co-operation of free citizens, each with an equal voice in the decisions which are adopted for the benefit of all.

After the War, in every country the struggle that is always going on between these two ideas, the idea of coercion and the idea of co-operation, will be intensified, and become the supreme issue, both in national and international affairs. In the international field the application of these ideas will be seen, on the one hand by a demand for larger armies and navies, a warfare of tariffs, and a more truculent dealing with the claims of rival nations. On the other hand will be a striving towards international arbitration and disarmament, and the building up of a league of peace to include all nations.

Our attitude towards the franchise issue will be one of the test questions which shall decide whether we are on the side of coercion or on that of co-operation.

At present the franchise qualification in this country is based on property. It is suggested that there should also be a qualification for naval and military service. The forms of service which human beings can render to the nation are infinite. Who shall measure them or decide between them? Every one of us should spend our lives in doing some part of the general service. The only qualification on which we should base our demand for the franchise is that of our common humanity. We should demand a vote for every human being of full age, without regard to property or sex.

The article which we publish from Martina Kramers, of Holland, shows us that the Dutch women have adopted the procedure which the Women's Suffrage Movement has hitherto followed here. When the men had only a narrow and restricted franchise, the Dutch women Suffragists asked that that narrow franchise should be extended to women also. Now that Manhood Suffrage has been extended to the men of Holland, the women at last are pressing for a vote for every woman. Hitherto, they have been sitting on the fence of compromise, and have refrained from declaring themselves for human suffrage. Only now are they making whole-hearted common cause with the forces of democracy.

In every country where the women have begun working for their enfranchisement before the enactment of Manhood Suffrage, the same thing appears to have happened. The women have not thought it expedient to demand human suffrage; they have asked for admission to the existing narrow franchise. *But in each country they have had to wait until the narrow franchise has been swept away.*

They have had the humiliation of seeing their demand for citizenship thrust aside again and again, whilst men have secured concession after concession, until at last, by the granting of Manhood Suffrage, the principle of human right to the franchise has been admitted. Then, in Australia, New Zealand, Finland, Norway, Denmark, Iceland, and thirteen States of America full human suffrage, including men and women, has been secured in a comparatively short time.

In no country, save the little Isle of Man with its handful of inhabitants, *have women succeeded in winning the vote before the property qualification for men had been abolished.*

This fact should not for one moment lead us to think that women should wait for the vote in this country until men have secured Manhood Suffrage. No, indeed! It should spur us on to throw ourselves unreservedly into the struggle for human Suffrage, for every woman and for every man.

Every property qualification must of necessity act more unjustly towards women than towards men, because so much of women's service receives no monetary recompense, because the husbands, and, not the wives, are householders.

It is true that the franchise on the men's present terms would give a majority of votes to women of the working class, because the working class is actually in such an immense majority; but an undue proportion of the women voters of every class would be elderly widows, whose time for developing new ideas, in most cases, has gone by. The young mother with her children growing up around her, who should be voicing the ideals of the coming womanhood, would be disqualified, together with the mass of women factory workers, who need the power of the vote most urgently.

How can we expect that such a restricted form of franchise should arouse that immense volume of popular enthusiasm that assuredly will be needed to sweep votes for women past the old political prejudices, on to the Statute Book?

Women who cling to the narrow demand for the old out-of-date form of franchise will be driven into the camp of the coercionists, and separated from the great democratic movement which, in spite of all attempts at restriction, is growing and consolidating and, perhaps even before the War is over, will arise in full force of overwhelming fervour to demand that the democratic principle shall be applied to every department of our national life.

People say: 'You cannot ask for a vote for every woman, because every man has not got one'; and add: 'You must not ask for a vote for every woman, because the men ought to get more votes, if they want them, for themselves.'

Such arguments are cramping and destructive, they should be cast away from us – lovers of freedom. Fight for freedom for all humanity – they make no distinction of sex.

Surely it is time that the British Suffrage movement should come together, reorganise its programme, and write on its banners: 'Human Suffrage – a vote for every man and woman of full age!'

MRS ALFRED SIDGWICK

For a woman who wrote numerous books and articles under the name of her philosopher husband (her own married name was Cecily Ullman Sidgwick), the writer here provides a wide-ranging and enlightened response to the still-vexing question of whether married women (especially those with children) should work.

Should *Married* Women Work?

1924, *Good Housekeeping*

No, they should not. They should sit at home while their husbands work for them. The nursery and the kitchen should be their kingdoms and the church their solace. We all take pleasure in the picture, but know in our hearts that it does not fill the bill. Some of us think the question itself tomfoolery. Who is to lay down the law for a class, the members of which are so diverse? Not public opinion in an age that is trying to liberate women, and not legislation in a country that no longer places them with children and lunatics.

At the end of the last century, a well-known novelist, interested in social questions, said that women did not want to work. They wanted to marry a man who worked for them. In the Ideal Home the man earns money in the market-place and the woman spends it in the house. His wishes are her law and his comfort her preoccupation. Where there are children, she devotes herself to them night and day, having neither wishes nor business of her own, but, becoming by marriage the contented slave of her family. This, again, is a picture we accept without question and admire exceedingly. We figure the smiling, slightly embonpoint matron, for ever busy, often tired, still the devoted wife, always the warm, tender mother, ready with stores of affection for the grandchildren about to come. A very pretty picture and, for all sorts and conditions, greatly to be desired.

The troublesome truth is that most pretty pictures bear an imperfect likeness to real life. They turn a blind eye to all the cases that are not pretty. If married women must not work outside the home, what are those women to do who have little mouths to feed and whose husbands fail them? Some men are ne'er-do-wells, some spend, some drink, some inconsiderately die. Their wives cannot sit at home, their children on their knees, singing little songs to them and teaching them their letters. They have to go out and earn what they may at any work they can do. I know one such who was a first-rate cook, earning high wages in rich men's houses and living in great comfort. She married a sickly little man, bore him three children, lost him, and now works as she never worked before, to add a little to the parish relief she gets and so keep her poor home together. For she cannot go back to her cooking because, even in these servantless days, people will not take a cook with three children attached: and the valiant creature will not leave them.

Other women find that their work makes just the difference between pinch and plenty in the home. The husband earns the bread and the wife puts butter on it. He pays the rent and she buys new cretonnes for the drawing-room. As a rule, marriages of this kind are harmonious and successful, for women who make money are not usually those who waste it; but all women want to spend it in ways that men may endure but cannot approve. I remember a case of a young couple taking a house in which the passages and the hall were papered with an atrocious varnished marbled paper in good repair. The woodwork was grained and in good repair too. The man and a legal friend advising him saw no reason for changing these things. The woman would have been depressed and exasperated by them constantly. In that case the husband was good-natured and let his wife have the white paint and fresh paper or distemper that she wanted. But even he, good-natured as he is, thinks his wife is extravagant when she buys new sheets or tablecloths. He would not like ragged house-linen, but he never wants to replenish the linen cupboard. So when that wife began to earn a little money, she had the pleasure of getting what was needed for the house without having to convert her man to her opinion – often a difficult process. He still twits her with her extravagance, but likes the look of a new stair-carpet when she puts one down because the old one was in holes.

Bachelor establishments are notoriously comfortable and do not have stair-carpets in holes: so bachelors must spend much what women do on wear and tear. But no one tells stories about their extravagance because they are spending their own money. A man who unwillingly pays for cretonnes reflects that the money might have backed a horse or bought a case of whisky.

Everyone who takes an interest in the welfare of women knows that their happiness and freedom hang on their economic independence. A woman should either own money or earn it. Otherwise, in honour or dishonour, she has to be maintained by men. But a woman who has trained carefully for a trade, an art, or a profession, and achieved success in it, does not always want to give it up when she marries. That she often does give it up is a common reproach. Money spent on training women is said to be wasted money, because when they are trained they usually marry and cease to practise what they have learned. Better, I say, that a thousand women should forget a wage-earning craft than that one, left destitute, should have none for her use. Every woman born without a silver spoon in her mouth should know how to get her daily bread. As for marriage, there are many vicissitudes in that estate, and it is not only the working-class woman who finds herself stranded, although a man has endowed her with his worldly goods.

In short, the question is unanswerable in terms of yes and no. Some married women should or must work, and some should not. It stands to reason that a woman who undertakes to make a home for a man, and rear as well as bear his children, should fulfil her contract: but it does not stand to reason that she will in all cases do this best by refusing to earn money. Often enough her time would hang on her hands.

Married women of energy, means, and leisure do an immense amount of voluntary work in this country and do not neglect their homes in consequence. Take a home from which the children have gone forth to school and in which servants do the work. How is the mistress to employ herself all day? We know very well how she does. She rises late, she writes a few letters and perhaps arranges a few flowers. After lunch she goes out for *to see*, either to shops or to friends. In the evening she sits at home with her husband, except when he or someone else will take her out. We all know how busy these women think themselves, how little time they have for anything they are asked to do, and how their trivial pastimes clash with their duties just as much or more than a working woman's work does: and by a working woman I do not mean what the Reds mean, but any woman, high born or low born, who pursues a craft, an art, or a business indoors or out and gets paid for her work.

The worst wives and mothers in the world are the gad-abouts and the fools – women so set on pleasure that they neglect all their duties, or so incapable that what they do is badly done. It is not the steady, intelligent women helping the family exchequer who have miserable homes. It is those who are set crazily on pleasure, or those who toil and moil to no purpose, nagging at their servants, muddling away money, stinting where they should be generous, buying bad bargains, spoiling good food. Regular work educates. No one can do it well without developing qualities of sense and application that are agreeable qualities in a house as well as in an office or a studio. That is partly why women trained to a job so often marry and give up their work. Men recognise that they will be helpmates and not hindrances in the struggle of life. Little bits of fluff marry too, no doubt, and they are not always what they seem. They sometimes turn out good housekeepers.

But in this controversy, and in others allied to it, I should like to know what those contending mean by 'work.' Some say servants are scarce because work in a private house is hard and enslaving: yet, if the mistress of the house does that work, she is 'fulfilling her mission,' and not neglecting it for paid work. Whether it is 'work' when a wife, and not a servant, does it and whether she should be legally entitled to payment are questions asked sometimes, but not yet answered. No one minds, as a rule, how much a woman drudges for her husband and children, but if she earns money in order to pay others to drudge she is a shirker and her employees are slaves. What nonsense! The best thing for a nation is for every man, woman, and child in it to do what they can do, well.

But women have never taken a step forward without a dust and a pother being raised around them. They have had to fight for education, for admission to trades and professions and, in our memories, for the Vote. Whatever they wanted was going to unsex them. When I enter a quiet balloting-room with my husband, put a cross on a slip of paper, say 'Good morning' to the schoolmaster sitting there, and walk out again, I always think of old speeches and prophecies representing this business as a disintegrating one performed by Mænads amidst a crowd of hooligans. The objections to married women working are just as futile.

Nature has settled the place of women in the universe and always will settle it. 'A woman wants a proper alliance with a man, a man who is better stuff than herself,' says Ann Veronica. 'She wants to be free – she wants to be legally and economically free so as not to be subject to the wrong man: but only God, who made the world, can alter things to prevent her being a slave to the right one.' However, Nature and modern civilised conditions are constantly in conflict and compromise ensues. The woman finds her man and goes on with her work, too, because she wishes it, or because together they need what she can earn, or because she is sane and sees work to do everywhere, outside her home as well as in it. Let women settle this question for themselves, each woman doing the duty nearest to her, after which the next will have become clearer. If her home fills her time and thoughts, so be it, for that woman. If her neighbour chooses otherwise, more power to her. We must live and let live.

MARY STOTT

1907–2002

As editor of the *Guardian* women's page, Stott revolutionized journalism, widening all notions of what might be considered appropriate subjects for female writers (see previous article for details). In the following piece she addresses the vexed question of men, women and money, and particularly the households of her contemporaries, in which men often withheld their wages and assets from their wives, allowing them only the minimum spending money on request. She discusses the infantilizing effects of this behaviour, and posits perhaps her pivotal question: 'Do men regard women as human beings?'

Woman Talking to Men

15 October 1964, *Guardian*

In the sad, bad days before the war, when the Jews were fleeing from Nazi persecution, I helped a gentle and timid young woman named Charlotte to find a home with an English family. I explained to them that it was not possible legally to pay her a salary for her help with their children, but that I hoped they would give her 'presents'. A few weeks later Charlotte wrote to me and asked if I would make her a loan against the security of her watch. The only present she had been given was a pair of bedsocks – not a penny for toilet needs, stamps, bus fares, stockings, or anything else – and she could not bear to ask for cash. I had Charlotte out of that house within days and I have never forgotten or forgiven.

It was this story of total lack of imagination and respect for human dignity that came at once to my mind when a reader told me the other day that after 30 years of married life she had persuaded her husband to give her a personal allowance. The sum was five shillings a week. When I said I was astounded and that he must be a rare relic of a dying breed, she promptly replied with a list of 19 of her friends and acquaintances in all parts of England only five of whom had any personal spending money. And they included two teachers who turned over the whole of their salary to 'the head of the house'.

I am not a warped spinster waving the feminist flag. I am a rather amiable married woman whose domestic arrangements are perfectly harmonious and who all her life has enjoyed the fun and stimulus of working with men, talking to them, being teased by them. But it makes me hopping mad when I hear of any man who regards a woman, especially his wife, as less than an adult human being.

Can any man who reads this column help me to understand? Do men regard women as human beings? A human being is not an animal on two legs who has learned certain tricks necessary to exist in a civilised society, but a creature different from the animals in being able to think, plan, and make a reasoned choice. And in a civilised society choice is dependent over and over again on the expenditure of money. Deprive a person of money of his own and you deprive him of the right of choice in a very large part of everyday life. And to deny a human being the right of choice is to humiliate and degrade him.

I know perfectly well that there are a great many men – I used to think happily that they were a majority; now I am not so sure – who regard their wives as equal partners, equal contributors to the wellbeing of the joint home. (My reader told me of a husband who refused to put their home in their joint names on the ground that *she had contributed nothing to it*.) But even they may be able to help me to see into the mind of the others – who, I fear, are not the sort of men to read a column written by a woman.

To try to get at what goes on in a household where the wife has no separate allowance, I picture the day when she thinks she needs a new coat.

Husband A may say: 'Any time you like. Have the bill sent to me.' (But suppose when she starts shopping around she finds that she would gladly make her coat do for another season if she could spend the money on an album of records, a pear tree, a couple of important books, and a dangling bauble for her little black dress. If it is his money she is spending, she has in all honesty, to ask her husband if he minds. Some would not. Some would.)

Husband B may say: 'I can't afford it.' (Often true; sometimes not. Not many wives who are kept informed of the state of the family finances would ask for a new coat unless there was money in the kitty, where every penny has to be used just for paying the rent, fuel, food, and clothes, and if the wife has a personal allowance it is a token payment only, for she will certainly spend most of it on the children. But that is her choice.)

Husband C may say: 'How much do you think you will need?' (It will depend on the relationship between them whether she puts the figure too high, too low, or just about right for her husband's means. But whatever sum he gives her the chances are that it will not be exactly right for the coat she finally wants to buy. If it is too much, does she return the balance or buy a new hat? If it is too little, does she borrow the balance from the housekeeping and ask later for a refund; cut down on the food shopping for a week or two to make up the difference; or defer the purchase until she can ask her husband if he is willing to spend more?)

I just cannot think myself into the skin of a man in circumstances like this and I need help to understand. I suppose there is many a man who thinks quite simply that as he alone brings money into the home he alone has the right to dispose of it, and that his wife is only his agent in doing the shopping, even for her own clothes. This seems to me to reduce the wife to the level of an unpaid employee (or slave, some would say), but I think that such a man tells himself that it is just because he does not regard the wife of his bosom as an employee that he does not want to have any kind of financial contract with her; that petty bookkeeping would make the whole relationship sordid and loveless.

But really, I think, these husbands subconsciously apprehend the truth that money means independence and that the wife with pennies in her pocket can cock a snook at him and go off on a bus to visit mamma, buy a highbrow magazine or a pop record, have a drink in a pub, or whatever she fancies. And this they cannot bear.

Why not? This is what absolutely baffles me. How can a man endure to share his home with someone who is of adult years but only of semi-adult status? I should loathe to be tied to someone whom I did not expect to spend time and money rationally and considerately. Some unfortunate people have to and manage heroically to carry the millstone around. But who in his right mind would choose to if he did not need to? In fact would insist on doing it?

And I certainly cannot imagine what it would be like to be the wife of a man who doled out money as to a backward child. But I could quite well imagine what it was like to be Charlotte . . . and I got her out of her cage within days.

JOREEN FREEMAN

1943–

Writer, political scientist and lawyer, Freeman's activism began whilst studying at Berkeley in the early 1960s, when she became involved with the growing civil rights movement. After graduating in 1964, she headed to Atlanta, where she worked for the Southern Christian Leadership Conference (SCLC) headed by Dr Martin Luther King Jr.

When Freeman first applied for jobs at mainstream newspapers she was told that they tended not to employ women, because 'girls couldn't cover riots'. In the final years of the 1960s, she formed the influential Westside group with fellow radical, Shulamith Firestone. It was this group that began the newsletter, *Voice of the Women's Liberation Movement*, and thereby gave the movement its name. The following article first appeared in this newsletter (which Freeman personally sent out to feminists all across the US) and has since become one of the key texts of feminism's second wave, stridently reclaiming the word 'bitch'.

The BITCH Manifesto

1971, *Voice of the Women's Liberation Movement*

. . . man is defined as a human being and woman is defined as a female. Whenever she tries to behave as a human being she is accused of trying to emulate the male . . .

Simone de Beauvoir

BITCH is an organization which does not yet exist. The name is not an acronym. It stands for exactly what it sounds like.

BITCH is composed of Bitches. There are many definitions of a bitch. The most complimentary definition is a female dog. Those definitions of bitches who are also homo sapiens are rarely as objective. They vary from person to person and depend strongly on how much of a bitch the definer considers herself. However, everyone agrees that a bitch is always a female, dog, or otherwise.

It is also generally agreed that a Bitch is aggressive, and therefore unfeminine (ahem). She may be sexy, in which case she becomes a Bitch Goddess, a special case which will not concern us here. But she is never a 'true woman.'

Bitches have some or all of the following characteristics.

1. Personality. Bitches are aggressive, assertive, domineering, overbearing, strong-minded, spiteful, hostile, direct, blunt, candid, obnoxious, thick-skinned, hard-headed, vicious, dogmatic, competent, competitive, pushy, loud-mouthed, independent, stubborn, demanding, manipulative, egoistic, driven, achieving, overwhelming, threatening, scary, ambitious, tough, brassy, masculine, boisterous, and turbulent. Among other things. A Bitch occupies a lot of psychological space. You always know she is around. A Bitch takes shit from no one. You may not like her, but you cannot ignore her.

2. Physical. Bitches are big, tall, strong, large, loud, brash, harsh, awkward, clumsy, sprawling, strident, ugly. Bitches move their bodies freely rather than restrain, refine and confine their motions in the proper feminine manner. They clomp up stairs, stride when they walk and don't worry about where they put their legs when they sit. They have loud voices and often use them. Bitches are not pretty.

3. Orientation. Bitches seek their identity strictly thru themselves and what they do. They are subjects, not objects. They may have a relationship with a person or organization, but they never marry anyone or anything; man, mansion, or movement. Thus Bitches prefer to plan their own lives rather than live from day to day, action to action, or person to person. They are independent cusses and believe they are capable of doing anything they damn well want to. If something gets in their way; well, that's why they become Bitches. If they are professionally inclined, they will seek careers and have no fear of competing with anyone. If not professionally inclined, they still seek self-expression and self-actualization. Whatever they do, they want an active role and are frequently perceived as domineering. Often they do dominate other people when roles are not available to them which more creatively sublimate their energies and utilize their capabilities. More often they are accused of domineering when doing what would be considered natural by a man.

A true Bitch is self-determined, but the term 'bitch' is usually applied with less discrimination. It is a popular derogation to put down uppity women that was created by man and adopted by women. Like the term 'nigger,' 'bitch' serves the social function of isolating and discrediting a class of people who do not conform to the socially accepted patterns of behavior.

BITCH does not use this word in the negative sense. A woman should be proud to declare she is a Bitch, because Bitch is Beautiful. It should be an act of affirmation by self and not negation by others. Not everyone can qualify as a Bitch. One does not have to have all of the above three qualities, but should be well possessed of at least two of them to be considered a Bitch. If a woman qualifies in all three, at least partially, she is a

Bitch's Bitch. Only Superbitches qualify totally in all three categories and there are very few of those. Most don't last long in this society.

The most prominent characteristic of all Bitches is that they rudely violate conceptions of proper sex role behavior. They violate them in different ways, but they all violate them. Their attitudes towards themselves and other people, their goal orientations, their personal style, their appearance and way of handling their bodies, all jar people and make them feel uneasy. Sometimes it's conscious and sometimes it's not, but people generally feel uncomfortable around Bitches. They consider them aberrations. They find their style disturbing. So they create a dumping ground for all who they deplore as bitchy and call them frustrated women.

Frustrated they may be, but the cause is social not sexual. What is disturbing about a Bitch is that she is androgynous. She incorporates within herself qualities traditionally defined as 'masculine' as well as 'feminine'. A Bitch is blunt, direct, arrogant, at times egoistic. She has no liking for the indirect, subtle, mysterious ways of the 'eternal feminine.' She disdains the vicarious life deemed natural to women because she wants to live a life of her own. [. . .]

Bitches were the first women to go to college, the first to break thru the Invisible Bar of the professions, the first social revolutionaries, the first labor leaders, the first to organize other women. Because they were not passive beings and acted on their resentment at being kept down, they dared to do what other women would not. They took the flak and the shit that society dishes out to those who would change it and opened up portions of the world to women that they would otherwise not have known. They have lived on the fringes. And alone or with the support of their sisters they have changed the world we live in.

By definition Bitches are marginal beings in this society. They have no proper place and wouldn't stay in it if they did. They are women but not true women. They are human but they are not male. Some don't even know they are women because they cannot relate to other women. They may play the feminine game at times, but they know it is a game they are playing. Their major psychological oppression is not a belief that they are inferior but a belief that they are not. Thus, all their lives they have been told they were freaks. More polite terms were used of course, but the message got thru. Like most women they were taught to hate themselves as well as all women. In different ways and for different reasons perhaps, but the effect was similar. Internalization of a derogatory self-concept always results in a good deal of bitterness and resentment. This anger is usually either turned in on the self – making one an unpleasant person or on other women – reinforcing the social clichés about them. Only with political consciousness is it directed at the source – the social system.

The bulk of this Manifesto has been about Bitches. The remainder will be about BITCH. The organization does not yet exist and perhaps it never can. Bitches are so damned independent and they have learned so well not to trust other women that it will be difficult for them to learn to even trust each other. This is what BITCH must teach them to do. Bitches have to learn to accept themselves as Bitches and to give their sisters the support they need to be creative Bitches. Bitches must learn to be proud of their strength and proud of themselves. They must move away from the isolation which has been their protection and help their younger sisters avoid its perils. They must recognize that women are often less tolerant of other women than are men because they have been taught to view all women as their enemies. And Bitches must form together in a movement to deal with their problems in a political manner. They must organize for their own liberation as all women must organize for theirs. We must be strong, we must be militant, we must be dangerous. We must realize that Bitch is Beautiful and that we have nothing to lose. Nothing whatsoever.

This manifesto was written and revised with the help of several of my sisters, to whom it is dedicated.

JUDY SYFERS

1937–

Born in San Francisco, Syfers was a prominent voice in the second wave of feminism, and has since written widely on other subjects including environmental issues and (since having breast cancer herself) women's experience of cancer.

The following article appeared in the very first issue of feminist magazine MS and is one of the standout texts of 1970s feminism. Using the classic satirical device of role reversal, Syfers imagines all she could do if she only had a wife.

Why I want a Wife

December 1971, MS. *Magazine*

I belong to that classification of people known as wives. I am a Wife. And, not altogether incidentally, I am a mother.

Not too long ago a male friend of mine appeared on the scene fresh from a recent divorce. He had one child, who is, of course, with his ex-wife. He is obviously looking for another wife. As I thought about him while I was ironing one evening, it suddenly occurred to me that I, too, would like to have a wife. Why do I want a wife?

I would like to go back to school so that I can become economically independent, support myself, and, if need be, support those dependent upon me. I want a wife who will work and send me to school. And while I am going to school I want a wife to take care of my children. I want a wife to keep track of the children's doctor and dentist appointments. And to keep track of mine, too. I want a wife to make sure my children eat properly and are kept clean. I want a wife who will wash the children's clothes and keep them mended. I want a wife who is a good nurturant attendant to my children, who arranges for their schooling, makes sure that they have an adequate social life with their peers, takes them to the park, the zoo, etc. I want a wife who takes care of the children when they are sick, a wife who arranges to be around when the children need special care, because, of course, I cannot miss classes at school. My wife must arrange to lose time at work and not lose the job. It may mean a small cut in my wife's income from time to time, but I guess I can tolerate that. Needless to say, my wife will arrange and pay for the care of the children while my wife is working.

I want a wife who will take care of *my* physical needs. I want a wife who will keep my house clean. A wife who will pick up after me. I want a wife who will keep my clothes clean, ironed, mended, replaced when need be, and who will see to it that my personal things are kept in their proper place so that I can find what I need the minute I need it. I want a wife who cooks the meals, a wife who is a *good* cook. I want a wife who will plan the menus, do the necessary grocery shopping, prepare the meals, serve them pleasantly, and then do the cleaning up while I do my studying. I want a wife who will care for me when I am sick and sympathize with my pain and loss of time from school. I want a wife to go along when our family takes a vacation so that someone can continue to care for me and my children when I need a rest and change of scene.

I want a wife who will not bother me with rambling complaints about a wife's duties. But I want a wife who will listen to me when I feel the need to explain a rather difficult point I have come across in my course of studies. And I want a wife who will type my papers for me when I have written them.

I want a wife who will take care of the details of my social life. When my wife and I are invited out by my friends, I want a wife who will take care of the babysitting arrangements. When I meet people at school that I like and want to entertain, I want a wife who will have the house clean, will prepare a special meal, serve it to me and my friends, and not inter-rupt when I talk about the things that interest me and my friends. I want a wife who will have arranged that the children are fed and ready for bed before my guests arrive so that the children do not bother us.

And I want a wife who knows that sometimes I need a night out by myself.

I want a wife who is sensitive to my sexual needs, a wife who makes love passionately and eagerly when I feel like it, a wife who makes sure that I am satisfied. And, of course, I want a wife who will not demand sexual atten-tion when I am not in the mood for it. I want a wife who assumes the com-plete responsibility for birth control, because I do not want more children. I want a wife who will remain sexually faithful to me so that I do not have to clutter up my intellectual life with jealousies. And I want a wife who understands that *my* sexual needs may entail more than strict adherence to monogamy. I must, after all, be able to relate to people as fully as possible.

If, by chance, I find another person more suitable as a wife than the wife I already have, I want the liberty to replace my present wife with another one. Naturally, I will expect a fresh, new life; my wife will take the children and be solely responsible for them so that I am left free.

When I am through with school and have a job, I want my wife to quit working and remain at home so that my wife can more fully and com-pletely take care of a wife's duties.

My God, who *wouldn't* want a wife?

BETTY FRIEDAN

1921–

Writer, speaker and academic, Illinois-born Betty Friedan came to international prominence in 1963 with publication of her seminal work, *The Feminine Mystique*, about women's financial, physical and emotional dependence on their husbands. Friedan's book became a rallying cry for a generation, and led directly to the campaigning and activism of the second wave feminism movement.

In 1966, Friedan was one of the co-founders of the National Organization for Women (NOW) which campaigned for women's equality. The following article is an extract from her account of America's first ever National Conference of Women, which underlines the event's many triumphs.

The Women at Houston

10 December 1977, *New Republic*

Eleven years ago, after delegates to a government conference on the status of women were told they had no right to take any action or even pass a resolution to make the government enforce the new law on sex discrimination in employment, a handful of women met in my Washington hotel room to start an independent women's movement. That was the National Organization for Women. Over the next decade an unprecedented revolution in women's consciousness produced laws and other concrete breakthroughs against sex discrimination. The constitutional underpinning needed to make these breakthroughs permanent and irreversible would be the Equal Rights Amendment, which expires if not ratified by March 1979.

In November 1977, with the Equal Rights Amendment stalled three states short of ratification by a right-wing backlash, and with the courts and President Carter backtracking on rights already won, another government conference on the status of women was held in Houston, Texas. The stated purpose of the conference was to adopt a 'National Plan of Action' for women.

The origins of the conference seemed harmless, straightforward: a bill introduced in Congress by Bella Abzug to provide five million dollars for women to meet in each of the 50 states and then nationally to implement for the United States the objectives of the International Women's Year, proclaimed by the United Nations in 1975. But the IWY conference in

Mexico was a fiasco. Some women became suspicious that various political powers were using the IWY to coopt and control and blunt the modern women's movement as it began to spread worldwide.

Some movement leaders felt similarly uneasy over the US government's espousal of this nation's women's movement at the apex of 10 years of unprecedented social change. No one could possibly object to being handed five million dollars and all kinds of logistical aid and comfortable perquisites to get more women together, at government expense, than could ever afford to meet independently. But it seemed almost too good to believe. If President Carter, who appointed the IWY Commission, was truly committed to women's equality, why was he showing such lassitude about mobilizing Democratic party power to counteract the right and get the ERA ratified in Democratic states like Florida, Illinois, Missouri, and even his own Georgia, where it is stalled? If the US government was going to take over the agenda of the women's movement in all sincerity, why the backtracking on federal funds for abortion? Why the backing and filling over affirmative action in sex discrimination programs, as in the *Bakke* case?

The uneasiness grew over the past year, as the energies of women were diverted from ratification of the ERA to the mechanics of running IWY conferences in every state. It was difficult to mobilize women before crucial votes on ERA in Florida and Illinois last Spring because they were working on their state IWY conference. Phyllis Schlafly's shrill 'stop ERA' squads with their red ribbons and Bibles almost had the men to themselves. John Birch groups, the Mormon church and the Ku Klux Klan partially took over IWY state conferences in Missouri, Utah, Illinois, Indiana, Mississippi, Alabama and other western and southern states, promoting anti-ERA and anti-abortion platforms. Phyllis Schlafly predicted that Houston would be 'the death knell of the women's movement.' On the other hand, some feminists felt the IWY Commission was being controlled by a small cabal whose real agenda was their own power. On the eve of Houston, when the Commission voted to put a resolution on lesbian rights ahead of other business, the suspicion arose that somehow, someone was trying to pit the extremists of 'women's lib' against the far right.

Nothing in the Plan of Action was new to feminists, nor in any way objectionable. But it buried the ERA in a catalogue of 26 other items ranging from 'women in the arts' to 'credit' and 'welfare.' If Houston were as ugly as all signs indicated it might be, who could blame Carter for backing off ERA – especially if he accepted a 26-point Plan of Action for Women, which included everything a feminist ever dreamed of, and endorsed a new Department of Women with a Secretary of Women (the provision of which was the 26th point of the Plan) to get the women out of the other departments' hair? [. . .]

The final Monday morning was to have been devoted to 'implementation' of this Plan – which, as proposed by the IWY Commission as its 26th item, involved the setting up of a Cabinet-level Women's Department. It was on this issue alone that most of the women delegates at Houston, including me, rebelled against control by the IWY commission. The very fact that so many members of that Commission, who should have known better, would have gone along with setting up a kind of Bureau of Indian Affairs for women, bespoke the dangers of cooption that come with government support, with comfortable perks, funding and the illusion of power. [. . .] To women on the floor, this proposal signified a retreat to tokenism, with relatively powerless female mediators interposed between their own organizations and the powers that be. Furthermore, the setting up of this Women's Department would be treated as a great new accomplishment for women, possibly to take Carter off the hook on the Equal Rights Amendment. All that last morning, the chair stalled, Bella kept reading announcements, introducing people; with a noon deadline for adjournment, the conference was an hour and a half late getting started. Plane departure times were nearing before a vote finally was called for. A move was made to extend closing time until 3 pm but the most ardent feminists joined the right wing delegates in their practical need to get home as planned. ('We all have to defrost our turkeys,' one said.) The Women's Department was soundly defeated. [. . .]

The women went home from Houston, elated at the realization of their breadth and diversity, their unity and their strength, their new confidence and skill and respect for each other – and their ability not to be provoked by their sworn enemies or coopted by their sworn friends. It was heady, invigorating, and infused the whole movement with new energy. The 'Plan' has no power whatsoever over Congress or the President. Whether or not any of it gets translated into new law – or enforcement of laws already on the books – probably depends, to be blunt, on the power of organizations like NOW, and the League of Women Voters, and AAUW and BPW and the churchwomen and the union women to achieve, within the next year and three months, ratification of the Equal Rights Amendment. The media, for the most part, reported Houston seriously and reported the ploys of Phyllis Schlafly for what they were. In the end, the Houston conference delivered its own promise: a new and visibly broad commitment to the goals of equality for women. Look at it as a kind of Woodstock of women, a happening that may never, and may never need to, happen again. What were we all so afraid of? If we didn't have Phyllis Schlafly to bring us together, we would have to invent her. Never underestimate the real power of women.

ERICA JONG
1942–

One of the most prominent voices of the 1970s sexual revolution (see previous article for more details), Jong has been one of the most ardent supporters of feminist principles. In the following article, written in the early 1980s, she considers the growing concept of 'post-feminism' and wonders whether the women of this generation face even greater pressures than their pre-feminist grandmothers. Was the whole notion of having it all an exhausting con?

The Post-feminist Woman – is she Perhaps More Oppressed than Ever?

30 December 1984, *Seattle Times*

Not long ago, on a flight to Los Angeles, I picked up an issue of *Town & Country* and, between the diamonds and the debutantes, the fall collections and the chateaux in France, found the most delicious article by the late Anita Loos, a.k.a. Lorelei Lee (of 'Gentlemen Prefer Blondes').

'In the middle twenties,' wrote Miss Lee – (the term 'Ms.' had not yet been invented, apparently was not needed) – 'when my book about a blonde like I was printed (against my better judgment), American gentlemen had a very different attitude toward females. They liked to support them in a better style than they were accustomed to, present them with gifts way above the category of flowers, perfume and candy, and never, in any circumstances, to go out and find them a job.'

When I read this article (apparently found in Loos' papers after her death in 1981), I was flying to the Coast to develop a TV series, doing interviews for my new novel, planning my daughter's sixth birthday party, renovating a town house in New York and making copious notes for my fifth novel, just beginning to percolate.

Other responsibilities I was facing included tax audits, legal problems and a number of article assignments I really wanted to fulfill. I had begun work on a musical comedy on one of my novels and an original screenplay.

How nice, I thought, things must have been for women (blondes or brunettes) in Loos' time. How nice to live in a world without alarm clocks, a world where women did not have to prove their prowess on the battlefield of the book tour, the tax audit, the pregnancy leave (such as mine) that lasts five days. I've been doing the superwoman stump for the past 10 years, and I'm ready to say those dames (such as Miss Lorelei Lee) had something on the ball. How nice, I thought, to sleep till noon (not to get up at six to feed the baby, walk the dog, catch the commuter train while reading articles about 'the female stress syndrome').

And then I thought: Am I crazy? All my prayers have been answered. I am 'having it all.' Why, then, do I feel like a victim of terminal exhaustion? Why do I find myself agreeing with Nora Ephron when she says that 'the main achievement of the women's movement is the Dutch treat'?

My story is the story of the post-feminist woman. We have won the right to be eternally exhausted. We go from reading Miss Loos in *Town & Country* to articles on female stress in *Working Woman*, and suddenly our contempt for those diamond-laden debutantes falters. What hath feminism wrought? We have taken on all the male burdens (breadwinning, mort-gage-paying, commuting) and all the female ones (baby-cuddling, man-coddling, self-beautification). The dilemma of the post-feminist woman is that there are only 24 hours in the day, and she needs 48 to get done all the things she wants to get done (and still find time to sleep, one hopes, not alone). Does this sound like a cry for counter-revolution? It is not. I would not turn back the clock to Anita Loos' day. If diamonds are a girl's best friend, then they should be the diamonds that she buys herself. But I often find myself wondering why things are so abundantly hard for women of my generation who are trying to have it all, why we so often feel so guilty and so unfulfilled (even in the midst of our successes), why we race like maniacs from the school play to the PTA meeting to the airport, then from the airport to the desk, then from the desk to the lawyer's or accoun-tant's office, feeling all the while that something is amiss, awry: We were not emotionally prepared for the lives we lead.

It's not that we would give up any part of them. Nor are we unaware that for most of history (except for a few aberrant periods) women have been like lionesses – responsible for both bearing and feeding the young. But most of us were reared in an aberrant period – the '50s. We carry within our teeming brains the values of the '50s ('Kinder, Kuche, Kinsey') and the values of the '70s (sex, sensitivity, social revolution) while we try to cope with the realities of life in the '80s.

Just what are those realities? Well, the truth seems to be that women have given up all their traditional protections without getting true equality in return. 'No more alimony,' Gloria Steinem said in the '70s, and indeed there is no more alimony (except perhaps for 'Hollywood wives'), but neither is there equal pay for equal work. Women still earn about 60 cents for each dollar men earn. Eighty percent of the divorced mothers in America receive no child support – whether it was mandated by the courts or not.

Yet when they work (as they must), they cannot count on adequate day care, after-school programs or meaningful tax breaks for child-care assistance. Add to that the fact that we do not work (as our great-grandmothers did) in the home, with grannies and aunts around to help rear the kids.

We are isolated in our single-parent households. We are not a footstep or two from our jobs, but a train ride or a car ride (or even a plane ride). We are not a footstep or two from our kids, but another train ride or car ride. Not only have our lives been transformed by the decline of the extended family, but also by the rise of the automobile and now by the epidemic of divorce.

The family unit, which shrank to one generation in the '50s, shrank to one lone parent in the '70s and '80s. There are only so many things one person (male or female) can do at once. They appear to be more than a body can do without screaming, 'Help!' In order to understand how uniquely difficult the lives of Americans have become in the '80s, one has only to transplant oneself into a different culture for a while – one that harks back to an older lifestyle.

Last July, I spent four weeks in Venice with my daughter, my lover and our surrogate grandma, Molly's nanny. We rented an apartment in a quiet residential section, ate at home (or in bistros or artists' cafes), walked everywhere, shopped at the Rialto (from a friend's fishing boat) and had an inkling of what life must have been like before the automobile and the decline of the grandma transformed it. We were on vacation, true, but we still had to get food, organize Molly's playtime, work on assignments we had brought along – while coping with a foreign language and supposedly alien customs. Life was made blissful chiefly by two things (aside from our familial bliss because we love one another): no commuting and the presence of our resident grandma. We could do our work at home; we did not need automobiles, and we had three generations in one house, so we could pair off in different ways so as to share responsibilities and give each other private time. The difference those things made to our otherwise stressful lives is incalculable.

Those powerful immigrant matriarchs, lately so celebrated in novels and films, who ran the family store, reared a dozen kids and made gefilte fish, liberating their men to study Torah, were not obliged to catch the 7:42 to Grand Central, or the noon flight to Los Angeles. Also, they had grandmas at home (or aunties) with whom they may have feuded, but on whom they depended for relief, assistance in basic survival tasks.

Human beings were not meant to live alone; even in the caves, they huddled. One lone, childless person may live alone and like it, but with kids (bless them) come food preparation, laundry and the organization of education and play (often the two are the same). One person can hardly organize it all alone.

Isolation is our contemporary plague. The separation of the workplace from the home has made all our lives more stressful, and the narrowing of the family to ever smaller and smaller units has made the bearing and rearing of children into a kind of marathon sport, rather than the joy it could be. The very use of the cliche 'quality time with one's child' betrays the unnaturalness of our attitude toward child-rearing. Those sainted Yiddish matriarchs (or Irish, or Italian or black or even WASP) didn't worry about 'quality time' with their kids. They brought up their kids *en passant* while the soup boiled, the store was kept, the piecework got done and the laundry got taken in. The family was a kind of ongoing three-ring circus, wherein things were accomplished in the din and companionship and confusion of daily life.

Different generations were there to help each other (and rile each other). Nobody had 'space'; the very term would have seemed laughable. They weren't there, after all, for self-expression, but for survival. There is no evidence that we are producing more creative geniuses because of our pre-occupation with 'space' and 'quality time.'

The bearing and rearing of the next generation is a communal effort. It is not a luxury by and for women. True, many women have a strong biological urge to have children (often, although not always, initially stronger than that of men). But, once the children are there, it takes 21 years of communal (not solitary) effort to bring them to something approaching maturity. If we are having fewer and fewer children (and we are), it is because, clearly, a society of single parents, step-parents and fragile marital and generational bonds is not equipped to rear more. If we really believe that children are our most precious resource, then why are we doing so little to make it possible for them to grow and thrive?

Women who work outside the home have been forced into the mode of male society rather than helping to feminize our culture (and thus humanize it). Many of us are frantic because we are trying to deny our femaleness, our maternity, in the name of corporate efficiency, rather than remaking the corporation in the image of female flexibility, resourcefulness, caring and caretaking. The corporation has become our social model, as the feudal estate was the social model in the Middle Ages, and the corporation insists on a denial of the existence of kids and their needs.

Except for a few avant-garde electronics firms that boast of their flex-time policies, American corporations tend to be bastions of the worst rigidities of the male power structure. Magazines that cater to female executives are full of tips about how not to let your femaleness 'interfere' with your corporate rise. The sick kid, the school play, the milk stains on the silk blouse are not part of the corporate image. They are to be kept out of sight in the name of 'efficiency' and 'corporate success.' Like wearing a bikini in the boardroom, these things do not enhance one's future. But what of the future of the human race? A nation of frantic mommies and half-neglected kids does not enhance its chance for survival. The time has not come to call for counter-revolution, but truly to change society so that it is responsive to the needs of women and children. If that means a revolution in the American corporation as well as in the American political system, so be it, for those are the only places where the revolution can make a difference. Feminists preaching to the already half-converted may raise consciousness, but they do not change the basic structures of our society.

And the fact is that the basic structures of our society are hostile to women and children. What would create real change is an understanding that children are precious to our society and that the work of raising and rearing them is a sacred trust. Since we are not going to go back to 'Kinder, Kirche, Kuche,' we are going to have to find ways to remake the workplace so that both men and women can work and also rear happy kids. A lot more of this depends on architecture, transportation, proximity of work and home, flex-time and a recasting of attitudes about what is 'male' and what is 'female' than we like to admit.

We could begin by acknowledging that children are everyone's business – even that of business! Private industry certainly loves to exploit children as consumers, but it gives back remarkably little to the short citizens to whom it owes its profits.

Government, for its part, likes to use children rhetorically, but when it comes to school budgets, day-care budgets, libraries, playgrounds, school lunches and the creation of new kinds of cities, new kinds of suburbs, new modes of transportation, even the rhetoric evaporates. If there ever was a year to insist that society begin to humanize, feminize and kiddicize itself, this is the year. Politically, the consciousness is ripe. Economically, the imperative is there. What is at stake is nothing more and nothing less than the future of our kids.

PAULINE KAEL
1919–2001

The daughter of Polish immigrants, Pauline Kael grew up in California, where she studied philosophy at UC Berkeley. Her first regular film review column, at the women's magazine *McCall's*, became infamous after she was fired for criticizing *The Sound of Music* ('We have been turned into emotional and aesthetic imbeciles when we hear ourselves humming the sickly, goody-goody songs').

Kael was uncompromising then, outspoken, never afraid to speak against the popular tide. Writing for the *New Yorker* for over three decades, she had a tough, witty, neologistic style that was peppered with biographical and cultural references and would become much copied – not just by other critics, but by political columnists and journalists in general. In the following article Kael eviscerates the film *Fatal Attraction*, damning its portrayal of women, which, she says, amounts to a 'hostile version of feminism'.

The Feminine Mystique

19 October 1987, *New Yorker*

Fatal Attraction is just about the worst dating movie imaginable – a movie almost guaranteed to start sour, unresolvable arguments – but long lines of people curl around the block waiting to see it. At a New York publishing party, a dull but presentable corporate lawyer (Michael Douglas), a settled married man, exchanges glances with a bold-eyed, flirtatious woman (Glenn Close), a book editor. She's wearing a Medusa hairdo – a mess of blond tendrils is brushed high off her forehead and floats around her face. She's made up to get attention, yet she resents it: the lawyer's plump pal (Stuart Pankin) tries a pleasantry on her, and she gives him a drop-dead stare. We see all the warning signals that the lawyer doesn't, and when he runs into her again, on a weekend when his wife and six-year-old daughter are out of town, we sense the hysteria behind her insinuating repartee and the hot looks she fastens on him. She makes all the overtures; he's not particularly eager, but she semi-transforms her frighteningness to sexiness, and he, being frightened, finds it sexy. She makes spending the night together seem casual and grownup – makes him feel he'd be a total wimp to say no – and he goes with her to her loft.

Like a femme fatale in a Cecil B. De Mille picture, she comes from hell: her loft is in the wholesale-meat district, where fires burn in the street. The director, Adrian (*Flashdance*) Lyne, puts on bravura demonstrations of frenetic passion. The two have sex, with her seated on the kitchen sink, and when she reaches for the faucet and splashes her hot face Lyne shoots it as if the water were wildly erotic. After more sex, they go to a Latin club for some (comically) supercharged dancing, then have sex in the elevator to the loft. By morning, the lawyer has had enough, but she pressures him, and he doesn't find it easy to get clear of her. When the weekend is over and he's determined to say goodbye and go back uptown she stops him, temporarily, by slashing her wrists. In the weeks that follow, she hounds him at his office and his home, insisting that he can't use her and then discard her. The picture is a skillfully made version of an old-fashioned cautionary movie: it's a primer on the bad things that can happen if a man cheats on his wife.

Once the woman begins behaving as if she had a right to a share in the lawyer's life, she becomes the dreaded lunatic of horror movies. But with a difference: she parrots the aggressively angry, self-righteous statements that have become commonplaces of feminist fiction, and they're so inappropriate to the circumstances that they're the proof she's loco. They're also Lyne's and the scriptwriter James Dearden's hostile version of feminism. (Dearden's script is an expansion of the forty-two-minute film *Diversion*, which he wrote and directed in England in 1979.) Glenn Close expresses the feelings of many despairing people; she plays the woman as pitiable and deprived and biologically driven. But in the movie's terms this doesn't make the character sympathetic – it makes her more effectively scary, because the story is told from a repelled man's point of view. Lyne and Dearden see her as mouthing a modern career woman's jargon about wanting sex without responsibilities, and then turning into a vengeful hellion, all in the name of love. They see the man as ordinary, sane, hardworking – a man who loves his beautiful homebody wife (Anne Archer) and bright little daughter (Ellen Hamilton Latzen). He's the opposite of a lech; he was a little tickled at being seduced. Yet the woman plays the *Madame Butterfly* music and doesn't regard it ironically; alone in her stark loft, she really sees herself as having been mistreated. When she seeks revenge, she might be taking revenge on all men.

The horror subtext is the lawyer's developing dread of the crazy feminist who attacks his masculine role as protector of his property and his family. It's about men seeing feminists as witches, and, the way the facts are presented here, the woman *is* a witch. She terrorizes the lawyer and explains his fear of her by calling him a faggot. This shrewd film also touches on something deeper than men's fear of feminism: their fear of women, their fear of women's emotions, of women's hanging on to them. *Fatal Attraction* doesn't treat the dreaded passionate woman as a theme; she's merely a monster in a monster flick. It's directed so that by the time she's wielding a knife (from that erotic kitchen) you're ready to shriek at the sight of her. But the undercurrents of sexual antagonism – of a woman's fury at a man who doesn't value her passion, doesn't honor it, and a man's rage at a woman who won't hold to the rules she has agreed to, a man's rage against 'female' irrationality – give the movie a controversial, morbid power that it doesn't really earn.

It's made with swank and precision, yet it's gripping in an unpleasant, mechanical way. When we first hear that the little daughter wants a bunny rabbit, an alarm goes off in our heads. And after the lawyer buys the rabbit we wait to see what obscene thing the demon lady will do to it. Educated people may want to read more into *Fatal Attraction*, but basically it's a gross-out slasher movie in a glossy format. (It has special touches, such as a copy of Oliver Sacks' *The Man Who Mistook His Wife for a Hat* next to the bed in the loft.) The violence that breaks loose doesn't have anything to do with the characters who have been set up; it has to do with the formula they're shoved into.

The picture has De Mille's unbeatable box-office combination – an aura of sexiness and a moral message. We know that the lawyer isn't going to chase after the blonde, because Lyne softens Anne Archer's features and sexualizes every detail of the cozy marriage. And the movie is edited so that the audience is breathing right along with the husband as he watches his wife put on her extra-moist lipstick. There are also bits of contrast, like the pal's making fun of himself, or the husband's experiencing a surreal embarrassment, trying to carry the blonde from her sink to her bed and being hobbled by his pants and shorts, which are caught around his ankles. Lyne uses these moments to break into the dreamlike tension of the male erotic reveries of the soft nest at home and of the tempestuous, kinky sex in the loft. The husband loves his wife and prefers her in every way to the interloper, whose rapacity scares him even before she threatens his way of life, even before she sends him porno tapes full of hate. The movie has its sex in the dirty sink, but it's pushing the deeper erotic satisfaction of the warm, sweet life at home. The key to its point of view is that dull, scared everyman husband. The woman was ready to go nuts; if it hadn't been this ordinary guy she tried to destroy, it could have been another. She carries madness, disease, the unknown. This is a horror film based on the sanctity of the family – the dream family. It enforces conventional morality (in the era of AIDS) by piling on paranoiac fear. The family that kills together stays together, and the audience is hyped up to cheer the killing.

NAOMI WOLF

1962–

Arguably the most controversial and outspoken feminist of her generation, Wolf graduated from Yale in 1984 and came to prominence with her book, *The Beauty Myth*, which tackled how society oppresses women by making them obsessed with their looks. The *New York Times* called it one of the seventy most significant books of the century. She followed that with *Fire with Fire* (about how to build a new feminist movement amongst younger women), *Promiscuities* (which looked at female desire), and *Misconceptions* (about birth and motherhood).

A prolific, much-respected voice, Wolf now writes regular essays for the *New Republic*, the *Wall Street Journal*, the *Sunday Times* and *New York* magazine.

Wolf has regularly lent a considered eye to changes in sexual mores, most notably in *Promiscuities*. In the following article, she discusses this and other subjects with Candace Bushnell, whose 'Sex and the City' columns inspired the eponymous TV show.

Sex and the Sisters

20 July 2003, *Sunday Times*

Sex and the City rules right now. It has such a fervent cult following in New York that rather than switch off the television and miss an episode, parents let their children watch. In Britain the final season has sparked a frenzy.

The woman behind this series has become as recognisable as her characters: Candace Bushnell, the 44-year-old, recently married one-time party girl who is famous in Manhattan for being at the centre of a scene that she has spun into literary gold.

She has become to the Noughties what Scott and Zelda were to the 1920s: a defining image and image-maker.

I met Bushnell on a hot summer afternoon in a swank hotel. Blonde and shimmery, she had not a hair out of place. I marvelled silently at how she had managed to do her eye makeup so professionally without, presumably, a makeup artist travelling with her. I noted the up-to-the-minute juicy lipgloss, the brocaded capri pants that I would later see in *Vogue*.

She was tiny, almost frail, beautiful with luminous blue eyes and peachy skin, and wore alarmingly elegant clothing – the pale blue trousers, lemony mules, a gauze shirt, a camisole; like one of her own characters, perfectly turned out. Her topaz ring was the size of a small principality.

Bushnell struck me – and I say this sympathetically – as someone in the great line of American self-inventors. Someone who decided to create a persona, even a CV, in order to enter the glamorous world that she describes so successfully to others who cannot get in. But she also struck me as someone who has yet to decide if she will take her place on the outside as the acute observer she can be, or if she will stay on the inside reeling out lucrative ephemeral copy as the mostly uncritical chronicler of the world she inhabits.

Bushnell ordered a shrimp cocktail and perched on a chair that seemed to dwarf her. She seemed a bit tense, poised and almost frustratingly smooth in her responses to my questions.

I recognised the tactics of a burnished media training: when a thorny question comes up, seamlessly change the subject; avoid defensiveness when the interviewer brings up a criticism; boost the positives.

The perfectly packaged woman frustrated me a bit, just as her fiction, including her new book, had frustrated me. There were glimpses of a dark, human, smart, cynical striver – an outsider looking in, with all the bristling insight that can bring – but these seemed a bit smothered under the media-genic brand-name creature she has so skillfully put together.

I had met Bushnell briefly before at the kind of socialites' event at which I am terrified I will use the wrong spoon. I was one of only two dark-haired women in a forest of real and faux blondes, and the only one wearing off-the-rack clothing.

At that event she had struck me at once as someone I liked: warm and sassy. Here we were again, but now her game face was on. I forged ahead. 'Do you consider yourself a feminist?' I asked.

'Completely,' she asserted with no hesitation. 'This is something I have been thinking about since I was a kid. In those days a girl could be a nurse, a librarian, a teacher, a secretary. Boys could be 10 things. Mothers were saying, at that time, they wanted to have a job. Men were asking: 'Don't I provide enough?'

She said *Sex and the City* came out of women's experience in the early 1980s, when they were told to have a career before marriage. This, plus the sexual revolution, created 'a huge amount of confusion for women'.

'Are the women in the show feminists, in your view?'

'Yeah,' she replied, again immediately. 'I think they're obviously feminists. Even Charlotte (the preppie character) in her way is a feminist.'

She added: 'These are really nice girls. They have a different attitude and morality. Being a feminist is not saying we are all the same!'

'How do you define feminism?'

'I think it's about taking care of themselves, not just relying on men,' she replied, eating a shrimp. 'You can be a feminist but that doesn't contradict the human desire for love. There is nothing wrong with that.'

To that, of course, the feminist in me can only say: 'Right on, sister.' Bushnell, whatever I would want her to do as a writer, has created a novel kind of female empowerment empire, and for that you have to give her credit.

Why do millions of women all over the world – after a long day of working in the secretarial pool in Slough or leading the charge in a corporate takeover in Munich or wiping bottoms in Omaha – tune in to *Sex and the City*? What could Miranda, Charlotte, Carrie and Samantha have to say to all of us disparate, girlish masses? Not what you may think.

Sex and the City, which is based on the columns Bushnell wrote for the New York *Observer*, has been derided as fashion fetishism, lightweight escapism, anti-feminist slush, a parable of the pathos of four oversexed women who can't hook a man, or even a gay saga.

In reality it is the first global female epic – the answer to the question posed in Virginia Woolf's essay, *A Room of One's Own*. What will women actually do when they are free?

Bushnell herself may think she is writing fluffy entertainment. But whenever a cultural product resonates like this – and *Sex and the City* has resonated worldwide – you can't help but wonder: what deeper nerve is this series touching?

Sex and the City is for several reasons a watershed, a series of female 'firsts' that speaks directly to women's fantasies today. These are the very opposite of the fantasies that the male-dominated mass media think the series is speaking to.

What is the storyline of the series, as recounted in the mainstream press? Four sexy, frantic women, alone in the mean city, looking haplessly for the happy ending – marriage with a stable, secure guy and family life.

But what do we really get, in show after show? The failure to find a marriageable man means the delicious prolongation of a late female adolescence: free and voluptuous, self-absorbed and female-centred. It means that the late-summer delight of unfettered female eroticism can proceed without restraint. It means nobody yells at the women for spending too much on their shoes.

The search for Mr Right is, I maintain, merely a pretext, a plot device to keep the action moving. It gives the women who are watching – most of them married – the chance to re-enact at length the fantasy of singleness, of unpunished sexuality, of paramount female friendships and autonomy. It is about Neverland for women, about not growing up and becoming responsible.

Sex and the City is a show about female choice, not female rejection. All the straight men are crazy. If the gender roles were reversed, the producers would be accused by feminists of rank misogyny. Women viewers get the naughty thrill of seeing their own gender portrayed for once as sane, sentient and decent, while the men are trolls and buffoons, mummy's boys and neurotics.

There is a strong element of revenge fantasy on those who have hurt us, stood us up, broken our hearts. When Miranda is stood up by a cute guy it turns out he is dead. Who can claim never to have wished such a sudden end on the cad who broke her heart?

Another element of the show's appeal is the theme of women's high standards and good taste. Far from being poor, post-feminist women who 'can't find love', in show after show they reject their suitors outright because the men suck as potential life partners. The moral is that it is not enough to be rich, handsome and able to offer marriage and a family; a suitable male has to be a decent person on the inside.

In one episode Carrie romps with a sexy young fellow who has to take his mother's call while they are in bed and assure her that he has given the dog its medicine. Another hot marriage prospect turns out to be lying about his job; he is not an agent, he is a house-sitter.

Many of the women in *Sex and the City*'s audience settled for home, for security, 'to have a man'. The mummy's boy, the cad, may be sitting on the couch next to them watching. But Carrie and co do not settle. They move on, because the sexual and women's revolution means that women have the right to select.

These are white, educated women who are economically independent; they no longer have to marry in order to eat or to feed their children. They can cut loose – and they do.

The show proposes but then subverts the ideal of married love as the happy ending. Look at Trey and Charlotte's marriage: while the rest of the women are shagging like bunnies, Charlotte can't have sex at all; Trey is inhibited with her though he can have a relationship with *Juggs*, his porn magazine.

Sex and the City also resonates because it is the first cultural document to treat women's concerns on an epic scale. I hear you laughing – but it is true. In what other novel or series do women's concerns mark and guide the dates, the events, the turns of the action? In the *Iliad*, war and battles set the pace. In the *Odyssey*, feats of seamanship determine the action. In a women's epic, sex and intimacy, fashion and matrimony are the landmarks on the horizon. Yet even the great women writers were not as narcissistically women-centred as the writers of *Sex and the City*.

One show featured the portentous sentence: 'The next day Samantha and I went to the Valley for Fendi bags. We had found fake Fendi paradise.'

You can go on laughing, but this sentence is as important, in its own way, as Virginia Woolf's iconic take on female friendship: 'Chloe liked Olivia.'

For women do secretly mark time and goals and accomplishments by fashion, bodies, children, sex, relationships. *Sex and the City* has the audacity to treat women's internal concerns as if they were actually important.

Then there is the sex itself. Having missed the series – which is only available to subscribers to the cable channel Home Box Office in America – I made the mistake of watching the videos in my bedroom where Gloria, our Latina cleaning lady, was working. As chatty scenes alternated rapidly with carnal moans, I blushed furiously, trying frantically to turn down the volume.

'*Necesito escribir algo sobre esta programa,*' I explained nervously in my high-school Spanish, as Samantha got energetically shagged . . . ('It's just research!' – the porn-watchers' famous cry.) 'Si, si,' Gloria nodded sceptically, one eyebrow raised while she folded sheets.

The fact is, my protestations to Gloria aside, I was indeed watching a kind of pornography. *Sex and the City* is revolutionary because it makes clear just how bawdy women really are. It portrays for the first time a genuine female sexual culture, unmediated by men, marriage, male porn and male rules. In this culture, food is part of sex ('He made sizzling scallops . . . after dinner, things got even hotter'). So is talking about sex, and anticipation of sex, and postcoital discussion of sex.

Dressing for sex is sex, and shopping for the clothes in which to undress is also part of sex, and grooming for sex is sex.

There is the famous Brazilian wax episode, in which Carrie gets shorn – completely – in a modish style of intimate depilation. The sexual payoff of the Brazilian wax technique is so temptingly rendered ('My Brazilian wax made me kiss him,' Carrie declares) that all of New York was abuzz a week later with the jump in demand for the procedure. Reports surfaced of the premier depilators in town, a pair of Latina sisters, having framed a thank-you note from Gwyneth Paltrow – 'Thank you for changing my life.'

Liberate the female pudendum and nobody is answerable for the ungovernable consequences. Or, as Carrie notes: 'Why hide your light under a bushel?'

The power of the show to set sexual trends for women is so great that once, when I was doing research – yes, really – about *Good Vibrations*, the right-on, women-run, women-centred sex toys catalogue, the woman who took the orders said that the famous Hitachi Magic Wand vibrator had sold out because it had been featured on the show.

Virginia Woolf asked what women would do if they had £500 a year and a room of their own.

Sex and the City has the answer: they'd f★★★ – a lot. And not always with the men they 'should'. And then they'd talk and talk and talk about it.

And I will say right here: this insight by the producers of the show is true to life. This is what women of a certain class and generation really do behind closed doors when they have the leisure, the confidence and the opportunity.

So, what of the woman who exposed this truth about her gender?

When I had first heard the biographical stories told about Candace Bushnell – that she had grown up in 'the lush pastures of Connecticut', that her father was a rocket scientist and that her ancestors had come over on the *Mayflower* – my bullshit detector had gone wild.

Even a parking lot in Connecticut is in a lush pasture – the whole state is a lush pasture. A rocket scientist? The only place we have rocket scientists working on rockets is in Florida, with Nasa. And the descendants of the *Mayflower* pioneers can be found in low-rent suburbs and trailer parks – you can trace your connection to them on the internet.

I was not unsympathetic: the great chroniclers of the American elite have always been self-created, and Fitzgerald – from the wrong street in St Paul – was the model Bushnell made me think of. But I wanted her to 'own' her roots.

As she nibbled her shrimp, I asked about the 'rocket scientist'. Her father, she explained, was a research engineer at Pratt & Whitney, which makes aeroplane and spacecraft engines in Connecticut: 'He has a patent for the fuel cell they used in the first Apollo rocket.'

'Your mother?' I asked.

'My mom was a businesswoman,' she explained. 'She started her own travel agency.'

Bushnell said she had grown up in Glastonbury, Connecticut, gone to the local high school, and studied at university for a year and a half.

A solidly middle-class background, I noted. But Bushnell rejected my assessment.

'We had horses, an old house,' she said. 'It was a mannered town. Everybody belonged to the country club.' Middle-class people then, she said, could live an upper-middle-class life.

Point taken – but to me, there is more drama and achievement in the gutsy rise to the top of a middle-class girl who is not to the manor born, who did not finish college, who survived for her first years in New York by waitressing.

'I know what it is like to go to a cash machine and hope you have $20 because without $20 you can't get any money out,' she said. To me, that story – of plugging away at the dream without the silver spoon – is Bushnell's really impressive biography.

When she arrived in New York she went to acting school and roomed with three girls who were actresses. That period of her life informs a great deal of her fiction and formed the basis of the column that became *Sex and the City*.

Now she has written a novel, *Trading Up*, in which the women are more cynical than the striving hopefuls of *Sex and the City*. In it, marriage is a berth to be manipulated by a lead character, Janey Wilcox, who turns out to have been a prostitute.

I told Bushnell I couldn't relate to the fear that underlies the women characters' drive for marriage – I mean, isn't that awfully retro?

'I don't think the world has changed so much,' she replied. 'Turn on the TV – these dating shows, reality shows – it is still a world in which women feel at a disadvantage.'

'My friends would never have sex with a man for money, or marry a man for money,' I protested. 'Are we just in really different worlds?'

'I listen to a lot of women,' she countered. 'I overhear things. Haven't you heard women saying, 'If he won't marry you, get pregnant'?'

I hadn't personally ever heard a woman I knew say this in seriousness. Which is why I relate much more to the reality of the *Sex and the City* world she describes – of confident professional women – than the gold-diggers in her latest fiction.

Bushnell herself has left the dating life; she was, famously, married recently. Bushnell's husband, Charles Askegard, is a principal dancer at the New York City Ballet.

'I met my husband,' she confided girlishly, 'at a gala for the New York City Ballet. I was sitting at a different table . . . we started talking . . . and I thought, "This guy is so nice, and so much fun." We both realised early on that this was something more. The truth is, you just know. We really talk about everything,' she sighed happily.

And now *Sex and the City* is being cancelled. Why? The British press has been full of speculation that the women were getting 'too old' to be sympathetic and sexy in their search for love.

Bushnell responded: 'That's a very English thing to say! I have not heard anything like that.'

The women were certainly not getting too old. 'It's never too late, that's really the point. We think that in America. They don't in England.'

The reason the show was being cancelled was that it 'has gone on for six great years and the actresses have been working incredibly hard'.

What will happen at the end of the current series? 'I know a little bit, but obviously cannot give it away,' she said firmly.

'What happened,' I asked, shifting approaches, 'in real life, to the women upon whom the four characters are modelled?'

'Loosely based,' she corrected me. 'Some are married. Some have achieved their aspirations – they are happy. The toxic bachelors are still toxic and looking worse every day. I think there's going to be a big percentage of women who are never marrying – and you know what? They are not unhappy.'

As the huge topaz on her finger sparkled in the later afternoon sun, she remarked: 'In your forties you are more accepting of your life and yourself. You are,' said the creatrix of *Sex and the City*, and a small female empire besides, 'able to find happiness in yourself.'

'What would a happy ending be for the women?' I asked. Meaning, of course, subtextually: would any of the single women get married?

'A happy ending,' Bushnell replied firmly, 'would be if they are happy.'

CHRISTINA LAMB

1965–

An award-winning journalist and author, Lamb has been a correspondent for the *Financial Times* in Pakistan and Brazil, a Nieman Fellow at Harvard University, and correspondent for the *Sunday Times* in South Africa. A fellow of the Royal Geographical Society, she is an inveterate traveller. She has published several books about her travels, including the *Sewing Circles of Herat*, about her love affair with Afghanistan, and *The Africa House*. She is now a correspondent reporting around the world for the *Sunday Times* and recently came back from Iraq.

In this article she goes to the heart of the dilemmas confronting working mothers – hers of course, is of a particularly extreme kind. What do you do when you've been trying to talk to your two year old all day from a satellite phone in the Hindu Kush and – when you finally get through – they want nothing to do with you?

My Double Life: Kalashnikovs and Cupcakes

23 January 2005, *Sunday Times*

The day I got out of hospital after having my first baby I went for tea with an evil dictator. My son Lourenço was in intensive care having been born at 29 weeks and my caesarean stitches felt as if they were tearing, but the first interview with General Augusto Pinochet under house arrest was a world exclusive.

When I returned to my son's incubator later, the nurses asked where I had been. When I told them they looked horrified. But I was 22 when I became a war correspondent and 12 years on I was determined that having a child would not change my life. I had cried when I found out that I was pregnant because it meant missing the war in Yugoslavia.

And perhaps, if I had to admit it, it was more scary watching a baby the size of my palm connected to an array of tubes and machines than doing what I know best.

Last Sunday the BBC screened *On the Front Line*, a documentary by Jeremy Bowen, a veteran BBC reporter, about being a war correspondent. To watch reporters like Fergal Keane talk candidly about resorting to drink or Jon Steele, a former ITN cameraman, on wandering round Heathrow babbling, was not comfortable for any of us who cover conflict for a living.

But apart from Christiane Amanpour of CNN they were all men. As a mother who keeps a terrible secret in her wardrobe – a flak jacket – and whose child's first words were 'bye-bye', it was decidedly guilt making.

For some time after Lourenço was born I thought about giving up foreign reporting. On September 9, 2001 we moved to Portugal, where my husband had been brought up, for me to start writing a book. Two days later I got a telephone call and switched on the television to see the World Trade Center in New York in flames and studio analysts talking about Osama Bin Laden and Afghanistan.

Afghanistan was where I had first started back in 1987. I had walked into the American Club in Peshawar and a group of whisky-drinking middle-aged men with blood-stained army jackets swivelled round on their stools to look me up and down.

Soon I was crossing back and forth along the Khyber Pass on donkeys or by foot, face darkened and dressed as a mujaheddin or disguised in a burqa. 'Going inside' we called it and we spent all our time trying to do it, then most of the time inside trying to get out. When I won young journalist of the year in 1988 it seemed an irritating distraction to go to London for the ceremony. The Afghan jihad was an adventure, it was like my first love affair, and when September 11 happened I knew that I had to go back even though Lourenço was just two.

When I finally returned home months later, his nursery manager asked me what I did. She said Lourenço kept telling everyone, 'My mummy lives on a plane.'

Of course it is difficult being apart. By luck I was there when he took his first steps. But I have yet to make a parents' evening and usually when I am away he refuses to speak to me. It may take hours to get through on the satellite phone from some mountain top in the Hindu Kush, only for him to say, 'I'm busy, Mummy.'

I think having a stable home life, a loving husband and child helps me to deal better with the horrors of being a war correspondent. It feels as though I have two separate lives. But sometimes those two worlds collide.

Two weeks ago a contact from Pakistan intelligence, who is close to some of the world's most wanted terrorists, was in town just for an afternoon. It was Lourenço's class 'bake sale' and I had arranged to pick him up from school. When I explained this, begging my contact to squeeze me in later, he said no problem, he would come too. He bought £10 of cupcakes. Last week we received the school newsletter congratulating Swan Class on a record total.

But generally the benefits for Lourenço seem few. His great-aunt gave him a globe and by the age of four he could point out Afghanistan and

Iraq. He regularly gives me his old toys for 'the poor boys in Afghanistan who don't have anything'.

Like most working mothers guilt is a part of life. When my son was born prematurely I was convinced that it was my fault. During my pregnancy I had gone everywhere – from the Siachen glacier, the world's highest battleground (where India and Pakistan are fighting), to the Niger Delta to cover clashes between the Ogoni people and the military. I was in South Africa covering the elections when I woke up in a bed covered in blood and was told by a gynaecologist not to move for the rest of my pregnancy.

Obviously there is no way that I could do my job if I did not have my husband. When I came back from months away covering the war in Iraq in 2003, we went to Marrakesh for a romantic weekend. I was woken by a 6a.m. phone call on the first day to be told that there had been an Al-Qaeda attack the night before in Casablanca and could I just hop on a plane. Reader, I am afraid I succumbed.

Employers, who in this business are generally male, are not always understanding. In a previous job I returned from three months away covering the war in Afghanistan not to a congratulatory bottle of cham-pagne but to a memo asking if it had really been necessary to phone home almost every day.

Amanpour talked openly to Bowen about 'the fear factor' increasing as she got older. Most of us are able to do this job by deluding ourselves that because we are witnesses, not participants, we lead a kind of charmed life. In Jalalabad I was in a convoy of three ambulances when the first was blown up, and there was the rock thrown through our back windscreen on a mountain road in Israel that missed smashing my skull by a whisker and then narrowly avoided my driver.

The first time I really felt scared was in Iraq. I had been bitterly against the war which I believed would provoke outrage across the Arab world. The day after it started I managed to sneak across the Kuwaiti border into southern Iraq with Jonathan Calvert, a colleague. I called the office, which was delighted and told us that the Ministry of Defence was reporting that Basra was under attack so we should head that way.

Apart from some brief sniper fire at a British checkpoint along the way we saw no signs of the British or American troops or the defecting Republican Guards that the defence ministry was claiming, let alone the helicopter gunships 'pounding the bridges', which one news agency was reporting. It felt wrong. In the end we turned back.

On the way we passed a car marked TV heading the way that we had gone. It was Terry Lloyd, the ITN reporter, and his crew. Later we saw his car overturned by the side of the road, riddled with bullet holes.

That evening I spoke to my little boy. 'Mummy, are you in the desert?' he asked excitedly. 'How many camels have you seen?' The reality was grey and gritty, not golden undulating dunes. I twisted around in the car, trying to find a comfortable position in which to sleep, and thought about Terry and whether I really wanted to risk my life covering a war that I believed was wrong.

Why do we do it? First, it's a privilege to have a ringside seat to history and we all hope that somehow what we see and report can change things. The reality is often frustrating. In Zimbabwe the situation just keeps getting worse. For all that I try to pen powerful words about rape and torture camps and an 80-year old megalomaniac starving his own people, it makes no difference. Worse, while I can jump on a plane and fly home, anyone I interview is likely to be harassed or tortured. 'What benefit do we get from talking to you?' is not an easy question to answer in a country towards which the world seems to have turned a blind eye.

And in places like Afghanistan or Angola, where everyone seems to have lost a son or a daughter, sometimes I just want to shut my notebook and flee.

I suppose the main reason we do it is because it's exciting. Being a war junkie is a kind of Peter Pan existence: the moment I step on that plane I am fleeing the mundane – paying bills, getting the living room decorated, dealing with banks and so on.

But I firmly believe that being a mother has made me a better reporter. After years in the developing world I had seen so many refugees that I was beginning to make Monty Python-style comparisons, unmoved by the plight of one group because, relative to another, they were not starving enough.

Once I had a child of my own, that changed. Meeting mothers who had been reduced to scraping the moss off rocks to try to feed their children, or telling them to suck their hair, made me imagine what it would be like to look my own son in the face and tell him that there was nothing to eat, nowhere to sleep.

It has also made me realise that the real story is not the bang bang but the mothers who somehow manage to feed, shelter and even educate their children in the midst of war. All too often the only way women are portrayed in war is as victims, not the heroes of the hour.

Being a mother has also made me more aware of danger. No story is worth someone having to tell my son that your mummy won't be around to watch you grow up because she went on a story and didn't come back.

But sometimes I forget because of a spur-of-the-moment opportunity. Such as during the war in Iraq, going into Basra in a taxi while it was still under Saddam Hussein's control and dodging Iraqi road-blocks.

Or because it's a big story, such as being smuggled on a motorbike in Baluchistan to meet Taliban ministers in hiding. And in September 2003, when an American military spokesman in Afghanistan described Shkin on the Pakistan border as 'the most evil place on earth', I knew I had to go there.

Over the years I have lost a number of friends, although more through plane crashes and traffic accidents than in fighting. Often it is only afterwards that we realise the danger. When Pakistani intelligence agents banged on my hotel room door in the border town of Quetta at 2.30a.m. one day in November, then forced it open and abducted me and Justin Sutcliffe, my colleague, I was too indignant to be scared.

It was two months later when Daniel Pearl, a reporter on the *Wall Street Journal*, disappeared the day after a meeting with the same Karachi cleric who we had met that we realised quite how much danger we had faced.

Pearl's execution highlighted how much the job has changed. As was shown by the attack last year on Frank Gardner, the BBC's security correspondent, and Simon Cumbers, his cameraman. Gardner was terribly wounded and Cumbers was killed. The truth is that we have become targets. The risks have never been greater – in the past two years 93 reporters have been killed.

Constantly bearing witness to man's worst evils has its psychological toll. Close colleagues have had nervous breakdowns or been through several marriages. Three friends have committed suicide. Suddenly everyone seems to be talking about post-traumatic stress syndrome.

Two things happened to me. Last autumn I had a miscarriage in Kandahar in Afghanistan while staying in a dirty guest house with a group of Bangladeshi telephone engineers. Then recently I was trying to be a proper mother and making Mr Men cakes with Lourenço. Afterwards he solemnly presented me one with a Little Miss holding a mobile phone to her ear. 'That's you, Mummy,' he said, 'Little Miss Journalist.'

That seemed to put things into perspective. But like all addictions it is hard to cure. A few days later I refused to go to cover the tsunami because it was the day after Boxing Day and my son was home on his Christmas holidays.

That afternoon I took Lourenço to a show about knights and dragons in a big top tent. All the way through, as Lancelot was slaying monsters, my hand was itching to text the office and ask, 'When's the next plane?'

CRIME & PUNISHMENT

MARTHA GELLHORN
1908–98

As a war reporter (see previous article for more details), Gellhorn built her career on her ability to lay bare the very darkest side of human nature, the psychic and social underbelly that allowed individuals and groups to commit – and justify to themselves – horrific crimes. In the following article, she finds herself being caught up in a lynching during a trip to Mississippi. The simplicity and detail with which she describes this scene underlines the incredible everyday horror of the American South during this period.

Justice at Night

August 1936, *Spectator*

We got off the day coach at Trenton, New Jersey, and bought a car for $28.50. It was an eight-year-old Dodge open touring-car and the back seat was full of fallen leaves. A boy, who worked for the car dealer, drove us to the City Hall to get an automobile licence and he said: 'The boss gypped the pants off you, you should of got his machine for $20 flat and it's not worth that.' So we started out to tour across America, which is, roughly speaking, a distance of 3,000 miles.

I have to tell this because without the car, and without the peculiarly weak insides of that car, we should not have seen a lynching.

It was September, and as we drove south the days were dusty and hot and the sky was pale. We skidded in dust that was as moving and uncertain as sand, and when we stopped for the night we scraped it off our faces and shook it from our hair like powder. So, finally, we thought we'd drive at night, which would be cooler anyhow, and we wouldn't see the dust coming at us. The beauty of America is its desolation: once you leave New England and the industrial centres of the east you feel that no one lives in the country at all. In the south you see a few people, stationary in the fields, thinking or just standing, and broken shacks where people more or less live, thin people who are accustomed to semi-starvation and crops that never quite pay enough. The towns or villages give an impression of belonging to the flies; and it is impossible to imagine that on occasion these languid people move with a furious purpose.

We drove through Mississippi at night, trying to get to a town called Columbia, hoping that the hotel would be less slovenly than usual and that there would be some food available. The car broke down. We did everything we could think of doing, which wasn't much, and once or twice it panted wearily and then there was silence. We sat in it and cursed and wondered what to do. No one passed; there was no reason for anyone to pass. The roads are bad and mosquitoes sing too close the minute you stop moving. And the only reason to go to a small town in Mississippi is to sell something, or try to sell, and that doesn't happen late at night.

It was thirty miles or more to Columbia and we were tired. If it hadn't been for the mosquitoes we should simply have slept in the car and hoped that someone would drive past in the morning. As it was we smoked cigarettes and swatted at ourselves and swore and hated machinery and talked about the good old days when people got about in stage-coaches. It didn't make things better and we had fallen into a helpless silence when we heard a car coming. From some distance we could hear it banging over the ruts in the road. We climbed out and stood so the headlights would find us and presently a truck appeared, swaying crazily. It stopped and a man leaned out. As a matter of fact, he sagged out the side and he had a bottle in one hand, waving it at us.

'Anything wrong?' he said.

We explained about the car and asked for a lift. He pulled his head into the truck and consulted with the driver. Then he reappeared and said they'd give us a lift to Columbia later, but first they were going to a lynching and if we didn't mind the detour . . .

We climbed into the truck.

'Northerners?' the driver said. 'Where did you all come from?'

We said that we had driven down from Trenton in New Jersey and he said, 'In that old piece of tin?' referring to our car. The other man wiped the neck of the bottle by running his finger around inside it, and offered it to me. 'Do you good,' he said, 'best corn outside Kentucky.' It was no time to refuse hospitality. I drank some of the stuff which had a taste like gasoline, except that it was like gasoline on fire, and he handed it to my friend Joe, who also drank some and coughed, and they both laughed.

I said timidly, 'Who's getting lynched?'

'Some goddam nigger, name of Hyacinth as I recollect.'

'What did he do?'

'He got after a white woman.' I began to think with doubt and disgust of this explanation. So I asked who the woman was.

'Some widow woman, owns land down towards Natchez.'

'How old is she?' Joe asked. Joe was in doubt, too.

'Christ, she's so old she ought to of died. She's about forty or fifty.'

'And the boy?'

'You mean that nigger Hyacinth?'

I said yes, and was told that Hyacinth was about nineteen, though you couldn't always tell with niggers; sometimes they looked older than they were and sometimes younger.

'What happened?' Joe said. 'How do you know she got raped?'

'She says so,' the driver said. 'She's been screaming off her head about it ever since this afternoon. She run down to the next plantation and screamed and said hang that man; and she said it was Hyacinth. She ought to of knowed him anyhow; he was working for her sometime back.'

'How do you mean; was he a servant?'

'No,' the driver said, 'he was working on her land on shares. Most of her croppers've moved off by now; she don't give them any keep and they can't make the crop if they don't get nothing to eat all winter. She sure is cruel hard on niggers, that woman; she's got a bad name for being a mean one.'

'Well,' Joe said, very gently, 'it doesn't look likely to me that a boy of nineteen would go after a woman of forty or fifty. Unless she's very beautiful, of course.'

'Beautiful,' the man with the bottle said, 'Jees, you ought to see her. They could stick her out in a field and she'd scare the crows to death.'

We bumped in silence over the roads. I couldn't think of anything to say. These men were evidently going to the lynching, but I didn't see that they were blind with anger against the Negro, or burning to avenge the honour of the nameless widow. Joe whispered to me: 'You know we can't just sit and take this. I don't believe the boy did anything to that woman. We can't just sit around and let a man get hung, you know.' I began to feel hot and nervous and I decided I'd like a drink even if it was corn whiskey. But I couldn't think of anything to do.

'How many people will be coming? A big crowd?' I asked.

'Yeah. They been getting the word around all evening. Some of the boys gonna go down and spring the jail. That's easy. Sheriff don't plan on holding that nigger till trial time anyhow. There'll be a lot of folks driving in from all over the county. They been telephoning around this afternoon and visiting folks and it gets around if there's trouble with a nigger. There'll be plenty of folks there.'

'But,' Joe said, this time desperately, 'you don't know that he did anything to that woman. You haven't any proof have you?'

'She says he did,' the driver said, 'that's enough for us. You gotta take a white woman's word any time before you take a nigger's. Helluva place it'd be if you said white folks lied and niggers told the truth.'

'But you said he worked for her,' Joe went on. 'You said she was mean and didn't give her share-croppers decent rations. He's so much younger than she is, too, and you said she wasn't any beauty. He may have been going to see her to ask for money for food and he may have gotten mad and raised his arm or something that made her think he was going to strike her . . .'

'Lissen, sonny,' the man with the bottle said quietly, finally, 'this here ain't none of your goddam business.'

We drove in silence, lurching against each other, and the driver took a drink, steering with one hand, and then the other man drank. They were sore, I could see that. They'd come out to get drunk and have a good time and here we were, asking questions and spoiling their fun. They were getting a grim drunk, not a laughing one, and they were sore about it. They didn't offer us the bottle any more.

The road widened and ahead we could see tail-lights. The driver stepped on the gas and the truck rattled forward. We passed a touring car with six men in it; I saw some shot-guns. 'That you, Danny?' the driver shouted. 'Hi, Luke, see you later.'

We were evidently going to an appointed meeting place. I asked about this. 'They'll bring him up from jail,' the man with the bottle said. 'We all are gonna get together at the Big Elm crossroads.'

There were more cars now and the road was better. 'Almost there,' the driver said, and for no reason at all the man with the bottle said, 'Attaboy,' and laughed and slapped his leg.

There was no moon. I saw an enormous tree and, though there were no doubt others, it stood by itself and had a curious air of usefulness. The roads forked and there were shapeless dark cars sprawled in the dust and men waiting in groups, laughing, drinking, and looking down the road for something to appear; something that would give this party meaning. I couldn't judge the crowd but there must have been about fifty cars, and these cars travel full.

Presently a line of cars came up the road. They were going as fast as they could over the ruts. They stopped and men poured out of them, not making much noise, apparently knowing what they had to do as if it were a ritual, or something they had practised often before. Some of these men seemed to be the poorest of white farmers: tenants or share-croppers themselves. Tattered clothes, the usual thin unhinged bodies, that soiled look of people who live in little crowded places. There were one or two men who seemed to be there on principle, as one would go to a dinner party because it was an obligation, but a very boring one, and a few men, rather more compact than the others, who directed the show. It was hard to tell in this light, but they seemed men of middle age mostly, householders, heads of families, reliable people. Joe was saying now, 'I'd like to kill somebody myself.'

I couldn't think of anything at all. I kept wondering why we were here. I hadn't seen Hyacinth yet.

But Hyacinth was there, surrounded by men. He had been brought in one of the last cars. I heard a man say: 'Hurry up before the bastard dies of fright.' Hyacinth was walked across the road, through an open space, to the great tree. He had his hands tied and there was a rope around his waist. They were dragging him; his legs curled under him and his head seemed loose and heavy on his neck. He looked small and far too quiet. They had torn off his shirt.

The men gathered around; they came without any commands and stood at a distance to give the leaders room to work. There was not any decisive noise, no cheering or shouting, but just a steady threatening murmur of anger or determination. The action moved fast, with precision.

A sedan drove up and stopped under the tree. A man climbed on to the top quickly. Another. They stood black against the sky. From beneath, a group of men, shoving and pushing, got Hyacinth's limp thin body up to them. Hyacinth half-lay, half-squatted on the roof. From the ground a length of rope sailed up, hung in the air, curved and fell. A man tried again and the rope caught and hung down from a limb. The noosed end was thrown to one of the men standing on the car-roof. He held it and shook Hyacinth. There were no words now, only vague instructions, half-spoken. The crowd stood still; you could hear the mosquitoes whining.

The other man held something in his hand; it looked like a great jug. He held it over Hyacinth, who shivered suddenly, and came to life. His voice rose out of him like something apart, and it hurt one's ears to listen to it; it was higher than a voice can be, not human. 'Boss,' he said. 'Boss, I didn't do nuthin, don't burn me Boss, Boss . . .' The crowd had trembled now, stirred by his voice, and there were orders to hurry, to kill the bastard, what the hell were they waiting for . . .

The two men held him up and put the noose around his neck, and now he was making a terrible sound, like a dog whimpering. The minute they let go, he slacked into a kneeling position and his whole body seemed to shrink and dwindle and there was this noise he made. The two men jumped down from the roof: the rope was taut now. The car started and the silly sound of the starter failing to work, then the hesitant acceleration of the motor were so important that nothing else was heard; there were no other sounds anywhere; just these, and a moment's waiting. The car moved forward, fast. Hyacinth skidded and fought an instant – less than an instant – to keep his footing or some hold, some safety. He snapped from the back of the car, hung suspended, twirling a little on the rope, with his head fallen sideways. I did not know whether he was dead. There was a choked sound beside me and it was Joe, crying, sitting there crying, with fury, with helplessness, and I kept looking at Hyacinth and thinking: it can't have happened. There had been a noise, a sudden guttural sound as of people breathing out a deep breath, when the rope carried Hyacinth twisting into the air. Now a man came forward with a torch made of newspaper, burning. He reached up and the flames licked at Hyacinth's feet. He had been soaked in kerosene to make it easy, but the flames didn't take so well at first. Then they got on to his trousers and went well, shooting up, and there was a hissing sound and I thought a smell. I went away and was sick.

When I came back the cars were going off down the road quietly. And men were calling to each other saying: 'So long, Jake . . .' 'Hi there, Billy . . .' 'See you t'morrow, Sam . . .' Just saying goodnight to each other and going home.

The driver and the man with the bottle came back to the truck and got in. They seemed in a good frame of mind. The driver said, 'Well there won't be no more fresh niggers in these parts for a while. We'll get you to Columbia now. Sorry we hadta keep you waiting . . .'

REBECCA WEST
1892–1983

London-born journalist, novelist and essayist, West began her career in 1911, aged nineteen, as a columnist for the feminist newspaper *Freewoman*. This was followed, in quick succession, by work at a number of more broadly socialist magazines as she established her reputation as a serious, though often very witty, essayist.

In 1918, West published *The Return of the Soldier*, the first of many well-received novels. She also began travelling more widely as a journalist. Never eager to report from war zones, West nonetheless established herself as one of the world's leading war reporters with her moving and incisive commentary on the Nuremberg Trials. Collected in *A Train of Powder*, these reports remain one of the most significant comments on the rise and demise of Nazi power. The following extract sets the scene and West's approach to her subject.

On the Nuremberg Trials

1946, *A Train of Powder*

1—There rushed up towards the plane the astonishing face of the world's enemy: pine woods on little hills, grey-green glossy lakes, too small ever to be anything but smooth, gardens tall with red-tongued beans, fields striped with copper wheat, russet-roofed villages with headlong gables and pumpkin-steeple churches that no architect over seven could have designed. Another minute and the plane dropped to the heart of the world's enemy: Nuremberg. It took not many more minutes to get to the courtroom where the world's enemy was being tried for his sins; but immediately those sins were forgotten in wonder at a conflict which was going on in that court, though it had nothing to do with the indictments considered by it. The trial was then in its eleventh month, and the courtroom was a citadel of boredom. Every person within its walk was in the grip of extreme tedium. This is not to say that the work in hand was being performed languidly. An iron discipline met that tedium head on and did not yield an inch to it. But all the same the most spectacular process in the court was by then a certain tug-of-war concerning time. Some of those present were fiercely desiring that that tedium should come to an end at the first possible moment, and the others were as fiercely desiring that it should last for ever and ever.

The people in court who wanted the tedium to endure eternally were the twenty-one defendants in the dock, who disconcerted the spectator by presenting the blatant appearance that historical characters, particularly in distress, assume in bad pictures. They looked what they were as crudely as Mary Queen of Scots at Fotheringay or Napoleon on St Helena in a mid-Victorian Academy success. But it was, of course, an unusually ghastly picture. They were wreathed in suggestions of death. Not only were they in peril of the death sentence, there was constant talk about millions of dead and arguments whether these had died because of these men or not; knowing so well what death is, and experiencing it by anticipation, these men preferred the monotony of the trial to its cessation. So they clung to the procedure through their lawyers and stretched it to the limits of its texture; and thus they aroused in the rest of the court, the people who had a prospect of leaving Nuremberg and going back to life, a savage impatience. This the iron discipline of the court prevented from finding an expression for itself. But it made the air more tense.

It seemed ridiculous for the defendants to make any effort to stave off the end, for they admitted by their appearance that nothing was to go well with them again on this earth. These Nazi leaders, self-dedicated to the breaking of all rules, broke last of all the rule that the verdict of a court must not be foretold. Their appearance announced what they believed. The Russians had asked for the death penalty for all of them, and it was plain that the defendants thought that wish would be granted. Believing that they were to lose everything, they forgot what possession had been. Not the slightest trace of their power and their glory remained; none of them looked as if he could ever have exercised any valid authority. Göring still used imperial gestures, but they were so vulgar that they did not suggest that he had really filled any great position; it merely seemed probable that in certain bars the frequenters had called him by some such nickname as 'The Emperor.' These people were also surrendering physical characteristics which might have been thought inalienable during life, such as the colour and texture of their skins and the moulding of their features. Most of them, except Schacht, who was white-haired, and Speer, who was black like a monkey, were neither dark nor fair any more; and there was amongst them no leanness that did not sag and no plumpness that seemed more than inflation by some thin gas. So diminished were their personalities that it was hard to keep in mind which was which, even after one had sat and looked at them for days; and those who stood out defined themselves by oddity rather than character.

Hess was noticeable because he was so plainly mad: so plainly mad that it seemed shameful that he should be tried. His skin was ashen, and he had that odd faculty, peculiar to lunatics, of falling into strained positions which no normal person could maintain for more than a few minutes, and staying fixed in contortion for hours. He had the classless air characteristic of asylum inmates; evidently his distracted personality had torn up all clue to his past. He looked as if his mind had no surface, as if every part of it had been blasted away except the depth where the nightmares live. Schacht was as noticeable because he was so far from mad, so completely his ordinary self in these extraordinary circumstances. He sat twisted in his seat so that his tall body, stiff as a plank, was propped against the end of the dock, which ought to have been at his side. Thus he sat at right angles to his fellow defendants and looked past them and over their heads: it was always his argument that he was far superior to Hitler's gang. Thus, too, he sat at right angles to the judges on the bench confronting him: it was his argument that he was a leading international banker, a most respectable man, and no court on earth could have the right to try him. He was petrified by rage because this court was pretending to have this right. He might have been a corpse frozen by rigor mortis, a disagreeable corpse who had contrived to aggravate the process so that he should be specially difficult to fit into his coffin.

A few others were still individuals. Streicher was pitiable, because it was plainly the community and not he who was guilty of his sins. He was a dirty old man of the sort that gives trouble in parks, and a sane Germany would have sent him to an asylum long before. Baldur von Schirach, the Youth Leader, startled because he was like a woman in a way not common among men who looked like women. It was as if a neat and mousy governess sat there, not pretty, but with never a hair out of place, and always to be trusted never to intrude when there were visitors: as it might be Jane Eyre. And though one had read surprising news of Göring for years, he still surprised. He was so very soft. Sometimes he wore a German Air Force uniform, and sometimes a light beach suit in the worst of playful taste, and both hung loosely on him, giving him an air of pregnancy. He had thick brown young hair, the coarse bright skin of an actor who has used grease paint for decades, and the preternaturally deep wrinkles of the drug addict. It added up to something like the head of a ventriloquist's dummy. He looked infinitely corrupt, and acted naïvely. When the other defendants' lawyers came to the door to receive instructions, he often intervened and insisted on instructing them himself, in spite of the evident fury of the defendants, which, indeed, must have been poignant, since most of them might well have felt that, had it not been for him, they never would have had to employ these lawyers at all. One of these lawyers was a tiny little man of very Jewish appearance, and when he stood in front of the dock, his head hardly reaching to the top of it, and flapped his gown in annoyance because Göring's smiling wooden mask was bearing down between him and his client, it was as if a ventriloquist had staged a quarrel between two dummies.

Göring's appearance made a strong but obscure allusion to sex. It is a matter of history that his love affairs with women played a decisive part in the development of the Nazi party at various stages, but he looked as one who would never lift a hand against a woman save in something much more peculiar than kindness. He did not look like any recognized type of homosexual, yet he was feminine. Sometimes, particularly when his humour was good, he recalled the madam of a brothel. His like are to be seen in the late morning in doorways along the steep streets of Marseilles, the professional mask of geniality still hard on their faces though they stand relaxed in leisure, their fat cats rubbing against their spread skirts. Certainly there had been a concentration on appetite, and on elaborate schemes for gratifying it; and yet there was a sense of desert thirst. No matter what aqueducts he had built to bring water to his encampment, some perversity in the architecture had let it run out and spill on the sands long before it reached him. Sometimes even now his wide lips smacked together as if he were a well-fed man who had heard no news as yet that his meals were to stop. He was the only one of all these defendants who, if he had the chance, would have walked out of the Palace of Justice and taken over Germany again, and turned it into the stage for the enactment of the private fantasy which had brought him to the dock.

As these men gave up the effort to be themselves, they joined to make a common pattern which simply reiterated the plea of not guilty. All the time they made quite unidiosyncratic gestures expressive of innocence and outraged common sense, and in the intervals they stood up and chatted among themselves, forming little protesting groups, each one of which, painted as a mural, would be instantly recognized as a holy band that had tried to save the world but had been frustrated by mistaken men. But this performance they rendered more weakly every day. They were visibly receding from the field of existence and were, perhaps, no longer conscious of the recession. It is possible that they never thought directly of death or even of imprisonment, and there was nothing positive in them at all except their desire to hold time still. They were all praying with their sharp-set nerves: 'Let this trial never finish, let it go on for ever and ever, without end.'

The nerves of all others present in the Palace of Justice were sending out a counter-prayer: the eight judges on the bench, who were plainly dragging the proceedings over the threshold of their consciousness by sheer force of will; the lawyers and the secretaries who sat sagged in their seats at the tables in the well of the court; the interpreters twittering unhappily in their glass box like cage-birds kept awake by a bright light, feeding the microphones with French and Russian and English versions of the proceedings for the spectators' earphones; the guards who stood with their arms gripping their white truncheons behind their backs, all still and hard as metal save their childish faces, which were puffy with boredom. All these people wanted to leave Nuremberg as urgently as a dental patient enduring the drill wants to up and leave the chair; and they would have had as much difficulty as the dental patient in explaining the cause of that urgency. Modern drills do not inflict real pain, only discomfort. But all the same the patients on whom they are used feel that they will go mad if that grinding does not stop. The people at Nuremberg were all well fed, well clothed, well housed, and well cared for by their organizations, on a standard well above their recent experience. This was obviously true of the soldiers who had campaigned in the war, and of the British and French civilians at work in the court; and it was, to an extent that would have surprised most Europeans, true of the American civilians. It never crossed the Atlantic, the news of just how uncomfortable life became in the United States during the war: what the gasoline shortage did to make life untenable in the pretty townships planned on the supposition that every householder had an automobile; how the titanic munitions programme had often to plant factories in little towns that could not offer a room apiece to the incoming workers; what it was like to live in an all-electric house when electric equipment was impossible to replace or repair. By contrast, what Nuremberg gave was the life of Riley, but it was also the water-torture, boredom falling drop by drop on the same spot on the soul.

What irked was the isolation in a small area, cut off from normal life by the barbed wire of army regulations; the perpetual confrontation with the dreary details of an ugly chapter in history which the surrounding rubble seemed to prove to have been torn out of the book and to require no further discussion; the continued enslavement by the war machine. To live in Nuremberg was, even for the victors, in itself physical captivity. The old town had been destroyed. There was left the uninteresting new town, in which certain grubby hotels improvised accommodation for Allied personnel, and were the sole places in which they might sleep and eat and amuse themselves. On five days a week, from ten to five, and often on Saturday mornings, their duties compelled them to the Palace of Justice of Nuremberg, an extreme example of the German tendency to overbuild, which has done much to get them into the recurring financial troubles that make them look to war for release. Every German who wanted to prove himself a man of substance built himself a house with more rooms than he needed and put more bricks into it than it needed; and every German city put up municipal buildings that were as much demonstrations of solidity as for use. Even though the Nuremberg Palace of Justice housed various agencies we would not find in a British or American or French law court, such as a Labour Exchange, its mass could not be excused, for much of it was a mere waste of masonry and an expense of shame, in obese walls and distended corridors. It recalled Civil War architecture but lacked the home-liness; and it made the young American heart sicken with nostalgia for the clean-run concrete and glass and plastic of modern office buildings. From its clumsy tripes the personnel could escape at the end of the working day to the tennis courts and the swimming pools, provided that they were doing only routine work. Those who were more deeply involved had to go home and work on their papers, with little time for any recreation but dinner parties, which themselves, owing to the unique character of the Nuremberg event, were quite unrefreshing. For the guests at these parties had either to be co-workers grown deadly familiar with the passing months or VIPs come to see the show, who, as most were allowed to stay only two days, had nothing to bring to the occasion except the first superficial impressions, so apt to be the same in every case. The symbol of Nuremberg was a yawn.

The Allies reacted according to their histories. The French, many of whom had been in concentration camps, rested and read; no nation has endured more wars, or been more persistent in its creation of a culture, and it has been done this way. The British reconstituted an Indian hill station; anybody who wants to know what they were like in Nuremberg need only read the early works of Rudyard Kipling. In villas set among the Bavarian pines, amid German modernist furniture, each piece of which seemed to have an enormous behind, a triple feat of reconstitution was performed: people who were in Germany pretended they were people in the jungle who were pretending they were in England. The Americans gave those huge parties of which the type was fixed in pioneering days, when the folks in the scattered homesteads could meet so rarely that it would have been tiring out the horses for nothing not to let geniality go all up the scale; and for the rest they contended with disappointment. Do what you will with America, it remains vast, and it follows that most towns are small in a land where the people are enthralled by the conception of the big town. Here were children of that people, who had crossed a great ocean in the belief that they were going to see the prodigious, and were back in a small town smaller than any of the small towns they had fled.

It might seem that this is only to say that in Nuremberg people were bored. But this was boredom on a huge historic scale. A machine was running down, a great machine, the greatest machine that has ever been created: the war machine, by which mankind, in spite of its infirmity of purpose and its frequent desire for death, has defended its life.

ROSE STYRON

A director of the American branch of the organization Amnesty International, Styron wrote this article to highlight the ongoing plight of the Chilean people under the dictator, General Pinochet.

Torture in Chile

20 March 1976, *New Republic*

It has been almost two years since I visited Santiago and talked with the kin of men, women and children who had been shot, had disappeared, were dying incommunicado or being physically and mentally destroyed in the stadiums, barracks, schools, mines, ships, hospitals, resorts and outposts that had been turned into detention centers, into houses of torture. Dawson Island, Chacobuco, Tejas Verdes, Quiriquina Island, the House of Bells, Lebu were the names I heard most often then. Scarcely a day has passed since I returned that I have not received a letter or call to augment my consciousness of the horror. Villa Grimaldi, Cuatro Alamos, Ritoque, Puchuncavi figure in more communiqués now. Scores of new documents concerning Chile are on my desk. They range from unanswered writs of habeas corpus, from manuscripts on genocide and nazism, the Chile Committee for Human Rights' excellent dispassionate, *Repression in Chile*, to a register of junta criminals that details the deadly acts and responsibilities of 40 Pinochet appointees. (Sample: 'Rodriguez, Christian; Lawyer. Murder and torture of General Alberto Bachelet. Santiago.' Sample: 'Vidal, Luis, Lieutenant. Torture and assault with bodily injury of José Flores, 14 years of age, and other children in arrest. Concepción.') There is Oriana Sanchez's heartbreaking account of following her daughter from one detention center to another, watching her slowly die under torture.

In addition, there are tapes of interviews with survivors of Chile's prisons: artist Gilberto Nuñez, safe in Paris after ordeals resulting from an exhibition of his work opened by the French embassy in Santiago; pre-med student Pedro Huertas Tapia, who became Chile's first refugee accepted in the US under the 1975 parole program, former parliamentarian Laura Allende, the president's youngest sister, witness to the cruel abuse of women and teenagers and little girls in the prison where she and her daughter were held, and former rector of the Technical University of Chile Enrique Kirberg, who was welcomed in a moving ceremony in Stamford, Connecticut on Human Rights Day by the Amnesty International group that had worked for two years for his release. Gentleness, not anger, was the tone of each. Each had come to understand that Pinochet's commander-in-chief was Fear. Not only were the poor and the hunted and the sensitive subject to the dictates of fear, but also those who had backed the general or worked for him now – the jailers, the police, the soldiers, the new mayors, the new military directors of factories and hospitals and schools, the once-smug members of Patria y Libertad, a Ku Klux Klan-type organization (also frequently compared to the elite Nazi youth) originally financed and encouraged by the CIA.

There is also on my desk a list of men, aged 16 to 76, imprisoned in Tres Alamos today. It includes the history of their maltreatment and a detailed description of places of their torture: La Discoteque, a house on 257 Iran Street in Nunoa: Villa Grimaldi, an estate that in the past six months has become the key torture center and from which many prisoners of both sexes have disappeared; Tejas Verdes, where for more than two years men and women have been held incommunicado, tortured and killed. The first letter smuggled out to me in Santiago was from a very young man in Tejas Verdes.

Of the 5,000 to 8,000 Chilean citizens classed as political prisoners today, the majority of them students and workers under 26, many have been guaranteed release if the United States and other nations would give them permanent residence and pay their way out. Other countries have taken upwards of l0,000 Chileans as refugees already. Last June Attorney General Levi signed a long-contested agreement that would permit 400 prisoners and their families to come to the US directly from prison. An immigration officer and a State Department official went from Washington to Santiago in July. With a Chilean who was attached to the US embassy there, they traveled to the camps to interview prisoners whose documented cases they had received from human rights organizations and prominent Americans and Chileans-in-exile. In July they interviewed at least 40 non-Communists in Tres Alamos who wanted to come to America. Working with the Intergovernmental Committee for European Migration (ICEM) more than 100 cases were processed, but by October not a single Chilean refugee had been accepted under the program. (Thousands of Vietnamese have been brought in, settled, launched.) Then in mid-October Edward Kennedy took the matter up on the floor of the Senate mentioning Chile's prize-winning boy scout, Pedro Huertas Tapi, who had once lived in California, a 20-year-old with no political connections or charges against him. Pedro had survived the torture that threatens every prisoner but was wasting away in Tres Alamos. Wasn't he qualified to come? The day after Kennedy's speech, Pedro was taken from prison and put on a plane to California.

I had gone out to see him, asking him about his return to Chile in 1972, following a year spent with a family in Mill Valley under a program called 'Beautiful Cities Exchange.' Pedro was from Viña del Mar, a coastal resort distinguished then by the president's summer house, now by the detention center called Ritoque. A slight, fair, shy young man with fine classic features and a quick smile, he told me the following: most students then were involved in politics at a grass roots level – community centers, student and faculty groups – and they were strong Allende supporters. After the coup Pedro decided to concentrate only on medical studies: he was neither an activist nor Marxist, and he knew none of the Movement of the Revolutionary Left (MIR) leaders. Yet after MIR leader Miguel Henriquez was killed and Carmen Castillo was shot, he was kidnapped from the apartment where he lived alone, at 3a.m. on November 18, 1974, because some unidentified neighbor had denounced him to the police. He was bound and blindfolded and taken to the torture center he later learned was Villa Grimaldi. The guards told him he was a revolutionary and demanded to know where his guns were hidden. They put him in a closet-sized cell and interrogated him for two weeks. He was hooded all the time, his hands shackled. After three days of sensory deprivation, he began to lose his sense of direction, of up and down and, after a longer spell of malnourishment, his sense of balance – physical and emotional – as well. He was then moved to a larger cell with four cots, where still hooded, he could talk to fellow inmates; one was always an informer, or a listener was posted by the door. For 45 days Pedro was subjected to a range of tortures standard in places like Chile, Uruguay and Brazil, from intensive electroshock to the wet and dry 'submarines.' In the wet submarine the bound victim is held upside down, totally immersed in a nameless liquid or excrement, to the brink of drowning. In the dry, a plastic bag is tied over the head and when the victim is near suffocation, ready to speak, he raises a finger to the tormentor. Accidental deaths via submarine are legion. Also standard are the mock executions complete with gunfire and threats to mutilate and kill one's family. Often Pedro, with constant nosebleeds, was so weak he fainted and thought himself dying; beaten, blindfolded and tied like a child, at the mercy of psychotic guards, he felt no relation to the real world, was certain no one knew or cared about him. He still has nightmares and nosebleeds, trouble with his ears and memory, and feels displaced. From there Pedro was taken to Cuatro Alamos, where, incommunicado, one's physical state is superficially repaired for eventual viewing by a judge or outside visitors.

After 10 days, he was transferred from Cuatro to Tres Alamos, out of the direct hands of the Direccion de Inteligencia Nacional (DINA), Chile's Gestapo. He could receive visits and get in touch with the Red Cross and the Committee for Peace. With public light on him, he felt he would not be killed. The Red Cross conducted limited questioning and agreed to take a message to Pedro's family. The Committee sent a lawyer, Ambassador Orlando Letelier's sister Fabiola to defend him. But Pedro never came to trial. After three months in Chocobuco, Pedro was taken to Ritoque, a detention center run by the air force.

In the three months since Pedro Huertas' arrival dispelled our conviction that the administration parole program was a sham (letters from Chileans with relatives here had painted a picture of utter confusion and/or deception in pertinent Santiago offices) nine more refugees have arrived with their families.

The State Department says that of 300 cases submitted by the Intergovernmental Committee for European Migration (ICEM) to our embassy, 217 were considered active in January and 61 were recommended by the Department for approval. What happened between 300 and 217, between 217 and 61? Since mid-January the Attorney General and Gen. Chapman of the Immigration Service have approved the expanding of the parole program to include a few of those who have been released from prison but wait in Santiag justly fearing rearrest.

Others fear death if their releases are delayed, dying from too much electroshock and too many beatings, as did 27-year-old Luis Alberto Corvalon (whom I saw alive and spirited in Mexico last March, released after eleven months of daily electroshock), of a premature heart attack, and Roseta Marinetti, who died on a Mexican operating table, her insides destroyed, the ruptures still in her vagina. (A friend who came to Mexico with her told of having been hung upside down by the heels for three days). They fear hemorrhaging to death after peculiar drug injections, as have a number of young prisoners from the *poblaciones*, the poor neighborhoods around Santiago. There were 180 young citizens arrested recently in the La Pincoya poblacion. One can only guess their plight today.

Human rights organizations and Chile solidarity groups around the world worked with enormous dedication in 1975 to expose the junta, to embarrass Gen. Pinochet into freeing victims. 'Hearings' have been held in Stockholm, Helsinki, Rome, Mexico City and Athens, and reports of their commissions have led a number of responsible European governments to cut political and economic ties with Chile. The United Nations spent months sifting complaints and listening to the testimony of survivors, and they organized a politically-balanced commission that left for Chile in early summer, with prior assurances of cooperation from

Pinochet. The commission was turned back at the Airport. Pinochet had changed his mind: it was not a good time to come. The UN, furious, unanimously decided to publish a full and damaging report. By thanksgiving it had pushed through a vote to condemn Chile for its violation of rights, 95–11, with 23 abstentions. Unlike the prior resolution which had gone 44–0 with the US and Chile abstaining, this resolve seemed to have both teeth and US support. In an indication of larger awareness, Secretary of State Kissinger suggested setting up a committee to study the nature and extent of torture in the world; and then-UN Ambassador Moynihan asked for amnesty for political prisoners everywhere. It remains for the US to implement these welcome freshly-sounded policies, and to see to it that 1975's Helsinki accords, which renew the spirit and letter of the 27-year-old Declaration of Human Rights, not be sidetracked by the temptations of détente, oil, power. Meanwhile, in Washington, Vietnam and Watergate past, Congress has shown its goodwill: it conducted a full-scale investigation of the CIA abroad, and recommended strong curbs on future activity. It passed Sen. Kennedy's bills to continue the cut-off of military aid to Chile and to put a $90 million ceiling on all other aid to Chile in 1976 (a far higher figure than the senator meant, but President Ford had committed that much and had planned the spending of many millions more). It passed the McGovern-Abourezk amendment to the Foreign Assistance Act, promising to deny aid to any country it decreed was violating human rights systematically. Sen. Jackson held hearings on the international freedom to write and publish.

On January 5th the *Christian Science Monitor* reported what may be the first crack in the junta façade: 10 senior generals, led by air force chief Gustavo Leigh, credited with being the brains behind the September 1973 coup, handed Pinochet an ultimatum demanding immediate and radical party changes, or resignation. They also asked for the dissolution of the DINA, reforms to save the economy from total collapse, and measures to improve the ugly image of Chile overseas. The wife of a general who exiled herself to Sweden gave out the story. Gen. Arellano Stark, the junta's military hero with a reputation for ruthlessness, 'resigned, over policy differences.' Like Minister of Interior Oscar Bonilla, the most accessible of Pinochet's cabinet until he was killed in a helicopter crash last spring, Stark had been an aide-de-camp to former President Frei. On January 19 the *New York Times* reported that Frei, who had refrained from speaking out after the coup, was publishing a booklet denouncing the junta for its violations of human rights. It was Frei the US subtly financed to defeat Allende a decade ago. Does he divine a new wind from Washington, blowing his way? This time we hope so.

Such signs have not visibly affected Augusto Pinochet. No voice he's heard has persuaded him to moderate his program of relentless repression. Two-and-a-half years after the coup there is still no civilian law, no right of assembly, no labor union, no school without a military director of a military-directed curriculum. Nearly 100,000 people have been arrested since 1973. The great majority have never been sentenced or even tried.

On June 20, 1975, Chile's dictator declared, 'There will be no elections in Chile in my lifetime nor in the lifetime of my successor.' The World Bank has just floated a loan of $30 million to the junta to facilitate its copper mines. When bank president Robert McNamara was asked by a delegation from church and human rights groups to postpone the loan, he said that the bank's only consideration was economic.

ANNE TYLER

1941–

Born in Minneapolis, Tyler was raised in North Carolina. Prodigiously academic, she began establishing herself as a writer whilst studying at Duke University, from which she graduated at just nineteen. From there, she went on to do graduate work in Russian studies at Columbia University.

Her first novel, *If Morning Ever Comes* (1964), established her as a major new voice, with the *New York Times* commenting that her 'touch is deft, her perceptions keen, her ear for speech phenomenal'. Since then she has continued to publish regularly.

Renowned for her narrative precision, it is this skill that she brings to the following piece. In charting the trial of Baltimore's Governor, Marvin Mandel, Tyler highlights the symbolism of all the characters and their situations, producing a report that reads like the very best short fiction.

Trouble in the Boys' Club

30 July 1977, *New Republic*

You can piece it all together from the *Baltimore Sun*, if you're willing to sit down with a few back issues. Here's this ordinary man, a low-key, pipe-chewing lawyer with a wife named Bootsie and two children. He grew up poor, selling newspapers at the Pimlico racetrack. He owns one green suit and a maroon sportcoat. You wouldn't guess it from his face (which is reassuringly benign, almost seraphic) but his clients are mostly characters on the Block – Baltimore's stretch of strip joints, massage parlors, and X-rated bookstores with peepshows in the back.

Then he falls into state politics, through a combination of circumstances. He knows the right people, he finds himself a seat in the House of Delegates. Then he's House Speaker. Then he's Governor – a little grayer, much better dressed, but still fond of an occasional kosher hot dog, still surrounded by the same old friends he's always had.

His friends. One looks like a stocky, pugnacious Columbo. Another has eyes like a lizard's, that appear to close in the middle. All are rich, but not so the Internal Revenue Service would notice. Their income depends upon certain bits of inside information, sudden government expenditures, suspiciously well-oiled glides through bureaucratic red tape. They draw much of their money from construction and racetracks – a combination that seems, at least from outside, as tough and sleazy and colorful as Baltimore itself.

Now, you have a good friend, the Governor figures – a fellow you've known half your life, gone fishing with, goose-hunting with – what's wrong with giving him a little boost, from time to time? A state contract here, a bit of legislation there? You've got to help each other out, in this world. Ease your friends' lives, and they'll ease yours: they'll send around a New York diamond cutter with a $4,500 diamond and platinum bracelet for your wife. They'll pick up the tab for your visit to a menswear store in Florida – couple shirts, ties, a few suits: $1,584.50. They'll hand you a little interest in some business ventures – free, or nearly free, but gifts can always be altered to look like payment for services.

Oh, accounts among the friends aren't all that closely calculated. It's just that occasionally, the Governor gets a dunning note from someplace, some little hotel or boutique that doesn't seem to understand these things, and he looks off in another direction a moment and the bill is somehow whisked away from him. A matter of caretaking, you might call it. What else are friends for?

But this has been a men's story, so far. (You don't find much talk of Bootsie.) And men's stories always have the same twist: a woman arrives, and trouble begins. The clubhouse falls to pieces. We could tell this part of the plot in our sleep.

So here comes this blond, divorced, from a lofty old Eastern Shore family. (Ah, her family. It's the combination that gets him, we feel: her brassy glittering hair, levitating about her head and then dripping in well-modulated scrolls; coupled with that Anglo-Saxon lineage. Later, he will spend their honeymoon searching the London museums for her ancestors.) Her ex-husband was in the state legislature. She herself has dabbled, at times, in real-estate selling – an occupation at once decorous and aggressive. She wears the sort of breezy, silken clothes that seem designed for lunch beside the golf course. She's irresistible.

Their courtship is not what is new in this story. That's been going on for years, or so we find out later. They've kept it quiet, but there've been some near misses. Back in 1971, that midnight auto accident in front of Rip's Restaurant and Motel . . . It was touch-and-go, for a while. Where was the Governor coming from, at such an hour? But either Bootsie never found out or (some rumors have it) she did find out but was placated by the aforementioned diamond bracelet. All nonsense, Bootsie says later. 'Do you think a woman like myself would be quiet for a diamond bracelet?'

No, we feel certain; not a woman like Bootsie. For when the Governor finally announces his divorce plans, Bootsie is far from compliant. She digs in her heels and stays on in the Mansion, alone. (The Governor moves to the local Hilton. State troopers are seen delivering his laundry.) She stays five and a half months, thereby losing much of the public sympathy she started out with. (We can identify with being wronged, but not with being undignified.) When she finally leaves, it's for a quarter-million-dollar divorce settlement, an air-conditioned Buick sedan, and a promise that her portrait will remain on the wall of the Governor's Mansion.

Maybe there was something to that bracelet story after all.

But the matter of the portrait, at least, is easily resolved. It has hung in the entrance hall, the end of a parade of first ladies. All you have to do is turn the parade around, send it up the stairs in the other direction, and Bootsie arrives on the landing, in the dark. Simple.

Nor is that all that's rearranged, once the blond marries the Governor. There's the furniture, too. There's the garden. And there's the Governor himself. Now he takes exotic trips, stays at exclusive resorts. The ketchup bottle is removed from the Mansion's dining table, and he develops a fondness for French cooking. He suddenly fancies Bordeaux with his meals. He likes to have the blond with him everywhere – not only at meals but also at private meetings, public meetings, and semi-political fishing trips.

Hear the mutters from the clubhouse.

She sends him secret signals in the middle of press conferences. She takes frantic notes during House debates. On every issue, she knows where she stands and she lets him know. She scolds his closest political associates, telling them to 'keep their lips zipped'; she freezes out others entirely, assists still others to positions of power. Life gets as complicated as a Chinese emperor's court.

But the Governor seems not to notice. He is beatific. His friends say he's grown absent-minded, careless, that political matters no longer claim his full attention. Where once he seized on any excuse to stay out late with the boys, he is now unbecomingly eager to get back home to the Mansion. He has changed, his friends say darkly. He's not the same man, since She came along.

Now, it may seem our story is trailing off here into a trickle of petty gossip, but take heart. There is a link between the Governor's private life and his public life.

Forced to scrounge for money to pay his divorce settlement, but living suddenly in a style that implies inordinate wealth, edged into the public's (and the federal government's) eye by scandal, and newly out of favor with some of his more influential supporters, the Governor is much like an overturned turtle. The federal prosecutor's office, therefore, pounces. Or so the Governor sees it.

For he is still, despite the French food and the Bordeaux wine, an unsophisticated man, and he appears honestly bewildered that plain old friendship should land him in court like a common criminal. After all, hasn't he been a good governor? Doesn't he run a tight ship? There must be some mistake. He chews his pipe a while and ponders how this could have happened. He thinks it might be because he's a newcomer, not old stock, and because he's given a helping hand to other newcomers. He casts his mind back to times when he's been persecuted, harrassed – that liquor raid on the Block, a while back, where they found a snapshot of the Governor with an underworld figure and circulated it everywhere, giving people the wrong idea. But he's sure it will work out, he says. You'll see.

Arriving at the Courthouse, where he will be tried for 20 counts of mail fraud and one count of racketeering, he is still chewing his pipe. The blond has a tan. Her son wears a T-shirt reading LUV THE GUV. A Baltimore fixture known as Mr. Diz takes it upon himself, as usual, to trumpet the arrival of all public figures appearing in court. There are plenty of them – but Maryland's grown used to that.

A spectator says, 'At least it keeps us on the map.'

The Courthouse can hold an audience of 46, and the seats are in great demand. Why wouldn't they be, for a trial that reads like an updated *Guys and Dolls?* There are fully grown witnesses with diminutives parenthesized at the centers of their names. There's Father Guido Carcich, no stranger himself to mail fraud, here to answer questions about 42,000 laundered dollars for Bootsie's divorce settlement. There's a jeweler who transacts his thriving business in cash, out of his coat pocket, and who testifies to receipt of over $3,000 in a 'lunch-looking bag with a rolled-over top' from a stranger in front of an airline counter.

He doesn't count the money then and there, though. 'In the middle of the waiting room of the Pan Am Airlines,' he says, 'you don't do that.'

We think this over, and we see his point. There are all sorts of rules and customs here that have not occurred to us – a whole world, meticulously organized. The trial, which has ceased to seem outrageous or even surprising, at least retains our interest because of this: a layer of life exists, occupying the same geographical space that our lives do, and we never even noticed, all this time.

Then the trial explodes. Somebody humdrum, a furniture salesman, no one you'd look at twice, has tried to bribe a juror. There is a lot of talk about 'tainting' and 'contamination.' The prosecution says that to call a mistrial would give the shark in our midst exactly what he wants, but the judge calls a mistrial anyhow. Some members of the defense team go out to lunch afterward and toast 'the shark,' and one gives a sharky, snaggled-toothed grin and winks at the others.

So much for Trial Number One.

Now, Trial Number Two will be, you'd think, an anticlimax, for we've been through it once before, had our taxes spent for nothing, and on top of that there comes a time when the sight of the same old item in the newspapers can bring on actual nausea. This little Governor, with his natty clothes and his courtly manners, has carried things too far. His continued declarations of injured innocence are orderly and reasonable, and the commas come in all the right places but we can't quite fix our attention on them. We wish he'd give up. We have, in fact, some of the same sense of weariness that we had during Bootsie's siege in the Mansion.

But then he falls ill: a jog in the plot. No trial, after all: He's had a small stroke, they think, or maybe it's a brain tumor. He is continually sleepy, his speech is slowed, he experiences headaches and gaps in his thinking. It's the stress, says the blond (blaming us, really). The doctors test and retest, probing his honesty along with his illness. He can feel a pin-prick in his leg, one doctor says which proves he isn't faking; for surely if he wanted to seem sick he would have said he *couldn't* feel it. It occurs to us that this pin-prick test appears to be unfailable; if he can't feel it, he's sick, and if he can, it shows he's not pretending. The unworthiness of this thought makes us feel terrible, eventually, when the doctors end up agreeing that he's truly ill. We hear he's in no condition to make any decisions whatsoever. We wonder what's going on, exactly.

Luckily, it has never seemed that having a functioning governor is all that necessary to our lives.

The blond is in her element. She tells a reporter that she is the Governor's eyes, his ears, and his legs; that she must do everything for him; that as long as he has her, he's fine. There are rumors that he has considered stepping down, but that the blond won't allow it. The boys in the clubhouse complain to anyone who listens that for a while there, she won't even let them in to see him. She just carries the bills he's signed back out to them. You can almost hear their teeth gnashing.

Then, inch by inch, the Governor returns. He is seen for brief periods, still chewing his pipe but looking a bit dimmer, with extra pleats of skin below his eyes. He walks in the garden. He takes a trip to Ocean City. He goes sailing on his yacht.

The blond reminds us that the Governor tires very easily, and that a trial would be injurious to his health. But no one seems to want to listen to her – not even the Governor, who still complains of headaches but seems resigned now, almost grim. He signs his duties over to the Lieutenant Governor, at least for the duration of the trial. The Lieutenant Governor seizes the reins enthusiastically and issues an immediate announcement that he is not in favor of political corruption.

From the indrawn breaths, your would think he slapped the Governor's face.

Now the Governor starts on Trial Number Two, stumbling as he trudges up the Courthouse steps. 'Oh, my God, he's falling!' the blond cries. There are tears in the Governor's eyes. We read all this in the paper, but not with the feelings you'd expect. Mainly, we're tired of it. We'd almost like to see the Governor back wheeling and dealing with his racetracks, happy as a little boy. And we tend, for some reason, to blame his tears not on his bruised knee, or on the trial that's awaiting him inside, but on the fact that just before he stumbled, the blond said, watching him narrowly, 'I just hope they don't hurt him.'

This second trial is a little hard to find jurors for. The judge keeps running into a problem: everyone's already decided on a verdict. And the proceedings themselves have the sketchy tone of a joke being told all over again, from the top, because somebody new walked in just before the punch line. In fact, a few of the witnesses merely have their statements from the last trial read into the records of this one. You picture the jurors mentally tapping their fingers, wondering how their gardens are doing without them. Bootsie will testify; Bootsie won't testify. Irving (Tubby) Schwartz, Father Guido Carcich . . . isn't this where we came in? The weather in Baltimore is hot and dark and still, and this trial seems motionless, timeless, a permanent fact of our lives. Who knows, maybe even the Governor himself is thinking of something else entirely, floating behind his bland, courteous face, dreaming of goose-hunts or of sailing on the Bay – in a good strong wind, on a cool afternoon, just he and a few of the boys.

JUNE JORDAN
1936–2002

Born in Harlem to West Indian immigrant parents, Jordan studied at Barnard College, before publishing her first volume of poetry, *Who Look at Me*, in 1969. There were many volumes to follow, as well as a huge variety of other work, as a teacher, writer and activist. Toni Morrison described her career as 'Forty years of tireless activism coupled with and fuelled by flawless art.'

In her determination to fight oppression, Jordan wrote extensively in support of the civil rights movement, feminism and the anti-war crusade. In the following essay, she brings some of these concerns to the fore, writing in support of Anita Hill, the African-American law professor whose charges of sexual harassment against Supreme Court nominee Clarence Thomas brought her national vilification.

Can I get a Witness?

12 December 1991, *Progressive*

I wanted to write a letter to Anita Hill. I wanted to say thanks. I wanted to convey the sorrow and the bitterness I feel on her behalf. I wanted to explode the history that twisted itself around the innocence of her fate. I wanted to assail the brutal ironies, the cruel consistencies that left her – at the moment of her utmost vulnerability and public power – isolated, betrayed, abused, and not nearly as powerful as those who sought and who seek to besmirch, ridicule, and condemn the truth of her important and perishable human being. I wanted to reassure her of her rights, her sanity, and the African beauty of her earnest commitment to do right and to be a good woman: a good black woman in this America.

But tonight I am still too furious, I am still too hurt, I am still too astounded and nauseated by the enemies of Anita Hill. Tonight my heart pounds with shame.

Is there no way to interdict and terminate the traditional, abusive loneliness of black women in this savage country?

From those slavery times when African men could not dare to defend their sisters, their mothers, their sweethearts, their wives, and their daughters – except at the risk of their lives – from those times until today: Has nothing changed?

How is it possible that only John Carr – a young black corporate lawyer who maintained a friendship with Anita Hill ten years ago ('It didn't go but so far,' he testified, with an engaging, handsome trace of a smile) – how is it possible that he, alone among black men, stood tall and strong and righteous as a witness for her defense?

What about spokesmen for the NAACP or the National Urban League?

What about spokesmen for the U.S. Congressional Black Caucus?

All of the organizational and elected black men who spoke aloud against a wrong black man, Clarence Thomas, for the sake of principles resting upon decency and concerns for fair play, equal protection, and affirmative action – where did they go when, suddenly, a good black woman arose among us, trying to tell the truth?

Where did they go? And why?

Is it conceivable that a young white woman could be tricked into appearing before twelve black men of the U.S. Senate?

Is it conceivable that a young white woman could be tricked into appearing before a lineup of incredibly powerful and hypocritical and sneering and hellbent black men freely insinuating and freely hypothesizing whatever lurid scenario came into their heads?

Is it conceivable that such a young woman – such a flower of white womanhood – would, by herself, have to withstand the calumny and unabashed, unlawful bullying that was heaped upon Anita Hill?

Is it conceivable that this flower would not be swiftly surrounded by white knights rallying – with ropes, or guns, or whatever – to defend her honor and the honor, the legal and civilized rights, of white people, per se?

Anita Hill was tricked. She was set up. She had been minding her business at the University of Oklahoma Law School when the senators asked her to describe her relationship with Clarence Thomas. Anita Hill's dutiful answers disclosed that Thomas had violated the trust of his office as head of the Equal Employment Opportunity Commission. Sitting in that office of ultimate recourse for women suffering from sexual harassment, Thomas himself harassed Anita Hill, repeatedly, with unwanted sexual advances and remarks.

Although Anita Hill had not volunteered this information and only supplied it in response to direct, specific inquiries from the FBI.

And although Anita Hill was promised the protection of confidentiality as regards her sworn statement of allegations.

And despite the fact that four witnesses – two men and two women, two black and two white distinguished Americans, including a federal judge and a professor of law – testified, under oath, that Anita Hill had told each of them about these sordid carryings on by Thomas at the time of their occurrence or in the years that followed,

And despite the fact that Anita Hill sustained a remarkably fastidious display of exact recall and never alleged, for example, that Thomas actually touched her.

And despite the unpardonable decision by the U.S. Senate Judiciary Committee to prohibit expert testimony on sexual harassment,

Anita Hill, a young black woman born and raised within a black farm family of thirteen children, a graduate of an Oklahoma public high school who later earned honors and graduated from Yale Law School, a political conservative and, now, a professor of law,

Anita Hill, a young black woman who suffered sexual harassment once in ten years and, therefore, never reported sexual harassment to any of her friends except for that once in ten years,

Anita Hill, whose public calm and dispassionate sincerity refreshed America's eyes and ears with her persuasive example of what somebody looks like and sounds like when she's simply trying to tell the truth,

Anita Hill was subpoenaed by the U.S. Senate Judiciary Committee of fourteen white men and made to testify and to tolerate interrogation on national television.

1. Why didn't she 'do something' when Thomas allegedly harassed her?
   The senators didn't seem to notice or to care that Thomas occupied the office of last recourse for victims of sexual harassment. And had the committee allowed any expert on the subject to testify, we would have learned that it is absolutely typical for victims to keep silent.

2. Wasn't it the case that she had/has fantasies and is delusional?
   Remarkably, not a single psychiatrist or licensed psychologist was allowed to testify. These slanderous suppositions about the psychic functionings of Anita Hill were never more than malevolent speculations invited by one or another of the fourteen white senators as they sat above an assortment of character witnesses handpicked by White House staffers eager to protect the president's nominee.

   One loathsomely memorable item: John Doggett, a self-infatuated black attorney and a friend of Clarence Thomas, declared that Thomas would not have jeopardized his career for Anita Hill because Doggett, a black man, explained to the Senate Committee of fourteen white men, 'She is not worth it.'

3. Why was she 'lying'?
   It should be noted that Anita Hill readily agreed to a lie-detector test and that, according to the test, she was telling the truth. It should also be noted that Clarence Thomas refused even to consider taking such a test and that, furthermore, he had already established himself as a liar when, earlier in the Senate hearings, he insisted that he had never discussed *Roe v. Wade*, and didn't know much about this paramount legal dispute.

Meanwhile, Clarence Thomas – who has nodded and grinned his way to glory and power by denying systemic American realities of racism, on the one hand, and by publicly castigating and lying about his own sister, a poor black woman, on the other – this Thomas, this Uncle Tom calamity of mediocre abilities, at best, this bootstrap miracle of egomaniacal myth and self-pity, this choice of the very same president who has vetoed two civil-rights bills and boasted about that, how did he respond to the testimony of Anita Hill?

Clarence Thomas thundered and he shook. Clarence Thomas glowered and he growled. 'God is my judge!' he cried, at one especially disgusting low point in the Senate proceedings. 'God is my judge, Senator. And not you!' This candidate for the Supreme Court evidently believes himself exempt from the judgments of mere men.

This Clarence Thomas – about whom an African-American young man in my freshman composition class exclaimed, 'He's an Uncle Tom. He's a hypocritical Uncle Tom. And I don't care what happens to his punk ass' – this Thomas vilified the hearings as a 'high-tech lynching.'

When he got into hot water for the first time (on public record, at any rate), he attempted to identify himself as a regular black man. What a peculiar reaction to the charge of sexual harassment!

And where was the laughter that should have embarrassed him out of that chamber?

And where were the tears?

When and where was there ever a black man lynched because he was bothering a black woman?

When and where was there ever a white man jailed or tarred and feathered because he was bothering a black woman?

When a black woman is raped or beaten or mutilated by a black man or a white man, what happens?

To be a black woman in this savage country: is that to be nothing and no one beautiful and precious and exquisitely compelling?

To be a black woman in this savage country: is that to be nothing and no one revered and defended and given our help and our gratitude?

The only powerful man to utter and to level the appropriate word of revulsion as a charge against his peers – the word was 'SHAME' – that man was U.S. Senator Ted Kennedy, a white man whose ongoing, successful career illuminates the unequal privileges of male gender, white race, and millionaire-class identity.

But Ted Kennedy was not on trial. He has never been on trial.

Clarence Thomas was supposed to be on trial but he was not: he is more powerful than Anita Hill. And his bedfellows, from Senator Strom

Thurmond to President George Bush, persist – way more powerful than Clarence Thomas and Anita Hill combined.

And so, at the last, it was she, Anita Hill, who stood alone, trying to tell the truth in an arena of snakes and hyenas and dinosaurs and power-mad dogs. And with this televised victimization of Anita Hill, the American war of violence against women moved from the streets, moved from hip-hop, moved from multimillion-dollar movies into the highest chambers of the U.S. government.

And what is anybody going to do about it?

I, for one, I am going to write a letter to Anita Hill. I am going to tell her that, thank God, she is a black woman who is somebody and something beautiful and precious and exquisitely compelling.

And I am going to say that if this government will not protect and defend her, and all black women, and all women, period, in this savage country – if this government will not defend us from poverty and violence and contempt – then we will change the government. We have the numbers to deliver on this warning.

And, as for those brothers who disappeared when a black woman rose up to tell the truth, listen: It's getting to be payback time. I have been speaking on behalf of a good black woman. Can you hear me?

Can I get a witness?

GITTA SERENY
1923–

Born a Hungarian in Austria, Sereny read Hitler's *Mein Kampf* aged eleven. Four years later, she heard him address the Viennese in person. In 1945, she briefly attended the Nuremberg war crime trials where she caught her first glimpse of Albert Speer – her future subject – in the dock. Half a century later, Ms Sereny befriended Speer and his wife to try to find out exactly how much he had known about the Holocaust while he was working for Hitler and in her acclaimed biography, *Albert Speer: His Battle with Truth*, she presented a damning portrait of him.

At the heart of her work lies an obsession with explaining evil and discovering why people commit monstrous acts. Since Speer she has written another book about the child killer Mary Bell and numerous pieces for newspapers about the nature of evil. This piece on the shocking murder of the toddler James Bulger by two young boys goes to the very heart of darkness.

On the Murder of James Bulger

30 January 2000, *Independent*

[. . .] Many in the court and beyond suspected that something terrible must have happened in these boys that finally drove them to this frenzy. But the legal system not only precluded the possibility of delving into their lives, it led to the suppression of evidence.

The intention was kind: to do everything possible to avoid adding to the suffering of James Bulger's parents. Thus an agreement was struck between prosecution and defence to the effect that, the forensic evidence entirely proving the case against the two defendants, certain injuries the child suffered would not be mentioned to the jury.

Under the system as it stands, it was a reasonable decision: this evidence, which certainly would have led to prurience in the media, was not necessary to the case. The prosecution had all they needed to prove murder. The fact that it was necessary in order to indicate the two boys' disturbance was, as we will see, not part of the case . . .

Robert Thompson – his police interrogators were to call him Robbie – and Jonathan Venables, known as Jon, had been arrested at 7.30am on Thursday, 18 February. During that afternoon and evening, and on the subsequent two days, each boy was interrogated three to four times every day, for about 40 minutes at a time. The police were extremely careful with the two children, before every interview meticulously repeating the prescribed cautions.

The interviews with Jon were conducted by Detective Sergeant Mark Dale and Detective Constable George Scott, with his mother or father and solicitor, Laurence Lee, present.

The police officers who interviewed Robert were Detective Sergeant Phil Roberts and Detective Constable Bob Jacobs. Robbie's mother and his solicitor, Dominic Lloyd, or his assistant, Jason Lee, were always present, except when Anne Thompson felt ill, when a policewoman replaced her.

The police's preoccupation with the sexual element of the crime had manifestly not escaped Robert's attention. On the second day when Anne came to see him in the child detention cell, Robert said at once: 'He (meaning a police officer) said I'm a pervert. They said I've played with his willy.' His mother had initiated such talk between them, by telling him the previous day what was being said about her. ('I told him that people were saying I had interfered with him,' she told me later, continuing: ' "You?" he asked. "What do they mean?" And I said, "They think I touched your private parts." "You did not!" he said.') Even so, it seemed surprising that he should bring the subject up about himself.

There was to be an enormous difference between the two boys' approach to the interrogations. Both their voices were tiny, light, almost toddler-age. But while in Jon one heard mainly his terror, in Robert, despite the infantile sound of his voice, there was energy. 'I found it . . .' tall, handsome Phil Roberts hesitated, 'frightening at times,' he said. 'Yes, frightening.'

Robert's story, as it starts, was not frightening. Moreover, as far as it went, it was almost true. 'He really was very intelligent,' said Phil Roberts. 'Very canny.'

They had sagged off from school on Jon's initiative, Robert said, gone walking along this road and that road, over a bridge, over a flyover on a backway to the Strand (Bootle Strand, the big modern shopping centre). Sometimes it took just an hour to get to the Strand, sometimes, like that day, he said, much more. Once they got there, they went to McDonald's – not to eat, just to keep warm and sit down. 'We went to about five shops, the Buckingham Bingo and the library.'

They had spent half an hour at the library, he said. They were allowed to read books there. He read nursery rhymes.

Jon's story was more expansive. He'd been walking to school that Friday, he said, 'and then he (Robert) came the back of me and . . . said do you want to sag off and I went, all right . . .' And Robert's brother, little Christopher had been along, too, he said, until six that night.

They had played 'in the subways' and in derelict factories, and in a park and under a bridge, and on swings, and in a big block of flats where they'd gone on the lifts, and then they'd gone 'robbing' in stores – Mars bars, which he liked, and trolls which Robert collected – and then they'd gone to the Liverpool football ground and then the cemetery, 'and Robert said let's look at the names and he said, do you want to get that flower, and I said no, no, it's people's memories . . . and then I showed Robert me nan's and grandad's (graves) and then he showed me his uncle's, his nan, his mum's uncle's . . . (gradually he gets confused) his dad's, dad's grave and his mum's, mum's grave . . . then there was a fire and then it was going darker and then we went to the video shop . . . and, I forgot: before that, we'd got the paint and he threw it over me . . . paint all over me arm and on me school pants and I said me mum's going to kill me . . .' (Here, he had realised that the police would have found the blue paint on his clothes which they had thrown at little James and tried, nowhere near as adroitly as Robert, to adapt his story accordingly.) '. . . and Christopher was laughing and then we went back to Walton Village and . . . Christopher said it was six o'clock he was going in now.'

And then, he said, they still went on for another hour, ending up in the video shop where his mum (who was sitting there, nodding) found them. 'And you (to his mother) took me to the police station and he (the duty officer there) said if you do it again, you'll go in a home. And then you took me home and then I went to bed.'

This story – little bits of truth mixed with large chunks of past experience and imagination – had taken almost an hour. Its whole purpose was to keep him away from the Strand, where Robert, much more defiant, and much more sure of his ability to outwit the police, in his account admitted arriving within minutes.

The second day, 19 February, was decisive. Both children were interrogated three times: Jon from 11.06 to 11.50; 12.23 to 12.56; and 15.57 to 16.30. Robert from 11.35 to 12.28; 14.14 to 14.57; and 15.00 to 15.11.

Throughout that morning – in Robert's case also the early afternoon – both boys desperately denied anything but the most marginal contact with James. In each 300-page transcript of each boy's interrogations, their denials, almost eerily voiced virtually in the same words, stretch over 100 pages.

Robert: 'I never took James on to the hill.' 'I never went on the hill.' 'I never had hold of his hand' (on four different occasions). 'I never had no paint.' 'I never touched the baby' (again in four different interrogations). 'I never killed him.'

Jon cried more often. His need for his mother's approval was paramount, and it was always her he addressed whenever he mentioned the baby: 'We never got a kid, mum.' 'We never.' 'I'm telling you, please.' 'I never got him.' 'Never a kid.' 'Mum, I never.' 'I never took him by the hand, I never even touched the baby.' 'I never touched a baby.' 'I never took the baby, mum . . .'

That afternoon, Detective Sergeant Roberts had been asking Robert Thompson about the things they had 'robbed' during their tour of the shops in the Strand that Friday, such as the tin of blue paint which Robert said Jon had 'thrown in James's eye'.

'Did he or you take anything else?' asked Phil Roberts.

'No.'

'Did either of you take some batteries?'

'No.'

'. . . You went all red in the face there.'

'What?'

'I noticed you went a little bit red in the face. What about these batteries?'

'I never took anything.'

'When somebody gets embarrassed about something, they go red in the face. Do you understand?'

'Yeah, but I never took no batteries.' (Cries wildly.)

'Well son . . .'

(Almost a screech:) 'I never took no batteries.'

'Who took the batteries, then?'

'I don't know' (sobbing), '. . . Yeah, well Jon might have took them . . . Why do we want batteries? It wasn't me . . . He might have stuck them in his pocket . . . I never. It weren't me . . .'

And that afternoon, questioned again about the batteries, Robert said again Jon might have taken them 'for his Game Gear, 'cos that's what he plays on most . . .'

'What are the batteries like he uses for those?'

'Pencil.'

'The little thin ones, are they?'

'Not the . . . little thin ones.'

'No?'

'They are about that thick.' (Indicates with his hands.)

'Are they the round ones – you know, are they shaped round?'

'Yeah, round.'

'How would you put it – with a little . . . nut . . . at the top?'

'A lump at the top . . . And no lump in the bottom . . .'

After six more pages in the transcript, Robert, with enormous deter-mination and skill, led the police officers away from the dreaded batteries by initiating a discussion about what one would think would be the worst thing for him to talk about – blood.

During the 33 minutes of Jon's second interrogation that day, he had become increasingly distressed, bursting into tears every few moments and beseeching his mother with that repeated 'I never touched him' to believe him. And Susan Venables tried desperately to help him: 'Calm down first,' she said.

'No, I can't, I never touched him . . . we just went home and I . . . I left Robert on his own until he came back to Walton Village.'

'Tell me the truth now, please Jon,' his mother urged.

'I never killed him, Mum. Mum, we took him and we left him at the canal, that's all . . .' (He now admitted for the first time taking James.) 'I never killed him, Mum.'

'I believe you,' Sue assured him.

'You think I done it,' he cried. 'I'm telling youse . . .' He starts almost to hyperventilate. 'Don't,' she tries to quiet him. 'We don't, Jon. Come on.'

'I want to go home. I've already told youse what I know. Ooh . . . you're going to put me in jail . . . I never mum,' he wails until his 'I never, I never' no longer sounds like words but one long cry.

'I know you wouldn't hurt a baby,' his mother says.

'This was where we broke it off,' David Tanner told me. It was early evening and we had been talking for an hour, sitting in his small office at the police station in St Helen's. Even though it was six weeks after the end of the trial, it had been extremely difficult to get any of the police officers who had been closely involved with the boys, to talk to me. Superintendent Kirby had finally persuaded a few of them to help me. 'Go easy,' he had warned me. 'Some are still very upset.'

David Tanner had been all right for that first hour while we discussed Liverpool, unemployment, violence, the decision he had made before all this happened to ask to be assigned where he was now, where it was quieter, and nearer home,

He is a powerful-looking man, but quiet, with warm eyes. The moment we began to talk about those days in February a year ago, they filled with tears. He tried to joke: 'just a reflex', he said. His wife would tell me there was a softy inside that big man. I didn't think so. There was a very human being inside that man.

'I had been listening in to the interrogations with Michelle Bennett,' Tanner said. Detective Sergeant Bennett, herself a mother of young children, had been assigned to look after Susan Venables and was to find it very arduous. 'We knew we had to do something,' David Tanner said, 'it was clear to us that the boy had a desperate need to confess, and the mother's reassurances were stopping him.'

They had taken Susan Venables to another room and explained to her that she wasn't doing Jon any good by helping him suppress what he was trying to get out. The police by this time knew that James's blood had been found on both boys' shoes and other things. 'It was particularly difficult,' David said, 'because we couldn't tell her about this evidence.

'We told her that what she and her husband had to do was to sit down with Jon and assure him that they loved him, and would continue to love him whatever happened. I think she trusted me. It took almost an hour, but then it dawned on her that what we were saying was right. She went to find Neil (Jon's father) and explained it all to him and he finally agreed.'

It was decided the parents would talk to Jon in the juvenile detention room where he had meanwhile been given lunch. As they went in, Susan turned around and told Tanner that she wanted him to come in with them. 'I hadn't expected it,' he said.

The experience, it was clear, had been extraordinarily upsetting. Tanner's lips kept trembling as he described it to me. 'There wasn't much of anything in that room,' he said. 'Just a mattress on the floor and a bench at the far side of it. That's where they sat down, with Jon between them. I sat down on the mattress, at the other end. They both put their arms around him and kissed and cuddled him.

'It wasn't very long at all,' he said, 'he ended up sort of curled up on Sue's lap and he was crying and crying and they said over and over that they loved him and would always love him and then, really very quickly, he said: "I did kill him." It was so quick and he was crying so hard, we thought perhaps he hoped we wouldn't hear but of course I did and Michelle and Mark Dale who were standing outside the door did too and it had an enormous impact on us . . .'

The parents came out then – Michelle took Susan to freshen up while David Tanner took Neil to the interview room. 'I told him that Sue had done enough for a bit and that it was time for him to take over. I said "It's time for you to be a man". He went back to Jon then and a little later he came out and he looked white. 'Do you know what they did?' he said, sounding stunned. 'My God, he just told me.'

'It really was all quite . . . quite terrible,' Tanner said, and we both sat quietly for a while.

'We really couldn't make do with Susan,' he finally said. 'We couldn't understand how she was . . . well . . . constantly repairing her make-up – it seemed so extraordinary.' A nervous reaction? I suggested. 'Well, it didn't feel like that to us.' Neil's weakness, too, he said, had made them feel uncomfortable. 'But they were honest, you know, in wanting Jon to tell the truth . . .'

Jon repeated his confession into the tape shortly afterwards. That afternoon, and the next day, they tried to lead him further, but – even worse than Robert – there was one thing he simply could not get out.

It took more than two hours not to say it; he told them everything in those hours: how it had been his idea in the Strand to walk towards James but ' . . . Robert's to kill him,' and then, bit by bit, he went over the whole walk and finally the railway yard and the bricks, and the metal bar, and the kicks, from both Robert and him, and the taking off of the trainers and socks – he did that – and his pants and his underpants – 'Robert done that' – and, and, and . . . 'There was something else, wasn't there?' Mark Dale eventually interrupted him. 'You left it out, haven't you, and you know it's important, don't you?' And it took another long detour, via yet more awful things he enumerated in his attempt to escape pronouncing what he just couldn't seem to bear saying.

'We found batteries there, didn't we,' Mark Dale finally said. And after countless more 'I never', 'no batteries, never batteries,' and 'Robert . . . not me,' he almost screamed, sobbing 'They're his batteries . . .' And then, at last, they ended it . . .

NICCI GERRARD

1958–

One damp evening in August, two little girls went missing in the English countryside. For two weeks, the nation was transfixed by their disappearance, and a shrine grew in the village where they lived. Then their naked bodies were found in a nettle filled ditch and the caretaker of the local school was charged with their murder, his girlfriend with conspiracy. Sixteen months later, after a trial filled with unbearable detail, Ian Huntley was found guilty of murder; Maxine Carr of perverting the course of justice. The case was a detective story and a sinister fairy tale rolled into one, a narrative of loss, horror and collective mourning, a myth which seemed to tell us something about the way we live now, and the fears that we all hold.

Nicci Gerrard spent weeks in Soham talking to the principle characters and wrote this moving piece for the *Observer* about what she found. A feature writer on the *Observer* for many years, she is best known as the co-writer of the 'Nicci French' thrillers (written with her husband Sean French) but has also published two novels of her own.

Holly and Jessica – we'll Never Know

21 December 2003, *Observer*

Guilty of the murder of Jessica Chapman, said the jury. Guilty of the murder of Holly Wells. Life, said the judge; life for the man who took life and showed 'no mercy and no regret'; whose only tears were shed for himself.

And so Ian Huntley, who for years has stalked the young and vulnerable, and who for six wretched weeks, for 16 months, has stalked our imaginations, is walked from the dock, face expressionless, and vanishes from public view. Now he will just become a ghostly name among all those other names that, when we think of them, send a frisson down the spine.

Remember him? In the dock, he looked like a tense-shouldered Russell Crowe, but with doughy, prison-pallid skin; duller eyes. He once had a slender girlfriend with a mop of hair and a crooked, pale, nearly pretty face. He once was the caretaker; the paedophile, the predator, the rapist, the murderer. The man who had for years been molesting and raping girls and young women, and who had fallen through all the cracks in the criminal justice system. The man who, one wet evening in August 2002, killed two 10-year-old girls. We know the story's end at last; the curtain's fallen on the long, heartbreaking drama. We now know too much, defiled by details, yet still we don't know. At the inky heart of the case, in that ghastly little hole in time, the silence remains. 'Take him away,' said the judge.

Justice Moses, turning to the parents, said their daughters had been 'bright and life-enhancing'. Their glowing young faces have haunted this trial. In their red football shirts, with their eager gaze, they stand under a clock that says it is four minutes past five, and we all know how that clock will tick away the short time that leads them out of the door, down the street, round the small town, into the house where they died. On the CCTV cameras, with its curious boiled-sweet colours and spasmodic, freeze-frame motion, they walk together along the wet roads; close together, shoulders touching, arms sometimes linked, giggling. It's 18.28 and 30 seconds; there they are. It's 18.28 and 41 seconds, and they're jerked forward, out of the frame – vanished, and the screen is empty, just lights shining on puddles.

Jessica Chapman and Holly Wells, sucked out of their familiarly happy present into the unfathomable black hole at the heart of this story. A few minutes later they were murdered by Ian Huntley, and then their bodies were rolled down a muddy ditch, limbs tangled, and they lay there among the nettles and the mud, and they didn't have a happy present or a mysterious future anymore, just a past. Forever 10.

Many of the murder cases that have gripped the nation in recent years possess the horror of the strange; the spooky dread of the unknown. Two 10-year-old boys snatch a toddler from outside a shop, walk him to a railway line and kill him there; a 'good' doctor gives lethal injections to dozens, hundreds, of his patients, and it's impossible to comprehend the mind that took pleasure in these blank and bureaucratic crimes; a couple sexually torture lost young women and their own children, then murder them and bury them vertically under the floor of their terraced slaughter-house; a little girl, running home across fields, is snatched by a stranger in a van, like a nasty modern fairy tale (many of us probably don't even recall Roy Whiting's name – rather than being an individual for us, he became the wicked wolf, the fictive bogeyman).

And Huntley exploded into view, in a violent transformation from an apparently sensible and steady young man to brutal killer. That he was dangerous and sick we now all know, a time bomb waiting to explode. On 4 August random events combined and touched off the fuse. A predator not a loner; a moment not a plan.

But in this case we have been gripped as well by the familiar, and that is why we care so much about them (and often so little about other murders). In the summer of last year, when Jessica and Holly first went missing, it was – to borrow one of the many clichés that filled the newspapers – 'every parent's nightmare'. They lived in the kind of village where, as residents said, 'these things just don't happen'; they went to the local school; they'd spent much of their last day playing computer games and going out to buy sweets (a half-eaten pack of Polos was found with their scorched clothes); they'd just had one of those very English BBQs, cooked under shelter and eaten in the kitchen. They were wearing Manchester United football shirts, trainers (Nike), tracksuit trousers (Umbro), underwear from Marks & Spencer and Tesco. They were well-behaved and popular at school, and liked their 'cool' young teaching assistant, Miss Carr. They were close to their parents, loyal to their friends (and one of them must have watched the other being killed). They seemed like a template for a proper, decent, safe and well-protected childhood – the way young girls, on the brink of adolescence but not yet there, should be; the way we'd like our own children to be.

It was this sentimental identification that filled the media, prompted the national outpouring of grief, and seemed to be trying to flood the great gap between those who knew the girls, and the strangers who spuriously felt they knew them. Yet, as Justice Moses sternly said, what the parents must feel cannot be imagined and cannot be shared. There is no emotional equivalent. They are alone with their grief and we cannot join them.

Tragedy usually happens when we're looking the other way – by the time the agonised and prolonged search had started, the little girls were two hours dead and dumped in that ditch (alder and birch, said the scientist who specialised in plants; common heather, yarrow, mudwort, meadow sweet . . .); Ian Huntley, after a drab Sunday (telly, a walk with the dog, a squabble by phone with Maxine Carr), entered a world of gothic violence, luring Holly and Jessica out of their ordinary Sunday evening and killing them, driving them to Lakenheath, returning to a village that had been transformed utterly in his absence. Kevin Wells stood by a field and called out their names, over and over again. Police arrived, with their vans and their dogs. Residents flocked to help and Ian Huntley joined in the hunt. Soham quickly became the centre of the biggest search this country has ever known, and it also became a media circus and a national shrine to which strangers flocked to lay their offerings ('Sweet dreams . . . We will miss you'), a glut of sorrow-lite next to the granite sadness of the family. Sniffer dogs, satellite dishes, a decaying mountain of flowers and cards. Detective story, horror story, easy tear-jerker, poignantly scripted tale of the way we live now and of the fears that we all hold.

And this case has been all about stories. The 11 days during which the girls were missing had us in the fist of its despairing mystery. There were all the classic ingredients: the small town; the cast of characters, including the tormented parents appealing to the world for help and the man who would eventually be charged with their murder; the search through the first grim night and on into the subsequent weeks; the misdirections, rumours, false hopes, scatter of clues, tattered hopes. It's a story that has become achingly familiar, an instant myth of the man-next-door, of if-we're-not-safe-here-then we're-not-safe-anywhere, as if in this world in which we live there's also a looming shadow world that can suddenly break into terrifying view.

Inserted in this larger, emblematic tale were the stand-alone, false stories told by the rather good-looking young caretaker who was the last one to see the girls before they vanished, and his girlfriend, the teaching assistant. We saw them, day after day, on our screens and in newspapers. They were such a well-matched double-act, so media savvy – their lies became more accomplished with practice; they gave the public what they wanted, and became, for a grossly ironic few days, a celebrity couple who both hated and courted the press, and were suspected and courted by them. Huntley liked to talk about 'the glimmer of hope' everyone should still feel. He spoke, with apparent sincerity, about how he was probably the last 'friendly face' that the girls had seen (and in court, pressed on this grotesquerie, he repeated it – 'I was,' he said, as if meaning it).

In the public imagination the pair became linked together, but Carr was in Grimsby when the girls died. He acted alone, and she was on the margin of the story. In the court they sat in the glass-sided dock and never looked at each other, not even when he edged past her on his way to the witness box. She was tipped away from him, her head slewed to the side and some-times leaning forward so her hair hid her face. He stared ahead. His expression never wavered, although once or twice he looked downwards, fiddled with a button on his jacket, tightened his knuckles.

'Psychopath,' some journalists said. 'Look at that brow.' How can you ever tell from a face what lies behind? The parents of Jessica and Holly also sat in court, day after day, week after week, and maintained a dignified demeanour even when Huntley told how he crammed the girls' bodies into his car boot. If there are lessons from this trial, one must be how much is concealed under the implacable surface and how hidden most people are from each other.

Paedophiles don't always look like the 73-year-old Arnold Hartley, battered to death in his house last month, who had a stubbly, jowly face and an eye-patch, like a down-at-heel bandit on a peeling 'Wanted' poster. They look like Huntley, too (but 'I know him,' cried Carr when she heard from the police that the man she had hoped to marry was charged with the murder); they look like us. This is one of the dreads of the case: that we keep so much of our strangeness and our turmoil secret, each of us unknowing and unknown. That you cannot protect your children because kindness and great cruelty often wear the same face.

The motif of clearing up and of cleaning away – Maxine was the spring-cleaner of all time, wielding her Flash, her bleach, her Mr Sheen, washing those curtains, scraping at the tiles until the paint flaked, desperately trying to erase the nasty stains of life – has its shadow version in the motif of dirt and ghastly disorder. Huntley, narcissistically clean in person, was a domestic slob and couch potato; he lay on his sofa, drinking lager and scattering crumbs. He didn't know how to use the washing machine (though he mysteriously managed to cram an entire duvet inside its tub). He left dishes in the sink, laundry in a heap. And then, in a nightmarish psychological version of squalor, he broke the bath, flooded the dining room, killed two little girls, vomited on the carpet, dragged their bodies through his house and into his car. Inner and outer worlds had all of a sudden collided like mucky breakers crashing over the sea walls, carrying with it the great sucking undertow.

In the story the trial told, conflicting versions jostled. The blizzard of details the prosecution produced was meticulous and almost irrelevant, because we knew from the start that the two girls had died in Huntley's house, and he had dumped their bodies. In a sense, the evidence provided the bricks and mortar of the case; Huntley had threaded his thin and frantic line of defence around their incontestability. Never mind the laminated maps, mobile-phone beacons, car tracks on the lonely lane in Lakenheath, fingerprints on the black bin bag; never mind the solid edifice of clues and circumstances – what dominated the trial was the hissing black hole at its centre. Which is still there now.

What always mattered was the tale that Huntley would tell and then how the prosecution would make him un-tell it, undoing the story, looking at the slippages through which truth might seep. The Huntley we glimpsed during other witnesses' brief statements was a fragile, weakly defended man, with few inner resources. He could be a bully (self-righteously chucking journalists out of the school where they were writing their copy), but was thin-skinned too. He stood stolidly enough in the dock, but in life he lost his temper, cried easily – cried in front of the vice-principal of the school where he worked; cried in front of the police when they came to ask questions.

Carr, in her garrulous original statements to the police, insisted that her boyfriend, even if he had killed the girls, would have broken down at once. He was an anxious, even depressive person (anxiety is one of the dominant impressions of him in photographs – tense, with a tight, vigilant smile) and had a prickly sense of his status – he was quick to insist that he was not a caretaker but a site manager, or even a 'senior site manager'.

What grabs you are the details – those sinister fissures through which the 'real' Huntley could be seen. When he was being led through his story by Stephen Coward, QC, he was calm and articulate. If you set aside the stunning ludicrousness of an account in which two fit girls both died because he panicked, the strangest aspect was his repeated use of the present tense when he talked about his life in Soham, with Maxine – 'We do this . . . we do that . . . we have a television in the kitchen.'

And he eerily repeated this under cross-examination, as if his domestic routine and his relationship was still going on and soon enough he would walk back into it in his chinos and his trainers, hair stiff and straight, and be senior site manager, couch potato and Maxine's boyfriend once again. (Later, during her testimony, Carr shoved Huntley firmly into the past tense, and while he called her 'Maxine' she referred to him as 'Mr Huntley', 'that man', and once, flinging out her hand towards the dock, even 'that thing'.)

But under cross examination the story cracked open and so, every so often, did he. Smooth talk stalled into silence, into 'I don't know'. 'I can't recall'. The dog-ate-my-homework excuse for the two deaths became a series of admissions: 'I killed Jessica . . .', 'She would have struggled . . .', 'It was inexcusable . . .' He lost his temper once, when pressed on the irrationality of his lie, and at times he seemed genuinely aggrieved with the prosecution, as if part of him believed his own unbelievable story.

'You've already made up your mind,' he snapped, bitterly. Self-pity has been one of the ugliest motifs of this trial; a gross narcissism that leaves no room for the sufferings of others. Pity – pity for the girls whose lives were blotted out; pity for the parents and family who sat day after day listening to this bleakest tale – was absent. Yet he said, with a Kafkaesque sanctimoniousness, that he had promised his mother he would make it through to this trial so that he could tell the truth to the parents about their daughters' deaths.

It seems plausible that Huntley's version of that Sunday evening was a relic of the truth he would not tell. The dog was probably dirty. Holly probably had a nosebleed. The girls wanted to know how 'Miss Carr' was. In some way he panicked. He didn't set out to commit murder, but having killed one he had to kill the other. He vomited on the carpet outside the bathroom. Maybe he actually did black out, as he claimed. An extraordinary 40 per cent of homicides cannot remember the moment of murder. The body revolts; the mind shuts down in horror at itself. 'I do not know' means 'I will not know': 'I cannot recall' means 'I must not remember'.

Bit by bit, from Huntley's inadequate version, another story emerged, one which could never be wholly spoken aloud during the trial but which lurked in the margins and between the lines. The great why? Why did they die?

Paedophiles, says Cleo van Velsen, a consultant psychiatrist in forensic psychotherapy who works a secure unit, are most usually age-specific, but Huntley's sexuality had unravelled into an undiscriminating compulsion to humiliate and control. Since 1995 he had been accused of nine sexual offences, including a string of rapes, an indecent assault of an 11-year-old girl, and unlawful sexual intercourse with four young girls. Who knows how many more unreported cases there were?

Now he has been convicted, the anecdotes and personal testimonies stream out, so that reading the papers the following day felt pornographically squalid and terrifying. He was a serial rapist, a despoiler of the young and vulnerable. He was consistently violent, controlling and abusive. He kept a girlfriend prisoner. He kicked a girlfriend in the stomach so she miscarried. He half-strangled another. He hit another down the stairs . . . The pattern gives terrifying evidence of a brutalising sexuality.

And then, on that August evening, he had an argument on the phone with Maxine about her going out that evening (she could, he said, get 'flirty' when she had too much to drink – and pictures after the verdict show him to be right there, for she was certainly on the razzle that particular night) and she sent him a curt text message at 18.31. Seconds later, Jessica and Holly came down the road. Somehow he lured them into his house – by saying Carr was there? He took them upstairs. At 18.46, if we are to follow the evidence of Jessica's mobile being turned off then, they were dead. We do not know what happened in those 13 or 14 minutes. We know they were in the bathroom, in the bedroom. We know he cut their clothes off their bodies, removed their underwear, tried to wash the duvet and cover.

While preparing to dump the bodies – collecting bin bags, rubber gloves, the petrol can to douse them and set them alight – Huntley changed out of his smart 'brushers' and into his trainers. Why? Because, he said, as if there was nothing odd about personal vanity in the middle of brutal double murder, he only wore his 'brushers' in the house: he didn't want to get them messy.

When, during the subsequent days of lying, he approached Kevin Wells, it was to say to him that he was very sorry, he hadn't known it 'was your daughter'. Under cross-examination, he denied this was playing with the emotions of the father. He had been speaking the truth: he hadn't known and he was sorry. This was mocked by Latham and used as evidence of his ruthlessness, used again in the judge's impassioned closing speech, but it had the eerie ring of truth. Huntley was, in this own way, apologising.

'Kev', he called him then. 'Kev', he called him again in court: 'Kev' – to the man whose daughter he'd killed. This is a psychopathic apology, emptied of sorrow and replaced instead with self – the same self that he paraded in his TV interviews, talking of the glimmer of hope and being the last 'friendly face', that felt self-righteously misunderstood by the prosecuting counsel, that changed out of his smart boots so as not to dirty them when dumping the little girls.

Is Huntley a psychopath then? We quickly rush to such labels, for our culture is fascinated by murders committed by emotionally perverted individuals driven by hidden inner compulsions. Crime is seen as the inevitable outcome of pathology – and then we can call some individuals evil and have done with it. It's so easy. Evil psychopath; bring back capital punishment (or, as one man who lived near Soham said to me: they shouldn't send him to prison; just set him down in the centre of the town and see what happens to him). The mourning crowd who laid flowers for the dead can too easily become the vengeful lynch mob.

The Hare psychopathy checklist (developed by Robert Hare, and originating in a book by Hervey Cleckley called *The Mask of Sanity*) has among the traits listed: glibness and superficial charm, a grandiose sense of self-worth, pathological lying, need for stimulation, proneness to boredom, cunning and manipulation, lack of remorse or guilt, lack of empathy, short-term relationships, criminal versatility. At first glance Huntley seems to fit almost too neatly. Cleo van Velsen agrees his behaviour falls into psychopathy – particularly his ability to compartmentalise. 'Not to be connected with what you're doing,' she says. 'Not to be overwhelmed by horror or guilt.' Psychopaths, she says, have a real capacity to seem sane and normal.

What lessons are there to be learnt from the case, apart from the gaping flaws in the system which allowed a man with a crowded history of violent, perverse sexual offences to end up as a school caretaker? Everything is simple in hindsight. We look at Huntley's life and see the signs of a murder that was bound to happen, as if the clock was always ticking forward to this moment. We can track back to see how we got here, but can't track forward to know where we're going.

Huntley grew up in Immingham, an industrial port for giant container ships where everything is looking away from the drab town centre towards the sea and where everything seems temporary; on its way somewhere else. Photographs show a boy with a pleasant face, a wide smile, but he was bullied at school (they called him 'Spadehead') and then became a vicious bully in his turn. He loved his mother (the same mother who has now said her son deserves to die), was jealous of his father (who says he will go on being there for him) and of younger brother Wayne (who, years later, would marry his brother's wife, Claire, after she left Huntley). His parents separated; he left school and drifted from job to job: he picked up girls; he had a temper that could flare suddenly.

All of this sounds wretched, but not psychopathic. Lots of children are bullied and are bullies, have complicated family relationships, come from broken homes. Yet this child became the man who molested, raped, killed, and yet wore a charming face.

He has shown no pity, nor admitted guilt; perhaps he doesn't feel it. Few killers take responsibility for what they have done: prisons are full of people who claim they are innocent. Huntley said it was an accident – and probably in his terms it was. Humans are infinitely good at blaming others and expressing their own emotional hurt (in the dock, Huntley was good at it too, charging his testimony with bitterness, the sense of being misunderstood) and bad at confessing guilt or feeling moral responsibility. The mind has all sorts of mechanisms for refusing to admit the truth to itself, and for making the perpetrator into another victim. The language of victimhood and fake-therapy flooded the trial. Huntley talked about 'coping mechanisms' and 'closure'. In a grotesque displacement, the 'real' hidden self feels betrayed by its own actions.

Huntley probably feels he's not a 'pervert' – Carr said they both agreed that paedophiles ought to be castrated and shot, and plausibly Huntley did believe this. Paedophiles are other people; rapists are other people; murderers are other people. It's hard for the mind to know itself as wicked. It tells itself a different story, keeping the darkness at bay. Week after week, Huntley listened to what he had done and didn't collapse. An accident, he said. Not something he did, but something that happened. What would it mean for him to accept that what he has done is also what he is? How could he live with this knowledge? In prison (and Wakefield, where he will probably be sent in the New Year, is known as 'the monster mansion'), Huntley will be in solitary confinement and on suicide watch. The celebrity days are over; all the ghastly pleasure and the horror. He is alone with his mind. Whether he stays alive, or he kills himself, his future is deathly.

Not guilty of aiding an offender, said the jury of Carr, but guilty of perverting the course of justice. Three-and-a-half years, said Justice Moses, condemning her selfishness and glib lies that added to the torment of the family. Carr's name has been linked to Huntley's; her future, as her counsel Michael Hubbard said before the sentencing, has been 'blighted'. She has been hounded, vilified, called 'Myra Hindley Mark Two', not only by the inmates of Holloway where she has been kept since her arrest, but also by newspapers. Words used about her were the same ones used about Saddam Hussein. Yet on Wednesday she was convicted of lying, but not of complicity – of ignorance and misplaced loyalty, not of wickedness. 'How much did she know?' was always the question, but we'll never have the answer and now we should leave her alone rather than go baying after her.

In court she named herself Huntley's victim; her own self-pity makes it harder for us to pity her. She appeared clever, chatty, tough and childish – not like a 26-year-old, more like a girl with a shallow understanding of the larger world, a narrow focus of her own. She too had learned the language of blame and popular therapy: she said she had been forced into lying by Huntley and that it was only after she had been away from him for months, out of his control, that she was finally herself again, freed from him at last.

And we are free of him, too. After the frenzy and public grief, he's been taken away, into the shadow realm and into silence. The doors close on him and his dark story. But the family of the murdered girls are not free of him and nor will they ever be, because for the rest of their lives they live with the legacy of what he did, without their daughters beside them. There will always be another dream world for them, in which the clock ticked on, the girls came home, back into their sunny lives, and they are not 10 any more, but growing up. Jessica and Holly: the two little ghosts who've haunted the country and should now be left in peace.

ROSE GEORGE
1969–

Yorkshire-born, George attended Oxford University and the University of Pennsylvania, before beginning her writing career with an internship at the *Nation* magazine in 1994. Since 1999 she has been living in London and freelancing for a wide range of publications.

In 2003, the *Guardian* published George's shocking account of the growing incidence of gang rape on France's most deprived estates. The following article, written a year later, uncovered the grim reality that this behaviour is far from unique to France, being equally prevalent in London's most deprived enclaves.

They don't See it as Rape. They Just See it as Pleasure for Them

5 June 2004, *Guardian*

Tamika Bravo is eating spare ribs in an east London noodle bar. She's 19 years old and has a one-year-old son. She's talking about gang rapes. 'They happen all the time, man. You hear about them in school – girls who went with a boy and his mate, who went with five boys. It's so common.'

A year and a half ago, Tamika was at a friend's house. Her friend liked to hang out with boys. There were five there that afternoon, and Tamika didn't like it. 'I have to know who I'm hanging out with. You can never be too safe, can you?' Tamika went home and phoned her friend an hour later. 'She was crying so hard, and she was dying to get out of her house, but she wouldn't talk about it over the phone. I thought okaaay, and I guessed what had happened, and when she came over, she told me what they'd done.'

What the five boys had done to this one girl was nothing unusual. What the girl did, or rather didn't do, was not unusual, either. 'What could she do, man? She was scared,' says Tamika. 'You know that if you talk about it, they can do it again. If they want you to be quiet, that's all you gotta do, just bite your tongue and continue. It's a sad thing but it's reality. Hard reality.'

In a north London McDonald's, I meet Kelly. She's 17 and originally from Jamaica, where she was gang raped when she was 13. 'It was lunchtime,' she says, hardly audible and ripping a bus ticket into tiny pieces. 'I was with three of my girlfriends: we'd gone home to change clothes.' Five boys came to her door and said they wanted to 'batter' – have sex with – one of Kelly's friends. 'I couldn't allow that, so I slammed the door. They kicked it in and beat me unconscious. My friends ran away.' When she woke up, it was obvious she'd been raped. 'I went to the hospital and got a report of my injuries and told the police. But I don't know what they did about it.'

She came to the UK later that year to live with her father in London, and she's heard that one of the rapists is here now, too. That's not her biggest worry any more: in July 2002, she was out with a friend in Hackney, east London, when two men with a gun abducted them and drove them to Southampton. They made the girls sell drugs for them, until 2.30a.m., when Kelly got a shopkeeper to call the police. 'They didn't rape us.' she says quietly. But they could have. She's getting counselling now, for the rape and the abduction, and she's stopped banging her head against the wall. 'I was thinking about it all the time, and I just wanted to get rid of it.' But where she lives, she can't get away from it, not really. 'I hear of other girls it's happening to, all the time. In school, when people would joke about it. I'd get mad and walk away. Finally I told my friend and she said I wasn't alone, that lots of girls get raped. But every time I hear about one, I get flashbacks.'

A year ago, I wrote an article in *Guardian Weekend* about gang rapes, tournantes, in France. In interviews, I confidently told people that nothing similar was happening in the UK. I was wrong. Last year, the following allegations were reported in the press: the gang rape of a 17-year-old girl in Bedford by four men aged 17–19 (the police decided not to proceed); the rape of a 12-year-old girl by four teenagers in Feltham (all were acquitted); the rape of an 18-year-old by three paratroopers who, it was said, recorded the incident on their mobile phones (no charges were brought). A group of young men in Greenwich filmed their 'rape' of a 15-year-old schoolgirl and entitled the video *Lethbridge X-rated Part One* (they pleaded guilty to unlawful sexual intercourse).

This year, the Old Bailey heard the case of seven men accused of raping an 18-year-old at gunpoint 'as a punishment'. The girl said she had been kept prisoner in a flat in Sudbury, Suffolk, where one man told her, 'If you want to go home, you have to do me and my friends.' After two trials (the first was thrown out for legal reasons) lasting eight weeks, the jury decided the girl wasn't telling the truth, despite the evidence of an electricity bill that proved the address of the flat.

In December last year, in a modern courtroom in the Old Bailey, a gang rape trial is being played out before a press bench containing one journalist. Me. The nation's media are filling a nearby court to hear a particularly scandalous murder case, but, in the words of a senior police officer, 'nobody gives a toss about gang rape'. The case concerns a winter night two years ago, when the two girls and the three accused boys were together in a London park.

'Emma,' now 16, is the first to testify. She gives her evidence via a TV link, as does her best friend, 'Lucy'. Because of the seriousness of the offence, juvenile rape cases are tried in adult court where attempts at informality are made, sometimes with unfortunate consequences. It's hard to take seriously a courtroom that allows a juror to wear an FCUK sweatshirt in a rape case. Or a judge who consistently gets Lucy's name wrong, and thinks it's civilised to give the jury the afternoon off, because a juror wants to go to a nativity play. The prosecuting barrister gets the girls mixed up – he's never met them before, because they have the status only of witnesses in their own case (the Crown is officially the wronged party). This may contribute to the appalling conviction rate of between 6% and 7% for rape (the introduction of specialist rape prosecutors, who are involved in the case all the way through, raised conviction rates in one New York borough to more than 80%).

The boys in the dock, though, are all formality. They sit impassively, three little heads close together, dressed to impress. They're boys, not men.

Emma: 'We were on the bus. Others got on the bus, and they started threatening us and calling us names. We got off the bus and they chased us. We ran into a cafe and hid there for half an hour. They said, 'Come out, we're not going to do anything.' The people in the cafe said, 'They won't do anything' and after about 10 minutes, they said, 'Sorry, you have to go.' They took us into a park. They made us have sex. After it happened, they took us into a block [of flats] and wouldn't let us go.'

Emma did not report the incident until 10 months later. Any CCTV evidence has long been destroyed, as have any forensics. There is little evidence to go on, so it comes down to what it usually comes down to in rape cases: words against words.

Emma's words do her no favours in the moral universe of the courtroom. She is feisty. She answers back. Easy for barristers to categorise as disrespectful. Lucy is sweeter, prettier and more distressed, but no match for the apparently polite, well-brought-up boys. They pepper their testimony with 'yes, sir' and 'no, sir'. They have good character records, bolstered by teachers and youth workers. They say it never happened. But their strongest defence lies in most people's perception of rape: that it's either made up, or it involves a stranger with a knife. Nice boys don't gang rape. Except they do, mostly with impunity. 'Group rape is a black hole,' said one senior London policeman I spoke to. 'It's a parallel universe where that kind of thing has become a way of living, and that's why it continues.'

Emma: 'He was trying to undo my trousers and I'd zip them back up. I wasn't having it. He just pulled them down. I can't really explain it. It was the threats, all the threats. He knows a lot of people and he'll do what he says he'll do. We was having sex and obviously I didn't want to do it and he had the cheek to say, 'Do you want me to stop?' The thing is, they don't see it as rape, as us being forced. They just see it as pleasure for them. Us, we're slags.'

Outside court one morning, a barrister's pupil pulls me aside. 'Why are you interested in this case? Is it because they're so young?' I don't tell her a 17-year-old defendant is old, as gang rapists go. There have been 13- and 14-year-olds. In 2002 in Croydon, five boys aged 11 and 12 were said to have raped a 10-year-old girl on her way home from school. One boy had been watching 10-minute free porn previews, according to a police officer, and copied what he saw.

The Metropolitan police are worried – enough to examine the statistics on 123 incidents in three London boroughs, involving over 900 assailants (including four gang rapes around the same school). Enough for Sapphire, the Met's three-year-old specialist rape unit, to recognise gang rape as a separate phenomenon, needing specific attention. Enough for a senior officer, Commander John Yates, tipped as a future commissioner, to speak on behalf of the Met on the issue. There has been a decrease in group rape reports, he tells me; nevertheless Met officers visited France late last year to compare notes.

I doubt his figures, and so does everyone I talk to. 'Gang rape is really common,' says a youth worker in Hackney. 'Girls won't talk about it because they think it's normal and there's nothing they can do about it.' Met commander Andy Baker, who used to be in charge of street crime, says, 'It's been going on for years. Before I was a policeman, I'd see boys coming out of a shed and a girl following later. Now, I'd know what that was, and so would you.'

'It's a taboo,' says Bernadette Brittain, counsellor at the Haven, London's first dedicated sexual assault referral centre. 'It's grim and it's not talked about.'

There is virtually no research on gang rapes in the UK. In the US, some work has been done on gang rapes by sportsmen and fraternity members. In 1985, a report entitled Campus Gang Rape: Party Games? – released by the Project on the Status of Education of Women – calculated that at least one gang rape per week took place on campuses. 'Fraternities are sporting clubs,' a professor was quoted as saying, 'and their sport is women.' Over here, the best data comes from the Haven, which was set up in mid-2000.

The Haven's database has collected details from 2,000 clients from in and around London. It doesn't make for optimistic reading. Among victims aged under 16 who visited in 2001 and 2002, 25% had had multiple assailants, compared with 13% among over-16-year-olds. Kids raping kids. The figures show a rise in gang rapes by a third between 2001 and 2002. 'We recorded 206 in two years,' says Peter Trail, an epidemiologist with the Health Protection Agency charged with collating the Haven's statistics. 'A lot of people in the field are angry about this, but they won't speak.'

I lose count of how many government agencies, schools and official establishments refuse to comment for this story. They say the same thing. 'Sorry. It's too sensitive.'

The added element in this is ethnicity,' says Trail. The Haven's statistics indicate that, in 2002, in the under-16 age group, 43% of the assailants were black, as were 33% of the victims. Even in an ethnically diverse population such as Lambeth-Southwark-Lewisham (LSL), this goes beyond demographics. It is controversial. When a documentary on juvenile gang rape was broadcast by Channel 4 in 1998, the channel was accused of racism. Trinidad-born writer Darcus Howe was a lone voice of support. Later, writing in the *New Statesman*, he recounted how his girlfriend Betty was gang raped for hours in Trinidad, and how – after he spoke out in support of the documentary – he got anonymous phone calls saying his daughter would get gang raped, too.

'For heaven's sake,' Trail says, 'this isn't about race, it's about rape.' He points to high numbers of sexually transmitted diseases in LSL, which also has the highest teenage pregnancy rate in Europe – problems that were also hampered by a refusal to look at the racial demographics, in the beginning. 'My line is lean, mean and clear,' Howe concluded, in the '*New Statesman*. 'I take a side in this war, the side of black women . . . There is nothing to discuss.'

There is much to discuss, but it takes courage. A Met press release from last year – which stated that black women are three times more likely than others to be raped, and black males aged between 10 and 17 are eight and a half times more likely to be charged with rape – was never released. And there has been little sign of the 'debate in the black community' promised by Ken Livingstone's race adviser, Lee Jasper (who was not available for comment).

The Commission for Racial Equality was hardly more forthcoming. 'We need more data and we need to know it is being collected in a robust and methodologically sound way,' a spokesman told me. 'If there is a problem, we need to know who is involved and who the victims are. We are also concerned that low levels of confidence in the police might mean that young ethnic minority women are less likely than other victims to report attacks.'

The majority of rapes are committed by adults at home, according to Women Against Rape. But young girls are being gang raped by young men or boys, who are – in reported cases – often black. Why? 'It's very difficult to explain things away with cultural factors,' says Peter Misch, a forensic psychiatrist specialising in adolescents at London's Maudsley hospital. He recalls visiting a young offenders' institute in Siberia in 1993, where each of the 20 offenders aged 14–16 was in for group rape. Camila Batmanghelidjh, who runs the children's charity Kids Company in Peckham, south-east London, thinks gang rapes go in clusters. 'It's not about race. You have to ask – is it because the black community is the most marginalised and pressurised, and does that lead to emotional consequences?' She prefers to concentrate on the state of mind of most boys she works with. She calls it 'emotional coldness'.

Poverty causes stress, which might contribute to emotional coldness. Add a macho culture and you might end up with a gang rape. Or not. No one has a simple explanation for why gang rapes happen, or why a third of all sex crimes are now committed by under-21-year-olds, according to recent Home Office figures.

'Some of the boys are pretty normal,' says Barry O'Hagan, who works with Misch on Southwark's Stop (Support, Treatment, Opportunity, Partnership) project for young sex offenders. 'That's pretty scary, but that's not what people want to hear.' In one notorious gang rape, the group played basketball together. They weren't a 'gang' in the street-gang sense of the word. For one of the boys, 'it was totally out of character,' O'Hagan says. 'He knew it was out of order, but in a group situation, it was just what happened. Groups are very powerful.'

The leader of the group might be antisocial or psychopathic, Misch says. 'They might think it's OK. Some boys are sadistic, some are altruistic.' He pauses. 'It's very complex. I've noticed that when a group of boys assault a girl, sometimes some boys want to help her afterwards. They somehow perceive there's something wrong. They'll help her put her clothes back on or something. They'll give her her bus fare. There is genuine altruism, which might be interpreted as an awareness that a crime has been committed (contrition), or a lack of awareness (the boy helps her because he thinks what has happened was in the context of a consensual relationship, however brief).' The almost standard use of condoms is equally open to interpretation. Misch thinks it's about self-preservation. 'Sometimes they use plastic bags. Whatever they can. It's about not leaving their DNA, not being caught.'

Cross-examination: 'Did they use condoms?'

Lucy: 'That's what I thought was weird. Usually when you hear about things like that, they look like boys who don't care about stuff like that. But I heard them opening a packet of condoms.'

One of the defence barristers, subsequently: 'My client apparently used a condom. You may think this is very sensible in one view and very polite in another. Two young people in a park and the boy is forcing himself on a girl who is not willing and he puts on a condom. That's not an easy task in a comfortable consensual setting, but in the cold in the park, and his victim doesn't run off – does that sound like rape to you?'

It sounds like rape to me. It sounds like rape to all the young women I talk to. 'Of course she'd get on a bus with her rapist afterwards,' says Tamika. 'She's scared, isn't she?' She tuts scornfully. 'These people need to get out and see what's happening in deep society.'

Patterns of behaviour recur. I mention certain scenarios from tournante cases to Baker at the Met. 'Have you come across boys sending text messages to get their mates to come along?' 'Oh yes.' 'Making home-made porn?' 'Yes.' 'Boyfriend handing girlfriend over to friends?' Yes. Déjà vu.

Most of this is inconceivable to most people, and that is why juries usually acquit. In the courtroom, as the prosecution barrister attempts to explain what 'wok it' has come to mean to kids (have sex, from the Jamaican slang 'work it'), and as the judge attempts to speak street, with every 'yeah' coming out as a 'yah', I am struck by the futility of it all. It is two worlds colliding. Outside the courtroom one morning, a solicitor on the defence bench says, 'I don't think it was a gang rape. They knew the boys. They always do.'

Most girls in gang rape situations know at least one of their attackers. Sometimes it's their boyfriend who hands them over, with sexual blackmail. 'If you don't go with my mates, I won't go out with you any more.' Sometimes it's the straitjacket of reputation. 'You get one person who says, "She gives head" or whatever,' says Tamika, 'and then every man wants it. It gets out of proportion.' Add to that high levels of alcohol consumption and drugs. 'You can build a picture,' Trail says. 'There's a bit of drinking, a bit of drug-taking, and at some point it turns into a rape.'

This is the reason the Met prefers the term 'group rape'. 'Gang sounds like marauders,' Yates says. 'This kind of offending is more subtle than that.'

I prefer the Australian term 'pack rape', because its predatory tinge is most accurate. The boys themselves, depending on where they're from, have a choice of terminology – line-up, pulling train, party rape. All cosy euphemisms for an activity that is twice as likely as single assailant rape to include debasing activities such as forced fellatio, biting, the use of implements and semen or excrement.

Lucy: 'There were two girls, C and T, who had rushed me at school. [That night in the park] They [the boys] said, "Oh, you know what, C and T live just up there, we can call them, we'll get them to bring knives and they're just going to come and kill you in the park. You're not going to get home alive unless you do that." He said, "It's so easy, you can do something with us, or you can never see your mum again. Take off your shoes and tights and get down on the floor." '

In some cases, such as an episode in Southend, the group of boys made an effort to charm the girls beforehand. 'The three girls had been a bit naughty,' someone involved in the case tells me. 'They'd told their parents they were going to the cinema. They'd drunk a litre bottle of wine between them, which the defence of course made a meal of.' They met a group of teenagers, aged from 11–17, and including two girls, who were down from east London. The girls were flattered to get the lads' attention, until 'they thought it was getting too heavy. They regrouped in a public toilet, but when they came out they were corralled across the road to the beach.' The allegations were that one girl was raped twice, another once, and the third sexually assaulted. It seemed like a strong case: there was DNA evidence in the condoms, there was CCTV evidence, the girls had reported it immediately, and the youths from the gang voluntarily turned themselves in, though without admitting guilt.

The first trial collapsed on a technicality. The second was thrown out when one witness discussed a minor detail – about a soft toy – with another (witnesses cannot discuss the case with each other). It might seem innocuous, but the judge had no choice but to dismiss the case. It can't be tried again. The girls were devastated, and in a letter to the investigation team, their parents thanked the police, and said they'd never again have any faith in the criminal justice system.

I don't have much, either. A dismal number of gang rape cases get to court; an even more dismal number result in convictions. One of the few that did – three young men were given six-year sentences this year for befriending and raping 13-year-old girls in Ilford shopping centres – inspired Judge Henry Blacksell to comment, 'This might be normal behaviour in Ilford, but the girls still need protection.'

Is it normal behaviour? According to official FBI profiling, 'Participants in a gang rape are generally driven by group motivations: camaraderie and competition, sustaining an image, sharing an experience with one's 'buddies', loyalty, and adopting and demonstrating a group identity and values.' This is why all-male environments, such as sports clubs, football teams, fraternities and the army, throw up a high proportion of group rape cases.

But so do our cities. LSL has a youthful population in a densely inhabited urban environment where it's easy to meet people and where boredom, listlessness and the stress of poverty are not uncommon. 'There is a chain of brutality,' Batmanghelidjh says. 'You have children who were brutalised when they were very young. I don't mean that as an excuse. They know what moral values are, but they don't have a belief system. If there's no quality contact between mother and baby, subtle areas of the brain don't develop, like empathy or any emotional repertoire.'

'Ha!' says a Harlesden youth worker when I tell him this. 'They just think it's fun, innit!' He'd begun by talking about black history, and went on to be fiercely critical of the black present. 'You're going to get called racist when you write this,' he says gloomily, 'because that's easier than talking about it. But it can only happen if their peers welcome it. Families defend their sons, but they're wrong and strong. Half the dads aren't there to tell them it's wrong to violate a woman. The kids don't have older role models. They don't have morals.'

One boy being treated in the Stop programme, involved in a notorious gang rape, never once, throughout months of therapy, changed his story that the woman had consented. 'He accepted responsibility for every other area of his life,' O'Hagan says, 'but not that. It was very striking.'

Experts will say it's simplistic to seek clues in pornography, but there are questions to be raised about sexual access, illusions, frustration. 'I'm no prude,' says Misch, 'but the level of sexualisation in our society is disturbing. Men's magazines perpetuate a myth of availability, yet this is not an open sexual society.'

Such solutions as have been suggested are mostly of the show–willing variety. A new inter-party parliamentary committee on sexual offences has been set up, of which Yates has hopes. 'Every school in France has to report every day to the Education Ministry any assault that's taken place in their schools. That's been in place 18 months. It's that type of initiative I suspect the committee will want to consider. There's a problem out there that we need to grapple with. But I suspect we deal with the symptoms, not what's causing it.'

There is always education, education. 'Sex education?' scoffs the Harlesden youth worker. 'What's the point? They already know every-thing. Unless you keep publicising it, nothing is going to change. We're saying our young women are worth nothing. We're saying you can go out and rape because you'll get away with it.' What needs to be taught, say psy-chologists, is boundaries. Respect.

Often, little respect is offered to a girl who's been raped. 'The mothers in our community are very scornful,' the youth worker tells me. 'You hear things like, "We hear say she invite them."' From then on, she's a slag. Kelly has had women calling her dirty because they've heard she was gang raped. She could take refuge in bravado, in joining a gang, but she doesn't. 'I stay home. I don't go out with boys. I don't want to.'

Emma: 'I assure you that I wouldn't be going through with this court case if I hadn't been raped.'

Cross-examination: 'We'll let the jury decide that.'

Emma: 'Yeah, let the jury decide that.'

In Lucy and Emma's case, the jury take one hour and 39 minutes to decide. This is a long time, for a rape verdict; however, the not guilty verdicts are no surprise. Most cases I researched didn't reach court, because the police decided no crime had been committed or the family dropped the charges, or the CPS decided not to prosecute. Most that did reach court were acquitted. The 12-year-old in Feltham? The jacket she was wearing had traces of DNA that were not the gang's. She said it wasn't her jacket; she wasn't believed. Not guilty. A woman in Coventry who had extensive injuries? She had given her number to one of the alleged rapists, so it must have been consensual. She claimed her rapists had gone out into the street and recruited two more. Not guilty. In his summing up, the defence barrister said, 'Some of the men hardly knew each other. You would not recruit people you did not know well to commit something as serious as a gang rape.'

In April this year, the home secretary announced a £4m fund for sexual assault victims, which would enable six more Havens to open. In the same month, the Met announced they were launching their biggest ever investigation into gang rape. They will reopen 2,000 old cases and attempt to establish patterns and trends. Victims who have stayed silent will be urged to report attacks, however old.

I wish them luck. Over her spare ribs in the noodle bar, I ask Tamika if her friend will talk to me about her gang rape. She laughs. 'No way! Who'd want to talk about something like that?' But Tamika, I say, someone has to. 'Yeah,' she says. 'I suppose. Someone's got to break the silence. But she's not going to start.'

SEX & BODY IMAGE

EMMA GOLDMAN
1869–1940

A radical advocate of birth control, during a period when distributing any information about the practice could lead directly to incarceration (see Goldman's previous article for more details) this article saw Goldman defying all government rulings to explain just why this issue is so crucial for contemporary women and, indeed, men. This short extract introduces her main points.

The Social Aspects of Birth Control

April 1916, *Mother Earth*, vol. XI, no. 2

It has been suggested that to create one genius nature uses all of her resources and takes a hundred years for her difficult task. If that be true, it takes nature even longer to create a great idea. After all, in creating a genius nature concentrates on one personality, whereas an idea must eventually become the heritage of the race and must needs be more difficult to mold.

It is just one hundred and fifty years ago when a great man conceived a great idea, Robert Thomas Malthus, the father of Birth Control. That it should have taken so long a time for the human race to realize the greatness of that idea is only one more proof of the sluggishness of the human mind. It is not possible to go into a detailed discussion of the merits of Malthus' contention, to wit, that the earth is not fertile or rich enough to supply the needs of an excessive race. Certainly if we will look across to the trenches and battlefields of Europe we will find that in a measure his premise was correct. But I feel confident that if Malthus would live today he would agree with all social students and revolutionists that if the masses of people continue to be poor and the rich grow ever richer, it is not because the earth is lacking in fertility and richness to supply the need even of an excessive race, but because the earth is monopolized in the hands of the few to the exclusion of the many. [. . .]

Malthus' theory contains much more truth than fiction. In its modern aspect it rests no longer upon speculation, but on other factors which are related to and interwoven with the tremendous social changes going on everywhere.

First, there is the scientific aspect, the contention on the part of the most eminent men of science who tell us that an overworked and underfed vitality cannot reproduce healthy progeny. Beside the contention of scientists, we are confronted with the terrible fact which is now even recognized by benighted people, namely, that an indiscriminate and incessant breeding on the part of the overworked and underfed masses has resulted in an increase of defective, crippled, and unfortunate children. So alarming is this fact, that it has awakened social reformers to the necessity of a mental clearinghouse where the cause and effect of the increase of crippled, deaf, dumb, and blind children may be ascertained. Knowing as we do that reformers accept the truth when it has become apparent to the dullest in society, there need be no discussion any longer in regard to the results of indiscriminate breeding.

Secondly, there is the mental awakening of woman, that plays no small part in behalf of Birth Control. For ages she has carried her burdens. Has done her duty a thousandfold more than the soldier on the battlefield. After all, the soldier's business is to take life. For that he is paid by the State, eulogized by political charlatans, and upheld by public hysteria. But woman's function is to give life, yet neither the State nor politicians nor public opinion have ever made the slightest provision in return for the life woman has given.

For ages she has been on her knees before the altar of duty as imposed by God, by Capitalism, by the State, and by Morality. Today she has awakened from her age-long sleep. She has shaken herself free from the nightmare of the past; she has turned her face towards the light and is proclaiming in a clarion voice that she will no longer be a party to the crime of bringing hapless children into the world only to be ground into dust by the wheel of capitalism and to be torn into shreds in trenches and battlefields. And who is to say her nay? After all it is woman who is risking her health and sacrificing her youth in the reproduction of the race. Surely she ought to be in a position to decide how many children she should bring into the world, whether they should be brought into the world by the man she loves and because she wants the child, or should be born in hatred and loathing.

Furthermore, it is conceded by earnest physicians that constant reproduction on the part of women has resulted in what the laity terms, 'female troubles': a lucrative condition for unscrupulous medical men. But what possible reason has woman to exhaust her system in everlasting child bearing?

It is precisely for this reason that woman should have the knowledge that would enable her to recuperate during a period of from three to five years between each pregnancy, which alone would give her physical and mental well-being and the opportunity to take better care of the children already in existence.

But it is not woman alone who is beginning to realize the importance of Birth Control. Men, too, especially workingmen, have learned to see in large families a millstone around their necks, deliberately imposed upon them by the reactionary forces in society because a large family paralyzes the brain and benumbs the muscles of the masses of workingmen. Nothing so binds the workers to the block as a brood of children, and that is exactly what the opponents of Birth Control want. Wretched as the earnings of a man with a large family are, he cannot risk even that little, so he continues on the rut, compromises and cringes before his master, just to earn barely enough to feed the many little mouths. He dare not join a revolutionary organization; he dare not go on strike; he dare not express an opinion. Masses of workers have awakened to the necessity of Birth Control as a means of freeing themselves from the terrible yoke and still more as a means of being able to do something for those already in existence by preventing more children from coming into the world.

Last, but not least, a change in the relation of the sexes, though not embracing very large numbers of people, is still making itself felt among a very considerable minority. In the past and to a large extent with the average man today woman continues to be a mere object, a means to an end; largely a physical means and end. But there are men who want more than that from woman; who have come to realize that if every male were emancipated from the superstitions of the past nothing would yet be changed in the social structure so long as woman had not taken her place with him in the great social struggle. Slowly but surely these men have learned that if a woman wastes her substance in eternal pregnancies, confinements, and diaper washing, she has little time left for anything else. Least of all has she time for the questions which absorb and stir the father of her children. Out of physical exhaustion and nervous stress she becomes the obstacle in the man's way and often his bitterest enemy. It is then for his own protection and also for his need of the companion and friend in the woman he loves that a great many men want her to be relieved from the terrible imposition of constant reproduction of life, that therefore they are in favor of Birth Control.

GLADYS HALL

1891–1977

Born in New York, Hall began her career in 1912, writing poetry and articles for fan magazines. From 1922, she wrote a syndicated column, 'The Diary of a Professional Movie Fan', which led the way to her interviewing many of the biggest Hollywood stars of the era (her subjects including everyone from Humphrey Bogart to Joan Crawford, Lucille Ball to John Wayne).

In the following piece, Hall interviews one of the most outspoken stars ever, Tallulah Bankhead, and her subject doesn't disappoint. In fact, Bankhead is so candid that the piece was to change the Hollywood system for ever. From its publication onwards, studios insisted that their stars be accompanied by minders, hence the ever-present PR managers of the modern media.

Tallulah Bankhead

September 1932, *Motion Picture*

Has Hollywood turned a cold shoulder on Tallulah Bankhead? Persons In The Know have it that Hollywood has given her a shoulder very cold and very rigid, indeed.

According to these women–about–town, Hollywood's most elite hostesses have run a blue pencil through the made up moniker of Bankhead.

These hostesses are pictured as confessing they are *afraid* of Tallulah. And the gossipers report that Marion Davies, Connie Bennett, and Bebe Daniels Lyon are among those who prefer not to be At Home to Tallulah.

It is said that, at formal dinner parties, where genteel elegance rests upon all, Tallulah is apt to give vent to words and expressions believed by our grandmothers to belong to truck drivers and longshoremen exclusively.

I am told that Tallul' is never decently hypocritical. She is never hypocritical at all. She conceals nothing. She reveals All – and more than all. She disguises nothing. She calls a spade nothing but a spade – in Hollywood, where dirt is dug with dinner forks. She gives to all the functions of living and loving, of body and soul their round Rabelaisian, biological *names*. Crimson faces and heaving bosoms and masculine guffaws slide off the bawdy Bankhead like oil off water. She is no respecter of persons and no respecter of personalities.

It is said that she speaks of her love affairs with equal frankness. She has a romantic interlude and, afterwards, discusses it with lurid details and complete unreserve. It matters not whether the recent recipient of her favors happens to be among those present or not. Whether he is or whether he isn't, she is said to dilate upon his ways and wiles, his abilities and disabilities, his prowess or his lack of prowess, with such consummate abandon that the unfortunate male, if present, can think of no recourse except immediate suicide.

No good hostess, I am informed, could dream of exposing her guests to such ribaldries. Tallulah's wit, I am told, is barbed. Her shafts and arrows fly wildly through the Hollywood atmosphere, striking willy-nilly, where least expected. She is like a gilded bomb invited to rest among lilies of the field. Thus I have been told.

But Tallulah denies all this. She denies it vehemently, amusedly, scornfully and – can it be? – a little sadly. She denies everything that has been said about her, rumored about her and printed about her.

She 'wears' an exterior as, for certain purposes, a mummer wears a mask. She wears this exterior for protection, to save her neck, her face, her feelings. She took it off for me.

She said, to begin with (and oh, the rapid, dynamite, restless things she said!): Hollywood has been divine to me. I don't know what you mean. If it *is* giving me the cold shoulder, I haven't felt the chill. It is news to me. It may be that I am suspected of giving *Hollywood* the cold shoulder because I accept so few invitations. Because I have never given parties. Because such hospitality as I have accepted I haven't returned. It has reached a point now where, if I gave a party at all, I would have to invite about five hundred people.

'But this is all absurd. Most of the things said about me and printed about me are absurd and untrue. Not that I mind what people say – it's all part of the game. They say, for instance, that Marlene Dietrich and I are furiously jealous, the one of the other. That we spend our spare time in brawling together like fish-wives all over the lot. I have just come, as it happens, from Marlene's dressing-room where we had a dish of champagne together . . .'

(On this I can confirm Tallulah. Marlene's dressing-room is next to Tallulah's. Just before Tallulah came in, I heard her call back, 'Thanks for the champagne, Marlene . . .')

'I am said to be lacking in seriousness, to have no serious side at all, to be unhurt by anything, to be incapable of hurt. Lies, of course. Here and now, for the first time, I deny that. I am serious. I am deadly serious.

I am serious about my work. I am serious about love. I am serious about marriage and children and friendship and the whole stuff of life. *I pretend not to be.*

'I have an inferiority complex. It is my defense mechanism working. So that, if I take a fall, if I fail here or fail there, if the movies or a man chuck me out on my ear, people will laugh it off and say, 'Oh, well, Tallulah doesn't care!' But I would care. I'd care all right, but not so much as if people knew that I cared. I can't bear pity. I can't endure sympathy. A kindly pat on my bowed shoulder would drive me nuts.

'I am deadly serious about my work. I'd have to be – anybody has to have any kind of lasting success. Nobody attains any kind of permanence unless he is serious. There are no such things as "the breaks". Not for long. I have had no "angels" in my life, nobody has ever helped me. I wouldn't be helped. What I have achieved, I have achieved by myself and I haven't done it by not caring.

'When I first started to make pictures, absurd stories began to circulate about me. I was said to be trying to "do a Garbo". A fatal thing to say about anyone. Words perfectly calculated to arouse the defensiveness and rage of thousands of Garbo fans. Do you think I didn't care about that? Don't be a fool. I was said to have ordered Adolph Zukor off the set, not knowing who he was. Do you think *I'm* a fool? I knew perfectly well who he was and what business he had there. I asked him to leave because I was working with a new medium, because I was frightfully nervous and edgy and because his presence, of all persons, made me more so.

'When I saw the preview of my first picture in the East, I managed to get out of the theatre, blind with tears as I was. I made my friends swear on my eyes (I'm superstitious about eyes, I'm something of an eye-worshiper) that they would never go to see that picture. I hadn't learned how to make up, how to be photographed. I was full of inhibitions and uncertainties.

'I am serious about money. I have my eye on a fixed sum. I may never reach it. I'm hideously extravagant. With all the money I made in London, I had to borrow a wad to get out of the place, skirts clean. I never leave a place owing bills. I'm serious about my credit, you know.

'I'm serious about my ambition. Know what it is? I'll give it to you – *to have no ambition.* To be without ambition of any sort is Heaven. Nirvana, the state of the blessed. I've been hag-ridden with ambition. It burns you up. It eats you alive. It drinks your blood and crumbles your bones. I want to be without it.

'I'm serious about love. I'm damned serious about it now, of all times. I haven't had an *affaire* for six months. Six months. Too long. I am not promiscuous, you know. Promiscuity implies that attraction is not necessary. I may lay my eyes on a man and have an *affaire* with him the next hour. But it is serious, The attraction is serious.

'I am serious about marriage – too serious to indulge in it. I know myself too well. I never fool myself. I do fool everyone else. I know that once I get a thing – or a man – I'll tire of it and of him. I am the type that fattens on unrequited love, on the unattainable, on the just-beyond-reach. The minute a man begins to languish over me, I stiffen and it is finis.

'I am serious about wishing I had children – beautiful children. I wouldn't care for the other variety. I love anything and everything that is beautiful. Perhaps beautiful is not the word – personality is more like it.

'Of course, I am an extremist. I'm in transports of mad delight with living one day and bored to a hellish desperation the next day. When I am in heaven, I'm liable to rip the stars out of the sky and gut the moon. When I'm bored – no hell is so dark-brown and odorous.

'I'm serious about the matter of good taste. Hollywood's cold shoulder or warm heart to the contrary, I would feel acutely if I thought I had hurt anyone. I am not religious, but I would make a wide detour and put myself to a lot of inconvenience before I would make a ribald remark about a minister, or priest or rabbi to one of the faithful. The things other people hold sacred I am careful of. I might offend morals, but never good taste – the more important of the two.

'My secretary says that I am mad, and tries to prevent me from saying it – and proving it – to the Press. At this moment she is making signs to me from the other room. Perhaps I am mad. How should I know? *I* think I am normal. I know that the things I do *seem* normal to me. And I repeat that I do not believe that mad people, or superficial people, or people who never take anything seriously get very far – or stay there.

'There is nothing more to say about this Hollywood cold-shouldering proposition. Other than that I've never heard of it, have not been aware of it. And certainly I feel no equivalent emotion in myself. I like Hollywood. I find the people interesting and, very often, especially delightful. I don't go around a great deal because it would bore me. I've done all the night-clubbing and partying I could swallow, in London and in Paris. It doesn't interest me any longer, that sort of thing. I've had some close and personal friends from London staying with me. I haven't needed outside entertainment. I play Bridge a little, very badly. I go to the movies, Garbo is a very great genius. I'm mad about her. *And I'm not, as a rule, very fond of women.* I'm crazy about Gary Cooper and Jackie Cooper, and Jack Oakie and Leslie Howard.

'If there's anything the matter with me now, it's certainly not Hollywood or Hollywood's state of mind about me, one way or the other.

The matter with me is – I WANT A MAN! I told you I haven't had an *affaire* for six months. I'm bored to the point of suicide when I'm not in love. When I am in love, I want to die. I always want to die when I'm on the top. When I'm down again, I want to fight back. I wish to God I could fall in love now – find someone to fall in love with. Six months is a long, long while. *I want a man!'*

I felt, when I left Tallulah's dressing-room, that I had been closed in with a feverish, very tired, very mundane and effete tigress. She wore scarlet pajamas, tailored coat and trousers. Her nut-brown hair was long-bobbed and flying. She wore no make-up. Her eyes were strained and weary. She paced the floor, back and forth, to and fro.

She brought to mind the gallant, maniacal *Mad Hopes*, the obsessed *Royal Family of Broadway* – all of the fiercely desiring, fiercely living desperadoes, male and female, of theatre, of history, of life. She may be mad. But she is serious about it. She may be without a soul. She is not without a heart. She may make mock of lovers as dead to her as the dead yesterdays. She would never make mock of love. Nor of life. And if life or love make mock of her, she will answer back with an ironic laugh and a bawdy phrase – and tears in her heart.

JOAN DIDION

1934–

Journalist, novelist and screenwriter, the California-born Didion began her career as a features editor at *Vogue*. Leaving in the early 1960s to work as a freelance journalist, she continued to produce some of the most iconic writing of the last century. The opening essay in her collection *The White Album* (1979), for example, is a mesmerizing evocation of California in the late 1960s, transferring the reader almost bodily to that paranoid place and era, in which the Manson murders of 1969 could be greeted with interest and gossip, but never, truly, surprise. Reading such essays underlines Didion's mastery of her own dictum for writing, which states that it's 'the act of saying *I*, of imposing oneself upon other people, of saying *listen to me, see it my way, change your mind.*'

In the following article, which deftly illustrates her style, Didion muses on the importance of self-respect.

On Self-respect

1961, American *Vogue*

Once, in a dry season, I wrote in large letters across two pages of a notebook that innocence ends when one is stripped of the delusion that one likes oneself. Although now, some years later, I marvel that a mind on the outs with itself should have nonetheless made painstaking record of its every tremor, I recall with embarrassing clarity the flavor of those particular ashes. It was a matter of misplaced self-respect.

I had not been elected to Phi Beta Kappa. This failure could scarcely have been more predictable or less ambiguous (I simply did not have the grades), but I was unnerved by it; I had somehow thought myself a kind of academic Raskolnikov, curiously exempt from the cause-effect relationships which hampered others. Although even the humorless nineteen-year-old that I was must have recognized that the situation lacked real tragic stature, the day that I did not make Phi Beta Kappa nonetheless marked the end of something, and innocence may well be the word for it. I lost the conviction that lights would always turn green for me, the pleasant certainty that those rather passive virtues which had won me approval as a child automatically guaranteed me not only Phi Beta Kappa keys but happiness, honor, and the love of a good man; lost a certain touching faith in the totem power of good manners, clean hair, and proven competence on the Stanford-Binet scale. To such doubtful amulets had my self-respect been pinned, and I faced myself that day with the nonplussed apprehension of someone who has come across a vampire and has no crucifix at hand.

Although to be driven back upon oneself is an uneasy affair at best, rather like trying to cross a border with borrowed credentials, it seems to me now the one condition necessary to the beginnings of real self-respect. Most of our platitudes notwithstanding, self-deception remains the most difficult deception. The tricks that work on others count for nothing in that very well-lit back alley where one keeps assignations with oneself: no winning smiles will do here, no prettily drawn lists of good intentions. One shuffles flashily but in vain through one's marked cards – the kindness done for the wrong reason, the apparent triumph which involved no real effort, the seemingly heroic act into which one had been shamed. The dismal fact is that self-respect has nothing to do with the approval of others – who are, after all, deceived easily enough; has nothing to do with reputation, which, as Rhett Butler told Scarlett O'Hara, is something people with courage can do without.

To do without self-respect, on the other hand, is to be an unwilling audience of one to an interminable documentary that details one's failings, both real and imagined, with fresh footage spliced in for every screening. *There's the glass you broke in anger, there's the hurt on X's face; watch now, this next scene, the night Y came back from Houston, see how you muff this one.* To live without self-respect is to lie awake some night, beyond the reach of warm milk, phenobarbital, and the sleeping hand on the coverlet, counting up the sins of commission and omission, the trusts betrayed, the promises subtly broken, the gifts irrevocably wasted through sloth or cowardice or carelessness. However long we postpone it, we eventually lie down alone in that notoriously uncomfortable bed, the one we make ourselves. Whether or not we sleep in it depends, of course, on whether or not we respect ourselves.

To protest that some fairly improbable people, some people who *could not possibly respect themselves*, seem to sleep easily enough is to miss the point entirely, as surely as those people miss it who think that self-respect has necessarily to do with not having safety pins in one's underwear. There is a common superstition that 'self-respect' is a kind of charm against snakes, something that keeps those who have it locked in some unblighted Eden, out of strange beds, ambivalent conversations, and trouble in general. It does not at all. It has nothing to do with the face of things, but concerns instead a separate peace, a private reconciliation. Although the careless, suicidal Julian English in *Appointment in Samarra* and the careless, incurably dishonest Jordan Baker in *The Great Gatsby* seem equally improbable candidates for self-respect, Jordan Baker had it,

Julian English did not. With that genius for accommodation more often seen in women than in men, Jordan took her own measure, made her own peace, avoided threats to that peace: 'I hate careless people,' she told Nick Carraway. 'It takes two to make an accident.'

Like Jordan Baker, people with self-respect have the courage of their mistakes. They know the price of things. If they choose to commit adultery, they do not then go running, in an excess of bad conscience, to receive absolution from the wronged parties; nor do they complain unduly of the unfairness, the undeserved embarrassment, of being named co-respondent. In brief, people with self-respect exhibit a certain toughness, a kind of moral nerve; they display what was once called *character*, a quality which, although approved in the abstract, sometimes loses ground to other, more instantly negotiable virtues. The measure of its slipping prestige is that one tends to think of it only in connection with homely children and United States senators who have been defeated, preferably in the primary, for reelection. Nonetheless, character – the willingness to accept responsibility for one's own life – is the source from which self-respect springs.

Self-respect is something that our grandparents, whether or not they had it, knew all about. They had instilled in them, young, a certain discipline, the sense that one lives by doing things one does not particularly want to do, by putting fears and doubts to one side, by weighing immediate comforts against the possibility of larger, even intangible, comforts. It seemed to the nineteenth century, admirable, but not remarkable, that Chinese Gordon put on a clean white suit and held Khartoum against the Mahdi; it did not seem unjust that the way to free land in California involved death and difficulty and dirt. In a diary kept during the winter of 1846, an emigrating twelve-year-old named Narcissa Cornwall noted coolly: 'Father was busy reading and did not notice that the house was being filled with strange Indians until Mother spoke about it.' Even lacking any clue as to what Mother said, one can scarcely fail to be impressed by the entire incident: the father reading, the Indians filing in, the mother choosing the words that would not alarm, the child duly recording the event and noting further that those particular Indians were not, 'fortunately for us,' hostile. Indians were simply part of the *donnée*.

In one guise or another, Indians always are. Again, it is a question of recognizing that anything worth having has its price. People who respect themselves are willing to accept the risk that the Indians will be hostile, that the venture will go bankrupt, that the liaison may not turn out to be one in which *every day is a holiday because you're married to me*. They are willing to invest something of themselves; they may not play at all, but when they do play, they know the odds.

That kind of self-respect is a discipline, a habit of mind that can never be faked but can be developed, trained, coaxed forth. It was once suggested to me that, as an antidote to crying, I put my head in a paper bag. As it happens, there is a sound physiological reason, something to do with oxygen, for doing exactly that, but the psychological effect alone is incalculable: it is difficult in the extreme to continue fancying oneself Cathy in *Wuthering Heights* with one's head in a Food Fair bag. There is a similar case for all the small disciplines, unimportant in themselves; imagine maintaining any kind of swoon, commiserative or carnal, in a cold shower.

But those small disciplines are valuable only insofar as they represent larger ones. To say that Waterloo was won on the playing fields of Eton is not to say that Napoleon might have been saved by a crash program in cricket; to give formal dinners in the rain forest would be pointless did not the candlelight flickering on the liana call forth deeper, stronger disciplines, values instilled long before. It is a kind of ritual, helping us to remember who and what we are. In order to remember it, one must have known it.

To have that sense of one's intrinsic worth which constitutes self-respect is potentially to have everything: the ability to discriminate, to love and to remain indifferent. To lack it is to be locked within oneself, paradoxically incapable of either love or indifference. If we do not respect ourselves, we are on the one hand forced to despise those who have so few resources as to consort with us, so little perception as to remain blind to our fatal weaknesses. On the other, we are peculiarly in thrall to everyone we see, curiously determined to live out – since our self-image is untenable – their false notions of us. We flatter ourselves by thinking this compulsion to please others an attractive trait: a gist for imaginative empathy, evidence of our willingness to give. *Of course* I will play Francesca to your Paolo, Helen Keller, to anyone's Annie Sullivan: no expectation is too misplaced, no role too ludicrous. At the mercy of those we cannot but hold in contempt, we play roles doomed to failure before they are begun, each defeat generating fresh despair at the urgency of divining and meeting the next demand made upon us.

It is the phenomenon sometimes called 'alienation from self.' In its advanced stages, we no longer answer the telephone, because someone might want something; that we could say *no* without drowning in self-reproach is an idea alien to this game. Every encounter demands too much, tears the nerves, drains the will, and the specter of something as small as an unanswered letter arouses such disproportionate guilt that answering it becomes out of the question. To assign unanswered letters their proper weight, to free us from the expectations of others, to give us back to ourselves – there lies the great, the singular power of self-respect. Without it, one eventually discovers the final turn of the screw: one runs away to find oneself, and finds no one at home.

KATHARINE WHITEHORN

1928–

London-born journalist and author, Whitehorn began her career at the *Picture Post*, before rising quickly to become one of the best-known columnists in Britain, writing for more than three decades (from 1960) for the *Observer* newspaper. Latterly she has reinvented herself as an agony aunt for *Saga* magazine.

The following column is one of the most famous examples of her work and demonstrates her personal style, which was hugely pioneering at a time when only business and 'hard' news were really considered appropriate subjects for newspaper coverage. Orginally turned down by *She* magazine, when the *Observer* ran it, the piece generated a huge response, primarily from women (like Whitehorn) trying to juggle the many aspects of their lives and relieved to find another, like them, who sometimes dropped a few balls.

Sluts I

29 December 1963, *Observer*

This article is dedicated to all those who have ever changed their stockings in a taxi, brushed their hair with someone else's nailbrush or safety-pinned a hem; and those who have not had probably better not read on.

Anyone in doubt, however, can ask herself the following questions. Have you ever taken anything back out of the dirty-clothes basket because it had become, relatively, the cleaner thing? How many things are there, at this moment, in the wrong room – cups in the study, boots in the kitchen, and how many of them are on the *floor* of the wrong room?

Could you try on clothes in any shop, any time, without worrying about your underclothes? and how, if at all, do you clean your nails? Honest answers should tell you, once and for all, whether you are one of us: the miserable, optimistic, misunderstood race of sluts.

We are not ordinary human beings who have degenerated as people think: we are born this way. Even at four you can pick us out: the little girls in the playground who have one pant-leg hanging down and no hair-slide; at ten we are the ones who look dirty even when we are clean (unlike the goody-goodies who look fairly clean even when they are dirty) and at fifteen, when black stockings are fashionable, we betray ourselves in the changing-room by legs spotted like a Dalmatian's, the inevitable result of using Indian ink instead of darning-wool.

People who are not sluts intolerantly assume that we must like things this way, without realizing the enormous effort and inconvenience that goes into being so ineffective: the number of times we have to fill a car's radiator because we don't get it mended, the fortune we spend on taxis going back for parcels we have left in shops, the amount of ironing occasioned by our practice of unpacking not so much when we get back from a weekend as four days later.

We acquire, it is true, certain off-beat skills: I am much better at holding a bottle of varnish between two fingers than those of my friends who do not paint their nails in the Tube, and they cannot cut their nails with a pen-knife, either; but nothing really makes up to us for the difficulties of our way of life.

However, I am not trying to make a soggy bid for sympathy so much as to work out what we can possibly do to improve our condition. And the first thing, it seems to me, is to inscribe *Abandon Hope All Ye Who Enter Here* over the lintels of all our messy houses; for it is our optimism that is principally our undoing. We keep hoping that we will remember to wash our white collars, or find time to comb our hair on the way to the office, or slide into the building and dump our coats before anyone can see that there are three buttons missing. More, it seems to me could be done if we could only face up realistically to all the things we never will be able to do.

We can realize, for example, that no power on earth is going to make us look well turned out all, or even most, of the time. We can therefore give up right away any New Year resolutions about fashion: a second pair of little white gloves will simply result in our carrying two right hands; wigs would be a waste of money because those of us who cannot keep our real hair tidy cannot keep our toy hair tidy either. Instead, we can wear reasonably sober clothes normally, go for stacked heels because we know we won't remember to get them reheeled before they are worn down, have only one colour of accessories, so that we cannot wear the brown shoes with the black bag.

And, having accepted that people are *not* going to say 'she's always so chic', we can concentrate every now and then on really dazzling efforts that will knock our audience sideways. Jane Austen was right when she said that no beauty accustomed to compliments ever felt anything like the thrill of an ordinary looker who was told she was looking terrific *that evening*.

We can give up making good resolutions about replacing things before they run out, which is absurd, and concentrate instead on bulk buying, so that the gap between demand and supply happens much more rarely.

We can also, of course, keep icing sugar, the wrong sort of rice, tea bags, a spearmint toothpaste and so on specifically to tide us over when we do run out of the real thing. It is true that we tend not to have any money either, but as we usually spend what we have at the beginning of the month like drunken sailors anyway, we might as well spend it on vast tubs of cleansing cream, acres of Kleenex (which we have to have, since clean handkerchiefs, let's face it, are beyond us), sugar in ten-pound bags.

Apart from this sort of grim realism, there are, I think, only two other things that can help us. The first is habit: odd as it may seem, even sluts do occasionally acquire good habits (we clean our teeth, for example, even if we sometimes have to do it with soap) and these, indeed, are all that hold us together. A slut who baths whenever she has time never baths at all: her only hope is to get up into one every morning; if she shops here and there for food there will never be any around, but a Saturday supermarket raid will settle a whole week's hash in one go.

And the second is money: for the only way a slut can really get things done is to get someone else to do them. Even the most domestic slut will find it worth earning a few pounds to pay for help in the house.

The only way to make up for missing the post is a long-distance telephone call; the only way not to have to go back to fetch things is to get them picked up by messenger. The only thing that will get a slut's carpets vacuumed daily is a daily. All sluts ought to be, or marry, rich people: and I treasure the hope that among the really rich there may be dozens of sluts lurking undetected by the rest.

Money, low cunning and a sense of realism may help us somewhat; but it is a hard life all the same. I wrote this article two years ago, but as it was felt that it hardly came well from the pen of a fashion editor, it was never printed. So I thought I had a soft option using it now; except that, of course, I couldn't find it, and have had to write the whole blasted thing again.

JILL TWEEDIE
1936–93

For a woman who went on to become one of Britain's foremost feminist commentators, Tweedie had a somewhat improbable background. Born into a wealthy Scottish family, she was denied a university education, being sent, instead to a Swiss finishing school. This led to a brief marriage, aged eighteen, to a Hungarian count, from which she fled with their two children to a Welsh hippie commune.

Whilst resident there, Tweedie was surprised to discover that, even in this apparently egalitarian setting, women were expected to do 'women's work' – which somehow amounted to *all* the work. Leaving again, she moved to London, where she lived in virtual poverty until her writing career took off.

Perhaps it was this varied background that gave Tweedie the insight and humour that distinguishes her writing. Compelling and passionate, but never aggressive or simplistic, Tweedie reached out to women who hadn't considered themselves feminists, and often changed their minds. In the following article she considers beauty and grooming and particularly the comparative aesthetic standard set for men and women.

Feminists and the Right to be Ugly

2 February 1970, *Guardian*

A Scottish father with Calvinist knobs on is the parent most likely to nip the first delicate buds of vanity in his daughter. My own Scottish father, if nagged to comment on my appearance, invariably replied that he supposed I looked better than a slap on the belly with a wet fish, or that I might pass with a push in a crowd with the light behind me. Human nature being what it is I managed to salvage enough vanity to get along with, though that early conditioning did make for a later ambivalence with the opposite sex: if a man compliments me on my cherry lips I think him boorish for overlooking my mind and if he says nice things about my mind I think him a cold fish for ignoring my cherry lips, which leads to alarums and exits all round.

Such an upbringing ought to make me feel at home with today's militant feminists who disdain make-up and other artifices designed to enhance their sexual attractions, on the grounds that these have for too long been the instruments of slavery. There's no doubt that it is humiliating to be dependent on so arbitrary a thing as physical appearance for any success or comfort in life, and many a girl has envied her brother for his freedom to operate in a haze of scruff and sweat where she is under constant pressure to groom herself like a Cruft's exhibit.

Apart from anything else, grooming oneself is a boring occupation and demands a more persistent dedication than I, at least, can muster. Once, overcome by a sudden desire for champagne and adoration, I presented myself at a model agency. An exquisite person looked me over, said go away, get your hair done, manicure your nails, iron your clothes and then come back. But I never did. Somehow champagne and adoration seemed too puny a reward for a lifetime of tweaking and peering at myself and I have now settled for looking like the curate's egg – good in patches, depending upon whether vanity or sloth has the upper hand that day.

One of the many Women's Liberation manifestos floating about London these days not only rejects positive grooming but demands the negative freedom for a girl 'to be able to be as funky in dress, body etc. as a man' and, after years of being urged, on pain of sexual ostracism, to keep myself as hairless, germless and odourless as a boiled bottle, by advertisers who believe, along with Saint Augustine, that women are vessels of uncleanliness, I see their point. As far as I am concerned, a natural slut can languish unwashed, hairy, germy and odorous, if that's the way she wants it, and other people should grin and bear it from her at least as much as they would with her male equivalent. And if a mother is going to impress hygiene on her daughter, she should do the same with her son.

In the past, a girl's face was her fortune and without some physical attractions she forfeited some of the necessities and all of the luxuries of life. Now, if a woman wants security, she can just about manage to provide it for herself and it seems eminently logical that the present revulsion of some women from self-titivation should coincide exactly with their maturing economic autonomy. But, as usual, logic appears to have little to do with it, because men are now taking more interest in their appearance than ever before and men have always had economic independence. All they have discovered is that being a meal ticket is not a sex symbol as it once was, and they are falling back on the oldest behaviour pattern of them all – roll up, roll up and look at lovely me.

Feminists also complain that, as women, they are expected to look attractive to all men, rather than just to the one man they choose and, certainly, this peacocking role is part and parcel of attracting and keeping a man. Many men are a good deal more interested in proving their masculinity to other men than they are in the woman herself and the need to feel sure their choice is applauded by other men too. One man I know goes doggedly out night after night with a series of interchangeable beauty

queens on his arm and though in the silence of his lonely room they bore
him to distraction this is apparently a small price to pay for the public envy
of other males. I doubt if jettisoning make-up is going to cure this hard-
ened case and anyway, beauty queens need outings, too.

In fact I doubt if jettisoning make-up will cure anything, though it
may make a passing point. Women are far more introverted about their
appearance than men and they need, on the whole, to think themselves
desirable before they can arouse, or even feel desire. At the age of ten
I wreaked havoc in the heart of a neighbourhood lad by setting my
cheeks aflame with pink chalk, scoring my eyebrows with black crayon,
stuffing two pairs of socks up my jumper and nursing a blind faith in my
own uncanny resemblance to Rita Hayworth. The blind faith did it, and
the fact that I looked uncannily like a deranged ten-year-old went unnoticed by either of us.

JILLY COOPER
1937–

Now internationally known and loved for her bestselling blockbuster novels (including *Riders*, *Rivals*, *Octavia* and *Appassionata*), British-born Cooper began her career on local newspapers, before writing a hugely-regarded column about the changing mores of middle-class life for the *Sunday Times* throughout the 1970s.

The following piece is typical of her witty and personal style. In it, she skewers Shere Hite's recently-published report into female sexuality.

If this is Sex, I'm Glad I'm English

1970s, *Sunday Times*

A glamorous man came round for drinks the other day, very euphoric, talking about two years he'd just spent in the States. American women, he announced smugly, were much better in bed than English ones. Why? asked I, bristling chauvinistically.

Well, he said, they look after their bodies better, read more sex books, experimented more and, above all, were prepared to tell you what turned them on. English women just let it happen, and were grateful if it worked.

A week of brooding later, a hefty tome arrived on my desk called *The Hite Report*, announcing itself as a nationwide study of female sexuality, in which 3,000 American women described their sex lives. Anxious to pick up a few tips, I fell to. All I can say is I'm jolly glad I'm English. Never have I met so many crosspatches bellyaching on about the rotten time they are having in bed. The book is so anti-men, it should be renamed *The Hate Report*.

Nevertheless, since one knows so little about other people's sex lives, it is an absolutely riveting read. One friend said she had an advance copy in the loo and people stayed in there for days. And if men can steel themselves against the bitching, they might learn a lot about female sexuality too.

All this information was gathered by a feminist lady, improbably named 'Shere Hite', who sent out 100,000 questionnaires asking some practical things like 'Do you orgasm?' and 'If so, how?' and some silly loaded ones like 'Can you imagine a woman you admire masturbating?' or 'Have you ever been afraid to say No, would you define this as Rape?'

Only 3,000 women replied (making one suspect that only those with a lousy sex life and a stamp bothered). They ranged from dog handlers and diamond cutters to housewives and a single proof reader – a pity they didn't employ her to check the book, the mistakes are terrible.

The most revolutionary finding seems to be that most of the women did not achieve orgasm from straight intercourse. And even if they did, orgasms from masturbation, *which 99 per cent could achieve*, were generally far more intense. QED the best sex is achieved without men. And, because Freud *et alia* had been telling them for years that ladies who didn't achieve vaginal orgasms were immature and psychologically flawed, they're absolutely livid about that too. 'It would give me great pleasure,' wrote one woman, 'to give Mr Freud a black eye.'

One has visions of poor Sigmund cringing behind God's skirts as hordes of bra-less hairy-legged ladies thunder through the pearly gates, brandishing vibrators and shrieking for vengeance.

What is sadder is that, as a result of fear that men would think them unfeminine, or get bored and impatient if asked to stimulate them in other ways, a horrifying number of women admitted faking orgasm, building up a mountain of guilt over the years. 'I cried when I first read the questionnaire,' said one. 'There was so much I'd lied about for so long.'

'I faked because men enjoyed seeing me pant,' admitted another.

Predictably far too much of the book is devoted to the pleasures of self-stimulation. One is surprised they haven't retitled it Mistressbation. Some eulogies sound like Ready–Brek commercials: 'I like masturbation more and more, physically it's quick, easy and satisfying.' Others claim more grandiosely that 'It preserves human dignity *vis-à-vis* other people.' The method of achievement is rather quaint, too: 'I bang my mons against the sink,' said one housewife.

To stress the universal normality of the pastime, Miss Hite also points out that a strange array of animals – including chinchillas, porcupines, squirrels, and elephants – indulge in it. Citing animal behaviour always seems a false argument. I know I'd never get away with it if I rushed out and bit the postman. One would have thought too that porcupines would have a wretched time indulging in any other form of sexual activity.

By stark contrast the descriptions of straight intercourse are joyless. 'How can I concentrate on my orgasm,' grumbled one girl, 'when someone is pushing themselves in and out of me.' Or even worse: 'They just jumped on and rode,' which sounds like a précis of 'How they brought the Good News from Ghent to Aix'.

Because the book builds up its evidence by a succession of similar quotes, it also tends to be terribly repetitive. Over and over, we hear complaints about the mechanical four-part nature of the male performance: Foreplay, Penetration, Intercourse, Ejaculation, stalking through female bedrooms spreading disaster like the Horsemen of the Apocalypse.

Even more grisly are the descriptions of couples trying to improve their sex lives. Most American males seem woefully ignorant of female geography. 'I don't think my husband knows where the clitoris is,' complained one woman. 'Usually we just try and find the damn thing,' said another. Putting a map on the bedroom ceiling seems the answer, particularly as American ladies prefer their guys underneath: 'A man on top is so political.'

But why do American women want to dominate so much? Is it because originally they went pioneering with their men, hammering in the tent pegs, carving out the land, fighting for survival side by side, and have always felt themselves to be more equal because of it? Or being such a young nation, are they still clamorously searching for their own identity?

They certainly know how to rape the language. One girl said she was 'devirginalized' at twenty-five, another found it hard to resist married men, 'because all my friends are adulterizing'. My favourite was the girl who described her private parts as 'plain but with charisma'.

The book will also comfort a lot of women. Sex is such a closed-door, private matter, they may well discover that something they've been ashamed of doing for years is standard practice. Or ignorance may be dispelled, as in the case of the poor woman who, never having seen another naked woman, always thought she was abnormally constructed until reassured, at the age of forty-six, by her gynaecologist.

One can't deny either, as Miss Hite claims, there is something askew about a coupling in which the man always achieves orgasm and the woman never does – like permanently being at someone else's birthday party.

But surely the essence of a good relationship is the sharing, the mutual dependency, the free exchange of pleasure. And how do you achieve this if you get all your kicks from solitary self stimulation? Good sex binds people together. At the lowest level, desire to make love forces one to make up a row.

What worries me also is the backlash. If on one side, the Clitoral-Orgasm-Only brigade now realize they're perfectly normal, the book is already quoting a poor girl who feels 'guilty about needing vaginal penetration because it's unfashionable'. Dear God.

And after all those clumsy men, Miss Hite even suggests we should try a little A.C. tenderness. There's a whole chapter devoted to Lesbianism as a blissful alternative to 'being a baby machine or under some man'.

We are also assured that guinea pigs, martens, pigs (not male chauvinist, I hope) and porcupines (they do get about) also indulge.

'If you dig a woman,' urges Miss Hite, 'let her know. It is important for women to recognize their potential for having sexual feelings for one another, it is essential for self love and accepting our bodies as good and beautiful.'

Oh dear, there's nothing wrong with pleasure from any source, but there is in making people feel guilty because they don't fancy that particular refinement. If women are expected to respond to their own sex, where does that put men? Sprinting into the nearest monastery, I should think.

The male is a fragile creature sexually. If women have been forced by the advent of the permissive society to feel prudish if they say no, the poor man has not only to 'get it up' and provide multiple orgasms on demand – but with all this fake rattle and roll around cannot even be sure he's giving any pleasure. No wonder the doctors' waiting rooms are full of cases of impotence.

If women go on haranguing men, they'll emasculate them. As Erica Jong pointed out, we lost more men to homosexuality than we ever did in two world wars. Or as my husband, having read the book and flung it across the room, pointed out, he can now understand why the retreat from Mons took place.

Finally an even more sinister alternative has reached our side of the river: the local sex shop has a special offer of three-speed electric vaginas at 25 per cent off. We must look to our laurels.

ANGELA CARTER
1940–92

A writer uniquely capable of describing the dark recesses of female psychology (see previous article for more details), in the following article Carter considers one of the darker periods of her own life. Reviewing a book on the subject of anorexia, she recalls her own struggle with this condition and her slow journey out of the morass.

Fat is Ugly

28 November 1974, *New Society*

Mara Selvini Palazzoli is a psychotherapist who has researched anorexia nervosa for twenty years and has had dozens of demented female emaciates pass through her, I should imagine, on the whole, healing hands. My qualification for reviewing her book is that I am an ex-anorexic myself and so, in spite of her massive research, and deep and informed sympathy for women like me, still I know a trick or two that she does not (or so I fondly believe, doctor).

Anorexia nervosa is clearly going to be one of the fashionable ailments of the seventies, just as schizophrenia was the mode of the sixties. (I was a student when Laing's *The Divided Self* came out to form an instant focus for self-identification for young people away from home for the first time; they had to open a new ward in the local madhouse to deal with the resulting plague.) It will not, however, be quite as widespread as schizophrenia, since its ravages are primarily confined to young girls – or, rather, since there are more young girls than young boys, it will be just as widespread but rather more particularised. There is also the possibility that famine will convert the symptoms to a form of socially beneficial behaviour.

A historico-cultural diagnosis of the increasing study of anorexia nervosa ought to take the woman's movement into account, because the relation of the anorexic to her physical being implies extreme dissatisfaction with the physical being itself. I would not say that Women's Lib afforded me the final therapeutic strength to cope with my own residual anorexia, but it certainly helped.

Anorexia nervosa is a form of compulsive fasting which organises a number of personal and interpersonal dilemmas around the desire to lose weight. 'The true cause', says Palazzoli, 'is a deliberate wish to slim.'

There is, as we all know, considerable pressure on young girls to conform to the cultural standards of conventional aesthetics in Western society. Fat is emphatically *not* Beautiful, as it is in cultures where there is less to eat. Woman, regarded as an item of conspicuous consumption (though that is becoming somewhat less true), has traditionally the sole creative function of Dandy; she is tacitly encouraged to sacrifice much for the sake of appearances. Dandyism is the last resort of the impotent, and the protracted attempted suicide by narcissism (which is how my anorexic experience now appears to me), can be regarded as a kind of batty exhibition of heroics, which ironically underlines the impotence it was adopted to combat.

Palazzoli appears to take this view. She quotes another researcher in the field: 'All severe anorexics she has treated show a paralysing sense of helplessness.' Child, usually, of an overprotective mother, docile and well behaved in a family with as many kinks as Laing's families of schizophrenics, the anorexic uses food as a weapon to establish some kind of autonomy. Reading this book is like reading a guidebook to a country I know very well, but where I never bothered to identify the major towns, or industries.

Palazzoli defines two specific traits of anorexics. First, an unusual sensitivity to the ambiguous cultural role of modern women; second, a heightened sense of lack of personal autonomy, due to the nature of familiar relationships. To the potential anorexic, menarche − the first menstruation − arrives like a thunderbolt. I am prepared to accept that it happened that way, but it doesn't quite tally with my memories, menarche didn't even affect my body much, obese from infancy. It was the entry into the world that caused the trouble.

Inside every fat man there is a thin man screaming to get out. I had a firm conviction that fat was ugly, ludicrous, and disabling. And thin was wonderful. My mother's attempts to reconcile me to obesity − she would flourish Rubens and Renoir nudes before me and read aloud enticing descriptions of fat women from Victorian novels − I regarded with extreme suspicion. I thought she was attacking my thin-equals-attractive equation for malicious reasons of her own. Nevertheless, since enough is enough, she got me a proper diet sheet from a doctor and, with encouragement from my family, I embarked on a disastrous course.

Because obsession, compulsion, narcissism took over from reason when I reached about size 14. In the spring of 1958, I weighed fifteen stone; by Christmas of the same year, eight stone. At this point, I became an anorexic. The following month, I went down to between five and a half and six stone. Meanwhile, I was working ten or twelve hours a day and, when I returned home, writing a novel full of the most horrifying Freudian symbols. (Overactivity – this checks with Palazzoli.)

Amenorrhoea, suicidal depression, frigidity, moroseness – the cadaverous symptomology of this bizarre affliction set in. From Rubens to Grünewald in nine months flat. Further – and how I now despise it – I had set out on this crazy species of self-mortification out of pure sexual vanity. Consciously, at least. Clearly, more was going on in my psyche than that, but sexual vanity was my justification. I assumed that no man in his right mind could ever have been attracted to Fat Angie; therefore I reduced myself to a physical condition – that of Walking Corpse – that only a chronic necrophile could have fancied. (I had, of course, tended to regard marriage as the only possible release from a home environment bulging with all those Renoir nudes, although my father had always told me a good job was actually a better bet.)

My parents, at this stage, concluded I was batty and left me alone; but time does heal. I fell in with a group of picturesque eccentrics; I was working on a local newspaper which, at that time, functioned as a kind of benign day-clinic, where my patent insanity was taken in good part. I ceased to be docile at home and became obnoxious: first sign of autonomy. (Confessions of an ex-anorexic.) Tentatively, at first, I began to menstruate again.

I didn't eat bread for ten years, which was the time it took me to get used to being thin; I haven't touched white sugar, or filthy cake, or things like that, for coming up to seventeen years. I have wonderful teeth and blood pressure and everything, and anorexia nervosa is *not* the end of the world and can have some splendid side-effects, if you get through it.

But, far more traumatic than menarche for the adolescent girl, says Palazzoli, are the conditions attendant upon it: ' – she experiences her feminine sexuality in a passive and receptive way; she is exposed to lewd looks, subjected to menstruation, about to be penetrated in sexual embraces, to be invaded by the foetus, to be suckled by a child'. She suggests it is this 'passive-receptive' aspect of feminine life which is revealed to the young girl at menarche, the 'concrete manifestation' of the passivity that has plagued her for so long.

The anorexic, in fact, is in desperate conflict with the woman's body she sees as a passive receptacle and the source of her own impotence; at the same time, she sees her own body – her sexuality? – as an all-powerful, invading force. Alienated, then, in totality from one's physical being. Yes, it felt like that. It did. But, thank God, nobody pumped me full of insulin or gave me electric shock therapy, as she says they do to other emaciates in her chapter on clinical treatment; that would have pandered much too much to the masochism inherent in the whole ghastly business. She herself believes only psychotherapy really helps. I should say so.

No, says Palazzoli, the anorexic does *not* reject femininity; she rejects only those aspects of adult femininity that 'conjure up the terrifying vista of turning into a succubus and a passive vessel'. Emaciation, therefore, equals emancipation; another false equation, but one way that presents itself to the baffled ego as a method of escaping a physical trap. Young men express the traumas of adolescence in other ways. I know it is not all jam for young men, far from it. But at least they cannot suffer unwanted pregnancy; and neither can a girl who does not menstruate.

And so we arrive where I suppose I must have started out, in the bosom of the 'anorexic family'. In 1967, Palazzoli founded the Milan Centre of Family Studies; in a chapter called 'The cybernetics of anorexia nervosa', she develops – I quote the flyleaf – 'an entirely new epistemology of the anorexic syndrome'. At this point, I pass. Get all the nutters responsible for provoking this particular manifestation of nuttery in one room and analyse the lot of them. Fine. I'm sure I'd have enjoyed it very much. But every family has two families behind it and so on *ad infinitum*. There were more nutters in my mother's family than mine, if only because it was a bigger family; and my father's too. Unlike Laing, Palazzoli acknowledges that you have to go on living with them after everybody knows the horrid truths they've spent so long concealing. But Aeneas fled Rome with his aged father on his back and so do we all.

I learned only by hindsight that I'd had anorexia nervosa. After the condition ameliorated, I attended the inquest on a fifteen-year-old girl who escaped from a mental hospital where she had been undergoing treatment for the affliction. She had laid down on the railway tracks at East Croydon station. (Anorexics *do*, I fear, commit suicide, though Palazzoli suggests they don't, or, at least, not often.) The evidence of her parents and her psychiatrists tallied with my own experience. Except, of course, that I hadn't been that bad; or else had somehow managed to conceal the extent of my folly from people who would have done something about it. But, you see, my parents, after verifying my amennorhea was not the result of pregnancy, concluded I was batty and left me alone. And perhaps I can attribute my survival in reasonable shape to that, as much as anything.

Palazzoli's book is, apart from anything else, a most valuable contribution to the field of woman's studies. The tone of this review may be attributed to that same gallows humour with which the seventeenth century approached the subject of syphilis; some existential ills are so savage, I believe one should approach them stoically. That is, lightly.

ERIN PIZZEY

1939–

A pioneering social reformer, writer and journalist, Pizzey was born the daughter of a British diplomat in China. Whilst still a child, she was captured by the Japanese in Shanghai, exchanged in return for a Japanese prisoner of war and allowed to leave China on the last boat. On her return to Britain, she completed her schooling.

In 1971, Pizzey decided to open the world's first refuge for battered women and their children, an idea that brought her huge international attention and prompted the ongoing shelter movement. Later, Pizzey broke decisively with the feminist sorority, disagreeing with many of their tenets, but particularly the suggestion that men were primarily, even solely, responsible for domestic violence. Pizzey argued that the women who had come through her refuges were equally prone to physical outbursts, and that many had been beaten by female lovers.

Throughout her career, Pizzey has written on a wide range of issues, some political, but many more personal. The following article is a compelling refutation of the cultural saw that being fat is synonymous with being unhappy.

Fabulously Fat

February 1980, *Cosmopolitan*

If you cough you'll be told it's because you're fat. If you laugh they'll tell you all fat people are jolly. If you are depressed they'll tell you it's because you are too fat. In fact anyone who doesn't look on the verge of anorexia is subject to millions of pounds of emotional blackmail.

The worst enemy of the whole conspiracy is other women. Seventy per cent of greetings between women start with a comment on whether or not one has put on or taken off weight followed by a long discussion on diets. Who has not had to sit next to something resembling a garden rake at dinner and watch her chase a limp piece of lettuce round her plate, making you feel positively porcine as you nosh your way through NW1 goulash.

However, I detect a change in the air. Just recently there was a report in the *Daily Mirror* where they had done a survey asking men whether they liked women fat or thin. I am delighted to tell you that the fatties did best.

But why or how did it ever get to a situation when to be fat actually meant that many women suffered serious emotional damage or feelings of dislike for themselves and an emotional round of crash dieting followed by midnight binges that very nearly destroyed their lives?

Fat women went out of fashion in a big way when photographers and fashion designers took the brushes out of the hands of artists. Now, most artists like women in all shapes, forms and sizes, especially in the Rubens era, when they were huge, rosy and smiling. Rubens knew a lot about women as well and it was his advice to all women that the best sexual exercise available to all was scrubbing the floor with a scrubbing brush – which may well be why their bottoms are rosy with exertion and could lead to a whole new line of make up. Of course those who take language seriously now know where the term 'scrubber' came from.

However, back to the serious subject of the conspiracy. People like photographers or fashion designers – who decided to dictate what a fashionable woman should look like – are not in the business of human relations but in the business of showing off clothes which actually need clothes-horses, or photographers who are usually so insecure that they lead a vicarious life hidden behind their camera lens and only relate to women so faint with hunger and malnutrition that they are unable to be any kind of threat.

It only took a short time for the media and manufacturing market to decide that here was a huge national neurosis that could be turned into a multi-million pound business and the whole 'make them guilty' act went into full swing.

The secret of being fat and feeling fabulous is that you spend a long time actually talking to yourself about the advantages and disadvantages of being fat or not. I started with the advantages. First of all, was I, with my genetic background of huge Irish potato diggers, prepared to live on a diet of lettuce, no alcohol and a climax of a lean piece of meat once a week? I imagined the effect it would have on my love life as I lay in the arms of some romantic lover muttering sweet nothings in my ear would be that all I could think of was a pound of rare steak and it's a pity it's only Wednesday. No, I was not prepared to diet to that extent and any other extent meant that I would not fit into the normal weight range. If I was going to be outsize, I might as well indulge in anything I liked to eat and drink, and just accept the size I am, enjoying the good things about it – like the fact that you can terrorise everybody because the sight of a large, angry woman maketh even the most outraged male feel quite faint. Or you can use the other warm, maternal side which cuddles and loves all things great and small and naturally they come your way for love and protection, so you're never short of friends.

Most fat people have beautiful skin and age very slowly because the fat under the skin stops wrinkles. It's nice not to suffer from spots and to know that your skin is soft and silky compared to your best friend who lives on vinegar and whose skin feels like rhino hide but looks just great in a leotard. Because I was always fat my mother would look at my twin sister with great pride and predict a glowing future for her, while adding that I wasn't to worry as I had 'character'. I decided that 'having character' was going to be a very positive asset and they have been trying to lock me up ever since.

Fat women usually have nice large breasts which fashion has made them so self-conscious about that they wear horrible punitive machines from awful places like Evans Outsizes, which always reminds me of a fatties remand centre. I decided either to have nice comfortable bras made or not to wear one at all. Lots of men love women with large breasts, and I must admit I did discover a sharp kick on the shin dissuades gropers.

On the subject of men, which is where most women believe they need their bones to protrude from their ribs, I must say that it is usually very insecurely sexed men, or men who are latently homosexual and can only relate to an androgynous female, that shy away from fat women. On the whole fat ladies are very cuddly and I have never felt my size to be a disadvantage. The only disadvantage is finding a man who is not totally narcissistic or, although six foot, makes me feel I'm dealing with a small boy.

Obviously if you have spent all your life looking at pictures of women with anonymously regular bodies, the idea of stripping off in front of the love of your life is not actually easy. There are various approaches like climbing into the wardrobe and coming out with a flannel nightie buttoned from the chin down to the feet. There is the 'night flying' approach which is to say that you are just going to tidy up – and get him to go ahead and get into bed. You then strip off in the loo, charge into the bedroom, switch off the light and make a crash landing on the spot where you hope he is not. If he is, you might be arrested, and under the circumstances – as one might put it – you would probably get off with manslaughter or, if the judge had a sense of humour, 'parking in an occupied zone'.

But as I said I just believe that if you are going to accept that you are going to be fat then both those approaches only prove that you haven't really come to terms with your size and the proper answer is to have really pretty nighties. I get old Victorian cotton nighties from a stall at Portobello market. They are lovely, fresh and enveloping and slowly you can gain confidence that whoever you are with will love you warts and all, bearing in mind that most lovers are not in the slightest bit worried about the other's imperfections, only their own. Along with liking yourself the way you are, it follows that you begin to take care of your hair and make up if you want to wear any. Most fat women have big, strong faces that take make up very well. It's fun to use kohl round your eyes and paint on a wide canvas. Get some good advice from someone like Mary Quant and wear her stuff; you can afford to be different and outstanding because nature made you that way.

On the subject of clothes in general you can only join my club by boy-cotting places like Evans Outsizes. There is no need to go there and feel dreadful. The shops are now full of excellent clothes that can really only be worn by big women.

I very often wander round maternity shops, too. Once you like your size and decide to enjoy it, then buying clothes becomes fun, not a terri-bly embarrassing business because the shop assistant looks at you as though you have a bad disease. It becomes a pleasure when you know where to go to find clothes that will fit anyone, and that you won't return home empty-handed and miserable.

I often go up to Shepherd's Bush market where they have the most beautiful Indian materials – anything from a glowing sari shot with gold to beautiful batik prints. I also enjoy jostling among the market stalls with the West Indian women, many of whom are as large as me and don't ever give it a thought. I must admit, though, that black fat is more beautiful than white fat. Next time round I want to be a Jamaican. Anyway, I buy enough to go round me, take it home and lay it on the floor doubled over into a square. I then cut straight up from the bottom to where I want the sleeves to be, and cut out one arm and then up the other side – and I have the outlines of a kaftan. I then make the neck into a 'V'. After a while I got very sophisticated and when I got to running up the sides with my machine I put in two darts from the sides to where I hoped my nipples would be. I had a bad time getting it right, but like everything else it comes with practice and I can make a sensational dress for very little money in an afternoon. You can line the neck with anything from soft fur to feathers. I gave up feathers because they made me sneeze and blew my false eye-lashes into my gin. I gave up gin because it makes me tell the truth, the whole truth and nothing but the truth – which tends to empty rooms and lose one friends.

Along with being large I like large things. It is much better to have a big car however old than crush oneself into a Mini. I have a Great Dane called Morgan who makes me feel very insignificant. I didn't realise how large they grew and it seemed like a good idea at the time.

As you get used to the idea of how special and unusual you are you can have fun practising grand entrances into restaurants – sweeping into the middle of the room, do a half turn and enjoy everyone looking at you. Watch out that you get it right or your partner may be found unconscious in the far corner and you will have to pay the bill. Thank God for the National Health – you can afford a few mistakes. You will never be denied a table. The last owner who said he was full changed his mind when I said I was paralysed with sorrow and he would have to carry me out himself. Rather than die of a coronary in front of his spell-bound audience he found us seats.

If you are very large, a very long cigarette-holder looks quite natural and indeed gives one an undisputed authority. Should anyone disagree with you, you can make your point very hotly felt with a quick jab in their direction. All of it is fun. Like all of yourself all the way round – even if it takes a wall-to-wall mirror – and you will enjoy life.

So far I've looked at the positive side. The negative side doesn't take long. Other women are my biggest problem. They run up to me with their little anxious faces asking, 'Why don't you diet?' 'Because I don't want to,' I say amiably. This usually sends them off into a frenzy. It is interesting, if I ever watch old interviews on the work I do at Chiswick, to see how women journalists go on at great length on how big I am and what I am wearing. Whereas male journalists get on with the job of talking about the mothers and kids. I do waste a lot of time defending myself over my utter lack of shame at not being the same size as everybody else – not really for my own benefit, but for all those beautiful put-down women who need to know that they can love and be loved and that attraction is not a physical thing. It is very mystical and comes from one warm loving human being to another.

Finally, here comes the government health warning bit. Fat makes you have high blood-pressure. Well – as Dr Nixon, who knows more about these matters than anyone else I know, points out – there are as many thinnies as fatties running around with high blood-pressure. You won't live as long as a skinny. I don't want to if I have to give up all the things I like.

A closing thought: the subject of exercise. Like many fat people I am very supple so I don't feel much actual need for exercise. Lately there has been this jogging craze, and I look out of my window and watch the red-faced puffing joggers go by. And I reflect that it is apparently a fact that an orgasm uses the same amount of energy as a five-mile run. So take your pick.

HELEN FIELDING

1958–

Born and raised in West Yorkshire, Fielding studied English Literature at Oxford, before starting work as a producer for the BBC. She remained there for ten years – producing everything from current affairs to children's programming. A documentary set in Africa led her to become increasingly involved with Comic Relief and she subsequently produced a number of documentaries for them.

It was this experience that led to Fielding's first novel, *Cause Celeb*, a satire on the world of celebrity fundraising. By the time of its publication, she had left television for print journalism, and was asked by the *Independent* to write a column about her life. Declining this offer ('because that's rather exposing') she agreed, instead, to come up with a fictional character.

The result was Bridget Jones, a hapless young single woman, struggling with life, love and litres of Chardonnay in mid-1990s London. Despite, or perhaps, because, as Fielding says, 'everyone else was writing about politics, and I was writing about why you can't find a pair of tights in the morning and losing weight', the columns struck a chord with a generation of women. In the following piece, Bridget rails against the silent enemy: 'smug marrieds'.

Bridget Jones's Diary

9 August 1995, *Independent*

THURSDAY 3RD AUGUST—14st (most likely), alcohol units 90, cigarettes 500 (feels like), calories 4 bloody million.

11.45pm Huh. Just got back from dinner party with ego size of lentil. It was me, four married couples and Jeremy's brother (forget it. Red braces and face. Calls girls 'fillies'). They obviously didn't know any unmarried girls to make up the numbers in the entire world except me. 'So,' bellowed Jeremy, pouring me a drink, 'How's your love life?'

Gurgh! Why can't Smug Marrieds understand this is no longer a polite question to ask? We wouldn't rush up to them and roar, 'How's your marriage going? Still having sex?' Everyone knows that dating in your thirties is not the happy-go-lucky free-for-all it was when you were 22 and that the honest answer is more likely to be 'non-existent' or 'actually last night my married lover appeared wearing suspenders and a darling little Angora crop top, told me he was gay/a sex addict/a narcotic addict/commitment phobic and beat me up with a dildo,' than 'Super, thanks.'

One of the best things about finally having a boyfriend was having a showy-offy reply ready. But unfortunately things have been going rather badly with me and Daniel this week and I'm not sure whether we're still going out or not. Not being a natural liar, I ended up mumbling shame-facedly to Jeremy, 'fine', at which point he boomed 'So, you still haven't got a chap! Bridget! What are we going to do with you!'

'Yes, why aren't you married yet Bridget?' sneered Woney (baby talk for Fiona), the wife of Jeremy's best friend Cosmo, with a thin veneer of concern while stroking her pregnant stomach.

Why do they do this? Maybe the Smug Marrieds only mix with other Smug Marrieds and don't know how to relate to individuals any more. Maybe they really want to patronise us and make us feel like freaks. Or maybe they're in such a sexual rut that they think, 'There's a whole other world out there' and hope for vicarious thrills by getting us to tell them the roller-coaster details of our sex lives.

'Seriously,' said Woney, 'why aren't you married?'

'Because I don't want to end up like you, you fat, boring, Sloaney milch cow', was what I should have said, or 'Because if I had to cook Cosmo's dinner then get into the same bed as him just once, let alone every night, I'd tear off my own head and eat it', or 'Because actually, Woney, under-neath my clothes, my entire body is covered in scales'. But I didn't, because ironically enough I didn't want to hurt her feelings, and merely simpered apologetically, at which point Jeremy piped up, 'Well, you know, once you get past a certain age . . .'

'Exactly. All the decent chaps have been snapped up,' said Cosmo, slapping his fat stomach and smirking so that his jowls wobbled.

At dinner, Magda had placed me, in an incestuous sex-sandwich sort of way between Jeremy and his crasher of a brother. 'You really ought to hurry up and get sprogged up you know, old girl,' said Jeremy, pouring a quarter of a pint of '78 Puillac straight down his throat. 'Time's running out.'

By this time I'd had a good half pint of '78 Puillac myself. 'Is it one in three marriages which end in divorce or one in two, Jeremy?' I slurred with a pointless attempt at sarcasm.

'Seriously, old girl,' he said, ignoring me, 'office is full of them, single girls over 30 – fine physical specimens. Can't get a chap.'

'That's not a problem I have, actually,' I breathed, waving my fag in the air.

'Ooh. Tell us more,' said Woney.

'So who is it, then?' said Cosmo.

'Getting a bit of a shag, old girl?' said Jeremy. All eyes turned to me, beadily. Mouths open, slavering.

'It's none of your business,' I said hoity-toitily.

'So she hasn't got a man!' crowed Cosmo.

'Oh, my God, it's 11 o'clock,' said Woney. 'The babysitter,' and they all leapt to their feet and started getting ready to go home. 'Will you be OK, Bridget?' said Magda pityingly. 'Actually, I'm going to, like this, club right?' I said, lurching out in the street. 'Thanks, for a really great evening.' Then I got into a taxi and burst into tears.

00.10 Just called Sharon. 'You should have said "I'm not married because I'm a Singleton, you smug, prematurely ageing, narrow-minded morons",' she ranted. 'And because there's more than one bloody way to live; one in four households are single, most of the royal family are single, the nation's young men have been proved by surveys to be completely unmarriageable and as a result there's a whole generation of single girls like me with their own incomes and homes who have lots of fun and don't need to wash anyone else's socks. We'd be as happy as sandboys if people like you didn't conspire to make us feel stupid just because you're jealous.'

'Bastards!' I shouted happily. 'Bloody bastards!'

00.30 Blimey. Daniel just rang. 'Bridge,' he slurred, 'I love you. Say you won't leave me.'

'No,' I said sulkily.

'Will you marry me?' he said.

'Ooooh, yes please,' I said, rather too quickly. At which point he burst into tears and said, 'My wife, my wife,' and put the phone down. What does this mean? Was he feeling so sentimental about the idea of me as his wife that he couldn't speak any more? Or has he just remembered he's already married? Am I engaged? To Daniel? Oh, my God. What have I done?

ANDREA DWORKIN

1946–2005

A highly controversial writer, campaigner and feminist, Dworkin was one of the most intensely radical voices of the twentieth century. An American Jew, born in New Jersey, she suffered a number of serious sexual and physical assaults in her youth and early adulthood, which led to her first book, '*Woman Hating,*' in 1974.

Dworkin went on to attract worldwide renown (and often unmitigated scorn) for her campaign against pornography, which saw she and fellow protestor, Catharine MacKinnon, draft a law defining pornography as a civil rights violation against women. Often quoted as saying that all heterosexual intercourse was rape, she always contended that this was a misinterpretation, and that her exact argument was that the use or expression of force in sex amounted to rape – a significant detail.

Despite coming in for huge criticism then (she sometimes seemed the prime focus of the cultural and social backlash against feminism) she always remained true to her political roots, writing iconoclastic yet clear-eyed accounts of society as she saw it. On her premature death in 2005, there was a vast outpouring of feeling and respect for her work, which led her friend MacKinnon to comment, 'I only wish they'd said it when she was alive.'

In the following article, Dworkin's last piece, she describes in brilliant detail the osteoarthritis that blighted her final years. The article provides a stark account of pain, disability and ageing, as Dworkin – a campaigner to the last – argues strongly for 'a determined policy of public access' to save the disabled from becoming a segregated group.

Through the Pain Barrier

23 April 2005, *Guardian*

The doctor who knows me best says that osteoarthritis begins long before it cripples – in my case, possibly from homelessness, or sexual abuse, or beatings on my legs, or my weight. John, my partner, blames *Scapegoat*, a study of Jewish identity and women's liberation that took me nine years to write; it is, he says, the book that stole my health. I blame the drug-rape that I experienced in 1999 in Paris. I returned from Paris and finished *Scapegoat* over a period of months while caring for my dying father.

Shortly after he died I was in hospital, delirious from a high fever, with infection and blood clots in my legs. I was there for a month. John had been told that I was dying. I forgot that in hospitals when one is dying, nurses abrogate the rules. John was allowed in after visiting hours; nurses would pull the curtain around my bed and let him lie with me. This was my happiness.

Doctors tell me that there is no medical truth to my notion that the rape caused this sickness or what happened after it. I believe I am right: it was the rape. They don't know because they have never looked.

A few months after I got out of the hospital, my knees began to change. They lost their flexibility. Slowly they stiffened. As they stiffened they became sore. They started to hurt terribly – as if injured but not visibly injured. I got a cellphone – this was before they were ubiquitous – so that if I couldn't walk any more I could call a car. I had given up on New York City subways: my knees could no longer bend enough to use them.

I went to an orthopaedic surgeon. I was diagnosed with osteoarthritis in my knees. I was treated with the anti-inflammatory Celebrex and, when that didn't work, its stronger cousin, Vioxx. Vioxx was recently taken off the market by its makers because of a risk of heart attacks or strokes; I was on it for three years. I had cortisone shots in my knees, followed by pred-nisone. The cortisone shots, which are painful, worked only once. Then I could walk without pain; in joy I sat on my front steps and talked with my neighbour – inconsequential chat. When I tried to stand up, my knees were rigid and excruciating. I managed to stand and swivel around; I took the remaining two steps up to my front door and used the door to drag me inside. I had had an hour-and-a-half of freedom.

My mobility lessened as the pain increased. Eventually I found myself housebound. I could walk only a few steps at a time, intimidated by the pain and the refusal of my knees to bend. John and I lived in a three-floor house. I could barely make my way up or down the steps. I'd crawl up the steps on hands and feet. I'd try to go down on my butt, step by step. The kitchen was on the first floor; the toilet on the second; my desk, books and shower on the third. My physical world became tiny and pain-racked. I stayed in my bed when I could. John brought me up food. I'd go out only to the doctors.

The orthopaedist started giving me narcotics, most of which contained acetaminophen, a common, nonprescription analgesic. My pharmacist persuaded the doctor that the liver damage caused by too much aceta-minophen was more dangerous to me than stronger drugs. Through her advocacy I got a drug normally given only to cancer patients. It was a little yellow lollipop and when in pain one was supposed to lick. I licked a lot. I was told that I had to have my knees replaced. The prostheses are made out of titanium and plastic. I had both knees replaced at once, a normal practice now but unusual even a few years ago. My surgeon would later tell me that if I had had one done, I would never have returned for the second. He got that right.

I still don't know what he did to me but I came to the conclusion that the operation was barbaric, involving as it did the sawing out of the arthritis, which meant sawing through bones. It was like being kneecapped, twice, or having one's knees and bones hammered and broken into bits. After the operation I was in a nightmare of narcotics and untouchable pain. There were morphine shots. I asked for them and got them often. Even morphine shots in the upper arm hurt.

I had a hallucination but it is still real as rain to me. I was in Virginia Woolf's house and I was happy. But 'they' wanted me to go down the stairs. I can't, I begged, I can't. My hospital bed was at the top of the stairs and I was afraid that they were going to push me down. I saw the steep decline of the steps. I couldn't get over my visceral fear of falling or being pushed or being turned over from the bed down the flight of steps. I kept experiencing my bed as being on the edge of a precipice.

One day, I remember, a nurses' aide braided my hair and I felt cooler, cleaner. I was on the bedpan, but raising myself up to use it – knees – was so fiercely painful that I would rather lie in my piss.

Then the day came when I had to walk. There was a vinyl chair next to my hospital bed. The physical therapist's name was Carl. He was like a tree trunk, big and solid. You can do it, he said. I'll help you; we'll just go over to the chair. It was impossible, outside the realm of the imaginable. Carl let me hold on to him in a desperate, tight embrace as he carried me over to the chair. My legs dangled, my knees twisted, I sweated, I screamed. See, you could do that, he said, without a shred of irony. I had to sit there for two hours, which meant knees bent but not weight-bearing. Nurses came by and gave verbal approval: good dog, good dog. Eventually Carl carried me back to bed.

Pain is a four-letter word. There is no way to recreate it through memory. It is not like the flashback arising from traumatic events such as rape or battery. The flashback is as if it is happening now, in the present, even if it is from decades ago. Pain can be recent yet inaccessible to immediate experience. Torturers know that people can't die from pain. The consequences of pain – for instance a heart attack – yes, but not from pain itself, however intense. The horror is that no one dies from pain. This means that suffering can be immeasurable, enduring, without respite. So it would be for me for the next two years.

I was taken to an institute for physical rehabilitation. A nurses' aide took me to shower in a wheelchair. I used a walker from the cot on which I slept

to the wheelchair, maybe two miserable steps. I had two responsibilities –
take my pain medications (Vicodin or Percocet) and show up at the right
room at the right time for the scheduled rehabilitative class. I was not
allowed to go to class if I did not take the painkillers. In fact, the pain was
unrelenting. I lived for the next pill.

Physical therapy is based on tiny movements, increments of change that
almost defy detection; it is built on the repetition of the minuscule. Yet to
the hurt person these motions or movements or minute steps are hard. The
first time is daunting and the 10th is like climbing Mount Everest. I sit in
a big room, my wheelchair in a big circle of wheelchairs. Big is good
because it means that my turn does not come often. I stand up by holding
on to a walker and take a step. Then I step back and sit down. The cycle
is hideous. The steps with the walker increase to two, then three. After
several weeks I am assigned a means of locomotion: crutches.

Rehabilitation also includes so-called occupational therapy: throw a ball
around in a circle; put round pegs in round holes; stand up, arms on a table,
and read a page of a magazine; water a plant; play checkers or cards; and
the pièce de résistance, cook and serve a simple meal. I am guided in the
intricacies of shopping while crippled; I learn how to use a 'grabber' to
latch on to things I have dropped or cannot reach; I am taught again how
to put on shoes and socks and tie shoelaces.

I also have to meet the institution's psychologist once. I keep getting
called back. When I ask why, I am told that I am 'interesting'. Well, yes,
I think, I used to be. The narcotics help me deal with the psychologist
but the physical pain simply marches on. It does not lessen or change
or stop.

I learn three rules in my occupational therapy classes: never hold on to
anything that moves; if it rains or snows, stay inside, even if that means
cancelling doctors' appointments (to those medicalised this is nearly
profane); and kick the cat – if a cat curls up in front of your feet, kick it
away. I learned to use my crutch to kick the cat. I will go to hell for this.

On discharge, social services are provided. My male partner is not
expected to be a care-giver. I am sent an itinerant nurse, a young, poorly
paid and badly trained social aide to help me with baths and to do light
housework, and a freelance physical therapist who will do the drill: stand
up, take steps, bend your knees, and – the killer – stand on your toes.

And on discharge a wreck like me is sent to a 'pain management centre'.
Despite my small successes at physical rehabilitation I am in agony. I spend
almost all my time in bed, a bed of nails, all through the knees. The pain
management centre is run by Curly, Larry and Moe. First there is a
10-page questionnaire. Rate from 1 to 10 your pain (I modestly assert an
8; my social conscience, atavistic as it is, tells me that there are others in

more pain). Rate from 1 to 10: is your mother dead; how many people in your family have died of cancer; how is your sex life; how many times a week do you have sex?

They want me to undress so they can examine me. This is absurd. I refuse. There is a table they want me to lie on that they claim lessens pain. The bottom line is that New York State regulates narcotics to such an extent that regular doctors are reluctant to write prescriptions for painkillers; and so Curly, Larry and Moe at pain management put you through whatever rigmarole and then write prescriptions, none of which, according to state law, can be refilled. So one is in a cycle of coming back for new prescriptions and new indignities every 30 days.

Curly eventually puts me on Percocet, fentanyl patches and methadone. I am on these drugs for nearly two years. I become slightly indifferent to the awful pain. My speech slurs and my memory is impaired. It is during this time that I write my memoir *Heartbreak*. I want to remember some good things in my life. I work for one hour a day. The narcotics do not make me Coleridge; but I hold my own.

One day I wake up and the pain is gone from my right knee – as if God had intervened. The pain in the left one is the same. I begin to go outside on my crutches. I can walk half a block to my local Starbucks. One day I sit there, still on my meds, and I see the ballet going on outside. The side-walk is heavy with pedestrian traffic. They are so unselfconscious, these normal walkers. They have different gaits; they move effortlessly; each dances without knowing it. I used to be one of them. I want to be again.

The anti-drama of small gesticulations continues, this time in physical therapy several blocks from where I live. My left knee is still rotten. After another year of physical therapy they give me a cane. I put away all the crutches and other signs of what I call 'disability chic'. I can sort of walk. The cane means victory. The pain in my left knee keeps me on my meds. Over the course of another year, that pain lessens. It's a whisper, a shadow – it goes. I give up the pills, though I go through a nasty with-drawal from methadone.

Alas, there is no happy ending. John and I move to Washington so that he can take a job as managing editor of a large-circulation magazine. We live in an apartment without steps. I am on the cane. I go into physical therapy because, unable to stand up straight, I hunch over the cane. A few days later I am at the kitchen table reading a magazine. I stand up to get something and my right knee cannot bear any weight, none. I can't use it because I can't step on it. I have no pain; I have had no warning. I get to my crutches, which are in a closet. I need both of them in order to move. My right knee remains useless. The physical therapist determines that the quadriceps above the knee has stopped working, because imperceptible pain occasions the quad muscle to give out. Then my knee buckles and I fall. It is dangerous to fall. I see the physical therapist twice a week.

The orthopaedic surgeon ('a genius with knees', says my internist) puts me in a restrictive brace that allows my knee to bend only so far. That way, if my knee fails, I am unlikely to fall. After nearly a year of physical therapy my quad muscle is not much stronger and my knee still buckles. The surgeon sends me to a rehabilitation hospital where they make me a new brace, specifically fitted to my leg. This brace works on the opposite principle to the first one: it immobilises the knee so that no buckling is possible, thus, no fall is possible.

It takes months for artisans to make the brace. It goes from beneath my calf to the top of my thigh. It is made of a black space-age material created to go to Mars or Saturn. Nothing makes it bend or stretch or break. It is completely unforgiving. I call it Darth Vader. It is the principle of evil incarnate. The straps that attach front to back are Velcro. I am supposed to lock it when I walk and unlock it when I want to sit. The brace is worn under my pants leg so no one can see it. Each manipulation is distinct: in public locking it makes me look as if I am masturbating, and unlocking it makes me look as if I am fondling my thigh. The brace must be very tight and positioned perfectly to work. It takes me nearly two months to learn how to put it on and use it. I lose my balance in efforts to lock it. Once I flip backward, magically landing on a chair.

Self-respect demands that I clean up the faecal mess that my cat has made. It is the immobilised knee that makes bending down to the floor fraught with peril. I start falling and know that I must not hit the floor. I fight against gravity, my fingernails clawing at the walls and my hand grasping for the door frame. I know that if I fall I probably will not be able to get up. Somehow I raise myself.

I was slow with the first brace. I had to remind myself to be patient. With Darth I make the turtle look like the hare. The landscape is one of hazard. Anything can reach up and bite me: a break in the sidewalk; leaves; sand; mud; a sudden slope up or down; a stone; some pebbles. Anything threatening balance is dangerous: first the brace itself; then wind, people running or bicycling or being too close or too many; a fast car; a step; a curb; a puddle; heavy doors; slick surfaces. Crowds are impossible and so are stairs.

I want to be able to carry a cup along with a plate to the kitchen sink in one trip. I don't want to have to make two trips. The cup slips and breaks. This happens several times. Is it a small thing? I can't bear it or accept it. I reject the extent of my disability. I find myself in a silent rage that stretches over weeks. I am utterly exhausted by my incapacity. I am worn out from walking. I am sick of physical therapy.

There are little humiliations. I keynote a conference on the Holocaust. The organiser picks me up. She is driving a truck. I try to climb up into it. She physically pushes me under my ass without permission, all the while talking to me in baby talk, put your tooshie there, keep your cute little fanny there. I turn to her and say, I am disabled, not stupid. A friend throws a party for me in Washington. I ask how many steps there are to the apartment. He doesn't know. I assume he will get back to me. John and I go to the party. There are three flights of steps. I can't get to the party being given for me. We could have given it in another venue, the friend says the next day. It cuts. I go to a bar and need to use the rest room. The men's is filthy, the bartender says; the women's is two flights up. I use the dirty one. I go to a new movie theatre that has elevators and disability bathrooms but the polished stone of the floor is so slick that my crutches cannot safely navigate it. I am walking with a friend who suddenly looks at my crutches and says, you don't want to be this way the rest of your life, do you? Her repulsion is barely masked. I feel unutterably alone.

Each disabled person has a story, often including pain, impairment, disorientation and loss of control. Each disabled person lives always on the threshold of separation, exile and involuntary otherness. Only a determined policy of public access can help to mitigate the loneliness. One needs to be able to enter buildings; have a cup of coffee; go to a restaurant, the theatre, cinema or a concert; attend school; go to lectures or readings; use public transport, bathrooms, hotel showers; go to museums and sporting events and political rallies. One needs equal opportunity in employment. One needs to be integrated into the world, not separated from it; yet one has special needs, ones that able-bodied people rarely consider. The low consciousness of the able-bodied increases alienation.

For mobility problems, one needs a new geography: kerb ramps; ramps in addition to steps; handrails; grab bars; high toilets; light doors; wheelchairs; room for wheelchairs in public bathrooms and hotel rooms; elevators; safety in floor surfaces including carpeting; entry and egress from public transport as well as acceptable seating; and a host of other considerations. Other disabilities require other remedies. In 1990 Congress passed the landmark Americans with Disabilities Act, which articulated in great detail the requirements for making the world available to disabled people. This is a civil rights law that recognises the exclusion of disabled people from the larger community as outright discrimination.

The law had its impact because disabled people found aggressive trial lawyers to sue commercial and private venues for noncompliance. The plaintiffs went after big-money damages for violating the civil rights mandated by the ADA. Eventually it became clear that compliance would be cheaper than continuing litigation. Losing money does put the fear of God into Americans.

I have to say that the ADA increases the quality of my life, Darth notwithstanding. I get through airports in a wheelchair provided by the airline; John takes me to the zoo a few blocks from where we live and the zoo provides a wheelchair; local coffee houses to which I gravitate have disability-standard bathrooms; there are special seats for me in cinemas and theatres and in rock venues; there are kerb ramps at pedestrian crossings and ramps or elevators in addition to steps and escalators in most public accommodations. In my neighbourhood I see many other disabled people outside all the time. We are not rare or invisible, because we are not hidden as if in shame.

And bless those nasty trial lawyers, whom George W Bush and the Republicans hate so much. Without them the ADA would be a useless pile of paper.

For myself – despite physical therapy, the breaking cups, and my immo-bilised knee – in the middle of the night, worn down, I listen to Yo-Yo Ma playing Bach or Loretta Lynn's *Van Lear Rose*; and I am, I think, healing. Surely music must be more powerful than bad luck.

INTERVIEWS & ICONS

ZELDA FITZGERALD
1900–48

Born in Montgomery, Alabama, Zelda Sayre was known locally as the most vivacious, reckless and beautiful of her peers, all qualities that would endear her to her husband, Francis Scott Fitzgerald. The two were married in 1920, just days after a publisher had accepted his first novel, *This Side of Paradise*. The book would become an instant bestseller, with its central character, Amory Blaine, leading the kind of wild, unfettered existence that Scott and Zelda became famous for in the early 1920s.

Although now considered a minor work, one of the interesting aspects of *This Side of Paradise* was Scott's lifting of large swathes of writing and dialogue from Zelda's personal diaries. Zelda was keen to write too, but, with Scott's fame secured at the very start of their marriage, it was generally more profitable for her articles to be published in both their names. Nonetheless, she went on to write the autobiographical novel *Save me the Waltz* (1932) and a play, *Scandalabra*, which Scott directed in 1933.

The following article sees Zelda musing on the fate of the iconic figure of the 'flapper', a gin-swilling, Charleston-loving young female stereotype, for whom she was the contemporary media's prime exemplar. It's interesting to note the article's date – 1925 – long before the 'Jazz age' is generally considered to have ended. As with all trends though, those who invented them moved on long before the general populus . . .

What Became of the Flappers?

October 1925, *McCall's Magazine*

Flapper wasn't a particularly fortunate cognomen. It is far too reminiscent of open galoshes and covered-up ears and all other proverbial flapper paraphernalia, which might have passed unnoticed save for the name. All these things are – or were – amusing externals of a large class of females who in no way deserve the distinction of being called flappers. The flappers that I am writing this article about are a very different and intriguing lot of young people who are perhaps unstable, but who are giving us the first evidence of youth asserting itself out of the cradle. They are not originating new ideas or new customs or new moral standards. They are simply endowing the old ones that we are used to with a vitality that we are not used to. We are not accustomed to having *our* daughters think our ideas for themselves, and it is distasteful to some of us that we are no longer able to fit the younger generation into our conceptions of what the younger generation was going to be like when we watched it in the nursery. I do not think that anything my daughter could possibly do eighteen years from now would surprise me. And yet I will probably be forbidding her in frigid tones to fly more than three thousand feet high or more than five hundred miles an hour with little Willie Jones, and bidding her never to go near that horrible Mars. I can imagine these things now, but if they should happen twenty years from now, I would certainly wonder what particular dog my child was going to. . . .

The flapper springs full-grown, like Minerva, from the head of her once-déclassé father, Jazz, upon whom she lavishes affection and reverence, and deepest filial regard. She is not a 'condition arisen from war unrest,' as I have so often read in the shower of recent praise and protest which she has evoked, and to which I am contributing. She is a direct result of the greater appreciation of beauty, youth, gaiety, and grace which is sweeping along in a carmagnole (I saw one in a movie once, and I use this word advisedly) with our young anti-puritans at the head. They have placed such a premium on the flapper creed – to give and get amusement – that even the dumbbells become Dulcies and convert stupidity into charm. Dulcy* is infinitely preferable to the kind of girl who, ten years ago, quoted the *Rubáiyát* at you and told you how misunderstood she was; or the kind who straightened your tie as evidence that in her lay the spirit of the eternal mother; or the kind who spent long summer evenings telling you that it wasn't the *number* of cigarettes you smoked that she minded but just the *principle*, to show off her nobility of character. These are some of the bores of yesterday. Now even bores must be original, so the more unfortunate members of the flapper sect have each culled an individual line from their daily rounds, which amuses or not according to whether you have seen the same plays, heard the same tunes, or read reviews of the same books.

The best flapper is reticent emotionally and courageous morally. You always know what she thinks, but she does all her feeling alone. These are two characteristics which will bring social intercourse to a more charming and more sophisticated level. I believe in the flapper as an involuntary and invaluable cupbearer to the arts. I believe in the flapper as an artist in her particular field, the art of being – being young, being lovely, being an object.

---

* Dulcy, the title character in the 1921 play by Marc Connelly and George S. Kaufman, is a featherbrained young wife.

For almost the first time we are developing a class of pretty yet respectable young women, whose sole functions are to amuse and to make growing old a more enjoyable process for some men and staying young an easier one for others.

Even parents have ceased to look upon their children as permanent institutions. The fashionable mother no longer keeps her children young so that she will preserve the appearance of a debutante. She helps them to mature so that she will be mistaken for a stepmother. Once her girls are old enough to be out of finishing school a period of freedom and social activity sets in for her. The daughters are rushed home to make a chaotic debut and embark upon a feverish chase for a husband. It is no longer permissible to be single at twenty-five. The flapper makes haste to marry lest she be a leftover and be forced to annex herself to the crowd just younger. She hasn't time to ascertain the degree of compatibility between herself and her fiancé before the wedding, so she ascertains that they will be separated if the compatibility should be mutually rated zero after it.

The flapper! She is growing old. She forgets her flapper creed and is conscious only of her flapper self. She is married 'mid loud acclamation on the part of relatives and friends. She has come to none of the predicted 'bad ends,' but has gone at last, where all good flappers go – into the young married set, into boredom and gathering conventions and the pleasure of having children, having lent a while a splendor and courageousness and brightness to life, as all good flappers should.

DOROTHY PARKER
1893–1967

Often remembered for her caustic wit, Parker was also a brilliantly accomplished journalist and, later, screenwriter, whose work crackled with pathos, subtlety and ideas.

Beginning her career at *Vogue*, she soon moved on to *Vanity Fair*, where she was initially thrilled to become New York's only woman drama critic, before realizing that the magazine wouldn't actually allow her to criticize any productions. Arguably her best work was her writing for the just-established *New Yorker* in the late 1920s to early 1930s, when the magazine and its founder, Harold Ross, were both, to some extent, saved from ruin by Parker's contributions to the first 'Talk of the Town' columns.

Parker was also the *New Yorker*'s first book critic, a role that she performed with typical panache. In the following column, she reviews Isadora Duncan's autobiography.

Poor, Immortal Isadora

14 January 1928, *New Yorker*

My Life, the posthumously published autobiography of Isadora Duncan, is to me an enormously interesting and a profoundly moving book. Here was a great woman; a magnificent, generous, gallant, reckless, fated fool of a woman. There was never a place for her in the ranks of the terrible, slow army of the cautious. She ran ahead, where there were no paths.

She was no writer, God knows. Her book is badly written, abominably written. There are passages of almost idiotic naiveté, and there are passages of horrendously flowery verbiage. There are veritable Hampton Court mazes of sentences. There are long, low moans of poetry, painstakingly interpolated. There are plural pronouns, airily relating to singular nouns. She knew all about herself as an author. She says, in her introduction, 'It has taken me years of struggle, hard work and research to learn to make one simple gesture, and I know enough about the Art' (that word she always capitalizes) 'of writing to realise that it would take me again just so many years of concentrated effort to write one simple, beautiful sentence.' But, somehow, the style of the book makes no matter.

Out of this mess of prose come her hope, her passion, her suffering; above all, comes the glamour that was Isadora Duncan's.

'Glamour' and 'glamorous' are easy words, these days. The, shall we say, critical writers scoop them up by the handsful and plaster the fences of the town with them. The, shall we also say, intelligentsia fling them about like coppers, for the urchins to dive for. The other day, I heard the term 'glamorous' applied three times within minutes. It was bestowed upon *(a)* a pretty little actress correctly performing a suitable little part in a neat little play; *(b)* an expensively dressed, nervous woman in whose drawing-room one may meet over-eager portrait-painters, playwrights of dubious sexes, professional conversationalists, and society ladies not yet quite divorced; and *(c)* a graceful young man ever carefully dropping references to his long, unfinished list of easy conquests. Well, there are always those who cannot distinguish between glitter and glamour, just as there are always those who cannot understand why you should desire real pearls when they can't be told from the imitations. But you can, you see, tell them from the imitations. The neat surfaces of the imitations shine prettily; the real glow from within. And the glamour of Isadora Duncan came from her great, torn, bewildered, foolhardy soul.

This book takes her up only to her departure for Russia to found a school of dancing, in 1921; it does not tell of her fantastically ill-advised marriage, and of her few blurred, dizzy years thereafter. There was to be another volume, but she never started it.

A little while after this one had reached her publishers, she was dead. She died as she should die, dramatically and without warning. It is curious that, almost on the first page of her book, she says, 'I was born by the sea, and I have noticed that all the great events of my life have taken place by the sea.' She died by the sea, on that shiny avenue of Nice that follows the Mediterranean. It is curious, too, that she died in an automobile accident, as did her two exquisite children. She never recovered from their deaths. Oh, she tried. You follow, in her ill-written pages, the way she tried to live again. She drank, and she loved, and she danced. But she never again became the Bacchante, the beloved, the high priestess of her Art. From the day they were killed until the day of her own death, she was Niobe.

I do not know how honest her book is. I am convinced that as she set down each event, she believed that she was representing it in absolute truth, for she was of the accursed race of artists, who believe each thing they say while they are saying it; yes, and who would go to the stake for that moment's belief. She speaks with frankness – though frankness, if you will forgive dogma, is no synonym for honesty – of her lovers. She had a knack for selecting the unworthy – perhaps all great women have; one and all, they treated her with an extraordinary shabbiness. She calls only

one by name. The others, she refers to by gloriously romantic titles –
'Romeo,' or the 'Archangel' (the Archangel, by the way, threw her flat for
one of the little girls in her band of dancers), or 'Lohengrin.' 'Lohengrin,'
whose true name we all know, was perhaps the most important figure in
her life; certainly he was the most frequent. He was generous to her only
with money, and he had so much of that that it was a tiny, an imperceptible, form of generosity. But she never writes of them ungallantly. She
does not whine, nor seek pity. She was a brave woman. We shall not look
upon her like again.

There is another heroine in her book, though I doubt if the author
realized it. That heroine is her mother. Dora Duncan, a little, prim, con-
vention-bound music-teacher who divorced her roving husband. But she
followed her children as anxiously and as loyally as a hen does a brood of
fluffy ducklings. Uncomplaining, she lived with them in bare studios,
where the only furniture, the mattresses upon which they slept, was
hidden by day under Isadora's famous blue curtains. She went with them
to Greece, donned, with them, tunic and chlamys and peplum – one
hears her saying, plaintively, 'How does this thing go on?' – and watched
her son, Raymond, who always was the boy to do the one thing too
much, kneeling down and kissing the soil, to the reasonable astonishment
of the natives. She saw Isadora come into fame and fortune; beheld the
contracts, that would have meant a secure old age for her, awaiting her
daughter's signature; and then saw Isadora tear them up because she was
interested, at the moment, in some transient young man. Finally, she
came back to America, to live the rest of her days – you see, in the book
you see only Isadora's version, but you can guess what a magnificent
battle it must have been – wanting no more to do with any of her
offspring. Isadora says that the elderly crabbedness, and the desertion, of
her mother was due to the fact that never, since her husband left, had she
taken a lover. But you can't help feeling that this is not quite so. Mrs.
Duncan must have been so tired. Oh, so very tired.

Please read Isadora Duncan's *My Life*. You will find you won't care how
it is written; you will find you will not be eager to trace to their sources
the current rumors that it has been expurgated. There is enough in these
pages. Here is the record of a grand person. Undoubtedly she was trying.
She could not do anything that was not dramatic. Take, for instance, the
occasion of her cutting her hair short. Other women go and have their
hair bobbed, and that is all there is to it. But Isadora – she was in Albania
with Raymond at the time – writes, 'I cut off my hair, and threw it in the
sea.' She was like that. It comes, again, from belonging to that accursed
race that cannot do anything unless they see, before and after, a tableau of
themselves in the deed.

Possibly I am unfair about the shabbiness of her lovers. Surely there is much to be said on their side. She must have been trying, with her constant drama, with her intensity, with her pitiful, undying hope that here was the love, the great, beautiful love, that was to endure for all time. But she gave them Excitement. She gave them Glamour. She gave them a glimpse of Beauty.

> Fortunate they
> Who though once only, and then but far away
> Have heard her massive sandal set on stone.

They were lucky men, they were. But she was not a lucky lady.

KATHERINE ANNE PORTER
1890–1980

Born and raised in Texas, Porter began her writing career as a journalist in Chicago, Denver and Colorado. In 1920, she gave this up, travelled to Mexico and concentrated on writing fiction. Her initial form was the short story, and she published her first collection, *Flowering Judas*, to great acclaim in 1930.

She was never prolific, so Porter's admirers were forced to wait for her first and only novel, *Ship of Fools*, which won her a much wider readership on its publication in 1962. Three years later her *Collected Short Stories* secured Porter the Pulitzer Prize.

Porter wrote occasional journalism throughout her life, writing that was infused with the purity and simplicity of all her work. In the following article this iconic writer profiles Jacqueline Kennedy and conveys her deep respect for the bereaved First Lady.

Jacqueline Kennedy

March 1964, *Ladies' Home Journal*

I saw Mrs. Kennedy only twice – first at the Inaugural Ball in the Armory in Washington; second, at the dinner in honor of the Nobel Prize winners, in the White House. In each of these glimpses she looked like all her photographs, those endless hundreds of images of her cast on screens and printed pages everywhere through the short, brilliant years of her public career beside her husband; only, in breathing life she was younger, more tender and beautiful. She had the most generous and innocent smile in the world, and her wide-set eyes really lighted up when she spoke to her guests. Old-fashioned character readers of faces believed that this breadth between the eyes was the infallible sign of a confiding, believing nature, one not given to suspicions or distrust of the motives of others. It might very well be true. On account of this feature, a girl reporter described her as resembling a lioness. I do not think she resembles a lioness in the least, but I am ready to say she is lionhearted. A merrier, sweeter face than hers never dawned upon the official Washington scene – so poxed with hardbitten visages, male and female, that bring joy to nobody – but even the swiftest of first glances could not mistake it for a weak face. It was and is full of strong character and tragic seriousness lying not quite dormant just under the surface, waiting for the Furies to announce themselves.

Certain members of her family, and long-term friends surmised these latencies, but could not name them – someone of them called her a 'worrier.' This is obviously not the word to name her special kind of hand-to-hand immediate concentration on the varied demands and emergencies of her days all through her life as we have known it – which may be called the ordeal by camera – but it is easy to see how a bystander, no matter how near the relationship, might misread her, never having seen in action the austerity, the reserve force and the spiritual discipline which no one expects in so young a creature. There had not been any occasion sufficient to call them out. She had been such a fashionable sort of young girl, brought up in the most conventional way: the good schools, the travel, the accomplishments and sports, the prepared social life. The whole surface was smooth as satin; she even wore clothes almost too well, a little too near the professional model. But she outgrew this quickly and was becoming truly elegant at an unusually early age. She had the mistaken daydream that many very nice girls do have, that to be a newspaper reporter and go about pointing cameras at perfect strangers was a romantic adventure. She got over this speedily too, and became herself the target of every passing camera and every eager beaver of a reporter who could get near her. And what a record they gave us of a life lived hourly in love with joy, yet with every duty done and every demand fulfilled: nothing overlooked or neglected.

Remember that veiled head going in and out of how many churches, to and from how many hospitals and institutions and official functions without number: that endless procession of newly sprung potentates to entertain royally! And always her splendid outdoor life – water-skiing with Caroline, both their faces serenely happy, fearless; driving a pony cartfull of Kennedy children, the infant John John on her lap; going headfirst off that hunter at the rail fence, and in perfect form too, her face perhaps not exactly merry, but calm, undismayed. An expert, trained fall that was; one would have to ride a horse to know how good it was, and what a superb rider Mrs. Kennedy is.

There is another snapshot of her going at a fine stride on her beautiful horse; and always that lovely look of quiet rapture in her high-spirited, high-stepping play. She never seemed happier than when swimming or skating or water-skiing, or sailing, or riding, or playing with her children. Who will forget the pictures of her in sopping wet slacks, bare feet, tangled hair, blissful smile, on the beach; with her husband nearby, rolling in the sand, holding Caroline, still in her baby-fat stage, at arm's length above him?

All of us heard, I'm sure, some lively stories of the pitched battles of early marriage, and there were dire predictions that little good would come of it. Nonsense! What would you expect of two high-strung, keen-witted, intensely conscious and gifted people deeply in love and both of them with notions of their own about almost everything? It was not in the stars for that pair to sink gently into each other's arms in a soft corner, murmuring a note of music in perfect key. It seems to have been a good, fair, running argument in the open – heaven knows there was no place for them to hide; eyes, ears and cameras were everywhere by then – and we know that things were coming out well. We could see it in their expressions as time ran on, and the cameras intercepted their glances at each other, saw them off guard at moments of greeting, of parting, their clasped hands as they came out of the hospital after Patrick was born – anybody could see that the marriage was growing into something grand and final, fateful and tragic, with birth and death and love in it at every step. Their lives were uniting, meshing firmly in the incessant uproar and confusions of the most incredibly complicated situation imaginable. But they were young, they were where they wanted to be, they loved what they were doing and felt up to it; and they dealt every day, together in their quite different ways, supporting and balancing each other, with a world in such disorder and in the presence of such danger, international and domestic, as we have not seen since Hitler's time. And the entertainments, the music, the dancing, the feasting – there hasn't been such a born giver of feasts in the White House, a First Lady who recognized that a good part of her duties were social, since Dolley Madison. Mrs. Kennedy had the womanly knack of making even dull parties appear to be pleasures. But the manner of the President and his wife to each other was always simple, courteous and pleasant, without gestures, without trying. It was a pleasant thing to see, and I began to be grateful for those swarming pestiferous cameras that could show me such reassuring steadfastness with such grace and goodness.

The only moment of uneasiness I ever saw in Mrs. Kennedy's pictured face was at the first showing of the *Mona Lisa* in Washington, when somebody concerned in the arrangements did something awkward, I forget what; she looked distressed. We know now she was expecting her fifth child, five within a period of little more than seven years: she had already lost two, and was to lose Patrick. Every child had cost her a major operation or a serious illness. This is real suffering, and yet she ceded nothing to the natural pains of women, but bore her afflictions as part of her human lot, rose and went about her life again.

I remember so vividly how she looked at the Inaugural Ball. In that vast place more fit for horse shows than balls, the stalls where we sat were railed in with raw pine, champagne was chilled in large zinc buckets such as they water horses in at country race tracks; there were miles and miles of droopy draperies and a lot of flags, and a quite impressive display of jewels and furs and seriously expensive-looking clothes. Also we listened to a peculiarly pointless program of popular songs: first, the Sidewalks of New York kind of stuff, then Negro jazz, not the best of its kind either; besides two or three bloodcurdling little ditties dedicated to Mrs. Kennedy; and I believe, I am not certain, that they were sung and played by the composers, young women who should have been warned off. It was acutely embarrassing; and altogether it was the oddest mixture of international grandeur and the tackiest little county fair you ever saw. I love county fairs, and I love grand occasions; but I don't like them mixed. So I remarked on the spot – still having the Coronation of Queen Elizabeth II in mind's eye – that we would never, it was clear, as a nation, learn how properly to conduct our ceremonial events.

The taking of the oath, outdoors in January, if you please, had been a series of gaffes. But that was over, and the young First Lady came to the big Ball at the Armory, one of five or six, I believe, going on all over town, and sat there in her white gown, motionless as a rose on its stem, watching her husband adoringly. She went away early, for John John had been born seven weeks before.

Later, by a year or more maybe, at the dinner given in the White House for the various Nobel Prize winners, and runners-up, we were having cocktails in the East Room, and I saw and greeted all sorts of delightful old acquaintances I hadn't seen for twenty years and may never see again – I seem nearly always to be somewhere else! – when the strains of 'Hail to the Chief' gave us the cue to set down our glasses and turn toward the great door. There was no roll of drums, no silver-trumpet fanfare, no; just a wistful, rather wiggly little tune, very appealing and sweet, and there stood the President and Mrs. Kennedy before us, amiable and so good-looking and so confident, with all the life and all the world before them, and why should it ever end? Very happily and easily we formed a long line and went past them shaking their hands lightly – think of all the hands they had to shake every day! – and then we went on to dinner and a merry party afterward, and it was all so gentle, and reassuring, in that lovely house, so well done and so easy.

Atmosphere, tone, are very elusive things in a house, and they depend entirely on the persons who live there . . . . The White House that evening was a most happy place to be, and I shall never see it again, for I wish to remember it as it was then. What style they had, those young people! And what looks . . . .

Then I went to Europe and came back a year later, on All Souls' Eve, to Washington. And now I am writing this, on the 22nd of December,

1963, on the day of the Month's Mind Mass, and the memorial lighting of candles at the Lincoln Memorial. The perpetual light that Mrs. Kennedy set at the President's grave can be seen from almost any point in this city. This light is only one of the many things Mrs. Kennedy asked for and received during that night of November 22.

I have a dear friend whose beloved wife died not long ago, and he wrote me an account of her going away, and he said: 'I never heard of, or imagined, such an admirable performance!' I knew exactly what he meant, and within a few days I witnessed Mrs. Kennedy's performance, at the great crisis of her life, and it was flawless, and entirely admirable; I have no words good enough to praise it. The firmness with which she refused to leave the body of her husband, keeping her long vigil beside him, but not idly, not in tears, planning and arranging for his burial to the last detail. What relentless will she showed, fending off the officious sympathy of all those necessary persons who swarm about tragic occasions, each anxious to be of service, true, but all too ready to manage and meddle. She refused to be cheated of her right to this most terrible moment of her life, this long torment of farewell and relinquishment, of her wish to be conscious of every moment of her suffering: and this endurance did not fail her to the very end, and beyond, and will not fail her.

What I think of now is the gradual change in that lovely face through the fiercely shattering years when she and her husband raced like twin rockets to their blinding personal disaster which involved a whole world. Among the last pictures I remember is Mrs. Kennedy as she stood with her two children in the cold light of a late-fall day – and you don't have such perfectly well-behaved children at their age unless you have known how to love them and discipline them! – watching the President's coffin being carried from the White House on its way to the Rotunda. She stood there staring a little sidelong, as if she could not dare to look directly. The first shock was over, that head-on collision with death in one of its most wasteful and senseless forms had taken place without warning, as it always does, but the dazed blind look was gone from her eyes, replaced by a look of the full knowledge of the nature of Evil, its power and its bestial imbecility. She stared with dawning anger in her eyes, in the set of her mouth, yet with the deepest expression of grief I have ever seen, a total anguish of desolation, but proud, severe, implacable.

No one who witnessed that three-day funeral service, in presence or by screen, can ever say again that we, as a nation cannot properly conduct the ceremonies of our state. We have been well taught.

CATHERINE STOTT

Daughter of the *Guardian* Women's Page editor, Catherine Stott brought a new style of interview to her mother's section in the 1960s, before moving to become Women's Editor of the *Sunday Telegraph*. Bold, searching and confessional, her interviews brought new vitality to the section, as well as the paper as a whole, with subjects opened up for the readers. In the following piece, Stott interviews one of the iconic magazine editors of the last century, Helen Gurley Brown.

The Iron Butterfly: Helen Gurley Brown

11 April 1968, *Guardian*

'There are girls who read *Cosmopolitan* and enjoy it as voyeurs. They don't want to be that driven, to have that many affairs; they don't want more than one man or one dress at a time. They don't care about jewellery and they don't want a sable coat or Paris for the week-end. They don't want to work as hard as I do. But 'my girl' wants it. She is on the make. Her nose is pressed to the glass and she does get my message. These girls are like my children all over the country. Oh, I have so much advice for them, and it's fun.'

Helen Gurley Brown was talking about readers of the magazine she edits with a stamp as personal as and not dissimilar from Hugh Hefner's on *Playboy*. It was Helen Gurley Brown who wrote the phenomenally successful *Sex and the Single Girl*, sold the title for $200,000 to a film company, and then began broadcasting its message for all it was worth through the columns of a moribund magazine which Hearst Publications asked her to edit, three years ago.

When she began, it was selling 650,000 copies. Now they are hitting the million mark and advertising has quadrupled; an unparalleled success with Madison Avenue. And all because this small, frail-looking woman they call 'the iron butterfly' has an uncanny eye for what women want, knows how to give it to them, edits every word herself, and spends ten hours a day and several hours a night working on it.

In a deceptively gentle voice she will explain to the listener that her success was motivated by fear not ambition. That she had a sad little childhood and a terrible growing-up. Although her simple little dress probably cost $100 a stitch and her jewellery may well come from Tiffany's, she looks as if she is afraid it may all be taken away, that she will be planted back in the Ozarks, a fatherless girl with acute acne giving dancing lessons to the other kids at 25 cents an hour to help to make ends meet.

Her philosophy is one of self-betterment, extremely subjective, virtually autobiographical. She thinks of herself very much as 'a girl who had very little going for her. As far back as I can remember, I thought I was physically barely adequate . . . in the 1940s bosoms were the big things; legs didn't matter . . . if you were small-breasted it was bad luck. Then I didn't have money going for me . . . nor an outrageously wonderful personality and I didn't go to college. I was a terribly average girl who inherited enough of a brain to do a few things. Being stupid is the worst thing that can happen to a girl; much worse than being ugly.'

Talking to Helen Gurley Brown in her Manhattan office is very much like reading her magazine; she explains her life very much in terms of what other people could achieve in the same way . . . 'I always say that anyone can do what I've done – not that it's all that much – but you can have a great career, make money and have some fabulous men in your life, and you don't have to be sensational to start with because I certainly wasn't.' She was the classic American dreamgirl who capitalised on what she had and finds it fun to watch others doing so.

It always charms her to see a girl who doesn't look like very much 'Coming on very sexy and maybe a little bitchy, but very attractive to men. My way would be to come on dynamic on the inside. To have something that gleams and burns inside you.'

What makes Helen burn? 'I think you get it because you feel deprived. You want to be more pretty, more of everything, more loved, perhaps. I wasn't ambitious when young, only frightened. I just got very scared during the Depression. Fear led me to do the best I could at everything. At school I was very competitive in a very quiet deadly way.

'I had to work the minute I got out of high school and all I could do was shorthand typing. I didn't think I should have been doing something better, only "if I get fired we'll all go down the drain". I was a secretary for 15 years, but always getting better until at 33 I was a whizz-bang executive secretary who got a whack at writing advertising copy.' She wrote sexy, girlish copy for seven years and was the highest paid woman in advertising in California. But the last agency she was with stopped giving her assignments, having stolen her from another agency for a vast sum, so she asked her husband, David Brown, vice-president of Twentieth Century Fox, what she could write a book about. 'He said I could write for the single girl. He said "When I first met you, you were a kind of a swinger, but you were also a solid citizen. You were very respectable with lots of friends and dates and parties." So I wrote it, and it sold millions.'

She says it wasn't that good a book – a sweet nice book on an idea whose time had come, about single girls having a good life. 'Single girls had been sleeping with men for a long time, quietly and without being run out of town. But secretively. Well, along I came with my little book and said that single girls did have a great sex life and were often much happier in bed than they ever would be as married women because they had more choice and variety and didn't have to stay with a man they didn't like.

'Mostly the message was "don't worry and feel guilty if you are having an affair because so is everyone else . . .", a sisterly book by a girl who was doing it herself, who seemed to understand how it was for others. Like a nice letter from home. More than this, *Sex and the Single Girl* actually conferred a new respectability on spinsterhood, making it appear glamorous.'

She believes every girl has one thing she can do really well and must find it, if she wants to succeed, 'and I have made this one exquisite little talent for writing sincerely in short, sharp sentences into quite a thing.' She doesn't necessarily approve of waiting as long as she did to marry (she was 37), 'I would think anyone who doesn't marry until 37 is quite neurotic. My neurotic drive towards work and success is perhaps a healthy one. The other neurosis was a bad one, in that the men who wanted to marry me I didn't want to marry and vice versa.

'I talk a great deal about success and you'll notice the word 'love' has scarcely entered this conversation. One is always criticised for that. Well, I adore my husband and I was in love with him when we married and there's not much point in going on about it! I don't say I wanted to marry a successful man – just I never would have married anyone who wasn't successful, and that's not the nicest thing you ever heard, is it? But if I'm going to work like a bunny rabbit I don't want a passive man, but my kind.

'Suddenly, when I was 40, I fell into a glamorous life . . . And I had earned it. And I've had some influence on other women. I work much too hard. I sound like a little girl from the Ozarks but I'm glad that at 46 things seem like fun and games to me. My forties have been my best years and I keep pounding the message home to my readers.'

JOAN DIDION

1934–

One of the most supremely evocative journalists of her, or indeed any, generation (see previous article for more details), Didion has brought her brilliantly incisive eye to a huge number of profile pieces. In the following article she turns her pen to the iconic and complex painter, Georgia O'Keeffe.

Georgia O'Keeffe

1979, *The White Album*

'Where I was born and where and how I have lived is unimportant,' Georgia O'Keeffe told us in the book of paintings and words published in her ninetieth year on earth. She seemed to be advising us to forget the beautiful face in the Stieglitz photographs. She appeared to be dismissing the rather condescending romance that had attached to her by then, the romance of extreme good looks and advanced age and deliberate isolation. 'It is what I have done with where I have been that should be of interest.' I recall an August afternoon in Chicago in 1973 when I took my daughter, then seven, to see what Georgia O'Keeffe had done with where she had been. One of the vast O'Keeffe 'Sky Above Clouds' canvases floated over the back stairs in the Chicago Art Institute that day, dominating what seemed to be several stories of empty light, and my daughter looked at it once, ran to the landing, and kept on looking. 'Who drew it,' she whispered after a while. I told her. 'I need to talk to her,' she said finally.

My daughter was making, that day in Chicago, an entirely unconscious but quite basic assumption about people and the work they do. She was assuming that the glory she saw in the work reflected a glory in its maker, that the painting was the painter as the poem is the poet, that every choice one made alone – every word chosen or rejected, every brush stroke laid or not laid down – betrayed one's character. *Style is character.* It seemed to me that afternoon that I had rarely seen so instinctive an application of this familiar principle, and I recall being pleased not only that my daughter responded to style as character but that it was Georgia O'Keeffe's particular style to which she responded: this was a hard woman who had imposed her 192 square feet of clouds on Chicago.

'Hardness' has not been in our century a quality much admired in women, nor in the past twenty years has it even been in official favor for men. When hardness surfaces in the very old we tend to transform it into 'crustiness' or eccentricity, some tonic pepperiness to be indulged at a distance. On the evidence of her work and what she has said about it, Georgia O'Keeffe is neither 'crusty' nor eccentric. She is simply hard, a straight shooter, a woman clean of received wisdom and open to what she sees. This is a woman who could early on dismiss most of her contemporaries as 'dreamy', and would later single out one she liked as 'a very poor painter.' (And then add, apparently by way of softening the judgment: 'I guess he wasn't a painter at all. He had no courage and I believe that to create one's world in any of the arts takes courage.') This is a woman who in 1939 could advise her admirers that they were missing her point, that their appreciation of her famous flowers was merely sentimental. 'When I paint a red hill,' she observed coolly in the catalogue for an exhibition that year, 'you say it is too bad that I don't always paint flowers. A flower touches almost everyone's heart. A red hill doesn't touch everyone's heart.' This is a woman who could describe the genesis of one of her most well-known paintings – the 'Cow's Skull: Red, White and Blue' owned by the Metropolitan – as an act of quite deliberate and derisive orneriness. 'I thought of the city men I had been seeing in the East,' she wrote. 'They talked so often of writing the Great American Novel – the Great American Play – the Great American Poetry . . . . So as I was painting my cow's head on blue I thought to myself, "I'll make it an American painting. They will not think it great with the red stripes down the sides – Red, White and Blue – but they will notice it."'

The city men. The men. They. The words crop up again and again as this astonishingly aggressive woman tells us what was on her mind when she was making her astonishingly aggressive paintings. It was those city men who stood accused of sentimentalizing her flowers: 'I made you take time to look at what I saw and when you took time to really notice my flower you hung all your associations with flowers on my flower and you write about my flower as if I think and see what you think and see – and I don't.' *And I don't.* Imagine those words spoken, and the sound you hear is *don't tread on me.* 'The men' believed it impossible to paint New York, so Georgia O'Keeffe painted New York. 'The men' didn't think much of her bright color, so she made it brighter. The men yearned toward Europe so she went to Texas, and then New Mexico. The men talked about Cézanne, 'long involved remarks about the "plastic quality" of his form and color,' and took one another's long involved remarks, in the view of this angelic rattlesnake in their midst, altogether too seriously. 'I can paint one of those dismal-colored paintings like the men,' the woman who regarded herself always as an outsider remembers thinking one day in 1922, and she did: a painting of a shed 'all low-toned and dreary with the tree beside the door.' She called this act of rancor 'The Shanty' and hung it in her next show. 'The men seemed to approve of it,' she reported fifty-four years later, her contempt undimmed. 'They seemed to think that maybe I was beginning to paint. That was my only low-toned dismal-colored painting.'

Some women fight and others do not. Like so many successful guerrillas in the war between the sexes, Georgia O'Keeffe seems to have been equipped early with an immutable sense of who she was and a fairly clear understanding that she would be required to prove it. On the surface her upbringing was conventional. She was a child on the Wisconsin prairie who played with china dolls and painted watercolors with cloudy skies because sunlight was too hard to paint and, with her brother and sisters, listened every night to her mother read stories of the Wild West, of Texas, of Kit Carson and Billy the Kid. She told adults that she wanted to be an artist and was embarrassed when they asked what kind of artist she wanted to be: she had no idea 'what kind.' She had no idea what artists did. She had never seen a picture that interested her, other than a pen-and-ink Maid of Athens in one of her mother's books, some Mother Goose illustrations printed on cloth, a tablet cover that showed a little girl with pink roses, and the painting of Arabs on horseback that hung in her grandmother's parlor. At thirteen, in a Dominican convent, she was mortified when the sister corrected her drawing. At Chatham Episcopal Institute in Virginia she painted lilacs and sneaked time alone to walk out to where she could see the line of the Blue Ridge Mountains on the horizon. At the Art Institute in Chicago she was shocked by the presence of live models and wanted to abandon anatomy lessons. At the Art Students League in New York one of her fellow students advised her that, since he would be a great painter and she would end up teaching painting in a girls' school, any work of hers was less important than modeling for him. Another painted over her work to show her how the Impressionists did trees. She had not before heard how the Impressionists did trees and she did not much care.

At twenty-four she left all those opinions behind and went for the first time to live in Texas, where there were no trees to paint and no one to tell her how not to paint them. In Texas there was only the horizon she craved. In Texas she had her sister Claudia with her for a while, and in the late afternoons they would walk away from town and toward the horizon and watch the evening star come out. 'That evening star fascinated me,' she wrote. 'It was in some way very exciting to me. My sister had a gun, and as we walked she would throw bottles into the air and shoot as many as she could before they hit the ground. I had nothing but to walk into nowhere and the wide sunset space with the star. Ten water-colors were made from that star.' In a way one's interest is compelled as much by the sister Claudia with the gun as by the painter Georgia with the star, but only the painter left us this shining record. Ten watercolors were made from that star.

CAMILLE PAGLIA

1947–

Writer, academic and iconoclast, the New York-born Paglia burst on to the cultural scene at the dawn of the 1990s, with her first book, *Sexual Personae*, and her newspaper and magazine essays on popular culture and feminism. Whether analysing film, television or Greek mythology, Paglia is always bold, original and combative, a style that has led some to call her the 'woman warrior'. Describing herself as a libertarian, she has no regard for the usual political divides. Subsequently, she has garnered a strong following amongst American conservatives who appreciate her support for the family and tradition, even whilst likely rejecting her enthusiasm for homosexuality, prostitution and fetishism.

In the following article, Paglia considers the figure of Princess Diana, in the wake of Andrew Morton's book *Diana: Her True Story*. At a time before Diana was considered a serious subject for cultural critics, Paglia explains her significance and defines a number of tropes that are now repeated as accepted facts. Reading the piece after Diana's death, it becomes both stunning and sad in its prescience.

Diana Regina

3 August 1992, *New Republic*

With the release of Andrew Morton's book, *Diana: Her True Story*, the decade-long Diana cult has become more than a sentimental fairy tale. Morton's book, first published in June, created a publicity storm unprecedented even for naughty, tell-all celebrity biographies. The June 7 edition of the *Sunday Times* of London, which contained the first serialized excerpt, sold a record number of issues, up 21 percent from the regular 1,143,000 sale. In the United States, the issue of *People* that contained the first excerpt for American audiences sold 4,001,100 copies, a record in the magazine's eighteen-year history. Simon & Schuster had to double its 200,000-copy print run of *Diana* within days of publication. The book flew to the top of the *New York Times* best-seller list, which also contains, at first place, a recent book by Lady Colin Campbell, *Diana in Private*, and at fifteenth, Nicholas Davies's *Diana: A Princess and Her Troubled Marriage*.

The book was shrouded in secrecy during production, but tantalizing tidbits began to leak out in the week before its serialization by the *Sunday Times*. The marriage of the Prince and Princess of Wales was over. Diana, weakened by bulimia, had tried to kill herself five times. Charles flaunted a mistress. There would be a divorce, a constitutional crisis, the collapse of the monarchy. The editor of the *Sunday Times*, denounced by members of Parliament and royalist hangers-on, stoutly defended the authenticity of the book, whose on-the-record sources are of unprecedented closeness to Diana, including her brother, Viscount Althorp. Because the book also uses a large number of unpublished family photographs, there was speculation that Diana herself had cooperated, however discreetly, with its production.

But as the American response to the news shows, the fascination with Diana is more than a British phenomenon. It is an international obsession whose scale and longevity show that it is more than high-class soap opera or a reactionary wish-fulfillment fantasy for American Anglophiles. Those who have never taken Diana seriously should take a new look. With this latest burst of press attention, Diana may have become the most powerful image in world popular culture today, a case study in the modern cult of celebrity and the way it stimulates atavistic religious emotions. It is increasingly obvious that Diana's story taps into certain deep and powerful strains in our culture, strains that suggest that the ancient archetypes of conventional womanhood are not obsolete but stronger and deeper than ever.

Cinderella. When we first met her, Diana was a shy, blushing teenager who had landed the world's most eligible bachelor, a dashing Prince Charming with a throne in his future. Morton's book reveals that Diana is Cinderella in more ways than one. Despite her privileged background, she had a desultory finishing-school education and earned money doing odd jobs as a charlady – 'vacuuming, dusting, ironing, and washing.' Bizarrely, we actually see her 'on her knees cleaning the kitchen floor' as she chats with a chum about her weekend plans. The Cinderella analogy continues in the way Diana is pushed around and undermined by real and step relations: her bossy, fast-track sister Sarah, her ruthless, showy step-mother Raine, and the snippy female royals. She is stonewalled, outwitted, criticized, particularly by a stiff and censorious Queen Mother, who had been publicly portrayed during the engagement as Diana's benevolent elder mentor.

The betrayed wife. Morton's book confirms rumors that have floated around for years about Charles's long-term mistress, Camilla Parker-Bowles, whom Charles dated before her marriage in 1973 to an army officer who is now Silver Stick in Waiting to the Queen, a peculiarly suggestive Tudor honorific. We now learn that Charles hardly spent a moment alone with Diana during the engagement. She seems to have been selected with clinical detachment as a brood mare to carry on the Windsor line. Like Mia Farrow in *Rosemary's Baby*, tricked and maneuvered into impregnation by Satan, she is isolated and conspired against by a faithless husband in league with a secretive, coldly smiling coterie. Most intolerably, her suitability as a mate was approved by Camilla herself, who deemed Diana the least threatening of rivals. Charles even proposed to Diana in the Parker-Bowles garden, as if under his mistress's aegis.

We are certainly getting only one side of the story. It is unlikely that the mature, athletic, tally-ho Camilla, whom Diana cattily calls the 'rottweiler,' is as merciless and scheming as she is presented here. But the tales we are told – photographs of Camilla falling out of Charles's diary, Charles on the royal honeymoon sporting new cuff links from Camilla with two 'Cs' intertwined, Diana over-hearing Charles in his bathtub professing eternal love to Camilla on his portable telephone, Camilla boldly presiding as hostess at the married Charles's country estate – inevitably make us sympathize with the young, fragile, and self-doubting Diana. Like Isabel Archer in Henry James's *The Portrait of a Lady*, Diana is an ingenue subtly manipulated by a cynical matron, a sexual sophisticate of insidious insideness.

The princess in the tower. Diana's story revives motifs of imperiled or mourning femininity that flourished in Victorian poetry and painting but that one had thought long dead in this era of aggressively career-oriented feminism. Having discharged his princely duty to marry, Charles apparently cut himself off from Diana emotionally. She seems orphaned, abandoned. Her old friends, outside the moat, joke, that 'POW,' Princess of Wales, really means 'prisoner of war.' Languishing in plush solitude, Diana resembles a whole series of melancholy pre-Raphaelite heroines painted by Holman Hunt and John Everett Millais: Tennyson's lovelorn Lady of Shalott caught in the threads of her loom, or his desolate Mariana, languidly stretching herself in her blue velvet gown; or Keats's half-mad young lover Isabella, watering the pot of basil with her tears. Like Andromeda chained to the rock – the theme of one of Burne-Jones's greatest paintings – Diana is both imprisoned and exposed. She is trapped in royal formulas of decorum, with the world's eyes upon her. Her immediate predecessor is another Diana: Julie Christie in *Darling* as a spirited young woman who leaves swinging Sixties London to become an Italian *principessa*, only to be buried alive in grandiose luxury and the unctuous obsequiousness of a hovering army of servants.

The mater dolorosa. Diana's children, William and Harry, give her image stature. Without them, and her widely noted physical tenderness toward them, her marital complaints would seem far more juvenile or petulant. It is ironic that Charles, who plucked Diana from obscurity and who has all the weight of rank and wealth behind him, seems helpless in the court of popular opinion against the ancient archetype of the sorrowing mother or *mater dolorosa*, which Christianity borrowed from the cult of Isis. Charles had sought and found, in Morton's words, 'a virginal Protestant aristocrat to be his bride' only to discover that his philandering attempts to remain himself produced a new Catholic Madonna, a modern Mary with a taste for rock and roll.

'Diana in tears' was the caption on the June 29 cover *of People* magazine – the second cover story in a row – which reproduced a photo now seen everywhere of the Princess of Wales at her first official appearance several days after the *Times* serialization began. Head bowed and biting her lip, she seems visibly shaken, but no tears are visible. This did not stop an American supermarket tabloid from artificially adding a tear streak and enhancing the drops, so that Diana resembles a Spanish Baroque Madonna with precious crystal tears sparkling down her cheeks. Weeping Madonnas are considered miraculous manifestations in Catholicism; like Diana, they draw rapt and unruly crowds. Morton matter-of-factly reports several dramatic instances of Diana's prophetic power to foretell death or catastrophic illness. For example, she publicly predicted her father's massive stroke the day before it happened, and she said aloud, while watching Charles gallop on his horse, Allibar, that it was going to have a heart attack and die – which it immediately did.

With the painful revelations of this book, Diana now assumes the international position once held by Jacqueline Kennedy after the assassination of her husband. Suffering redeems, and the world honors grace under pressure. Diana's dislike of the sporting life at Balmoral, the royal family's hallowed vacation retreat in Scotland, recalls the soft-spoken Jackie's hard knocks in the early years of her marriage: trying to fit in with the hyperkinetic, competitive, rough-housing Kennedys, she broke her ankle in a touch-football game and never went that route again. The supreme moment of Jackie's public life was her dignified deportment at John Kennedy's funeral, where, draped in a misty black veil, she stoically stood with her two small children, gazing at the flag-draped casket. In Morton's book, Diana is significantly shown alone with her children. Though she is smiling, the somber black-and-white of the photographs suggests her mourning for a dead marriage.

The pagan goddess. Diana's conflict with her husband's mistress has Greco-Roman echoes unusual for the British royal family: Diana, a fierce Italian goddess of the woods, versus Camilla, Virgil's Amazon, the militant Volscian horsewoman. A photo in Morton's book shows the young Diana Spencer dreamily reading a hunting magazine, *The Field: The Stalking Review*, with grazing stags on its cover. The caption informs us, 'While she has a reputation for being unenthusiastic about blood sports, Diana does enjoy stag hunting.' Throughout art history, the ancient Diana, hot on the chase with her dogs, is almost invariably depicted with a stag or doe. Do names contain their own fate?

The Hollywood queen. Morton tells us that Charles, exasperated by his wife's 'histrionics,' has often accused her of feigning 'martyrdom.' Indeed, in reserved upper-class British terms, Diana's behavior has an operatic Mediterranean theatricality. In her quarrels with Charles, the pregnant Diana threw herself down the Sandringham staircase, where she was found by the 'Queen Mum,' as the London dailies put it in June. On other occasions, she slashed her wrists with a razor blade, cut herself with a lemon slicer, stabbed herself in the chest and thighs with Charles's penknife, and hurled herself against a glass cabinet at Kensington Palace. These may have been, as the *Times* headline said, 'Cries for Help' rather than serious suicide attempts, but Diana's lurid private exhibitionism, so different from her public introversion, is reminiscent not only of the sensually gory lives of the saints but of Hollywood at its garish high point, the era of the 'women's pictures' of Lana Turner, Susan Hayward, and Jane Wyman, which featured flawed, gallant, tormented women loyal to gorgeous but callow men.

The old Hollywood studio system was like the Vatican in the way it manufactured stars and promoted its ornate ideology. The House of Windsor still functions like a studio in the way it sequesters its stars and subjects them to inhumane rules that make them more than human. Although she is still called 'Di' in America, as if she were magically ever-virgin, Diana at her marriage ceased to be a private person and became Her Royal Highness, the Princess of Wales, one in a long succession of women holding that title. She merged with her function. Similarly, the movements of the royals are recorded daily in the *Times* under the rubric of their residences, as if the palace itself has a greater living authority.

Diana's enormous glamour springs from the tension between energy and structure. Going about her public duties, she radiates a magnetic power that is directly produced by her disciplined containment within class and rank. Her staggering worldwide popularity demonstrates the enduring power and significance of hierarchy, a power that fashionable academic paradigms – influenced by feminism, Marxism, Foucault, and the Frankfurt School – cannot understand and whose enduring mystique can only be explained by Roman Catholicism or Hollywood history.

Diana's sole contemporary parallel as an international pop diva is the second Madonna, who, like Diana, expresses herself best through dance, the universal language. Both Diana and Madonna have trouble with words, which fail them in public. Diana even stumbled over her wedding vows, when she reversed the order of Charles's names. It is remarkable how Diana has projected her personality without the use of words. Photographs and video footage are her medium. She may be the last of the silent film stars. Morton's book reveals Diana's secret private life as a solitary ballet dancer: we see her gracefully poised *en pointe* on the rotting stone balustrades at the 'creepy' ancestral Althorp estate, which symbolize, as in *Last Year at Marienbad*, the ambivalent burden of history. Diana's classical dance training has given her an aplomb and distinction of carriage that make for great photographs even when she is simply getting in and out of cars – a talent conspicuously lacking in the lumbering, bottom-heavy Sarah Ferguson. Like the great stars of the Hollywood studio era, Diana exists for us as primarily a visul presence.

The beautiful boy. The stunning childhood color photographs in Morton's book, lavishly reproduced with the care normally reserved for old-master paintings, reveal an element in Diana we may have been only subliminally aware of: her boyish androgyny. With her refined Greek profile and ethereal expression, she looks remarkably like the seraphic Antinous. Staring vacantly at the television in a half-dozen different pictures, she has the eerie, blank, contemplative 'Attic look' of Athenian divinities.

Charisma springs from a presexual narcissism that is both male and female. It is Diana's androgynous charisma that makes her so photogenic; the camera is picking up her perfect, glowing, self-enclosed childlikeness – not to be confused with childishness, a behavioral flaw. Morton's book provides startling new information to explain this phenomenon: 'I Was Supposed To Be a Boy,' reads one chapter title. A badly deformed male baby was born to the Spencers, after two healthy girls, and soon died. Diana, the third girl, born a year and a half later, disappointed everyone's expectations. The fifth child was the long-awaited male heir, christened with great fanfare in Westminster Abbey, with the Queen as god-parent. Brought up with her brother in a divorced home, with her two older sisters soon off to boarding school, Diana seems to have merged with him in gender: standing in the photos next to his athletic, long-legged sister, he seems plump, girlish, and abashed.

Very beautiful people have an autoerotic quality plainly visible in the Diana pictures, which border on kiddie porn. The young Diana, in boots and creased, crotch-tight overalls, leans back against a fence rail in an attitude of solicitation normally associated with boy prostitutes. We see a good deal of the ample developing bosom and a great array of peekaboo shots in towels and bathrobes, including one in a Paris hotel bed. Aquatics offer all the charms of semi-nudity, and so we repeatedly watch Diana diving or posing, with the precise leg position of Botticelli's Venus, at poolside. There has been a persistent, half-conscious provocativeness in Diana's big public moments. In her first candid photo session at the London kindergarten where she worked, the newly engaged Diana was caught against sunlight in a see-through skirt that revealed her willowy legs. For her first official appearance with Charles, she chose a strapless, low-cut, lushly bust-revealing black ballgown that enamored the world but – we now learn – surprised and annoyed Charles.

One of the principal, much-debated issues relating to the cult of Greek youth was *paideia*, or education. Child-rearing emerges as a major theme in Morton's book. Diana was raised with the 'formality and restraint' typical of British upper-class families. Her brother never had a meal with his father until he was seven. The kind of constant parent-child contact that is the norm, for better or worse, in poorer, smaller homes was missing from both Diana's and Charles's upbringing. Nannies, ranging 'from the sweet to the sadistic,' as Morton puts it, are the parent substitutes. One nanny punished the Spencer girls by mixing laxatives in their food; another beat Diana on the head with a wooden spoon. The children retaliated by putting pins on the nannies' chairs or throwing their clothes out the window. Privileged British children are soon packed off to boarding school, in an enforced separation from their homes that would be considered cruel and traumatic in contemporary America. Diana is determined to treat her sons differently: 'I hug my children to death and get into bed with them at night.' Is this enlightened or suffocating?

The book's striking dust-jacket photos illustrate Diana's duality. On the front, she kneels in a fountain of white chiffon. She is wearing what looks like a stripped-down wedding dress from which every adornment has been torn, after battle on the field of love. The bodice is daringly off-the-shoulder, in her usual unsettling subtext of sensuality. On the back, in her androgynous mode, Diana wears a bohemian black turtleneck and pants. With her tousled hair, she looks like the Beatles on their first album cover. This reminds us that, with the failure of the Wales' marriage, the popular imagination has suffered its bleakest awakening since the Beatles broke up.

Diana's multiple personae, from princess and mother to Greek ephebe, are rich and far-ranging but also mutually contradictory, and they are clearly consuming her. No one, least of all a nervous, vulnerable young woman, could sustain the voyeuristic laser beam of the world's adulation. Deification has its costs. The modern mega-celebrity, bearing the burden of collective symbolism, projection, and fantasy, is a ritual victim, cannibalized by our pity and fear. Those at the apex of the social pyramid are untouchables, condemned to horrifying solitude. There may have been many unhappy wives in royal history, but they did not have to live their emotions under the minute scrutiny of the telephoto lens. Mass media have made both myth and disaster out of Diana's story. We have created her in our own image. And, pursued by our best wishes, Diana the huntress is now the hind paralyzed in the world's gun sight.

LESLEY WHITE

One of Britain's top interviewers, White is particularly well-known for her lengthy profiles of politicians. She has worked for the *Sunday Times* since 1987 and in 1998 was named Interviewer of the Year.

This interview with Bill Gates caused an immense fracas: Gates hated it and specifically mentioned it later in an article for *GQ*. As ever, Lesley White had managed to get under her subject's skin. It also shows that the deference female interviewers were expected to show to their subjects earlier in the century has evaporated – you get the sense with this article that it was the first time anyone had dared to question Gates for a long time.

Net Prophet

12 November 1995, *Sunday Times*

Never let it be said that Bill Gates, the richest man in America, give or take a skirmish on *Fortune* magazine's Top 500 has become complacent. Though all about him are strewn the signs of massive wealth, global fame and the whispering reverence of his staff at Microsoft, he is looking over his shoulder for an early glimpse of the guy who might steal his crown.

Gates is ready. 'Success is a lousy teacher: it seduces smart people into thinking they can't lose,' says the man whose company provides 90% of the world's computers with software; a 40-year-old guru whose vision of the future is accepted as the most reliable version of what our lives will be. 'I'm not good on self-congratulation. It has no value. The more successful I am the more vulnerable I feel. I can't tell you the number of business plans that have been formulated on, "Hey, we're gonna beat Microsoft" – thousands. When you do something well, people expect even better next time round. We sell 7m copies of Windows 95 (his company's new software package, launched in a firestorm of publicity earlier this year) and some people think we should sell more. Jeez! I don't know if I can go beyond that expectation but I gotta try.'

Staying ahead for Bill Gates means looking ahead, craning further and further into the unknown. He is bored by the temporal; he spends his life in the future, and he can't wait to get there, racing through his schedules, anticipating problems and questions, talking over the slow responses of people around him.

He has even tired of explaining the information superhighway and his 'vision' of the next century which for the common man is Dr Who territory. He wrote his new book *The Road Ahead*, serialisation of which begins in the *Sunday Times* next week, because he wanted to stop repeating himself.

'I thought there's got to be some way of getting this out there and move on. Let's get these debates going, let's tell people about what it means for the house, for school, for children.'

The miracles of the future are detailed in his book: the wonder of the wallet-sized PC that will make cash redundant; of telecommuters and video-conferencing; of hiring entertainment, ordering shopping, making friends, playing Scrabble without meeting another person; of pen-based computers that recognise handwriting and software that can 'remember' like an assistant.

This is a world where we can select how the movie ends and speak to its characters; where electronic 'agents', like spirit guides, will lead us by the hand through cyberspace; where we can summon up a Picasso, hold a sick baby before the screen for diagnosis, commit our whole lives to the system so that when we are accused we can say, in Gates's words: 'Hey buddy, I have a documented life.' The Internet, he enthuses, will even vet our friends in a dangerous world; randomness – the Microsoft insult – will be a mere memory. 'I think this is a wonderful time to be alive,' Gates says. 'There have never been so many opportunities to do things that were impossible before. It's the best time ever to start new companies, advance sciences such as medicine that improve the quality of life.'

He wants the world to share his optimism and he sees his book as a way of inviting everyone to join the discussion 'about how we should be shaping the future'.

'The network will draw us together, if that's what we choose, or let us scatter ourselves into a million mediated communities. Above all, the information highway will give us choices that can put us in touch with entertainment, information, and each other.'

Is he on a mission to convert, to sell us a dream as well as an operating system? He laughs: 'Sell? The only way I want to sell this stuff is to actually deliver it.'

When Gates founded Microsoft Corp (market value: $57 billion) 20 years ago he was a brilliant skinny kid with a great idea – make the software, not the computers – and dismissed by the microcomputer grown-ups who now couldn't get five minutes of his time. As a feted maker of the next century, he is constantly solicited for advice; moves in the hallowed business league of men like Rupert Murdoch, Mike Ovitz, Barry Diller; he is asked to meet celebrities, world leaders, politicians; he plays golf with Bill Clinton and is consulted by them all on the shape of the future. Does he enjoy it? He splutters: 'Gee well, it's not as if I go round asking them for their autograph. I'm no groupie of powerful men, but yeah, I get to meet some smart people, though it all calls on my time.'

And what about un-smart people? The ones he has to woo into his new world if it is to work? Like me. Two days before our meeting I sat at home in London staring at Windows 95 and blinked as the screen cleared itself twice without being asked. The auto-save mutinied. The mouse was on crack.

That night his corporate PR called about the forthcoming interview. Did I require extra information: biographies, transcribed lecture tours for close study? Gates, in his heady, hothouse existence, light years from the lives of his customers, is handled with care.

In a bid for light relief I asked her, an English woman, how she found working at Microsoft in Seattle. Great, she gushed, you get up in the morning and you know you are going to meet someone smarter than yourself. Amazing, I lied.

Over the next three days an endless stream of material arrived by bike and fax: CD-Rom packages, three sets of Gates's press cuttings, 18-page articles, two videos of the great man addressing a swooning conference on interactive film, two copies of his speeches, all with the adjoining notes that I would want to be 'well prepared', to have 'done my homework', since, by the silent assent of all but myself, I was about to meet God.

What was he like, I asked a fan. 'He is simply the cleverest person you will ever meet.' A letter from his publisher expressed admiration at my calmness in the face of this great event. I realised I could be his biggest challenge to date.

On the top floor of building eight on the Microsoft 'campus' in Seattle, where you don't give the receptionist your name but type it into a desktop computer, I asked William Henry Gates III if some people were allergic to computers in which case his whole take on the future might run up against human fallibility.

He looked at the carpet, pondering. 'There are only people who psyche themselves out of it because in adult life they are not used to being confused,' he says seriously. 'When you're a kid and you're learning it's okay because a lot of things are confusing and you persevere with it.'

But how does Gates deal with the average person's grasp of computer science? Throughout our precisely adjudicated hour together he was polite, bemused, like he was switching into first gear for the irksome business of communicating with a mortal. Strange, in a way, that a man whose life's work is communication, finds it problematic in the flesh but any old pop psychologist could tell you this empire was built as a wall of compensation for a personal inadequacy. Gates isn't hot on social skills. He rocks to and fro in his chair so violently that I feared motion sickness, was sure at least twice that the straight-backed figure in a sweat-stained monogrammed shirt would soon catapult itself into my lap. Eye contact is mostly avoided; his glasses were so mucky on one lens that perhaps he couldn't see and he laughs low and loud at points where no laughter is expected.

We know how the world thinks about Bill Gates: 'nerd or not?' is the gist of the debate but what does he think about himself? Gates, however, is not big on emotion ('What do I feel?' he will repeat in mild disbelief); he is a creature of logic and reason, phobic about sloppy thinking.

So for a definition of genius, a label as familiar to the multibillionaire as his junk food habit and economy air tickets, we turn to Microsoft's dictionary, Bookshelf, for Ezra Pound's 'A man of genius has a right to any mode of expression'. And a rich one, I think to myself, even has a right to bizarre hair, soapy tastes (he loved *The Bridges of Madison County*), and an affection for *The Great Gatsby* that speaks more of his dreams of self-reinvention and glittering prizes than his conversation would ever allow.

Does he mind being called a nerd? 'If it means you can enjoy understanding the innards of a computer and sit there for hours and play with it and go, 'Wow, this is cool', then I am a nerd.'

Why should he care, anyway? Gates is so rich it was once rumoured in jest that he was buying the Catholic Church. Microsoft is indeed the perfect refuge for a man not blessed with the usual enhancers of human advancement: charm, charisma, obvious strength, impressiveness, in short. Instead he did it another way, on inspiration and defiance, building his own Camelot on a personal belief in PCs, a place he leaves late at night and to which he is connected at all times by a modem and an obsession. After our meeting I asked his people if I might talk to him on the phone if I had any queries. Was I mad? Bill is not a phone guy, he sets aside the hour from 9a.m. to 10a.m. for answering world-wide e-mail (address: billg@ microsoft.com); I could take my chances with the rest.

Although Gates is 40, the importance of youth is stamped all over the Microsoft campus, as if, while generating a wealth beyond dreams, it is still somehow all about needling the grown-ups. 'Who wants to be part of the establishment,' he sighs. 'Jeez, they're there to be overthrown, that's how the world works. You're young and establish a new way of looking at things.'

Microsoft's baby programmers barely know they are out of college. In the staff canteen, overworked youths, many with shares in the company to enhance effort, are snacking on sushi and mango juice. They work like demons, sleep in the office, driven by ambition and obsession. 'If they want, we will give them a sleeping bag, but, you know, there is something romantic about just sleeping under the desk; they want to do it,' says the boss, though the point to remember is that nobody, even if they kill themselves in the effort, can be more committed than he is.

Does he pine for the old days when he quit Harvard at 19 so that he and his friend Paul Allen could design software, notably the MS-DOS system that would operate IBM's computers and launch the company in 1974?

'Oh yeah, sure, who doesn't want to be 19 again? Today, PCs are everywhere. I look back and it's like WOW! We must really have meant that when we said it and people believed us. WOW! Looks like we were right.'

Gates may be rocking like a caged psychotic, but when you are worth $13 billion, when more millionaires go to work at your company than anywhere else in the world; then believe me, in America, it's the others who are weird. And Gates has the Zeitgeist on his side; if Gordon Gecko was the fictional father of the 1980s yuppie hustlers, so this underwhelming maths major is the role model for a generation of clever kids, over whose awkward introspection he has cast a hip gloss.

In the 1980s they talked about things being 'cool'; now they talk about being 'smart'. At Microsoft, intelligence is a whizzy, supernumerate, boffin braininess: Joe 90 in a baseball cap and sneakers has been raised to the level of fashion. Gates uses the word as a mantra. Smart people, smart idea, smart business.

Does he prize intelligence above all other human qualities? The reply, like so many of Gates's, is cautious. 'It has never been quantified well, it comes in different forms.' His definition? 'Say you have a meeting and someone goes home at night and the next day there's a 10-page memo that's crisp in evaluating the ideas: that's a smart piece of work. In software, it's not like ditch-digging where the best is two or three times faster than the average. The best software writer is the one who can make the program small, make it clever.'

But alongside the brains there is also his killer instinct, the need to win, to be the biggest and the best. He sits dead still at this suggestion, says he created his own market, enjoys proving the sceptics wrong more than anything. He thinks it dangerous to apply words like win and lose to business. 'Because your products are always gonna be obsolete so you'd better enjoy doing the next version. It's like pinball: if you play a good game, the reward is that you get to play another game. There is no ultimate gain.'

His book's analogies lean on the pioneering past of his country, the Internet likened to the building of the national highways, and technological

advances to the Oregon trail to the gold of California, on which many are
wounded, some left behind, but the bravest and the best march on to
conquer a new frontier, Gates's wagon at the head. 'I tell the people here
that there are two possibilities, success and failure, but it's the possibility of
both that creates the best results. Risk-taking is fun when you succeed . . .
but I don't know as much about the other side of that equation as I should.'
Could he have lived with failure? He shrugs. 'If people fail a lot they put
their wild ideas into their hobbies instead. I'd have moved in a different
direction.'

Gates's wildest idea of late is the house he is building for himself and his
newish wife Melinda French, a Microsoft manager who was wooed with
e-mail. A huge and extravagant project overlooking Lake Washington, it
has relit the comparisons with Howard Hughes and Welles's *Citizen Kane*.
But this monument to greatness will not be stuffed with the standard trophies; it is more a repository for the 'Killer Apps', the must haves of the
next century, with video walls, pass-card entertainment, and a reported
two screens in the trampoline room: one image for up, another for down.

'I'm not interested in money for its own sake; what's important is to
keep moving ahead, keep changing, keep fresh . . .' His home will be the
proof that marriage has not smoothed his edge, merely enticed him to
longer vacations: two years ago it was Africa, for his honeymoon, the first
time he had taken more than a week, and when we met he had just
returned from a three-week trip to China. Did he work? 'No – well, maybe one day, but it was fun.'

All the big questions he shakes off with a shimmy of irritation. Does he
feel like a man of destiny? Was he born to monumental success? Did he
just luck out?

The Gates family were uptown Seattle, he a lawyer, she a former regent
at Washington University: culture, success, expectations, a private school
with an early computer, a passion for maths, straight As, a rebellious
period.

'The normal path would have been for me to go into science, but then
I had this computer hobby and I also read *Fortune* magazine and I knew
from my dad that you were supposed to make a profit. In the end I combined all three in this company.'

What moral values did his privileged background confer? 'My dad
taught me that in business long-term goals are the important thing.'
Fairness, kindness, justice? 'Hey, I never joined the Communist party,
I never gave it a second thought, I happen to believe in capitalism.'

As a boy, however, he worked as a Democrat page, sitting on the floor
of the Congress, learning the names of 242 congressmen whom he
greeted, pouring drinks at their cocktail parties, delivering notes. 'I was

for McGovern, who was very liberal. Perhaps it was just a rebellion thing. I was fascinated and at the time wanted to go into politics but there isn't the slightest fascination now.'

The Microsoft campus is where he is happy, where he makes sense, a theme park of fun-time capitalism with its own hall of fame in the brass plaques that are laid every time a product is shipped. This is his empire, but who could run it when he has gone? He has said he will retire at 50, leave 95% of his fortune to charity (not to his future children), but could he ever go? 'This is my life,' he says. 'It's what I am, what I get excited about . . . but maybe in a decade or so I'd be wise to turn over the leadership role. It's hard for me to imagine a 50-year-old running this company.'

And when he is 70? He couldn't imagine. If the future is where he wants to be, old makes no sense to him. 'Are you asking where I'll be if I'm dead by then?'

Cyberheaven, I guess. He smiles doubtfully, implying that the opposite place is more likely. It is odd that, despite the iconic achievements, Gates seems drawn to the anti-hero role, referring to his 'notoriety' rather than celebrity. I ask him how he wants to be remembered. He doesn't.

Some predict that the Microsoft party must wind down eventually. There have certainly been problems: an investigation by the Justice Department into the question of the company's possible monopoly, the fear that the demand for PCs will plateau and that a phalanx of imitators will be harder to keep at bay as the third wave of the digital revolution takes shape. Gates speaks of caution but he is so wrapped in the potential and possibilities of the Information Age that his excitement is almost childlike, his prophecies extraordinary.

Most transforming of our personal lives will be the wallet PC, a combination of purse, credit card, universal entry ticket and best friend: we will no longer need to carry keys, cash, cameras, concert tickets, cellular phone – all will be contained in one small computer. 'Rather than holding paper money, the new wallet will store unforgeable digital money,' says Gates, who likens it to his boyhood Swiss army penknife. There will be no queues at airports, theatres or anywhere one is expected to show a ticket; the 'wallet' will connect to the venue's system and prove we have paid.

It will tell us precisely where we are on any inch of the earth's surface at any time, via the Global Positioning System of satellites; currently used by jetliners and cruise missiles, but soon to be just as available for an orienteering trip through the countryside. Driving on a motorway, it will speak to us, warning of danger spots, traffic conditions, or that the junction we need is approaching. Its maps will be overlaid with specific regional information: where's the nearest Italian restaurant, we could ask it, the closest casualty department, or dry-cleaner?

It will tell us, make our order, show us the way there, and see us safely home. If we need help, it will find the appropriate services at the touch of a panic button.

And consider, enthuses Gates, perfecting the way we navigate on the information superhighway. For home banking, say, we will simply need to go to a drawing of a high street and point a mouse at the picture of a bank. We will be able to 'walk' through an art gallery, summoning extra information on the exhibits that interest us, create our personal gallery by tracking down a remembered painting of, say, a young woman in a black evening dress, even if we know neither the artist nor the title. Using virtual reality we may even be able to travel through the human body, 'perform' surgery, take the lead in the latest blockbuster.

The history of the future is littered with ludicrous predictions and equally with those who defied and denied progress even as it was happening. Gates gleefully tells the story of the Oxford professor who in 1878 dismissed electric lighting as a gimmick.

The point of genius like Gates's is being absolutely, arrogantly certain that you, just you, have got it right.

LYNN BARBER

1944–

A veteran interviewer, Barber has worked for most British newspapers and for magazines all over the world, including *Vanity Fair*. Her interviews are renowned for their fearless approach to their subjects and mix humour with penetrating insight. In the following interview Marianne Faithfull (singer, actress and Rolling Stones groupie) gets the harsher end of Barber's pen.

'You Know, I'm Not Everybody's Cup of Tea!'

15 July 2001, *Observer*

Marianne Faithfull once said, 'I am a Fabulous Beast, and as such, I should only be glimpsed very rarely, through the forest, running away for dear life.' How wise she was. If I were ever asked to interview her again, I would turn into a Fabulous Beast myself and hightail it to the forest. I first glimpsed Her Fabulousness ages ago at a restaurant in Notting Hill, 192, where she was sitting all alone at lunchtime reading the papers. 192 is a very sociable sort of table-hopping restaurant, so I thought there was something faintly sad about her solitude. But then a man joined her – it might even have been my future nemesis, François – and she simply handed him a slice of newspaper and carried on reading right through lunch. It was so devastatingly drop-dead cool that all the chattering at the other tables somehow died – we farmyard animals knew we were in the presence of a Fabulous Beast.

So when I heard she was coming to London (she lives in Dublin) to publicise the film *Intimacy*, I jumped at the chance to interview her. It all seemed quite straightforward: she would go to David Bailey's studio at 12.30pm to have her photo taken – she likes David Bailey, they 'go back a long way', to the 60s – and I would pick her up at 4pm and interview her till 6pm when a car would take her to the airport for her flight back to Dublin. My only worry (ha ha, in retrospect) was where I could take her between 4pm and 6pm, because I thought as a reformed junkie she wouldn't fancy a wine bar. Silly old me.

At 1pm, the publicist phones to say Marianne has not yet arrived at Bailey's – she was still in bed when they rang at 12.45pm – so everything has been put back an hour. Fine, or fine-ish. I arrive at Bailey's studio eager-beaver at 5pm, and walk into an atmosphere you could cut with a knife. Marianne, trussed like a chicken in Vivienne Westwood with her boobs hanging out, ignores me, Bailey likewise; half a dozen assorted stylists, hairdressers, make-up people stand around looking tense. The PR is friendly but apologetic – she says the photographs will take at least another hour and I should push off and have coffee. A Frenchman who looks like Woody Allen but without his suavity and charm introduces himself as François Ravard, Marianne's manager. I wait for some apology or explanation of why they are running two hours late – it never comes. Finally I say, 'You're running late?' 'Ah yes,' he says with a shrug. 'You know how it eez – it eez always the same.' Really? 'But don't worry,' he adds, 'we have dinner later.' Thanks a million, *mon frère* – I was supposed to be having dinner with friends. I push off to make calls cancelling my evening.

When I return to Bailey's, the atmosphere is even worse. No sign of Marianne – she has gone off to change – Bailey looks like thunder. Various *sotto voce* conversations are going on around me and I hear the ominous phrase from Bailey 'as long as it takes'. Time for my tantrum, I feel. Choosing my spot carefully, I stamp my feet like a flamenco dancer and address the studio at large. 'There is no point in taking photographs,' I warble, 'unless there is an article to stick them in. And there is no article unless I get my interview now.' The hair and make-up people stare blankly – so uncool! – but Bailey's assistant and the PR seem to get the point and agree that they will shoot one more pose and finish at 6.15pm. This news is relayed to Bailey with much fierce muttering and hostile staring at me. I decide to go outside and do some deep breathing.

When I get back, Bailey is at the camera; Marianne, in a black mac and fishnet tights, is sprawling with her legs wide apart, her black satin crotch glinting between her scrawny 55-year-old thighs, doing sex kitten moues at the camera. Oh please, stop! I want to cry – this is sadism, this is misogyny, this is cruelty to grandmothers. I wonder if Bailey actually hates her – I wonder if this is her punishment for turning up late. I hear the agent and the Frenchman muttering behind me – 'They won't use this, they can't.' So why is Bailey shooting it then?

Suddenly, the session is over, and we – Marianne, the Frenchman, the PR and me – emerge into the street where a chauffeur-driven limousine has been waiting all this time. It is now 6.45pm and Faithfull has still barely said hello. The PR says we can eat at the Italian restaurant at the end of the street. Marianne says she can't possibly walk, so we pile into the limousine to drive 50 yards to the corner. It is a sweet, friendly, family-run Italian restaurant that has no idea what hell awaits them. No sooner have we been ushered into a private room downstairs than Marianne is muttering, 'What do you have to do to get a drink around here?' Order it, seems the obvious answer, but that's too simple – François has to order it for her. Unfortunately – my huge mistake – I have let him and the PR eat downstairs with us, albeit at a separate table, and even more unfortunately I have placed Marianne against the wall, where she can see François over my shoulder. I could smack myself: what's the use of serving all these years in the interviewing trenches if you still make such elementary mistakes?

Suddenly, Marianne is shouting at François: 'Get it together!' and he is shouting back: 'What do you want, Marianne?' 'I don't know. What have they got?' she counters, drumming her feet under the table and moaning: 'I. Can. Hardly. Bear. It.' François keeps asking whether she wants wine or a cocktail. I'm thinking rat poison. Eventually she tells François a bottle of rosé. The waiter brings it with commendable speed and starts pouring two glasses. She snatches mine away – 'We don't need that. Where's the ice bucket?' The waiter goes away and comes back with an ice bucket. 'I'll have the veal escalope,' she tells him. He waits politely for my order. 'Veal! Vitello!' she snaps – she can't understand why he is still hanging around when he should be off escaloping veal. 'I'll have the same,' I say wearily.

I'm already fed up with her and we haven't even started. But at this point – a tad late, in my view – she suddenly flicks the switch marked Charm and bathes me in its glow. 'Cheers!' she says. 'Sorry I yelled. A slight crise there. It's been a long day.' (Really? She was still in bed at one, it is now seven, hardly a full shift at the coalface.) But anyway, she is – finally – apologetic. And I in turn put on my thrilled-to-meet-you face and tell her that I deeply enjoyed her autobiography *Faithfull* (1994), which I did. It is a truly amazing story – a pop star at 17, a mother at 18, Mick Jagger's girlfriend at 19, reigning over Cheyne Walk – and yet by her thirties she was a heroin addict living on the street in Soho. Even if she didn't write a word of it (David Dalton was co-author), she deserves some credit just for living it. For a while she basks in my compliments and then switches off the charm and snaps, 'But I'm not going to talk about the book, I want to talk about the film.' Huh? Too late I realise my mistake with the placement – obviously there has been some signal from François.

So then she launches into her spiel about *Intimacy* – how she saw Patrice Chéreau, the director, in a Paris restaurant and rushed over to tell him she loved his film *La Reine Margot* and to ask: Can I be in your next film? He said yes, and started writing a part for her that night. It is quite a small part, as a loopy bag lady, but Chéreau evidently convinced her it's the pivot of the film. Did she mind having to look so unglamorous? 'I did and I didn't. The first time I saw it, it was a shock. But I would jump off a cliff for Patrice. I don't know why, but I really fell in love with him and I want to work with him again. He's one of the reasons I'm doing this interview.

I want the film to be a success – I want Patrice to go on making films in English so I can work with him again.'

Actually, I would have thought that Patrice Chéreau's career could survive without the services of a ratty old rock chick. But let that go – she is very good in the film, however briefly. She has always had the potential to be a good actress, but four years ago she told the *Radio Times*, 'I was never an actress. That's a waste of my time.' So is she an actress or isn't she? 'Well, you know I love acting, but I haven't ever made it my priority. Maybe that was a mistake. But I couldn't help it. Music really is my life. And nearly every film I've been on has been crap, except *Hamlet* [with Nicol Williamson], which is brilliant. And I've ended up very fond of *La Motocyclette* [Girl on a Motorcycle] although it was a horrible experience to make. But honestly, the rest of the filmwork I've done has been ghastly. So I used to feel, till now, that I hadn't had the opportunity to be in really good films with really good directors. Because I could have been a really good actress – and I still could.'

Yet, judging from her book, she had endless opportunities to be a good actress, but invariably blew them away by turning up to work drugged to the eyeballs or not turning up at all. It might have been an obscure desire to punish her mother who had huge ambitions for her little princess. But also she was hell-bent on becoming a junkie from the moment she read *The Naked Lunch* – she wanted to be a junkie more than she wanted to succeed as an actress or to marry Mick Jagger. Jagger was surprisingly patient for a long time – he took the rap for her in the notorious drugs bust at Redlands when he claimed her pills were his. (Incidentally, she says about the drugs bust that, yes, she was naked under a fur rug – but it was a very large fur rug – and no, there was no Mars bar involved. But she hasn't eaten one since.)

She split with Jagger in 1970 and became a full-time heroin addict, living in squats and on the street. But she was lucky in that friends got her on an NHS drugs programme, which meant she could get her daily fix on prescription from the chemist. She had one of the highest dosages going – 25 jacks of heroin a day. It left her with poor circulation which is still evident in her angry red, mottled arms.

It is a mystery what she lived on in the 70s – she says it's a mystery to her, too. 'I don't know how I survived. There was a time after the 60s, when I was – I call it depressed – where there was absolutely no income. But I managed somehow. My parents didn't have any money. I didn't sell my body. I don't know how I managed. Flying through life on charm, I suppose. But I never took unemployment, welfare, ever. I have a thing about it.' Scratch an old hippie, find a Thatcherite, as Julie Burchill always says. Faithfull was far too hoity-toity to do anything as common as signing on. She always made sure people knew her schoolteacher mother was a baroness (Austro-Hungarian, natch). There is a theory that Jagger only embarked on his social mountaineering to impress Faithfull, because she sneered at him for being middle class – of course he totally gazumped her within months. Anyway, she 'lived on her wits' and according to Chris Blackwell of Island was very good at touching people such as doormen for the odd fiver or tenner.

What drove her to drugs? 'I don't know that anything drove me. I didn't even like it that much either; I just think it was like a good anaesthetic.' But she says in her book that she always had an attraction to the 'Dionysian' life. 'And I still do!' she grins. 'I'm always going to be drawn to that sort of fantasy. Though nowadays I don't do anything about it.' Does she still take drugs?

'Occasionally. I'm not going to go into it. Obviously no heroin. And I don't at all trust all these new drugs; they're not a good idea. But you know I'm a very decadent person, I really am. Whether I'm on drugs or not, it doesn't change anything. I can see why I liked them, and I can't sort of put that down. It's just if you want to do anything else in your life, it doesn't really go.'

She had one failed detox in England in the early 80s, and then went to Hazelden, the Minnesota clinic, in 1985 and cleaned up. She stayed completely clean, and went to NA meetings for five-and-a-half years. She also moved to Ireland, to the remote and beautiful Shell Cottage on a country estate in County Wicklow, and lived very quietly, alone. She had friends three miles down the road, but she couldn't walk that far and couldn't drive. 'It felt very lonely, and I was there nine years, and it's a long time to be all on your own. But I'm very glad I did and it was really great for my spiritual life.'

But four years ago she moved in to Dublin. The papers reported that she was chucked out of Shell Cottage after a rowdy birthday party caused £5,000 worth of damage. She says not so. 'I gave it up because I was lonely. It did have rats. And I'd lived there just long enough. It was self-protection, and there was a moment when it was over. I know the landlord didn't really like me. But you know, a lot of people don't really like me. I'm not everybody's cup of tea!'

I like her for saying that. Unfortunately, liking someone, with me, always provokes a disastrous urge to give good advice, and out it pops. Surely, I tell her, she shouldn't be drinking, surely Hazelden taught her that sobriety was the only salvation? 'I'm not going into all that,' she snaps. And somehow she must have signalled an SOS because suddenly the PR is beside us, telling Marianne, 'I'm really sorry to interrupt, but I do think we need to lead it slightly more to *Intimacy*. I know you've got lots to say about the film.' François simultaneously explodes behind me, 'I knew it! I knew this would happen! It's always the same – this is going to be the last time, Marianne.' 'Why don't you join us, François?' I say, thinking I'd rather have him in sight than shouting over my shoulder, but Marianne says quickly, 'Oh, you don't want that!'

Heroically, like a good Girl Guide, she pulls herself together and starts yakking about *Intimacy* until everyone has calmed down. We both rave about the sex scenes between Kerry Fox and Mark Rylance – she says they remind her of Lucian Freud paintings – she says they're almost like seeing sex for the first time. And, she adds, the orgy scene is brilliant. 'Though of course I've never been to an orgy.' Oh come, Marianne! 'In my mind. I've never actually physically been to an orgy. But it does fascinate me – how do you show decadence onscreen? And I'm sure that it's not about chandeliers and opulent surroundings, it's exactly like in *Intimacy*. True decadence is an empty room with one bare lightbulb.' In the book, she confesses that sex was always her Primal Anxiety. Every 60s male fantasised about going to bed with the Girl on a Motorcycle – but she suffered terrible stage fright before the act and would do almost anything to put it off. She once spent days hanging around Bob Dylan, seeing off the other groupies, until he finally made his move and then she told him, 'No – I'm pregnant.' Was it performance anxiety? Did she think she was a lousy lay? 'No. I am sexy, we all are – but people saw me as some kind of illusion and I always had a problem with that. But it doesn't really come up any more because, you know, I have a lover and I don't have to worry about it.'

'Who is it?'.

'I'm not telling you. I just thought I should explain that when I say I'm not worried about it any more, that doesn't mean I don't have sex any more. It's just not an issue in the sense that one isn't having to take one's clothes off and go to bed with strangers.' Is this a long-term relationship? 'Yes. A deeply committed and serious relationship. But private.' Might they marry? 'I'm not the marrying kind.'

' It is a man, is it?' I blurt, suddenly remembering that her book includes several scenes with women. 'Yes. I'm not gay. I would never rule it out, but it's obviously not my thing – although very nice and perfectly sexy and so on. And anyway I've moved on from that, because I'm in love.'

No amount of questioning from me will yield any more, and she segues smoothly into talking about her life in Dublin. 'I take care of myself. I go swimming. I read a lot. I see my friends. I talk on the phone. I watch telly. I go to bed quite early.' She is scared to live in London because 'it's too on' and she thinks she would be pestered by paparazzi. But she sometimes dreams of having a second home in London so she could see more of her son and grandchildren. She had her only child, Nicholas, when she was just 18, and lost custody of him when she became a junkie. But they are on good terms again now. 'I'm really glad I had Nicholas – though I never ever meant to have children. But I had this sort of force that guided me and I knew that if I didn't have Nicholas I'd never have a child – and I never would have, either. But I could see myself going out with my beautiful grown-up son. And I did that last night – we went to see Beck at the Brixton Academy and it was wonderful. I never quite saw the grandchildren!'

Over coffee, I ask her about François. 'Darling François!' she exclaims, 'I'm sorry he's a bit grumpy – he's had so much of it. He's been my manager for seven years.' Just for acting, or for music as well? 'The whole thing. The whole treatment.' She says this almost with a wink and suddenly – how can I have been so slow? – bells ring, scales fall from eyes, and I squeal, aghast, 'Is he The Man?' She says she won't talk about it, but the answer is all too obviously Yes. Good God. 'Well, I find him very difficult,' I tell her. 'Yes,' she says, 'but that's partly his job.'

François has obviously been earwigging again, because he suddenly looms over me and shouts, 'Are you talking of me? I hate this fucking tabloid paper. Sex and drugs and all that. I just allowed this interview for Patrice, because Marianne loves Patrice. If I could put it back, I will.' Marianne hisses at the PR, 'You let him get drunk, you fool.' François, meanwhile, grabs the bill from the waiter and plonks it in front of me. 'Oh,' says Marianne sarcastically, 'is this on the *Observer* – that dreadful tabloid newspaper? Sorry, Lynn.' François shouts at her, 'Don't be sorry, Marianne. Don't apologise. You will see the piece, it will just be sex and drugs, always the same shit. Trust me, for seven years I am telling you the truth.' The PR intervenes brightly, 'I think everything's OK', only to get a blistering from Marianne: 'Well, no. Everything is not OK. I mean, I'm cool, but François is not pleased. Don't let's go into denial – it's not a river in Egypt.'

So then François snarls some more insults at me and I pay the bill and flounce out. The poor chauffeur is still waiting outside and for a moment I think, 'Tee hee, I could take the limo home and leave them to grub around for a taxi.' But then I think how furious François would be and how he'd take it out on Marianne, and decide I don't really want to punish her quite that much. Though remembering her performance with the waiter I'm fairly torn. I don't for a minute believe in their nice cop-nasty cop routine. If François is bad, she's bad too – in fact, maybe worse: she chose him, after all.

Oh, she is exasperating! She is so likeable in some ways but also such a pain. The question that was spinning round my head the whole time was: Who does she think she is? She is a singer with one good album (*Broken*

English) to her credit, an actress with one or two good films. Really, her main claim to fame is that she was Mick Jagger's girlfriend in the 60s, but of course she would never admit that. She thinks she's a great artist who has yet to unleash her full genius on the world. Maybe one day she will, and then I will beg to interview her again on bended knee. Till then, back to the forest, you tiresome old Fabulous Beast.

JULIE BURCHILL

1959–

Born in Bristol to working class parents, Burchill moved to London in 1976, aged seventeen, in response to an ad in *NME* for 'hip young gunslingers' to cover the punk scene. Her journalism career was an immediate success, and by her early twenties she had written for a slew of publications and was employed as a columnist at the *Sunday Times*.

During the 1980s, Burchill became arguably the most famous journalist in Britain, with her legendarily substance-fuelled nights out earning her the sobriquet, 'Queen of the Groucho Club'. She shored up her fame with a bestselling blockbuster, *Ambition*, and her own magazine, *The Modern Review* (slogan 'Low Culture for Highbrows'). Although it only ran for four years, from 1991–5, the magazine's premise proved hugely influential and prescient.

Burchill has always been most famous for her wild, iconoclastic style and an ability to make even the most outlandish arguments seem plausible. In the following article, she profiles the oft-reviled Margaret Thatcher and explains just why she's always admired her.

Slimeballs Always Hate a Strong Woman

14 October 2004, *The Times*

I've had some inappropriate liaisons in my time, but somewhere in the Eighties, I slipped, tripped and fell like a ton of bricks into the mother of all crushes. And this time, the object of my affections was supremely unsuitable – a woman, married, much older than me. And, if a good number of my friends were to be believed, the Antichrist.

Margaret Thatcher! Even the very name can still set me on fire/set my teeth on edge. In 1984, when I first fell, I'd watch the latest communiqués from the front lines of the miners' strike on the TV news, and then I'd see those imperious eyes and that impervious mouth, and a line from an old Smokey Robinson song would jump, unbidden, into my mind: 'I don't like you – but I love you!' I didn't love her, of course. And I liked barely anything she did – apart from take the rise out of herself, like the time she walked into the meeting of the heads of the EC countries after the evil axis of France and Germany had been giving us a particularly hard time, and said: 'Now, gentlemen – I've only got time to lose my temper and get my way,' Oh, and her broad-mindedness and lack of finger-pointing when it came to private conduct and petty vices – I liked that too.

Perhaps, having married a divorcé at a time when nice girls didn't do such things and also having a strong Protestant faith, she believed that only he/she who has no sin has the right to cast the first stone at people living in glass houses and all that jazz. Despite the left-wing slurs, sneers and witch-hunts, determined to find a neurotic repression at the root of all that bossiness, Mrs T was never an old-fashioned girl; voting for her, if you were part of the moral minority, was a bit like buying a Cliff Richard LP, getting it home and finding a Beastie Boys record inside.

If anything, she erred a little too much on the side of *laissez-faire* lechery: she could never understand what all the fuss was about poor Cecil and the Daughtergate scandal, or even over Jeremy Thorpe, whom she barely knew yet defended hotly to more strait-laced colleagues. When a minor Tory whom she was not particularly close to was convicted of shoplifting during a funny turn, she sought him out the day his shame was splashed across the red-tops and paraded arm-in-arm with him through the lobby. She had, in short, the non-judgmental moral attitudes of a woman who is happy in her marriage – in every department, nudge nudge.

That's another thing I liked about the Thatcher phenomenon – her marriage to her Denis. How modern and feminist-triumphalist was that! – Queen Bee and Old Buffer. And how strange to find such a gender-flexible marriage on the Right, when it has always ostensibly been the Left that championed the rights of women; the right to stand by your man making goo-goo eyes at him, bake cookies on TV and overlook his ceaseless adultery, it seemed, judging by the behaviour of Cherie Blair (the first of the above rights) and Hillary Clinton (all three, sad cow). Denis, on the other hand, was so supremely self-confident/drunk that he didn't give a fig about being seen as an alpha woman's consort: with the quiet, amused, ceaseless tolerance of the little woman's little ways typical of the real man, he was a tower of strength disguised as a bumbling buffoon – never the cretinous yes-man caricature portrayed by some weird lefties who, while paying lip service to feminism, seemed decidedly uncomfortable at the sight of a man walking behind a woman.

Another thing I loved about her – she didn't like a yes-man in any way, shape or form, unlike most prime ministers before and since. Arguing was a delight to her ('Be constructive, Enoch!'), contradicting the accepted wisdom that she was no sort of intellectual. Oh, and her philo-Semitism, always the mark of excellence in a Gentile. Not for Margaret Thatcher the sly, shameful sneers of Labour's Old Etonian Tendency about the hidden powers of Jewish 'cabals' or of the slimeball who said of her Jew-heavy Cabinet that it owed more to Lithuania than

Leeds. Oh, and her sheer bloody-mindedness – a fine and rare thing in a woman.

OK, so I liked quite a lot of things about her. But what I liked more than anything was what she brought out in other people; how she just had to stand there being herself and they'd divest themselves of their civilised veneer, unbidden. A whole host of characters who had previously passed for decent revealed themselves as sneering snobs when they applied themselves to Thatcher. Mary Warnock said it made her feel sick to hear that Mrs T bought her pussy-bow blouse at Marks & Spencer, Jonathan Miller whipped himself into a self-righteous frenzy over 'her odious suburban gentility'. A few years later, of course, he would be banging on about the ghastly 'feral', ie working-class, children disturbing the peace of his precious NW Twee neighbourhood, as suburban as any retired colonel. And who can forget the caring, anti-sexist Labour Party and its 1983 'Ditch The Bitch' campaign? She got it from her own side, too – the drunken Tory grandee who asked her at a Number 10 luncheon while she was Edward Heath's Education Minister if there was any truth in the rumour that she was a woman.

I didn't like, of course, what she was doing to the miners. Since I was brought up a communist my heart was with those heroes, fluttering with their beautiful banners, piping mournfully with their brass bands. But my head . . . my head was somewhere else, mutinously thinking even as I cheered them on: 'Well, is it REALLY the best way for men to live their lives, like trolls or moles in the dark, dying young of lung disease?' Hearing public schoolboys banging on about the importance of preserving the pits, I couldn't help but wonder sourly why none of them was actively attempting to pursue a life lived underground and ending prematurely in a painful hacking death, coughing up bits of lung on the laps of their loved ones.

So even on this apparent sticking point, I was eventually in two minds. And I couldn't help coming back to the fact that the level of criticism aimed at Margaret Thatcher was often unbelievably babyish and bullying. It highlighted a tendency that the Left has always pretended was a weakness of the Right – silliness about sex. I've noticed over the past few years that when some poor liberal clown wants to deal what he fondly imagines to be the 'killer blow' to the Bush-Blair alliance, he'll draw a cartoon of the Titan Two apparently bending, blowing, buggering and generally being gay with each other. In this easy assumption that calling him a homosexualist is the most devastating thing you can do to an enemy, certain sections of the Left reveal their shocking lack of sexual health and sophistication – no wonder some of them have hopped so easily into bed with woman-oppressing, gay-executing Islamic (funda)mentalists. Personally, I like Bush and Blair, and do you know what? If I thought they really were serving it to each other on a regular basis, I'd like 'em even more.

Similarly, Margaret Thatcher was often accused of being 'in love' with Ronald Reagan; one monumentally silly poster portrayed them as Rhett Butler and Scarlett O'Hara, him scooping her up in his arms. '*She promised to follow him to the ends of the earth: he said that could easily be arranged!*' scaremongered the slogan. (Quite ironic, the accusations of sabre-rattling thrown at Reagan and Thatcher, when we compare the relative level of world stability then to the Islam-induced mayhem now.) '*Mrs Thatcher – you love Ronnie, you do!*' sneered 'socialist' pop stars from their tax exile in Switzerland. Believe me, as one who was there – that was the level of the debate in many circles.

Of course the lady had her faults. She wasn't uncaring and cruel, as the liberals made out, but she was naive. She simply couldn't comprehend how absolutely useless, helpless and hopeless quite a lot of people are, often through no fault of their own, and was cursed with an almost surreal optimism and romanticism regarding the capabilities of the individual. If she kicked away the crutches, it wasn't for pleasure or profit – but because she genuinely believed that everyone had the ability to walk without them.

This messianic fervour meant that very early on in her premiership she became no longer a politician but a leader; like de Gaulle she was a master of illusion who could not fight crime or reduce the deficit but could make her country FEEL BIG. She moved to a place above politics, probably after we won the Falklands conflict which may have been why she didn't get along with the Queen; Olympus wasn't big enough for both of them. She was the longest-serving British Prime Minister of the 20th century because she retained our vote long after we seriously expected the policies to work, because of what she meant to our sense of nation: quite rightly, she believed that Britain should see itself as an important world player, easily as hard as the US, France and Germany, rather than a country such as Belgium or Luxembourg whose finest hour was coming second in the Eurovision Song Contest.

And now she is merely the New Look: after all that blood, sweat and tears, she is a style statement to be oohed and aahed over by a gaggle of frock-cutters. 'First you're another sloe-eyed vamp/ Then someone's mother/ Then you're camp,' sang Stephen Sondheim's superannuated starlet-survivor in the song *I'm Still Here*, and it has even happened to the Iron Lady. She has gone from being the fatal woman referred to so lasciviously by François Mitterrand as possessing 'the mouth of Marilyn Monroe and the eyes of Caligula', to the solitary, widowed *mater dolorosa* making the headlines only when her useless son gets himself into hot water, to the fashion icon of whom Marc Jacobs said: 'This season is all about finding the Margaret Thatcher look sexy' and whose straight skirts and pussycat bows are now being plucked off the rails at Zara, Hennes and Topshop by 16-year-old girls to whom she is history. But because of her, and only her, those 16-year-old girls have grown up knowing that there is no job in this country – outside the Church, shamefully – that they cannot do. Today they're only dressing like her, but tomorrow . . .

Margaret Thatcher has walked a hard and lonely path. She has done harsh things and had a great deal of faith in herself – and, being a woman, this more than anything is why she remains so unforgiven by certain sections of society. But that she is now mocked as a mad old bat, Miss Havisham forever frozen in time, waiting in her faded finery until her country calls to her once more, says more about the sheer woman-hating sliminess of her erstwhile enemies than it does about her.

It is said with relish by civilians that all political careers end in failure, but if Margaret Thatcher's career can be judged a failure – to come from nothing, and do all that! – then only the good Lord knows how history will judge the rest of us and our miniature, mediocre achievements. Let us only hope, when we too reach the twilight of our years, that our critics will be more merciful to us than we have been to her.

A footnote: just a couple of weeks ago, Taki reported in *The Spectator* that, at a dinner given in her honour by Annabel Goldsmith, Lady Thatcher refused to say a word in criticism of the Government when the international white trash gathered round the table began to bitch about the number of immigrants being let in by Labour. Apparently, it is a rule of hers never to criticise the government of her country at social gatherings, which demonstrates to me an awesomely self-possessed and rare ability to know what is and what is not appropriate. It also doesn't seem the type of discretion habitual to the deranged or drunk, as Lady Thatcher is so often cruelly and falsely accused of being.

All political careers end in failure? Perhaps. But if any British politician can claim, in the style of that other great fallen fighter, Muhammad Ali, to be 'loser and still champ', it is this boldest, strangest and somehow most undefeated of women. God bless you, ma'am!

SOURCES AND ACKNOWLEDGEMENTS

All of the articles are copyright in the name of the individual writers, their estates or their organisations as follows. Every effort has been made to trace the holders of copyright. In the event of any inadvertent transgression of copyright, please contact the editors via the publisher.

Barber, Lynn. 'You Know, I'm Not Everybody's Cup of Tea!', *Observer*, 15 July 2001. Reprinted by permission of the author. All rights reserved.

Barnes, Djuna. 'How it Feels to be Forcibly Fed', *New York World,* 6 September 1914.

Baxter, Sarah. 'My Brave, Wounded New World', *Sunday Times*, 11 November 2001. Reprinted by permission of NI Syndication Ltd/The Times Newspapers Ltd.

Bly, Nellie. 'Ten Days in a Madhouse', *New York World*, 1888.

Burchill, Julie. 'Slimeballs Always Hate a Strong Woman', *The Times*, 14 October 2004. Reprinted by permission of NI Syndication Ltd/The Times Newspapers Ltd. Copyright © Julie Burchill.

Carter, Angela. 'Fat is Ugly', *New Society*, 28 November 1974. This is taken from an article, which first appeared in *New Society*. Copyright © *New Statesman*. All rights reserved.

Carter, Angela. 'Notes from a Maternity Ward', *New Statesman*, December 1983. This is taken from an article, which first appeared in the *New Statesman*.

Colvin, Marie. 'The Arafat I Knew', *Sunday Times*, 14 November 2004. Reprinted by permission of NI Syndication Ltd/The Times Newspapers Ltd.

Cooper, Jilly. 'If this is Sex, I'm Glad I'm English', *Sunday Times*, 1970s. Reprinted by permission of NI Syndication Ltd/The Times Newspapers Ltd.

Crittenden, Danielle. 'AmandaBright@home', *Wall Street Journal*, 25 May 2001. Reprinted from the *Wall Street Journal* © 2001 Dow Jones & Company. All rights reserved.

Cunard, Nancy. Report from the Spanish Civil War, *Manchester Guardian*, 1939.

Didion, Joan. 'George O'Keeffe', *The White Album* by Joan Didion. Copyright © 1979 by Joan Didion. Reprinted by permission of Farrar, Straus and Giroux, LLC.

Didion, Joan. 'On Self-respect', American *Vogue*, 1961. 'On Self-respect' from *Slouching Towards Bethlehem* by Joan Didion. Copyright © 1966, 1968, renewed 1996 by Joan Didion. Reprinted by permission of Farrar, Straus and Giroux, LLC.

Drew, Elizabeth. 'A Watergate Diary', *Atlantic Monthly*, August 1973. Copyright © Elizabeth Drew 1973. Reprinted by permission of the author. All rights reserved.

du Maurier, Daphne. 'Letter Writing in Wartime', *Good Housekeeping*, September 1940. Reproduced with permission of Curtis Brown Ltd, London, on behalf of The Chichester Partnership. Copyright © The Chichester Partnership.

Dworkin, Andrea. 'Through the Pain Barrier', *Guardian*, 23 April 2005. Copyright Guardian Newspapers Limited 2005.

Eastman, Crystal. 'Mother-worship', the *Nation*, 16 March 1927. Reprinted with permission from the March 16, 1927 issue of the *Nation*. For subscription information, call 1-800-333-8536. Portions of each week's *Nation* magazine can be accessed at http://www.thenation.com.

Ehrenreich, Barbara. 'Nickel-and-Dimed: On (Not) Getting By in America', *Harper's*, January 1999. Reprinted by permission of International Creative Management, Inc. Copyright © 1999 by Barbara Ehrenreich.

Fielding, Helen. 'Bridget Jones's Diary', *Independent*, 9 August 1995. Copyright © Helen Fielding 1995.

Fitzgerald, Zelda. 'What Became of the Flappers?', *McCall's* Magazine, October 1925.

Flint, Julie. 'Mountainsides of Hell', *Observer*, 14 April 1991. Copyright © Guardian Newspapers Limited 1991.

Freeman, Joreen. 'The BITCH Manifesto', *Voice of the Women's Liberation Movement*, 1971. Reprinted by permission of the author. All rights reserved.

Friedan, Betty. 'The Women at Houston', *New Republic*, 10 December 1977. Reprinted by permission of the *New Republic* © 1977 the *New Republic*, LLC.

Gellhorn, Martha. 'Dachua', *The Face of War*, 1945. Copyright © by Martha Gellhorn, reproduced by kind permission of Gillon Aitken Associates, Ltd.

Gellhorn, Martha. 'Justice at Night', *Spectator*, August 1936. Copyright © by Martha Gellhorn, reproduced by kind permission of Gillon Aitken Associates, Ltd.

George, Rose. 'They don't See it as Rape. They Just See it as Pleasure for Them', *Guardian*, 5 June 2004. Copyright © Guardian Newspapers Limited 2004.

Gerrard, Nicci, 'Holly and Jessica – we'll Never Know', *Observer*, 21 December 2003. Reprinted by permission of the author. All rights reserved.

Goldman, Emma. 'The Promoters of the War Mania', *Mother Earth* (vol. XII, no. 1), March 1917.

Goldman, Emma. 'The Social Aspects of Birth Control', *Mother Earth* (vol. XI, no.2), April 1916.

Hall, Gladys. Interviews Tallulah Bankhead, *Motion Picture*, September 1932.

Heaton Vorse, Mary. 'The War in Passaic', the *Nation*, 17 March 1926. Reprinted with permission from the March 17, 1926 issue of the *Nation*. For subscription information, call 1-800-333-8536. Portions of each week's *Nation* magazine can be accessed at http://www.thenation.com.

Higgins, Marguerite. On the American Invasion of Inchon, Korea, *New York Herald Tribune*, 18 September 1950.

Jong, Erica. 'Hillary's Husband Re-elected: the Clinton Marriage of Politics and Power', the *Nation*, 25 November 1996. Reprinted with permission from the November 25, 1996 issue of the *Nation*. For subscription information, call 1-800-333-8536. Portions of each week's *Nation* magazine can be accessed at http://www.thenation.com.

Jong, Erica. 'The Post-feminist Woman – Is She Perhaps More Oppressed Than Ever?', *Seattle Times*, 30 December 1984. Copyright © Erica Jong 1984. Reprinted by permission of the author. All rights reserved.

Jordan, June. 'Can I get a Witness?', *Progressive*, 12 December 1991. Copyright © June Jordan; reprinted by permission of the June M. Jordan Literary Estate Trust, www.junejordan.com.

Kael, Pauline. 'The Feminine Mystique', *New Yorker*, 19 October 1987. Reprinted by permission; © Pauline Kael. Originally published in the *New Yorker*. All rights reserved.

Kinnan Rawlings, Marjorie. 'I Sing While I Cook', American *Vogue*, 1930s.

Kirkpatrick, Helen. On Surviving the London Blitz, *Chicago Daily News*, 9 September 1940.

Knight, India. 'Thank God I Let my Baby Live', *Sunday Times*, 25 April 2004. Reprinted by permission of NI Syndication Ltd/The Times Newspapers Ltd.

Lamb, Christina. 'My Double Life: Kalashnikovs and Cupcakes', *Sunday Times*, 23 January 2005. Reprinted by permission of NI Syndication Ltd/The Times Newspapers Ltd.

Leslie, Ann. Report on the Fall of the Berlin Wall, *Daily Mail*, 1989. Reprinted by permission of the author. All rights reserved.

Lorde, Audre. 'That Summer I Left Childhood was White', *Zami*, 1982. Copyright © Audre Lorde 1982.

McCarthy, Mary. 'Report from Vietnam I: The Home Program', *New York Review of Books*, 20 April 1967. Copyright © Mary McCarthy, 1967.

Mills, Eleanor. 'Putting her Best Face on a Murky Business', *Sunday Times*, 10 October 1999. Reprinted by permission of NI Syndication Ltd/The Times Newspapers Ltd.

Mitford, Nancy. 'The English Aristocracy', *Encounter*, September 1955. Extracts from 'The English Aristocracy' by Nancy Mitford (Copyright © The Estate of Nancy Mitford, 1955, 1968) are reproduced by permission of PFD (www.pfd.co.uk) on behalf of the Estate of Nancy Mitford.

Paglia, Camille. 'Diana Regina', *New Republic*, 3 August 1992. Reprinted by permission of the *New Republic*, © 1992 the *New Republic*, LLC.

Pankhurst, Sylvia. 'Human Suffrage', *The Woman's Dreadnought*, 18 December 1915.

Parker, Dorothy. 'Poor, Immortal Isadora', *New Yorker*, 14 January 1928. The editors wish to thank the National Association for the Advancement of Colored People for authorizing the use of Dorothy Parker's work first published in the *New Yorker*, January 14, 1928.

Phillips, Melanie. 'Everybody Wins and All Must Have Prizes', *Daily Mail*, 22 September 2003. Copyright © Melanie Phillips, 2003. Reprinted by permission of the author. All rights reserved.

Picardie, Ruth. 'Before I Say Goodbye', *Observer*, 24 August 1997. Copyright © Guardian Newspapers Limited 1997.

Pizzey, Erin. 'Fabulously Fat', *Cosmopolitan*, February 1980. Reprinted by permission of the author. All rights reserved.

Porter, Katherine Anne. 'Jacqueline Kennedy', *Ladies' Home Journal*, March 1964. From *The Collected Essays and Occasional Writings of Katherine Anne Porter* (New York:

Delacorte Press/Seymour Lawrence, 1970). Originally published in *Ladies' Home Journal* (March 1964). Reprinted with the permission of Barbara Thomson Davis, Literary Trustee for the Estate of Katherine Anne Porter.

Roosevelt, Eleanor. 'My Day', United Feature Syndicate Inc, 11 November 1938. Copyright © United Feature Syndicate Inc.

Sereny Gitta, 'On the Murder of James Bulger', *Independent*, 30 January 2000. Reprinted by permission of the author. All rights reserved.

Sharp, Evelyn. 'The Rebel on the Hearth', *Manchester Guardian*, 4 March 1924. Copyright © Guardian Newspapers Limited 1924.

Sidgwick, Mrs Alfred. 'Should *Married* Women Work?', *Good Housekeeping*, 1924.

Sontag, Susan. 'Regarding the Torture of Others', *New York Times*, 23 May 2004. Copyright © Susan Sontag, 2004. Reprinted with the permission of the author's estate c/o the Wylie Agency.

Stott, Catherine. 'The Iron Butterfly: Helen Gurley Brown', *Guardian*, 11 April 1968. Copyright © Guardian Newspapers Limited 1968.

Stott, Mary. 'Learning to be a Widow', *Guardian*, 27 July 1968. Copyright © Guardian Newspapers Limited 1968.

Stott, Mary. 'Woman Talking to Men', *Guardian*, 15 October 1964. Copyright © Guardian Newspapers Limited 1964.

Styron, Rose. 'Torture in Chile', *New Republic*, 20 March 1976. Reprinted by permission of the *New Republic*, © 1976 the *New Republic*, LLC.

Syfers, Judy. 'Why I want a Wife', *Ms*, December 1971. Reprinted by permission of the author. All rights reserved.

Tweedie, Jill. 'Feminists and the Right to be Ugly', *Guardian*, 2 February 1970. Copyright © Guardian Newspapers Limited 1970.

Tyler, Anne. 'Trouble in the Boys' Club', *New Republic*, 30 July 1977. Reprinted by permission of the *New Republic*, © 1977 the *New Republic*, LLC.

Vegtel, Maddy. 'Forty – when the Baby was Born', American *Vogue*, 1930s.

Walker, Alice. 'The Right to Life: what can the White Man…Say to the Black Woman?', the *Nation*, 22 May 1989. Reprinted by permission of the Wendy Weil Agency, Inc. First published in the *Nation*. Copyright © 1989 by Alice Walker.

West, Rebecca. On the Nuremberg Trials, 'Greenhouse with Cyclamens I', 1946. Reproduced from 'Greenhouse with Cyclamens I' in *A Train of Powder* by Rebecca West (Copyright © Estate of Rebecca West 1955) by permission of PFD on behalf of the Estate of Rebecca West.

White, Lesley. 'Net Prophet', *Sunday Times*, 12 November 1995. Reprinted by permission of NI Syndication Ltd/The Times Newspapers Ltd.

Whitehorn, Katharine. 'Sluts I', *Observer*, 29 December 1963. Copyright © Guardian Newspapers Limited 1963.

Wolf, Naomi. 'Sex and the Sisters', *Sunday Times*, 20 July 2003. Reprinted by permission of NI Syndication Ltd/The Times Newspapers Ltd.